D0118664

RESEARCH METHODS
FOR
ORGANIZATIONAL STUDIES

RESEARCH METHODS
FOR
ORGANIZATIONAL STUDIES

Second Edition

Donald P. Schwab
University of Wisconsin-Madison

Routledge
Taylor & Francis Group

LONDON AND NEW YORK

Senior Acquisitions Editor: Anne Duffy
Editorial Assistant: Kristin Duch
Cover Design: Kathryn Houghtaling Lacey
Textbook Production Manager: Paul Smolenski
Full-Service Compositor: TechBooks

This book was typeset in 10/12 pt. Times, Italic, Bold, Bold Italic. The heads were typeset in Americana, and Americana Bold Italic.

First published by
The Haworth Press, Inc.
10 Alice Street
Binghamton, N Y 13904-1580

This edition published 2011 by Routledge

Routledge   Routledge
Taylor & Francis Group   Taylor & Francis Group
711 Third Avenue   2 Park Square, Milton Park
New York, NY 10017   Abingdon, Oxon OX14 4RN

Library of Congress Cataloging-in-Publication Data

Schwab, Donald P.
Research methods for organizational studies / Donald P. Schwab.—
    2nd ed.
        p.   cm.
Includes bibliographical references (p.) and index.
ISBN 0-8058-4727-8 (casebound : alk. paper)
1. Organization—Research—Methodology.   I. Title.

HD30.4.S38 2005
302.3′5′072—dc22   2004013167

Contents

Preface   xv

About the Author   xxi

I: OVERVIEW   **1**

  1. Introduction   3
          Research Activities   6
          A Point of View   8
          Objectives and Organization   8
          Summary   9
          For Review   10
              Terms to Know   10

  2. A Model of Empirical Research   11
          Research Variables   12
              Conceptual and Operational Variables   12
              Dependent and Independent Variables   12
          The Model   13
              Conceptual Relationships   14
              Operational Relationships   14
                  Empirical Relationships   14
                  Causal Relationships at an Empirical Level   14
              Conceptual to Operational Relationships   16
          Generalizing From the Model   17
              Statistical Generalization   17
              External Generalization   19
          Summary   19
          For Review   19
              Terms to Know   19
              Things to Know   20
              Issues to Discuss   20

II: MEASUREMENT: UNDERSTANDING CONSTRUCT VALIDITY   **23**

  3. Measurement Foundations: Validity and Validation   25
          Construct Definitions   26
              Construct Domain   26
              Nomological Networks   26
          Construct Definition Illustration   27
          Construct Validity Challenges   27

Random Errors	28
Systematic Errors	29
Scores are Critical	29
Construct Validation	30
Content Validity	31
Reliability	32
Types of Reliability	32
Reliability and Construct Validity	32
Convergent Validity	32
Discriminant Validity	33
Criterion-Related Validity	34
Investigating Nomological Networks	34
Summary	36
For Review	36
Terms to Know	36
Things to Know	37
4. Measurement Applications: Research Questionnaires	38
Questionnaire Decisions	39
Alternatives to Questionnaire Construction	39
Secondary Data	40
Questionnaires Developed by Others	40
Questionnaire Type	40
Self-Reports Versus Observations	40
Interviews Versus Written Questionnaires	41
Questionnaire Construction	42
Content Domain	43
Items	43
Item Wording	43
Item Sequence	44
Scaling	44
Questionnaire Response Styles	45
Self-Reports	45
Observations	46
Implications for Questionnaire Construction and Use	47
Pilot Testing	47
Summary	47
For Review	48
Terms to Know	48
Things to Know	49
Part II Suggested Readings	49
III: DESIGN: ADDRESSING INTERNAL VALIDITY	**51**
5. Research Design Foundations	53
Causal Challenges	54
Causal Direction	55
Specification: Uncontrolled Variables and the Danger of Bias	56
Bias	56
Spurious Relationships	57

Suppressor Variables	57
Noise	57
Mediators	58
Moderators	59
Using Design to Address Causal Challenges	61
Sampling: Selecting Cases to Study	61
Restriction of Range	61
Comparison Groups	62
Measurement Decisions	62
Control Over Independent Variables	62
Measurement and Statistical Control	63
Administering Measures to Cases	63
Matching	63
Random Assignment	64
Design Types	64
Experiments	64
Quasi-Experiments	65
Field Studies and Surveys	65
Summary	65
For Review	67
Terms to Know	67
Questions for Review	68
Issues to Discuss	68
6. Design Applications: Experiments and Quasi-Experiments	69
Basic Designs	70
Design A1: Cross-Sectional Between-Cases Design	70
Design B1: Longitudinal Within-Cases Design	70
Threats to Internal Validity	72
Threats From the Research Environment	72
Demands on Participants	72
Researcher Expectations	73
Threats in Between-Cases Designs	73
Threats in Longitudinal Designs	74
Additional Designs	75
Design C1: Longitudinal Between-Cases	75
Design D: Cross-Sectional Factorial Design	77
Design E: Cross-Sectional Design with Covariate	79
Design Extensions	80
Summary	81
For Review	82
Terms to Know	82
Questions for Review	83
Issues to Discuss	83
7. Design Applications: Field Studies and Surveys	84
Basic Designs	85
Design A2: Between-Cases Design	85
Design B2: Within-Cases Time Series	86
Design C2: Longitudinal Between-Cases Panel Studies	87
Design Extensions	88

Threats to Internal Validity   88
    Concerns About Causal Direction   89
    Biases Introduced by a Single Source and Similar Method   89
Praise for Surveys and Field Studies   90
    Internal Validity May Not Be a Concern   91
    Causation May Not Be a Concern   91
    Design Constraints   91
Summary   91
For Review   92
    Terms to Know   92
    Questions for Review   92
    Issues to Discuss   93
Part III Suggested Readings   93

IV: ANALYSIS: INVESTIGATING EMPIRICAL RELATIONSHIPS   95

8. Data Analysis Foundations   97
    Data Analysis and Statistics   98
        Statistical Information   98
        Statistical Purposes   99
    Properties of Scores   99
        Levels of Measurement   99
        Discrete and Continuous Variables   101
    Conventions   101
    Summary   103
    For Review   103
        Terms to Know   103
        Questions for Review   103
    Appendix 8A: On Clean Data   104
        Errors Made on Measuring Instruments   104
        Data File Errors   104
        Missing Values   105
        Evaluating Secondary Data Sets   105

9. Analysis Applications: Describing Scores on a Single Variable   106
    A Data Matrix   107
    Tables and Graphs   108
        Tables   108
        Graphs   108
    Statistical Representation of Scores   110
        Central Tendency   110
        Variability   110
        Shape   111
            Skew   112
            Kurtosis   113
    Relationships Between Statistics   113
        Skew and Central Tendency   113
        Skew and Variability   114
    Summary   114

For Review   115
   Terms to Know   115
   Formulae to Use   115
   Questions for Review   116
   Issues to Discuss   116

10. Analysis Applications: Simple Correlation and Regression   117
   Graphical Representation   119
   Simple Correlation   121
      Correlation Formulae   121
         Covariance   122
         Standard Scores 123
      Variance Explained   124
   Simple Regression   126
      Regression Model   126
      Regression Formulae   127
   Nominal Independent Variables   128
   Summary   131
   For Review   131
      Terms to Know   131
      Formulae to Use   132
      Questions for Review   133
      Issue to Discuss   133

11. Analysis Applications: Multiple Correlation and Regression 134
   Graphical Representation   135
   Multiple Correlation   135
      Multiple Coefficient of Determination 136
      Examples of the Multiple Coefficient of Determination 138
   Multiple Regression   139
      Intercept and Partial Regression Coefficients 140
      Partial Beta Coefficients   140
      Examples of Multiple Regression 141
   More Than Two Independent Variables   142
   Nominal Independent Variables   143
      One Nominal Variable With More Than Two Values 144
      Other Independent Variables   145
   Summary   146
   For Review   147
      Terms to Know   147
      Formulae to Use (Text)   148
      Formulae to Use (Appendix A)   149
      Questions for Review   149
   Appendix 11A: Contributions of Single Independent Variables in Multiple
      Correlation   150
      Squared Semipartial Correlation Coefficient 151
      Squared Partial Correlation Coefficient 151
      Examples   151
   Appendix 11B: Another Way to Think About Partial Coefficients 152
   Part IV Suggested Readings   154

V: STATISTICAL VALIDATION   155

12. Statistical Inference Foundations   157
  Probability   159
    Random Variables   159
    Independent Random Variables   160
  Probability Distributions   160
    Discrete Probability Distributions   160
    Continuous Probability Distributions   162
  Sampling Distributions   164
    Statistics and Parameters   164
    Sampling Distribution of the Mean   164
    Other Sampling Distributions   168
      Students' t Distributions   168
      F Distributions   168
  Summary   168
  For Review   169
    Terms to Know   169
    Formulae to Use   170
    Questions for Review   170
    Issues to Discuss   171

13. Statistical Inference Applications   172
  Statistical Hypothesis Testing   173
    Hypothesis Testing Logic and Procedures   174
      Specify Statistical Hypotheses and Significance Levels   174
      Draw a Probability Sample   175
      Estimate the Sampling Distribution If the Null Hypothesis Is True   175
      Identify Critical Region(s) of the Null Sampling Distribution   176
      Use Sample Statistic to Decide If the Null Sampling
        Distribution Is False   176
    Hypothesis Testing Example   177
    Hypothesis Testing Outcomes   179
    Statistical Power   179
      Statistical Power Conventions   180
      Other Power Determinants   183
  Confidence Intervals   184
    Confidence Interval Logic and Procedures   185
      Set Confidence Level   185
      Draw a Probability Sample and Calculate Sample Statistic   185
      Estimate Sampling Distribution Assuming the Statistic Represents
        the Parameter   185
      Identify Probable Region of the Sampling Distribution   185
      Infer That the Population Parameter Falls Within the
        Probable Region   185
    Confidence Interval Example   185
  Confidence Intervals Versus Hypothesis Testing and Power   187
  Internal Statistical Validity   188
    Randomization Tests   188
    Concluding Cautions   189
  Summary   191

For Review 192
Terms to Know 192
Formulae to Use 192
Questions for Review 193
Issues to Discuss 194
Appendix 13A: Formulae for Statistical Inference 194
Sampling Distributions 194
Statistical Inference Tests 194
Simple Correlation Coefficient 194
Simple Regression Coefficient 197
Multiple Coefficient of Determination 198
Partial Beta Coefficients 199
Incremental R^2 200
Part V Suggested Readings 200

VI: GENERALIZATION: ADDRESSING EXTERNAL VALIDITY 201

14. External Validity 203
External Generalization Challenges 204
Generalizing From Single Studies 205
Replication 206
Replication Roles 206
Narrative Reviews of Replications 207
Meta-Analysis 208
Example 210
Illustrative Data 210
Meta-Analysis Interpretations 211
External Statistical Inference 212
Internal Statistical Inference 212
Evaluation 213
Contributions of Meta-Analysis 213
Meta-Analysis Reservations 214
Closing Observations 214
Summary 214
For Review 215
Terms to Know 215
Questions for Review 215
Issues to Discuss 215
Part VI Suggested Readings 216

VII: RESEARCH REPORTS 217

15. Research Report Writing 219
Research Report Format 220
Introduction 220
Methods 220
Cases 220
Measures 221
Procedure 221
Analyses 222

Results   222
Discussion   223
Alternative Research Report Formats   223
Additional Suggestions   224
Begin by Organizing   224
Rewrite, Then Rewrite   225
Draft a Critic   225
Take a Scout's Oath   225
Summary   225
Appendix 15A: On Table Construction   226
When to Use Tables   226
Table Characteristics   226
Integrate Tables and Text   226
An Example   226
Descriptive Results   227
Substantive Results   227

VIII: EXTENSIONS   229

16.   On Incomplete Data   231
Avoid Incomplete Data   232
Evaluate Nonresponse   233
Address Missing Data   233
Dependent Variables   233
Independent Variables   234
Delete Variables   234
Delete Cases   234
Mean Substitution   235
Alternative Methods   236
Identify "Missingness"   237
Reporting Incomplete Data   237
Current Reporting Practices   237
Recommended Practices   238
Summary   238
For Review   239
Terms to Know   239
Questions for Review   239
Suggested Readings   239

17.   On Reliability   240
Reliability Defined   241
Estimating Reliability   242
Internal Consistency   242
Interpreting Coefficient Alpha   243
Stability   244
Interrater Reliability   244
Reporting Reliability Estimates   244
Consequences of Unreliability   245
Simple Correlation and Regression   245
Demonstrations   245

	Correlation Coefficients	246
	Correcting for Unreliability in Correlation Coefficients	247
	Regression Coefficients and Intercepts	247
	Unreliability in X	247
	Unreliability in Y	247
	Correcting for Unreliability in Regression Coefficients	248
	Unreliability in Multiple Correlation and Regression	248
	Summary	249
	For Review	249
	Terms to Know	249
	Formulae to Use	249
	Questions for Review	250
	Exercise	251
	Suggested Readings	251
18.	On Multicollinearity	252
	Consequences of Multicollinearity	252
	A Demonstration	253
	Population Parameters	253
	Sample Statistics	254
	Multicollinearity Misconceived	256
	Addressing Multicollinearity	257
	Summary	258
	For Review	258
	Terms to Know	258
	Formula to Use	258
	Questions for Review	258
19.	On Causal Models and Statistical Modeling	260
	Causal Models	261
	Illustrative Data Set	261
	Evaluating Causal Models	261
	Four Illustrative Models	262
	Direct Effects Models	263
	Mediated Models	264
	Moderated Models	266
	Subgrouping	266
	Moderated Regression	267
	Centering	269
	A Final Requirement	271
	Hierarchical Models	271
	A Closing Caution	273
	Summary	273
	For Review	274
	Terms to Know	274
	Questions for Review	275
	Suggested Readings	275
20.	On Statistical Modeling Challenges	277
	Specification	278
	The Conceptual Model	278

The Statistical Model	278
Importance of Independent Variables	279
Variance Explained and Coefficient Size	279
Correlation and Variance Explained	279
Regression Coefficients	279
Measurement Issues	280
Reliability	280
Construct Validity	280
Representativeness of the Cases Studied	282
Design and Statistical Inference	283
Summary and Conclusions	284
For Review	286
Terms to Know	286
Questions for Review	286
Issues to Discuss	286
Suggested Readings	287
21. On Good Research	288
What Makes Research Good?	289
An Illustration Using The Research Model	290
Causal Conceptual Relationships	290
Generalizability of Causal Conceptual Relationships	292
Elements of a Persuasive Research Study	293
Theoretical Justification	293
Contributions of Theory	293
If There Is No Theory	294
Prior Research Evidence	294
Research Design	294
Research Execution	295
Sensitivity Analysis	295
The Research Report	296
Summary	296
Causal Relationships	296
Generalization	297
For Review	297
Terms to Know	297
Questions for Review	298
Issues to Discuss	298
Suggested Readings	298
Glossary	299
References	311
Author Index	315
Subject Index	319

Preface

This book introduces social science methods as applied broadly to the study of issues that arise as part of organizational life. These include issues involving organizational participants such as managers, teachers, customers, patients, and clients and transactions within and between organizations. The material is an outgrowth of more than 30 years of teaching research classes to master's and doctoral students at the Universities of Wisconsin and Minnesota and at Purdue University. Although these classes have been offered in management and/or industrial relations departments, students participating have come from many other programs, including industrial/organizational and social psychology, educational administration, sociology, marketing, communication arts, operations management, nursing, health care administration, and industrial engineering.

Naturally, my views about research and about what constitutes good research practice have strongly influenced the content of this book. However, experiences while teaching have had the most significant impact on the organization, emphases, and tone of the book. Many students experience anxiety when they begin a course in research methods; not all students begin such a course enthusiastically. This book aims to reduce anxiety by presenting research methods in a straightforward and understandable fashion. It aims to enhance student motivation by providing practical skills needed to carry out research activities.

Responses to the first edition have been very positive on these points. Published reviews, correspondence, and personal communications have all indicated that the first edition achieved the objective; the volume has been uniformly viewed as "student friendly." I am particularly pleased with the unsolicited letters and e-mails received from students and instructors on this characteristic of the book.

An important aid to students is the use of an integrative model explicated in Part I of the book. I initially developed this model in a paper on construct validity (Schwab, 1980). However, the model is useful as a way of viewing empirical research generally. Its use was well received in the first edition and I continue its use throughout the second edition to explain and integrate major research activities. This model, shown as Exhibit P.1, is a powerful way to communicate key research concepts, challenges, and outcomes. The model distinguishes between empirical activities carried out at an operational level and the interpretations we make of those operations at a conceptual level. It thus illustrates the critical need for valid measurement and underscores the challenges researchers face in obtaining useful measures. The model also distinguishes between independent and dependent variables. Although not always explicitly stated in research reports, most organizational research is designed to draw causal inferences; the distinction between cause and consequence is essential for conducting research and, especially, for interpreting research findings.

By combining these two dimensions of research, the model clearly illustrates contributions and limitations of empirical research outcomes to conceptual understanding. It shows that the only outcome directly observable from empirical research is the relationship between scores (line d). All other relationships involve inferences as implied by the broken lines. Inferences are required to conclude that relationships between scores are causally or internally valid (line c).

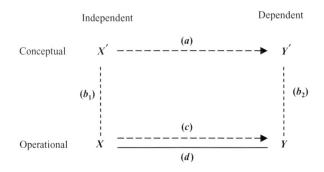

EXHIBIT P.1.   Empirical research model.

Inferences are also required to conclude that the scores obtained from measures represent their respective constructs, that they have a high degree of construct validity (lines b_1 and b_2). Finally, inferences about causal conceptual relationships (line a) require supportive evidence from all the other relationships and inferences. The model is extremely useful for showing the roles and limitations of each of the major research activities.

The model also serves as a foundation for drawing generalizations from research results. For example, it is used to show how statistical inference can be used to draw generalizations about the relationship observed by line d. The model also serves as a foundation for the discussion of external validity where generalizations that transcend statistical inferences are at issue.

OBJECTIVES AND ORGANIZATION

My major objective in a research methods course is to help students develop skills needed to conduct empirical research and to critically evaluate research conducted by others. This, in turn, requires that students spend a substantial portion of their time engaged in research activities. This book is designed to facilitate that objective in several ways.

First, the book has an applied orientation. Although it explicitly acknowledges the centrality of conceptualization to research understanding, it focuses primarily on empirical research activities. Major parts are devoted to measurement, design, analysis, and the inferences to be drawn from research results. Typically, each part begins with a chapter on foundation issues. These chapters include a discussion of how the activity fits into the framework provided by the model and identify objectives for, and challenges to, the activity. A chapter or chapters on applications then elaborates on procedures used to address objectives and challenges.

Second, the book is designed and organized to address a serious challenge for research methods instructors. Specifically, research understanding is interactive in the sense that the more a student knows about design, for example, the easier it becomes to understand analysis or measurement, and vice versa. Yet, classes must be organized in a sequential fashion. This book addresses this problem by first providing an overview of *all* research activities in part I of the book. The model is used to show the roles for measurement, design, analysis, and inference. The book then proceeds sequentially through each of these topics. The discussion of measurement in part II, for example, does not require knowledge from part III on design or part IV on data analysis beyond what has been discussed in part I. The discussion of design does not require additional knowledge about analysis or inference.

The last portion of the book, part VIII, covers topics that draw on knowledge presented in two or more of the previous parts. In particular, measurement and design issues that require knowledge of data analysis methods are discussed at the end of the book. For example, chapter 17 on reliability draws on information from parts on measurement and analysis. Chapter 19 on modeling draws on information from parts on design, data analysis, and inference.

The extension chapters at the end of the book serve an additional purpose. These chapters can be used selectively as suggested by specific course objectives and student interests and capabilities. From semester to semester, even when teaching the same class, I discuss these special topics selectively depending on the unique characteristics of each class.

NEW FOR THIS EDITION

The major changes in this edition are the addition of two entirely new chapters. In the first edition, chapter 19 served as a capstone of sorts by describing modeling using regression and correlation. It also included a brief discussion of challenges to modeling that focused on the interpretation of statistical inference.

This material has now been substantially augmented and made into two chapters. Chapter 19 now focuses just on describing the modeling process and outcomes. The description of moderator models has been enhanced with an explanation of how to use and interpret centering. While it retains its focus on ordinary least squares, it also introduces structural equation modeling.

An entirely new chapter 20 now addresses challenges to modeling. It goes substantially beyond a discussion of statistical inference. It also discusses issues in interpreting variance explained estimates and standardized and unstandardized regression coefficients. It additionally returns to design and measurement and shows roles they play in the interpretation of modeling outcomes. Thus, chapter 20 draws from issues spanning the entire model and accordingly is more integrative.

Indeed, chapter 20 might have served as an appropriate way to end the book. However, I believe the new chapter 21 is a true capstone. Starting with a review of the model and material in preceding chapters, chapter 21 describes conditions needed to conduct persuasive research. Given a topic of interest, it identifies two major research criteria. Using the model as a point of departure, it then shows how components of the research process are linked to produce persuasive research. The chapter thus serves not only as a summary of the entire book, it also provides a guide for evaluating the research of others as well as a guide for conducting research.

Numerous other changes have been made in this second edition with the objective of further clarification. Also, a number of additions (and a few deletions) have been made to improve this edition. A definition and discussion of criterion-related validity is added to chapter 3. The discussion of bias in chapter 5 is now improved and integrated with a discussion of bias resulting from other sources. Chapter 5 also has a more appropriate discussion of restriction of range; it notes that restriction typically creates more problems than it solves as a design option. Chapter 17 extends the discussion of unreliability to include its implications for multiple correlation and regression output. In the first edition, chapter 19 described empirical modeling (stepwise procedures) at some length. In this edition, empirical modeling is described briefly in a Research Highlight consistent with my belief that empirical modeling is generally to be discouraged. The instructor's manual retains material on empirical modeling for instructors who still wish to cover this topic.

I chose not to include a chapter on qualitative research, although at least two published reviews faulted the first edition for not having one. First, I am not an expert in qualitative research methods. Second, qualitative research methods are at least as complex as the quantitative methods described in this book. I fear even an expert would be challenged to write a chapter that was useful in the spirit with which this volume seeks to provide students with usable research tools. Consequently, I acknowledge qualitative methods in chapter 1 and point out that this book simply does not address them as it does not, for example, address analytical research methods.

Although two chapters have been added, the book remains relatively short. I believe it is easy for students to get information overload when reading encyclopedic methods volumes. Because my objective is to help students learn how to conduct research, I prefer to give them only information that is essential to initiating quality research projects. Much of our class discussion and study time is spent carrying out research.

In addition, I find that from semester to semester there are substantial student differences in sophistication and substantive interests. I use outside readings along with this book—some are substantive to serve as fodder for research critiques and some discuss research methods issues. The content and level of these papers vary depending on class composition. Consequently, this book is tightly focused; I use it as an organizing schema for the other class activities and readings.

SPECIAL FEATURES

The second edition retains a number of additional features; although they are not unique, they are all designed to make information about research methods more accessible to students and to help teachers in the instruction process. Key terms are defined and highlighted when introduced in the text. These terms are also included in the chapter-ending review section and are organized alphabetically in a glossary at the end of the volume. Chapter endings also contain review questions and, where appropriate, exercises to reinforce learning of chapter material. I was very pleased with one published review that commented on these features. Written by an instructor, the review noted that these features of the book were found to be very useful by beginning doctoral students.

Chapters usually have one or more Research Highlights; a number of new ones have been added to this edition. These typically elaborate briefly on points related to a central theme in a chapter. They may serve as a basis for further class discussion. Briefly annotated bibliographies are also provided at the end of each part of the book and, in the case of the integrative chapters in part VIII, at the end of chapters. These are highly selective; only readings that I believe will be accessible to students are included.

Several of the chapters included are novel but are consistent with the applied objectives of the book. A separate chapter is devoted to research report writing. This chapter is as useful to me as to students because it helps to improve papers that students submit as their major class project. There are also separate chapters on how to address nonresponse and missing data and on how to cope with multicollinearity.

The treatment of design is comprehensive and I believe a special strength of the book. Chapter 5 sets out the major causal challenges for design and shows how three major design decisions address these challenges. A separate chapter then describes experiments and quasi-experiments and another describes surveys and field studies. These latter chapters explain how threats to internal validity popularized by Cook and Campbell (1979) differ substantially by the type of design at issue.

Finally, an instructor's manual has been updated and is available to teachers who use this book. This manual has sections containing lecture notes and suggestions, transparency masters, test items, and recommendations for test construction and grading; it also has a number of cases. Some of these are designed to be used as exercises for learning on just one or two topics; others can serve for semester projects to be performed by individuals or teams. Data for these cases are also provided on a computer disk. Data sets are provided that can be used for class demonstrations.

ACKNOWLEDGMENTS

Both editions of the book have benefited enormously from the help and encouragement provided by colleagues and students. Colleagues at other universities who provided valuable help on one or both editions, often by reading major portions of the manuscript and in some instances class testing one or more chapters, include Alison Barber, Michigan State University; Mike Campion, Purdue University; Bob Eder, Portland State University; Jeff Edwards, University of North Carolina; Jack Fiorito, Florida State University; Dave Harrison, Pennsylvania State University; Rob Heneman, Ohio State University; John Hollenbeck, Michigan State University; Pat Joynt, Henley Management College; Tom Lee, University of Washington; Tom Mahoney, Vanderbilt University; Craig Olson, University of Illinois; Marc Orlitzky, University of Sydney; Jon Pierce, University of Minnesota-Duluth; Craig Pinder, University of British Columbia; Barb Rau, University of Wisconsin—Oshkosh; Sara Rynes, University of Iowa; and Paul Sackett, University of Minnesota.

Students and colleagues here at Madison who provided valuable assistance include Melissa Arronte, Paula Bassoff, Linda Brothers, Gil Churchill, Barry Gerhart, Bob Giambatista, Herb Heneman, Bob Miller, Anne Miner, J. Paul Peter, Andreas Schwab, Frank Siciliano, Charlie Trevor, and Mary Zellmer. Special thanks to Janet Christopher and Dongseop Lee for their help in editing, preparing, and managing the manuscript.

About the Author

Donald P. Schwab, PhD, University of Minnesota, is a faculty member at the University of Wisconsin–Madison. He is currently Rennebohm Professor of Business Research and the Chair of the Management and Human Resources Department. He has also been the Donald Slichter Professor of Business Research and is a Romnes Faculty Fellow. Professor Schwab has also been a Visiting Professor at the University of Kentucky, University of Minnesota, and Purdue University.

Professor Schwab is a Fellow of the Academy of Management and of the American Psychological Association. He is a Past Chair of the Human Resources Division of the Academy of Management. In 1994, he received the Career Achievement Award from the Human Resources Division of the Academy, only the second individual so honored.

Professor Schwab's research has appeared in publications including the *Academy of Management Journal, Academy of Management Review, Journal of Applied Psychology, Industrial and Labor Relations Review, Industrial Relations, Organizational Behavior and Human Decision Processes, Personnel Psychology*, and *Psychological Bulletin*. He is a co-author of nine other books. He has also served on the Editorial Board of the *Academy of Management Journal* and *Organizational Behavior and Human Decision Processes*; he is currently on the Board of *Human Resources Management Review*. He currently teaches graduate courses in research methods.

RESEARCH METHODS
FOR
ORGANIZATIONAL STUDIES

I

Overview

1
Introduction

Chapter Outline

- *Research Activities*
- *A Point of View*
- *Objectives and Organization*
- *Summary*
- *For Review*
  - *Terms to Know*

Consider these courses of action:

- An elementary school principal establishes a set of difficult teacher goals to improve students' academic performance.
- A medical director has staff members make suggestions anonymously to encourage participation.
- A company president joins an alliance with other firms in the industry to improve returns from research and development expenditures.
- Parents take their children to a concert to stimulate an interest in music.
- A union leader calls for a strike vote to increase members' solidarity.
- A basketball coach has team members take dancing lessons to improve agility.
- A director of marketing recommends that a product be renamed, repackaged, and increased in price to attract more affluent customers.
- A captain in the Salvation Army posts names of the bell ringers who obtain the greatest contributions each day to encourage bell ringer solicitations.
- A human resource manager proposes a flexible benefit plan to reduce employee turnover.

These decisions have several things in common. They all take place in an organizational context, as does most human activity. These may be educational organizations such as elementary schools, health-related organizations such as clinics, business organizations such as manufacturing firms, volunteer organizations such as charitable agencies, and biological organizations such as families.

The examples also illustrate courses of action that are undertaken as a result of expected relationships between two or more factors. A school principal believes that setting goals will influence teachers, who, in turn, are expected to influence students. A human resource manager believes a flexible benefit plan will make the organization more attractive to employees and hence increase their motivation to retain their membership in it.

Each of the expected relationships is causal. In **causal relationships** one factor influences another. The school principal expects the introduction of teacher goals will cause student achievement. The human resource manager expects flexible benefits will cause employee retention. These and other expected causal relationships for the examples mentioned are summarized in Exhibit 1.1.

Emphasis is placed on the word *expected.* All these illustrative actions are based on expected relationships between factors; these expectations may or may not hold. Student achievements

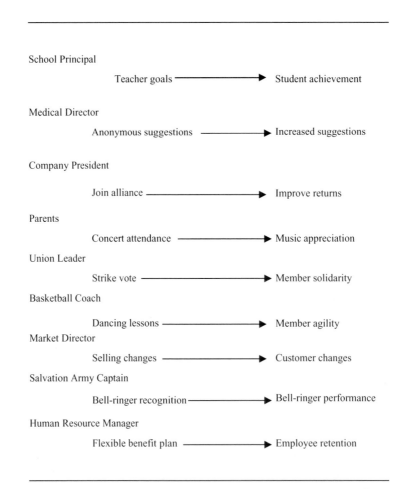

EXHIBIT 1.1. Causal representation of illustrative actions.

may increase after the principal establishes goals for the teachers, but they may not. Flexible benefits may increase employee retention, but they may not.

Empirical research can help obtain evidence on the veracity of expected causal relationships of the type described here. ***Empirical research*** addresses expected relationships through the systematic study of relationships between scores obtained from cases on measures.

This book describes methods for conducting empirical research on issues of the type illustrated in the preceding paragraphs. Topics covered explain how the three key elements in the definition of empirical research, as shown in Exhibit 1.2, are addressed in research. ***Cases*** are the entities investigated in research. Cases may be individuals interacting in organizations such as customers, patients, and students, who agree to be studied. Cases also may be organizations such as political parties, business firms, hospitals, libraries, government agencies, and religious groups. They may be formal or informal groups within organizations such as executive policy teams in business firms, sports groups in schools, SWAT teams in police departments, and production quality improvement teams in manufacturing firms. Cases also may be events or transactions made within organizations, or linking organizations, such as sales invoices, bank

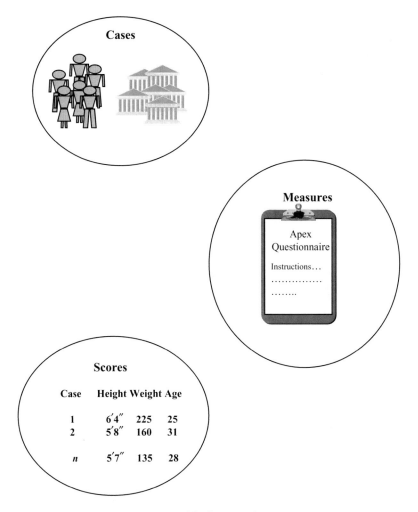

EXHIBIT 1.2.   Empirical research components.

RESEARCH HIGHLIGHT 1.1

Not All Research Is Empirical

Empirical research involves observation; it requires cases, measures, and scores. Not all types of research are empirical. For example, computer simulations generate scores from random number routines. Cases and measures are not involved. Analytical researchers use mathematical operations to work from initial assumptions to conclusions. There are no cases, measures, or scores.

This book is about empirical research methods only. Hereafter, *research* and *empirical research* are used interchangeably.

---

checking account balances, contractual provisions, stock prices, grocery receipts, records of hospital patient prescriptions, and golf scores.

Measures are instruments used to obtain scores on the cases studied. For example, measures may be items or questionnaires that individuals complete, or they may be items on forms that researchers fill out after they review sets of transactions or events. Finally, *scores* (or *data*) represent information obtained from cases on the measures used. Typically, scores are recorded in numerical form. Researchers use these scores to identify whether relationships exist as expected.

To illustrate, a researcher believes increases in education lead to increases in financial success; this represents an expected causal relationship. The researcher investigates this expectation by soliciting the cooperation of a group of adult workers (cases). A questionnaire (measure) is developed that asks participants to record their highest year of education and gross income earned in the previous year. Participants' responses constitute scores the researcher studies to see if a relationship exists as expected.

RESEARCH ACTIVITIES

The scenario described indicates that empirical research involves three activities: measurement, design, and analysis. *Measurement* involves activities associated with measuring the factors that form the expected relationship. In the example, the researcher develops questions about education and income specifically for the study conducted. In other situations, a researcher may begin with measures already developed and assess their suitability for a study at hand.

Research design establishes procedures to obtain cases for study and to determine how scores will be obtained from those cases. In the example, the choice of adult workers to study and the choice of measures and procedures to obtain scores on those measures are illustrative of the research design.

Empirical research also involves analyses of scores. *Analyses* are performed to describe scores on single measures and, especially, to identify relationships that may exist between scores across different measures. In the example, the researcher is particularly interested in the relationship between scores on the measures of education and income. Analysis methods typically involve the use of statistics.

Measurement, design, and analysis are the three major activities of empirical research as shown in Exhibit 1.3. This book describes methods to develop and evaluate measures, design research, and analyze relationships between scores.

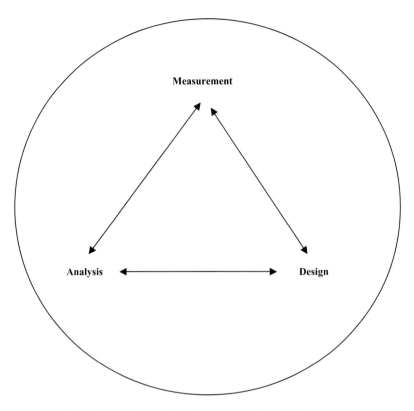

EXHIBIT 1.3. Empirical research activities.

The lines linking the three research activities signal two things. First, they signal that these research activities are related in practice. For example, decisions about design influence both measurement and analysis decisions. Second, they signal that knowledge of any one research activity is helpful in learning about the other activities. For example, the more you know about analysis, the deeper can be your understanding of measurement and design.

RESEARCH HIGHLIGHT 1.2

Not All Empirical Research Is Quantitative

As with the research methods described in this book, *qualitative research* is also empirical. Qualitative researchers also use measures to obtain scores from cases within a research design. Good qualitative research is also systematic. However, qualitative researchers typically study relatively small numbers of cases and often involve themselves in substantial interaction with the cases studied. Analyses also usually involve greater use of the researchers' subjective interpretation and judgment. Statistical procedures such as those described in parts IV and V are less likely to be used by qualitative researchers. Qualitative researchers use a variety of research designs, methods for measurement, and procedures for analysis. Those procedures have evolved from the humanities as well as the social sciences; they typically differ substantially from methods discussed in this book. As a consequence, no attempt is made to describe qualitative research methods in this book.

A POINT OF VIEW

Research is sometimes described as a major tool of "the scientific method," and that method is described in terms so abstract as to be nearly incomprehensible. Research methods may then be seen as a mysterious set of practices that only a chosen few can accomplish, probably in cloistered laboratories.

This book is written with a less deferential view of research methods. Research methods are easily accessible. These methods do not differ qualitatively from our everyday practices of observing events and making sense of them.

This book takes the view that research methods have two advantages for obtaining knowledge and that these are only advantages when research is appropriately conducted and reported. First, research methods properly conducted address questions *systematically*. Researchers carefully collect scores from cases with measures that are suitable for the question asked. Analysis of these scores is thoughtfully performed, and results obtained are carefully interpreted; probable limitations are acknowledged.

Second, research properly performed is a public process; it is *transparent*. The methods used are reported along with the results and interpretations. This characteristic is desirable so that others may evaluate research results and, if desired, repeat the research under similar or different conditions.

These are modest claims. Single research studies do not answer questions definitively. At best, research investigations are limited by researchers' assumptions and expectations, by the cases studied, by the measures used, and by the methods of analysis used. Furthermore, studies involving human interactions are always bounded by context, such as the organizational setting in which they are conducted. To paraphrase Winston Churchill's view of democracy, research is the worst way to acquire knowledge except for the alternatives.

OBJECTIVES AND ORGANIZATION

Although this perspective for research is admittedly modest, it reflects a view adopted by many practicing organizational researchers. Furthermore, this perspective hopefully will suggest that you can acquire the skills needed to be a successful researcher. The book is written to help you acquire skills to conduct research with this view of research methods and outcomes in mind. The systematic nature of the research enterprise is emphasized. This applies to all three major research activities: measurement, design, and analysis. Part VII of the book is devoted to reporting research studies, the public portion of the research process.

Acquiring skills to conduct research will help you be a more thoughtful and critical consumer of research performed by others, a second objective of the book. Most knowledge, even knowledge obtained by professional researchers, comes from research conducted by others. Thus, skills to critically evaluate research often are more useful than skills to conduct it.

The book is organized into eight parts consistent with its viewpoint and objectives. Part I includes this and the next chapter. Chapter 2 presents a model of the entire research enterprise. This model introduces research objectives and shows how measurement, design, and analysis contribute to knowledge generation.

Part II contains two chapters on measurement. These chapters describe measurement objectives and introduce criteria used to evaluate measures against these objectives. These chapters also describe measurement procedures commonly used in organizational studies.

Part III addresses research design. Chapter 5 identifies challenges for research design and identifies major decisions that researchers make when designing empirical research studies. The chapter also shows how these decisions affect conclusions that can appropriately be drawn from research studies. It concludes by introducing major types of designs that researchers use. Chapters 6 and 7 elaborate on these major design types.

Chapters in part IV focus on data analysis. Chapter 8 provides an overview of data analysis and introductory material on important characteristics of scores for analysis purposes. Chapter 9 describes methods for summarizing information about scores obtained from a single measure. These include statistics of central tendency, variability, and shape. Chapters 10 and 11 describe simple and multiple correlation and regression, respectively. These statistics provide useful ways to summarize relationships between scores from two or more measures.

Part V has two chapters on the use of statistics and probability theory for drawing inferences that transcend the relations observed on scores. These statistical inferences are made to address causal relationships and to address whether a statistic observed on the group of cases studied likely applies in the broader population from which the sample group was drawn. Chapter 12 introduces the statistical inference process. Chapter 13 describes two methods for performing generalizations: hypothesis testing and confidence intervals.

Part VI has a chapter on other types of inferences researchers seek to make from their research. It discusses the important role of repeating research studies to obtain information on the likely generalizability of research findings. It also describes two methods that researchers use to make these sorts of generalizations: narrative reviews and meta-analysis.

Part VII contains a chapter on research report writing. Research reports have a special obligation to satisfy the second advantage of research mentioned earlier—namely, to provide a public record of the research for evaluation. Chapter 15 identifies the elements of research that should be included in a report to meet this obligation.

Part VIII contains six chapters that extend topics covered earlier in the book. The first three of these address incomplete data sets, a challenge facing nearly every empirical study; reliability, a challenge for nearly all measurement efforts; and mutlicollinearity, an analysis issue that typically confronts researchers in even moderately complex studies. Two chapters follow that draw on earlier chapters to show how researchers carry out research studies to address causal questions and the challenges they confront when doing so. Finally, the last chapter draws on all earlier chapters to suggest what makes for conducting a persuasive research study. This chapter also serves as a guide for evaluating whether research conducted by others is persuasive.

SUMMARY

Organizational research questions usually involve *causal relationships* in which it is anticipated that one factor influences another. *Empirical research* activities contribute to causal understanding by investigating relationships between *scores* obtained from *cases* on *measures* of concepts. Three activities are needed to conduct empirical research: measurement, research design, and analysis. *Measurement* activities are aimed at obtaining scores on measures that correspond to the concepts studied. *Research design* establishes procedures to obtain participants and to determine how scores are obtained on measures. *Analyses* are performed to describe scores on single measures and to identify relationships between scores across measures.

This book takes the perspective that research methods are not greatly different from other methods for drawing conclusions about events that are observed. Research is generally superior to alternative methods because of its systematic and public nature.

Given this perspective, the book is designed to help you achieve two objectives: to learn how to conduct research and to learn how to evaluate other people's research. It does so by explaining how to perform and to record activities associated with measurement, research design, and analysis.

FOR REVIEW

Terms to Know

Causal relationship: When variation in one factor is responsible for variation in another.

Empirical research: Systematic study of relationships between scores obtained from cases on measures.

Cases: Entities (e.g., individuals, groups, organizations, transactions) investigated in research.

Measures: Instruments used to obtain scores from participants.

Scores (also, *data*): Numerical information about cases obtained on measures.

Measurement: Activities associated with measuring cases.

Research design: Overall plan of a study; establishes procedures to obtain cases for study and to determine how scores are obtained on measures of cases.

Analyses: Used to describe scores on single measures and to identify relationships that may exist between scores across different measures; typically involve the use of statistics.

Qualitative research: Empirical research procedure that investigates a small number of cases, typically with substantial interaction between the cases and researcher.

2

A Model of Empirical Research

Chapter Outline

- *Research Variables*
  - *Conceptual and Operational Variables*
  - *Dependent and Independent Variables*
- *The Model*
  - *Conceptual Relationships*
  - *Operational Relationships*
    - *Empirical Relationships*
    - *Causal Relationships at an Empirical Level*
  - *Conceptual to Operational Relationships*
- *Generalizing from the Model*
  - *Statistical Generalization*
  - *External Generalization*
- *Summary*
- *For Review*
  - *Terms to Know*
  - *Things to Know*
  - *Issues to Discuss*

Chapter 1 points out that many decisions are based on expected causal relationships. For example, a decision is made to establish goals for teachers expecting these goals will influence their behaviors and subsequently influence students' academic achievement.

Chapter 2 develops a model that explicates such causal relationships and shows how empirical research contributes to causal understanding. Master the model in this chapter, and you will see research questions just as practicing researchers see them. The model will also help you understand researchers' frames of reference when you read research reports. Most important, the model provides a good way to think about issues as you conduct and evaluate your own research.

The chapter begins by discussing variables; relationships between variables represent the core of research and the core of the model. The model links variables in two ways that correspond to research as typically performed. One way links variables understood at a conceptual level with variables measured and observed at an empirical or operational level. The second way links variables in a causal chain. Combined, these two methods for linking variables form a powerful way to think about empirical research methods and outcomes. The chapter also discusses issues associated with the generalization of research outcomes beyond the cases investigated in a specific study.

Topics covered in this chapter are important for the organization of this book. The model described serves as the organizing theme for parts II through IV. The description of generalization serves as the basis for parts V and VI.

RESEARCH VARIABLES

Variables are characteristics of objects or events that can take on two or more values. Age, height, and weight are variables used to describe people. Number of employees, number of accounts outstanding, gross receipts, and total assets are variables used to describe organizations. All these characteristics are variables, because they can take on different values.

Variables are central to research. Most research is concerned with relationships between variables. For example, is there a relationship between education (one variable) and financial success (another variable)? A relationship in this case means that persons with different levels of education experience different levels of financial success.

Conceptual and Operational Variables

Empirical research activities and our understanding of research outcomes exist at two different levels of abstraction. We understand at a conceptual level. To say, "I know that education leads to financial success," expresses a belief about a causal relationship at a conceptual level.

At this level of abstraction variables are called *conceptual variables* or *constructs*. Constructs are mental definitions of objects or events that can vary. Definitions of characteristics such as education and financial success are examples. To illustrate, the construct *education* may be defined as the knowledge and problem-solving abilities one acquires from formal learning environments. The term *construct* is used to denote conceptually defined variables from this point forward.

Empirical research activities are carried out at an operational level of abstraction. Empirical research obtains scores from cases on measures. These measures represent *operational variables*. Variables are made operational by the measures used to obtain scores from the cases studied. For example, a question that asks respondents to report the number of years they have attended school is an operational measure of education.

Dependent and Independent Variables

Another way to distinguish variables involves their location in a causal sequence. *Dependent variables* are outcomes or consequences; they are variables that researchers seek to understand, explain, and/or predict. *Independent variables* are those thought to influence or at least predict dependent variables. For example, a researcher may seek to understand why some athletic

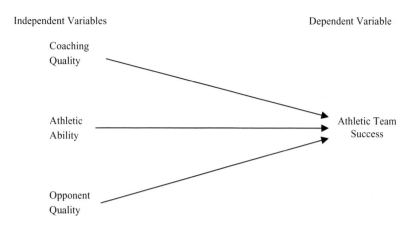

Independent Variables   Dependent Variable

Coaching
Quality

Athletic   Athletic Team
Ability   Success

Opponent
Quality

EXHIBIT 2.1.   Relationship between independent and dependent variables.

teams succeed more than others. Athletic program success is the dependent variable. Coaching quality may be an independent variable. Variation in coaching quality is expected to influence variation in athletic team success.

Dependent variables typically are influenced by more than one independent variable. For example, athletic success depends on the athletic ability of team members and the quality of opponents as well as on coaching quality. Exhibit 2.1 provides a representation at the conceptual level.

Variables can be dependent in one context and independent in another. Athletic success, the dependent variable just mentioned, may serve as an independent variable in a study of athletic department revenue. Research interests determine the dependent variable in any study.

Researchers are usually interested in causation. In such research, the independent variable represents a cause; the dependent variable represents the consequence. However, independent and dependent variables are not necessarily causally linked. Independent variables may simply predict dependent variables without causal linkages. For example, birds often begin to sing shortly before sunrise; their singing predicts the sunrise but does not cause it.

THE MODEL

A model of empirical research that accounts for the two distinctions just made is shown in Exhibit 2.2. The distinction between conceptual and operational variables is represented vertically; the distinction between independent and dependent variables is represented horizontally. Only two constructs are included in the model, although it can easily be extended to more than two.

Exhibit 2.2 uses three conventions utilized throughout the remainder of this book:

1. Independent and dependent variables are identified by X and Y, respectively.
2. The symbol *prime*, ' , is used to designate that a variable is specified at the conceptual level.
3. Arrows represent the direction of influence or cause.

The set of variables in Exhibit 2.2 shows three types of relationships; all are important in research.

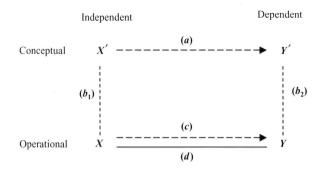

EXHIBIT 2.2.   Empirical research model.

Conceptual Relationships

The top horizontal line (*a*) represents a causal conceptual relationship. A ***causal conceptual relationship*** describes a situation in which an independent construct is thought to influence a dependent construct. The school principal believes that teacher goals enhance student achievement. This illustrates a belief about a causal conceptual relationship.

Researchers usually have an expectation about this relationship before conducting a study. In research, such expectations are called ***hypotheses***, tentative beliefs about relationships between variables. Research is done to obtain information about whether the hypothesized relationship is valid.

Validity refers to the truth of a research conclusion. In this case, validity refers to the truth of the causal conceptual relationship between X' and Y'. Because this relationship is conceptual, its validity is necessarily tentative. Line (*a*) in Exhibit 2.2 is broken to signal this tentative nature of the validity of the relationship.

There is always a degree of uncertainty when a conclusion or inference is held to be valid. ***Verisimilitude***, meaning something having the appearance of truth, is a good way to think about validity and truth in research.

Operational Relationships

Exhibit 2.2 shows two lines connecting scores on X and Y at the operational level of measurement.

Empirical Relationships

An ***Empirical Relationship***, represented by line (*d*), refers to the correspondence between scores on measures of X and Y. Line (*d*) is solid to signal that this relationship can actually be observed, typically by using some statistical procedure (see part IV).

Causal Relationships at an Empirical Level

When causality is an issue, research must do more than establish an empirical relationship; it also must provide evidence of causation. Line (*c*) signals a causal relationship between X and Y. Scores on the two measures are related, and it is because variation in X scores leads to variation in Y scores. ***Internal validity*** is present when variation in scores on a measure of an independent variable is responsible for variation in scores on a measure of a dependent variable.

1. Independent and dependent variables are meaningfully related.

2. Variation in the independent variable is contemporaneous with, or precedes, variation in the dependent variable.

3. There is a reasonable causal explanation for the observed relationship and there are no plausible alternative explanations for it.

EXHIBIT 2.3.   Internal causal criteria.

Line (c), as (a), is broken, because internal validity cannot be established with certainty. *Internal validation* procedures (see part III) are used to infer internal validity indirectly. Internal validity is assessed with the three criteria shown in Exhibit 2.3. The first criterion states that a relationship must be observed between scores on measures of X and Y. Although not sufficient, an empirical relationship is necessary for causation.

Furthermore, this relationship must be meaningful; it must be greater than what might be expected to occur by chance or coincidence. An empirical relationship has *internal statistical validity* when it is not due to chance. *Statistical validation* (see part V) uses probability theory to assess internal statistical validity.

The second criterion follows from a linear time perspective. It is based on an assumption that things occurring later in time are not responsible for those occurring earlier. A causal (independent) variable occurs before a consequence (dependent) variable.

The third criterion has two parts. First, it requires that there is a reasonable conceptual explanation for why X causes Y. Researchers often use *theory* to help them in this process. A theory provides a tentative explanation for why a causal relationship(s) obtains (see Research Highlight 2.1). For example, a theory may explain that education causes financial

RESEARCH HIGHLIGHT 2.1

Many Faces of Theory

The definition of theory adopted in this book—a tentative explanation for why selected causal relationships obtain—is widely shared. However, it is not the only way the term is used. For example, some researchers regard typologies (hypothesized sets of categories to describe groups of objects or events) or taxonomies (empirically derived sets of categories) as theories. These researchers assess their theories against criteria such as whether the resulting categories are mutually exclusive and exhaustive. Others view the derivation of consequences (theorems) from a set of postulates or axioms as theory building. Tests of theory in this context involve logic and mathematical rules. Other definitions for theory exist as well.

These alternative definitions may not address causation and typically do not involve an explanation for the *why* of causal relationships when they do. As a consequence, the expression "causal explanation" is typically used in this book rather than the term "theory" to avoid confusion.

success because it provides people with knowledge, skills, and abilities that are valued in the marketplace.

The second part of the third criterion states that there must be no plausible rival conceptual explanations that account for the relationship observed. This issue is typically evaluated by entertaining alternative explanations involving some third variable(s) that may account for the relationship observed between X and Y. For example, education and financial success may be related among a group of participants only because both are related to the financial success of the parents of those studied.

The two parts of the third criterion are closely related. A compelling theory places a greater burden on what may be considered a plausible alternative, and vice versa.

Conceptual to Operational Relationships

Conceptual validity requires that activities conducted at the operational level be linked to the conceptual level. This link depends on relationships between measures and their respective constructs; these are represented by lines (b_1) and (b_2) in Exhibit 2.2.

The construct X' is measured by the set of operations X; the construct Y' is measured by the set of operations Y. **Construct validity** is present when there is a high correspondence between the scores obtained on a measure and the mental definition of the construct it is designed to represent. Lines (b_1) and (b_2) are also broken to show that construct validity is also tentative.

Construct validation (see part II) involves procedures researchers use to develop measures and to make inferences about a measure's construct validity. Three steps are involved in the construct validation process as shown in Exhibit 2.4. Step 1, define the construct, is central. The definition guides the choice or development of the measure (Step 2); it also provides criteria for any investigations performed on the measure (Step 3).

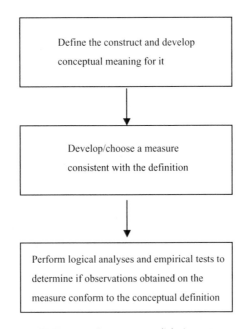

EXHIBIT 2.4.   Construct validation steps.

RESEARCH HIGHLIGHT 2.2

A Research Example Using the Model

A researcher hypothesizes that work experience (X') has a positive impact on work attitudes (Y'). This expectation is studied on a group of managerial employees in a public-sector organization. Work experience is measured by the number of years participants have worked for this organization (X) and work attitudes (Y) are measured with a questionnaire that managers complete.

Support for the researcher's hypothesis is obtained if three conditions are met:

1. An empirical relationship is found. Participants who have worked for the organization longer provide more favorable work attitude scores, on average, than those who have worked less time.
2. Evidence is obtained to suggest that the relationship is internally valid. It must be reasonable to suppose the relationship observed results because experience scores cause work attitude scores among the participants.
3. There is evidence that the measures X and Y validly represent their respective constructs X' and Y'.

GENERALIZING FROM THE MODEL

Empirical research provides information about relationships among scores obtained on a group of cases at one point in time. Researchers and research consumers usually are not particularly interested in this relationship, per se. They usually are more interested in knowing how the relationship generalizes beyond the specific situation studied. For example, does the relationship generalize to groups of cases, to other times, and to other ways of assessing the relationship?

Statistical Generalization

Researchers have two methods to obtain validity evidence about research generalization. One, *statistical validation* (see part V), uses probability theory to generalize a relationship observed on a sample of cases to the relationship that applies to the broader population from which the sample was drawn. *Statistical generalization validity* is obtained when the empirical relationship observed on a sample of cases validly estimates the relationship in the population of cases from which the sample was drawn. (Statistical validation relies on probability theory for both internal and statistical generalization validity.)

Exhibit 2.5 illustrates statistical generalization. An inference is made from an empirical relationship observed on a sample (d) to the corresponding, but unknown, empirical relationship (D) in the population. Public opinion polls illustrate a well-known use of statistical generalization procedures.

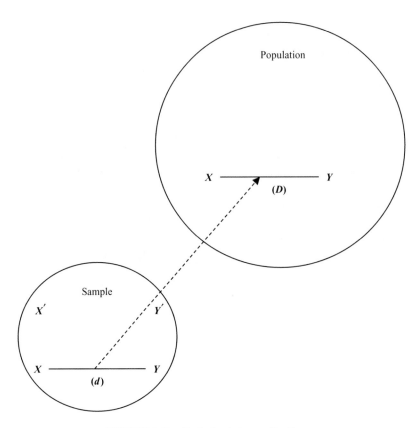

EXHIBIT 2.5.   Statistical generalizations.

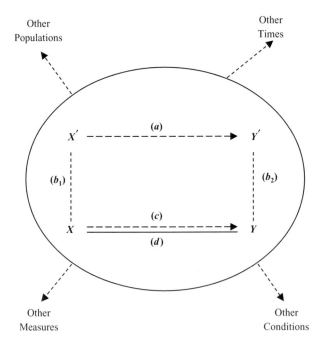

EXHIBIT 2.6.   External generalizations.

External Generalization

External validation (see part VI) refers to procedures researchers use to investigate all other types of research generalization. ***External validity*** is present when generalizations of findings obtained in a research study, other than statistical generalization, are made appropriately. Exhibit 2.6 provides examples of external generalization.

Substantial progress has been made in methods to address external generalization during the last three decades. This external validation technology usually goes by the name ***meta-analysis***. Meta-analysis is a research procedure designed to provide quantitative estimates of the generalizability of relationships across studies.

SUMMARY

Research is concerned with relationships between variables. ***Variables*** are characteristics of things that can take on two or more values.

A main objective of research is to assess causal relationships among conceptual variables called ***constructs***. Research does so by addressing three issues: First, is there an ***empirical relationship***, a relationship observed between scores on a measured ***independent variable*** (cause) and a ***dependent variable*** (effect)? Second, is it reasonable to think that the relationship is causal? ***Internal validation*** procedures are used to address this question. ***Internal validity*** is supported when the answer is affirmative. Finally, is it reasonable to suppose that scores on measures represent their respective constructs? ***Construct validation*** procedures are used to address this question. ***Construct validity*** is supported when it is reasonable to think scores on the measures represent their respective constructs.

Once a research study has been performed, it is often of interest to know whether the results obtained generalize beyond the cases and scores at hand. ***Statistical validation*** procedures are used to generalize from an empirical relationship observed on a sample of cases to the population of cases from which the sample was drawn. When the generalization is warranted, there is ***statistical generalization validity***.

All other sorts of generalization are called external. ***External validation*** procedures are used to generalize to other populations, other times, and other research methods. When such generalizations are warranted, there is ***external validity***.

A final caveat to the discussion in this chapter is appropriate. Many types of validity have been described. Validity refers to truth. However, research validity and truth are always tentative; they are at best provisional, subject to change as new evidence is obtained. Researchers must settle for ***verisimilitude***, the appearance of truth.

FOR REVIEW

Terms to Know

Variables: Characteristics of objects that can take on two or more values.
  Conceptual variable; also a ***construct***: A mental definition of an object or event that can vary.
  Operational variable: Variable with a measure to obtain scores from cases.
  Dependent variable: Research outcome; the consequence in a causal relationship.
  Independent variable: Variable that helps explain or predict a dependent variable; it is a cause in a causal relationship.

Causal conceptual relationship: A relationship where variation in the independent construct is responsible for variation in the dependent construct.

Hypothesis: An expected relationship between an independent and a dependent variable.

Validity: In research, when a conclusion or inference is true.

Verisimilitude: Having the appearance of truth. In research, validity is best thought of as verisimilitude.

Empirical relationship: The correspondence between scores obtained from cases on measures.

Internal validity: Present when variation in scores on a measure of an independent variable is responsible for variation in scores on a measure of a dependent variable.

Internal validation: Methods used to determine whether internal validity is likely.

Internal statistical validity: Present when an empirical relationship is not due to chance.

Statistical validation: The use of probability theory to investigate internal statistical validity or statistical generalization validity.

Theory: Provides a tentative explanation for why a causal relationship(s) obtains.

Construct validity: Present when there is a high correspondence between cases' scores on a measure and the mental definition of the construct the measure is designed to represent.

Construct validation: Methods used to estimate a measure's construct validity.

Statistical generalization validity: Present when an empirical relationship observed on a sample of cases provides a correct estimate of the relationship in the population of cases from which the sample was drawn.

External validity: Present when findings obtained in a research study, other than statistical generalization, are correctly generalized.

External validation: Methods used to estimate external validity.

Meta-analysis: Procedures to review and evaluate prior research studies that depend on quantitative research methods.

Things to Know

1. Understand the model (Exhibit 2.2) and its extensions. Be able to define terms in the model. Also, be able to discuss how the constructs in the model are related. For example, how are empirical relationships and internal validity related? (An answer could point out that an empirical relationship is one of several requirements for internal validity. An empirical relationship is necessary; scores on the measure of the independent variable must be associated with scores on the dependent variable for internal validity. However, because internal validity also requires evidence of a causal relationship, an empirical relationship is not sufficient. Note that this answer defines both constructs, a good idea when you are asked to compare, contrast, or otherwise connect two constructs.)

2. How do construct validation procedures address construct validity? How do internal validation procedures address internal validity?

3. What role does measurement play in the contribution of empirical research to causal conceptual validity?

Issues to Discuss

1. Territoriality is a presumed characteristic of some animals; the animal or group claims a certain territory as its own and seeks to protect it from invasion or threat by other animals, especially from members of its own species. Different animals engage in territorial behavior in different ways. Some birds sing vigorously. Some animals mark their territory with a scent, often urine.

Sociology researchers at Pennsylvania State University did a study of territoriality among humans (reported in the *Wisconsin State Journal,* 5/13/1997). They observed people leaving shopping mall parking places in their automobiles. They found that individuals drove out of their parking spots more quickly when no one was waiting in an automobile to take their parking spot (32.2 seconds from the time they opened the door). They left more slowly (almost 7 seconds longer) when someone was waiting and more slowly still (10 seconds longer) if the waiting person honked his or her horn. The researchers concluded that humans, as many other animals, are territorial.

 a. What are the independent and dependent ***constructs*** in this illustration?

 b. What are the ***operational*** independent and dependent variables in this illustration?

 c. Is this study convincing regarding the expectation that humans are territorial? Why or why not?

2. Describe the following about a causal relationship of your choice involving one independent and one dependent variable.

 a. In one sentence, state the causal relationship at a conceptual level. Be sure the independent and dependent constructs are clear and be sure the direction of the relationship is clear.

 b. Define the independent and dependent constructs in a sentence or two.

 c. Describe a measure for each of your two constructs in a sentence or two.

—

II

Measurement: Understanding Construct Validity

3

Measurement Foundations: Validity and Validation

Chapter Outline

- *Construct Definitions*
  - *Construct Domain*
  - *Nomological Networks*
- *Construct Definition Illustration*
- *Construct Validity Challenges*
  - *Random Errors*
  - *Systematic Errors*
  - *Scores Are Critical*
- *Construct Validation*
  - *Content Validity*
  - *Reliability*
    - *Types of Reliability*
    - *Reliability and Construct Validity*
  - *Convergent Validity*
  - *Discriminant Validity*
  - *Criterion-Related Validity*
  - *Investigating Nomological Networks*
- *Summary*
- *For Review*
  - *Terms to Know*
  - *Things to Know*

Part I described how empirical research contributes to knowledge by investigating relationships between scores on measures. However, the value of such research depends largely on whether scores obtained are construct valid. Relationships among scores are meaningful only when there is a close correspondence between the scores and researchers' mental representations of the variables investigated.

Unfortunately, construct valid measurement is confronted by an inescapable challenge. There is no direct way to measure constructs, because they are conceptual phenomena. As a consequence, there is no direct way to assess construct validity; it must be inferred from a variety of criteria. These inferences are made by examining scores on measures and comparing them with theoretical propositions about how the scores should perform.

This chapter introduces the foundations of measurement and construct validation. It begins with a discussion of conceptual definitions and then introduces research procedures useful in construct validation.

CONSTRUCT DEFINITIONS

Measurement produces numerical values that are designed to summarize characteristics of cases under study. A measure is an instrument to record such scores. Construct valid measures yield numerical values that accurately represent the characteristic. For example, if a score of 5 represents "very satisfied," then a measure of satisfaction should obtain scores of 5 for all individuals who are very satisfied; individuals who experience other levels of satisfaction should receive other numerical values. In short, construct valid measurement results in a close correspondence between the construct of interest and the scores provided by the measure.

Defining constructs at a conceptual level is an essential first step in the development of construct valid measures. Good construct definitions are also needed to identify appropriate empirical procedures for evaluating the validity of results obtained from measures. The most useful conceptual definitions have two elements.

Construct Domain

First, useful conceptual definitions identify the nature of the construct by specifying its meaning. This element explains what a researcher has in mind for the construct; it contains a dictionary-like statement that describes the construct domain. It speaks to what is included in the construct. If there is potential confusion about what is not included, this too should be addressed in the definition.

Nomological Networks

A second element of a good construct definition specifies how values of the construct should differ across cases and conditions. For example, should the construct remain about the same over time, or is it expected to vary? Some constructs, such as human intelligence, are expected to be relatively stable over time. A measure of intelligence administered at different times should provide the same approximate estimate of an individual's intelligence. Others constructs, such as opinions about current events, are expected to be more volatile. Scores on measures of such constructs are not necessarily expected to be similar from one administration to another.

The second element also should specify how the construct of interest relates to other constructs in a broader web of relationships called a ***nomological network.*** A nomological network is identical to a conceptual model in form; it differs only in purpose. In contrast to conceptual models, nomological networks are used to draw inferences about constructs and construct validity.

CONSTRUCT DEFINITION ILLUSTRATION

The following example may help solidify the ideas just developed and illustrate construct validation methods described in the following section. Suppose a researcher seeks to measure satisfaction that owners experience with personal laptop or desktop computers. The researcher may be interested in characteristics that influence satisfaction and thus view it as a dependent variable. Or, the researcher may be interested in consequences of satisfaction with computer ownership and thus view satisfaction as an independent variable. In either event, the researcher defines the construct as:

> Personal computer satisfaction is an emotional response resulting from an evaluation of the speed, durability, and initial price, but not the appearance of a personal computer. This evaluation is expected to depend on variation in the actual characteristics of the computer (e.g., speed) and on the expectations a participant has about those characteristics. When characteristics meet or exceed expectations, the evaluation is expected to be positive (satisfaction). When characteristics do not come up to expectations, the evaluation is expected to be negative (dissatisfaction). People with more education will have higher expectations and hence lower computer satisfaction than those with less education.

This example is explicit about the domain of the construct. Computer satisfaction as defined refers to speed, durability, and price. It is also explicit that satisfaction with appearance is not a part of the definition.

The definition goes on to state that the evaluation leading to satisfaction or dissatisfaction depends on a comparison of peoples' expectations for computers with their actual experience. The researcher anticipates that satisfaction will differ among participants because their computers differ in power, durability, and price, and because expectations for these three computer characteristics differ. A measure of satisfaction might ask for the evaluation directly, or it might be constructed from responses about computer expectations and computer experiences.

Finally, the definition includes a primitive form of a nomological network by relating expectations to education level. The definition states that those with higher education levels will have higher expectations and hence lower satisfaction, other things equal.

Suppose that after defining the construct the researcher finds a measure of computer satisfaction that is already developed, as shown in Exhibit 3.1. The researcher decides to perform construct validation on this measure. This measure represents an operational definition of the construct. It has six items, each anchored by a 5-point rating scale ranging from 1 (very dissatisfied) to 5 (very satisfied).

CONSTRUCT VALIDITY CHALLENGES

Two major challenges confront construct validity. One involves **random errors,** completely unsystematic variation in scores. A second, more difficult, challenge involves **systematic errors,** consistent differences between scores obtained from a measure and meaning as defined by the construct.

Decide how satisfied or dissatisfied you are with each characteristic of your personal computer using the scale below. Circle the number that best describes your feelings for each statement.

Very Dissatisfied	Dissatisfied	Neither Satisfied nor Dissatisfied	Satisfied	Very Satisfied

My satisfaction with:

1. Initial price of the computer   1   2   3   4   5

2. What I paid for the computer   1   2   3   4   5

3. How quickly the computer performs calculations   1   2   3   4   5

4. How fast the computer runs programs   1   2   3   4   5

5. Helpfulness of the salesperson   1   2   3   4   5

6. How I was treated when I bought the computer   1   2   3   4   5

EXHIBIT 3.1.   Hypothetical computer satisfaction questionnaire.

RESEARCH HIGHLIGHT 3.1

Multidimensional Constructs

Throughout this chapter, assume that researchers are interested in *one-dimensional constructs*. Whatever the construct, it is assumed to represent a single domain.

However, there are circumstances when *multidimensional constructs* are of interest. One-dimensional and multidimensional constructs differ in level of abstraction; multidimensional constructs represent combinations of related and more specific one-dimensional constructs. In the example, computer satisfaction is considered one dimensional. However, a researcher could disaggregate computer satisfaction into three components: satisfaction with computer speed, satisfaction with computer durability, and satisfaction with computer price. In that case, computer satisfaction, consisting of the three components, would be multidimensional. Researchers choose levels of abstraction consistent with their research interests.

Random Errors

Random or unsystematic errors are nearly always present in measurement. Fortunately, there are methods for identifying them and procedures to ameliorate their adverse consequences. Because these procedures involve the use of statistics, their formal discussion is postponed to chapter 17. However, one such procedure is illustrated by the measure shown in Exhibit 3.1.

The questionnaire has more than one item related to each characteristic of computer ownership. Items 1 and 2 relate to satisfaction with price, items 3 and 4 relate to satisfaction with speed, and so forth.

The use of more than one item to measure a construct is common, and it acknowledges that random errors are a common problem. Taking an average of several items designed to measure the same thing is one way to address random errors. Random errors tend to "average-out" across multiple items; errors that inflate scores on one item tend to be offset by errors that understate other items. The more items, the more successfully this type of random error is controlled.

Systematic Errors

Items from the measure shown in Exhibit 3.1 also suggest two types of systematic errors that reduce construct validity. Items 5 and 6 ask about satisfaction with the purchasing experience; these are not part of the researcher's conceptual definition of the construct. A measure is *contaminated* if it captures characteristics not specifically included in the definition of the construct.

A measure can also have systematic errors because it is *deficient*—that is, when it does not capture the entire construct domain. The measure in Exhibit 3.1 is deficient because there are no items capturing satisfaction with computer durability.

Scores Are Critical

The discussion so far actually understates the challenges faced in developing construct valid measurement. The computer satisfaction illustration identifies differences between a construct definition and a measure. Yet, construct validity (or invalidity) is not established by measures alone; it is ultimately determined by scores. Construct validity refers to the correspondence between the construct and the *scores* generated from a measure, not the measure per se.

Consequently, anything that influences scores can influence validity, often adversely. To illustrate, contamination may result from sources other than the measure. In the computer satisfaction example, participants may be motivated to systematically under- or overestimate their satisfaction. They may systematically report greater satisfaction than they truly feel if a representative of the computer manufacturer is present while they complete the questionnaire. The administrative environment (location, noise levels, temperature, etc.) also may influence errors regardless of the specific items in a particular measure.

Challenges for construct validity are summarized in Exhibit 3.2. The solid circle represents variability associated with the construct. In the example, this is the variability expected in satisfaction as defined conceptually. It includes the characteristics of computer speed, durability, and initial price.

The circle starting on the far right represents variability in scores obtained on the measure from a group of participants. Variability in these scores is due to differences in participant responses to the items on the measure at the time completed and in the environment where the measure was administered. These scores contain both systematic and random elements.

Finally, the middle circle represents variability that reflects the consistent (systematic) variance in the observed scores. Construct valid variance must be systematic by definition. However, systematic variance may not be construct valid, because it may be contaminated or deficient. Systematic variance is sometimes called *true score* variance. This is a misnomer because it means only systematic variance, not necessarily construct valid variance.

Scores on a measure are construct valid (area represented by crossed lines) to the extent that systematic observed score variance overlaps with the construct valid variance. The objective

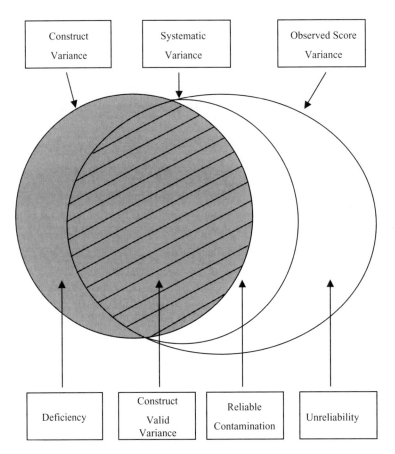

EXHIBIT 3.2.   Construct validity challenges.

of construct validation is to investigate measures and scores and ultimately to maximize this overlapping area.

Exhibit 3.2 also shows three sources of construct invalidity:

1. Scores on a measure may be less than construct valid because of deficiency. In the example, observed scores are deficient because the measure does not capture satisfaction with computer durability.
2. Scores may be less than construct valid because of systematic contamination. In the example, observed scores are contaminated because the measure includes satisfaction with the purchasing experience.
3. Finally, scores on a measure are less than construct valid to the extent that they include random errors.

CONSTRUCT VALIDATION

Because construct validity cannot be assessed directly, it cannot be directly established. However, there are procedures available to help researchers develop construct valid measures and to help evaluate those measures once developed. Six such procedures are described here.

RESEARCH HIGHLIGHT 3.2

Measurement by Manipulation

Measurement issues, language, and technologies have developed largely around measures that call on research participants to complete some sort of questionnaire. Examples include measures of ability, attitudes, and opinions.

However, construct validity issues are equally relevant when researchers actively manipulate values of independent variables. For example, a researcher wants to know whether "decision complexity" influences the quality of decision making. Two hypothetical decision scenarios are created to represent two levels of decision complexity. Groups of research participants are assigned to one or the other of the two scenarios; decision quality of the two groups is then compared.

All the measurement questions and issues raised about questionnaires are appropriate in this case. Is decision complexity adequately defined at the conceptual level? Is the manipulation subject to random errors? Is it deficient or contaminated? For example, the scenarios may manipulate more than just decision complexity and hence be contaminated. Good research using manipulations takes steps to obtain information about the quality of the manipulations used.

Content Validity

A measure is **content valid** when its items are *judged* to accurately reflect the domain of the construct as defined conceptually. **Content validation** ordinarily has experts in the subject matter of interest provide assessments of content validity.

For example, a researcher develops a measure to predict performance among computer programmers. The organization wants to use this measure to help identify job applicants most likely to perform effectively if hired. As a part of development, the researcher has a panel of experts in computer programming review the measure for its content. Content validation of this sort provides information about potential systematic errors in measures. Expert judges can be especially helpful in identifying items that potentially may contaminate a measure.

RESEARCH HIGHLIGHT 3.3

The Appearance of Validity

A measure is *face valid* when its items appear to reflect the construct as defined conceptually. In contrast to content validation, estimates of face validity are usually obtained from persons similar to those who serve as research participants. A measure should appear valid to participants to help motivate accurate responses.

Either content or face validation likely would identify that the computer satisfaction questionnaire (Exhibit 3.1) is both deficient (no computer durability items) and contaminated (purchasing experience items).

Content validation can help improve the items that form a measure. Nevertheless, it is not sufficient for construct validity. In particular, content validation procedures may not provide information about potential deficiency, nor can subject matter experts provide much information about random errors that may be present in the scores that are obtained.

Reliability

Reliability refers to the systematic or consistent variance of a measure; it thus indicates the degree to which measurement scores are free of random errors. **Reliability statistics** provide estimates of the proportion of the total variability in a set of scores that is true or systematic. Reliability is shown in Exhibit 3.2 as the proportion of observed score variability (circle on the far right) that is overlapped by the middle circle representing true (systematic) score variability.

Types of Reliability

There are three common contexts in which researchers seek to assess the reliability of measurement. Chapter 17 describes statistical procedures for estimating these types of reliability.

1. **Internal consistency** reliability refers to the similarity of item scores obtained on a measure that has multiple items. It can be assessed when items are intended to measure a single construct. In the computer example (Exhibit 3.1), satisfaction is measured with six items. The internal consistency of that questionnaire can be estimated if scores are available from a set of cases.

2. **Interrater reliability** indicates the degree to which a group of observers or raters provide consistent evaluations. For example, the observers may be a group of international judges who are asked to evaluate ice skaters performing in a competition. In this case, the judges serve as measurement repetitions just as the items serve as repetitions in the computer satisfaction questionnaire. High reliability is obtained when the judges agree on the evaluation of each skater.

3. **Stability reliability** refers to the consistency of measurement results across time. Here measurement repetitions refer to time periods (a measure is administered more than once).

Reliability and Construct Validity

Reliability speaks only to a measure's freedom from random errors. It does not address systematic errors involving contamination or deficiency. Reliability is thus necessary for construct validity but not sufficient. It is necessary because unreliable variance must be construct invalid. It is not sufficient because systematic variance may be contaminated and because reliability simply does not account for deficiency. In short, reliability addresses only whether scores are consistent; it does not address whether scores capture a particular construct as defined conceptually.

Convergent Validity

Convergent validity is present when there is a high correspondence between scores from two or more different measures of the same construct. Convergent validity is important because it must be present if scores from both measures are construct valid. But convergent validity is not sufficient for construct validity any more than is reliability. Exhibit 3.3 shows why. The solid circle on the left represents construct variance; this variance is necessarily unknown to a researcher. The two open circles on the right represent variance in scores on two measures designed to assess the construct.

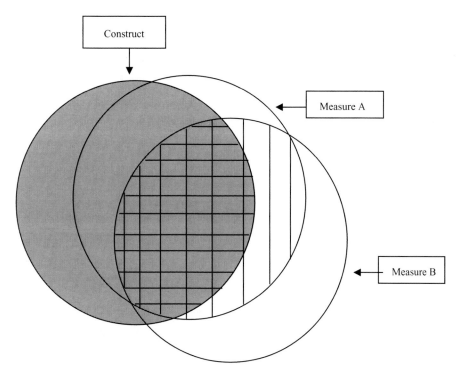

EXHIBIT 3.3.   Convergent validity.

The area crossed with vertical lines shows the proportion of variance in scores from the two measures that is convergent. However, only the area also crossed with horizontal lines shows common construct valid variance. The area covered only by vertical lines shows where the two measures share variance that represents contamination from a construct validity perspective. Convergent validity also does not address whether measures are deficient. Nor does it provide construct validity information about the proportion of variance in the two measures that do not converge. Exhibit 3.3 shows that more of the variance unique to the measure A overlaps with construct variance than variance from measure B.

Despite these limitations, evidence of convergent validity is desirable. If two measures that are designed to measure the same construct do not converge, at least one of them is not construct valid. Alternatively, if they do converge, circumstantial evidence is obtained that they may both be construct valid. Evidence of convergent validity adds to a researcher's confidence in the construct validity of measures.

Discriminant Validity

Discriminant validity is inferred when scores from measures of different constructs do not converge. It thus provides information about whether scores from a measure of a construct are unique rather than contaminated by other constructs.

The researcher defined computer satisfaction to exclude an evaluation of the appearance of the computer. Evidence supportive of this definition would be provided by a discriminant validity investigation. If scores on the researcher's measure of computer satisfaction show little or no relationship with scores from a measure of satisfaction with computer appearance, then discriminant validity evidence is obtained.

An investigation of discriminant validity is particularly important when an investigator develops a measure of a new construct that may be redundant with other more thoroughly researched constructs. Proposed constructs should provide contributions beyond constructs already in the research domain. Consequently, measures of proposed constructs should show evidence of discriminant validity with measures of existing constructs.

Criterion-Related Validity

Criterion-related validity is present when scores on a measure are related to scores on another measure that better reflects the construct of interest. It differs from convergent validity, where scores from the measures are assumed to be equivalent representations of the construct. In criterion-related validity the criterion measure is assumed to have greater construct validity than the measure being developed or investigated.

Why not just use the criterion measure if it has greater construct validity? Typically, criterion-related validity is investigated for measures that can be administered more economically and/or more practically than the criterion measure. For example, suppose a human resource manager is interested in developing a measure of a construct that represents the effectiveness of employees performing some complex task. The manager develops a measure that will be administered to supervisors of the employees who perform the task. Criterion-related validity is assessed by comparing scores obtained from supervisors with scores obtained from a panel of job experts who carefully observe a small sample of employees over a two-week time period. The manager reasons that the job experts provide valid assessments of employee performance. A strong relationship between supervisor and job expert scores (criterion-related validity) provides evidence that supervisor scores can be used among the entire group of employees performing this task.

The expression criterion-related validity has also been used in another sense. Historically, researchers used the term to describe relationships between a construct (represented by the measure under consideration) and a measure of another construct that is thought to be conceptually related to the first. This situation is now more frequently discussed under the heading of nomological networks, a topic considered next.

Investigating Nomological Networks

Nomological networks have been described as relationships between a construct under measurement consideration and other constructs. In the chapter example, the researcher's expectation that education is related to computer satisfaction illustrates a simple nomological network, as shown in Exhibit 3.4. This nomological network is indistinguishable from a

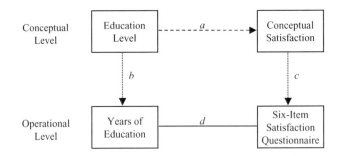

EXHIBIT 3.4. Nomological network: computer satisfaction and education level.

conceptual model used by researchers concerned with the relationship between education level and computer satisfaction constructs. The difference is in underlying motivations and assumptions.

Researchers with a conceptual orientation are interested in the conceptual relationship between the independent and dependent variable constructs (line a in Exhibit 3.4). Such researchers use a relationship observed between scores from participants on measures of education and satisfaction (line d) to infer to the conceptual relationship (line a). To make this inference, they must assume construct validity for both education level and satisfaction (lines b and c). Given the assumptions, a negative relationship between years of education and the six-item satisfaction questionnaire is consistent with the conceptual validity of the relationship between the two constructs.

A researcher interested in the construct validity of the six-item measure of computer satisfaction may use the same model to draw different inferences. Specifically, the measurement researcher assumes the conceptual relationship is true (line a). Further, in the example, the measure of education level is assumed to be construct valid (line b). Given these alternative assumptions, results from an investigation of the relationship between scores on years of education and the six-item satisfaction questionnaire (line d) provide evidence about the construct validity of the questionnaire (line c). A negative relationship between years of education and the six-item satisfaction questionnaire is consistent with construct validity for the satisfaction questionnaire.

A relationship observed between one measured construct and a measure of another provides only limited evidence for construct validity. Thus, researchers usually seek to create more elaborate nomological networks. These may include several variables that are expected to vary with a measure of the construct. It also may include variables that are expected not to vary with it to show evidence of discriminant validity.

Evidence for construct validity mounts as empirical research supports relationships expected from a nomological network. The richer the network and the more support, the greater a researcher's confidence that the measure is capturing variance that is construct valid.

Information obtained in the construct validation process also may lead to modification of the construct. For example, in contrast to the initial definition, the researcher may consistently find that computer appearance is related to a measure of computer satisfaction. If so, the definition of the construct may be changed to include appearance given this empirical information.

RESEARCH HIGHLIGHT 3.4

A Common Misconception

Sometimes research reports include a claim that a measure(s) is construct valid; such claims are unwarranted.

Good research studies report evidence on construct validity. They may conduct many of the construct validation steps outlined in this chapter. However, the criterion in construct validation research, the construct, cannot be observed directly. Inferences about construct validity are, therefore, necessarily tentative. Conclusions about the validity of a measure may be modified when more evidence about it is obtained.

SUMMARY

Measurement represents the main link between constructs that motivate research and the empirical procedures used to address relationships between them. Definitions of constructs serve a key role in construct validation because they serve as the principle criteria for evaluating measures. A good construct definition contains a dictionary-like statement of the construct domain and a statement of how scores on a measure of the construct should behave, including how they should relate to other constructs in a ***nomological network.***

Construct validity is challenged by random and systematic errors. ***Random errors*** produce unsystematic variation that can inflate scores in some instances and deflate them in other instances. ***Systematic errors*** may result from ***contamination,*** when scores from a measure get at characteristics that are not included in the construct. They also may result from ***deficiency,*** when scores from a measure do not capture a portion of variance that is in a construct. Both random and systematic errors are present in scores of all measures.

Researchers engage in construct validation to learn about and improve construct validity. Random errors in measurement are assessed by estimating ***reliability*** that refers to the systematic or consistent portion of observed scores obtained on a measure. Common types of reliability include ***internal consistency*** (consistency of measurement across items), ***interrater reliability*** (consistency of measurement across observers or raters), and ***stability reliability*** (consistency of measurement across time periods).

Evidence for construct validity also is obtained by assessing other types of validity. These include ***content validity,*** expert judgments about the validity of a measure; ***convergent validity,*** the correspondence of scores from two or more measures of the same construct; ***discriminant validity,*** present when scores from measures of different constructs that should not be related are not related; and ***criterion-related validity***, present when the measure of interest is related to another measure judged to be more construct valid. Finally, evidence for construct validity is obtained when research provides support for the nomological network established for a construct.

FOR REVIEW

Terms to Know

Nomological network: Relationships between a construct under measurement consideration and other constructs. It is the measurement analog to a conceptual model of interest to causal research.

Random errors: In measurement, also called ***unreliability,*** errors in scores on a measure that are unsystematic. Random errors are uncorrelated with ***true*** (***systematic***) scores.

True scores: Also called ***systematic,*** the consistent (repeatable) portion of scores obtained from participants on a measure.

Systematic errors: In measurement, when scores from a measure consistently vary from construct validity because of contamination and/or deficiency.

> ***Contamination***: In measurement, the portion of scores that measures something other than the defined construct.
>
> ***Deficiency***: In measurement, the portion of the defined construct that is not captured by scores on a measure of the construct.

Content validity: When a measure is judged to be construct valid, usually by individuals who are thought to be subject matter experts.

Content validation: Procedures used to obtain content validity.

Face validity: When a measure appears to be construct valid by individuals who use it, including participants.

Reliability: Refers to the consistency of measurement.

> *Internal consistency*: A form of reliability that addresses the consistency of scores from a set of items in a measure.
>
> *Interrater reliability*: A form of reliability that addresses the consistency of scores from a set of observers.
>
> *Stability reliability*: A form of reliability that addresses the consistency of scores across time periods.

Convergent validity: Is present when there is a high correspondence between scores from two different measures of the same construct.

Discriminant validity: Is present when measures of constructs that are supposed to be independent are found to have a low correspondence.

Criterion-related validity: Is present when the measure of interest is related to another measure judged to be more construct valid.

One-dimensional constructs: Construct that represents a single domain or dimension.

Multidimensional constructs: Construct that contains more specific but related one-dimensional constructs.

Things to Know

1. What construct validation purposes are served by the definition of the construct?
2. Be able to discuss how true scores are similar to constructs. How do they differ?
3. Unreliable variance in the scores from a measure are not construct valid by definition. How can reliable variance in scores not be construct valid?
4. Compare and contrast content and face validity.
5. Procedures to estimate reliability require that there be repetitions of scores. What are the repetitions in estimates of internal consistency, interrater reliability, and stability?
6. Two measures of a construct show convergent validity. Why is this not sufficient for construct validity? In what sense can you argue it is necessary? If two measures do not show evidence of convergent validity, does this mean that neither has construct validity?
7. How are conceptual models similar to nomological networks? How do they differ?
8. Provide an example of a criterion and a measure that would be appropriate in a criterion-related validity study.

4

Measurement Applications: Research Questionnaires

Chapter Outline

- *Questionnaire Decisions*
  - *Alternatives to Questionnaire Construction*
    - *Secondary Data*
    - *Questionnaires Developed by Others*
  - *Questionnaire Type*
    - *Self-Reports Versus Observations*
    - *Interviews Versus Written Questionnaires*
- *Questionnaire Construction*
  - *Content Domain*
  - *Items*
    - *Item Wording*
    - *Item Sequence*
  - *Scaling*
- *Questionnaire Response Styles*
  - *Self-Reports*
  - *Observations*
  - *Implications for Questionnaire Construction and Use*
- *Pilot Testing*
- *Summary*
- *For Review*
  - *Terms to Know*
  - *Things to Know*
- *Part II Suggested Readings*

A remarkable variety of measures are used in organizational research. Some are designed to capture characteristics of organizations, such as information about size, longevity, organizational success, quality of products or services, and policies and practices. Some are designed to identify characteristics of individuals who interact with organizations, such as clients, customers, investors, suppliers, employees and volunteers. Measures of the latter sort, in turn, may be designed to obtain information about a variety of individual characteristics, such as their knowledge, abilities, motivations, opinions, and behaviors.

There are also many measurement methods to obtain scores for organizational research. This chapter discusses issues involved with one general and widely used form of measurement—namely, *questionnaires*. Questionnaires are measuring instruments that ask individuals to answer a set of questions. If the questions ask for information about the individual respondents, they are called *self-report questionnaires*. Information obtained in self-report questionnaires include biographical information, attitudes, opinions, and knowledge. As examples, self-report questionnaires are used to obtain information about employee reactions to employment policies, consumer satisfaction and buying intentions, student evaluations of instruction, and investor evaluations of investment opportunities.

Individuals may complete self-report questionnaires by responding to written questions or to questions shown on a computer terminal. Self-reports also may be obtained through an *interview* in which another individual (the *interviewer*) asks the questions verbally and is responsible for recording responses.

Questionnaires also are used to obtain information from individuals who serve as *observers*. Observers use questionnaires to record descriptions and evaluations of organizational and individual variables. For example, questionnaires of this sort may ask supervisors to describe and/or evaluate performance behaviors of individual employees. As another example, observers may complete questionnaires to describe interaction patterns between sales personnel and customers.

These examples indicate that questionnaires have wide applicability in organizational research. This chapter discusses issues related to questionnaire construction and use. It describes decisions researchers make when they seek information to obtain from questionnaires. Much of the chapter is devoted to questionnaire construction. However, recall that construct validity refers to the scores obtained from measures, not the measures themselves. Thus, behavior (called *response styles* in this context) of individuals who complete questionnaires is also discussed. Finally, the important role of pilot testing is discussed, because questionnaire construction is invariably an imperfect research activity.

QUESTIONNAIRE DECISIONS

Constructing a questionnaire is time-consuming and challenging. It is particularly challenging when abstract constructs are measured. As a consequence, researchers should first consider alternatives to questionnaire construction. There are two additional questions to address if it is decided that a questionnaire must be developed to carry out a research project. One, should information be obtained with a written questionnaire or an interview? Two, if the questionnaire is designed to obtain information about individuals, should the questionnaire obtain it from outside observers or from individuals reporting on themselves?

Alternatives to Questionnaire Construction

Choosing measures depends foremost on the topic a researcher seeks to investigate. Given a topic, a starting point is to see if the data you are interested in studying may already be available. If not, a second step is to see if a measure(s) is available that will serve your research interest.

Secondary Data

Much organizational research is conducted with **secondary data**, data collected for some other purpose. Such data are available from many sources. They are collected by organizations for other internal purposes, such as maintaining records to monitor and improve the quality of services or products. Secondary data are also collected by organizations to meet external requirements such as safety, affirmative action, and tax regulation. Secondary data relevant to organizational research are also collected by outside organizations, such as industry trade associations and organizations that collect and sell information about other organizations (e.g., Standard & Poor's financial reports) and individuals who interact with organizations (e.g., A. C. Nielsen's ratings of television viewing). In addition, governments at all levels collect information that is of interest to organizational researchers. At the federal level alone, agencies such as the Census Bureau and Departments of Health and Human Services, Education, Commerce, Transportation, and Labor all collect large amounts of data that may be used for research.

Use of secondary data is advantageous from both a cost and a time perspective if available and applicable. However, availability alone should not drive a decision to use secondary data. Construct validity issues identified in the previous chapter are as relevant here as to any other measurement situation. Consequently, you need to evaluate the measures used to generate the secondary data as you would evaluate alternative research measures.

Questionnaires Developed by Others

There is a second alternative to questionnaire construction. Another researcher may have already developed a questionnaire that addresses your research questions. Although data may not be available, a questionnaire may be available that you can use to collect your own data. Questionnaires measuring constructs relating to many individual characteristics such as ability, personality, and interests are readily available. Questionnaires are also available for measuring characteristics of individuals interacting with organizations, such as employee satisfaction. A good method for finding these measures is to examine research reports on topics related to your research interests.

If suitable for your research interests, questionnaires already constructed are obviously advantageous in the time and effort they save. They are especially attractive if construct validation research as described in the previous chapter has already been performed.

Questionnaire Type

Often secondary data or questionnaires already developed are simply not viable options. This is necessarily true when a researcher chooses to investigate a construct that has not been previously defined. It is also true in many applied situations in which research is aimed at investigating a topical issue, often one that applies to a specific organizational characteristic, such as a product or service. These situations call for the construction of questionnaires as a part of a research investigation.

Self-Reports Versus Observations

Researchers are often curious about relationships that include behaviors or characteristics of individuals interacting with organizations. For example, a researcher may want to know whether academic achievement of students is related to teaching styles. Both variables in this example represent individual behaviors, one of students and one of instructors. As another example, a researcher may want to know whether employee performance levels are influenced by an organization's system for providing financial rewards. An individual behavior, employee performance, represents one variable of interest.

In these situations, researchers must decide whether they should obtain the information from the participants studied. Some constructs require that the information be measured with responses provided by research participants. In particular, constructs that address internal mental states of individuals often can be measured only by asking research participants to provide them. Attitudes and opinions, intentions, interests, and preferences are all examples of such constructs.

However, there are other constructs that can be measured either internally through self-reports or externally by observation. These constructs typically involve overt behaviors, characteristics of individuals that can be observed directly. For example, the researcher interested in employee performance could ask employees to complete a questionnaire reporting on their own performance. Or, the researcher could obtain the information by having an observer complete a questionnaire that reports on employee performance. (There may also be ways to measure performance that do not involve the use of questionnaires. For example, quantity of performance may be recorded mechanically or electronically for employees in jobs that produce an observable output.)

Observations are typically preferred when constructs can be assessed directly. External observers are more likely to provide consistent assessments across research participants. Furthermore, external observers may be less likely to bias responses in a way that characterizes the behavior in a favorable light.

However, the choice of using self-reports or external observers has no necessary implications for the form of the questionnaire per se. The same questionnaire can be used for self-reports or by external observers if the information sought is the same.

Interviews Versus Written Questionnaires

A distinction is sometimes drawn between the development of interviews and the development of questionnaires. This distinction is largely unwarranted. The difference between the two procedures resides primarily in the way information is obtained from research participants. Interviews elicit information verbally; questionnaires elicit information in written form. The same care must be taken in developing interview questions and response formats as is taken in developing questionnaires.

A case can be made that interviews allow greater flexibility. Interviewers can follow up on answers with questions that probe respondents' thinking in greater depth. Interviewers can record responses and interviewee behaviors that are not available as formal questionnaire responses.

These are differences that make interviews attractive in the early stages of instrument development. Interviews can help researchers refine questions to be asked and the response formats to be used. However, when finalized, when a researcher is ready to collect data that will be used to investigate the main research expectations, a typical interview schedule will look much like a typical questionnaire.

The decision about whether to use an interview or questionnaire as the final measurement instrument depends on other criteria. Assuming the same care in construction, questionnaires usually are less expensive to administer. The decision to use an interview or a questionnaire also must take account of respondents' abilities and motivations. Reading abilities among some members of heterogeneous populations may make the use of questionnaires problematic. Interviews may also be advantageous from a motivational perspective. The interaction that takes place between the interviewer and interviewee may be used advantageously to motivate participation and complete responses.

Interaction between interviewers and interviewees also poses dangers for interviews. There is a greater risk that the administration of questions differs from interview to interview. Furthermore, because there is interaction, interviewee responses may be influenced by the particular individual conducting the interview.

It is generally desirable to use questionnaires when possible. The importance of uniformity in questions and response coding favors questionnaires. When interviews are used, it is important that they be conducted as systematically as possible.

QUESTIONNAIRE CONSTRUCTION

Questionnaires, whether administered in written form or through interviews, have two essential characteristics. First, they have items designed to elicit information of research interest. Second, they have a protocol for recording responses. For example, Exhibit 4.1 shows sets of items and response scales from the pay portions of two well-known job satisfaction questionnaires. The Minnesota Satisfaction Questionnaire (MSQ) has five items designed to measure satisfaction with pay. Each has a 5-point response scale ranging from very dissatisfied to very satisfied.

Question	Response Format				
Minnesota Satisfaction Questionnaire	VD	D	N	S	VS
1. The amount of pay for the work I do	☐	☐	☐	☐	☐
2. The chance to make as much money as my friends	☐	☐	☐	☐	☐
3. How my pay compares with that for similar jobs in other companies	☐	☐	☐	☐	☐
4. My pay and the amount of work I do	☐	☐	☐	☐	☐
5. How my pay compares with that of other workers	☐	☐	☐	☐	☐

Cornell Job Descriptive Index

Question			
1. Income adequate for normal expenses (+)	Yes	?	No
2. Satisfactory profit sharing (+)	Yes	?	No
3. Barely live on income (-)	Yes	?	No
4. Bad (-)	Yes	?	No
5. Income provides luxuries (+)	Yes	?	No
6. Insecure (-)	Yes	?	No
7. Less than I deserve (-)	Yes	?	No
8. Highly paid (+)	Yes	?	No
9. Underpaid (-)	Yes	?	No

Note. Minnesota Satisfaction Questionnaire from Weiss, Dawis, England & Lofquist (1967). Items are scaled from Very Dissatisfied (VD) = 1, Dissatisfied (D) = 2, Neither Dissatisfied nor Satisfied (N) = 3, Satisfied (S) = 4 to Very Satisfied (VS) = 5. Cornell Job Descriptive Index from Smith, Kendall & Hulin (1969). Positive (+) items are scaled Yes = 3 and No = 0. Negative (-) items are scaled Yes = 0 and No = 3. For both positive and negative items ? = 1. Both scales shown are with permission from the authors.

EXHIBIT 4.1. Two questionnaires designed to measure satisfaction with pay.

The Cornell Job Descriptive Index (JDI) has nine items to measure satisfaction with pay. Participants respond by indicating only whether each item applies (yes), does not apply (no), or they cannot decide whether the item applies in describing their pay (?).

Content Domain

A properly designed study will identify the variables to be measured by the time questionnaire development becomes an issue. If one or more constructs are included, these should be carefully defined as described in chapter 3. Items should follow closely from the definitions.

Typically, researchers also want to obtain additional information from their questionnaires. At the very least, information will be sought about personal descriptive characteristics of the questionnaire respondents, such as their organizational role (e.g., manager, student, customer), education, age, and gender. Respondents in the role of describing characteristics of organizations typically will be asked to provide descriptive information such as size, location, and type of products or services provided.

Interesting side issues are likely to occur while the questionnaire is being developed. As a consequence, it is often tempting to add items that are not central to the research investigation. Resist this temptation. Attend to developing a set of items that focus directly and unequivocally on your research topic. Diverting attention to related items and issues will likely reduce the quality of items that are essential. Furthermore, response rates inevitably decline as questionnaire length increases.

Items

Item wording and the arrangement of items obviously affect the responses obtained. Indeed, the content of the questionnaire influences whether research participants provide responses at all. There is a great deal of research showing the importance of item wording and item arrangement on questionnaire responses.

Item Wording

Despite this research, recommendations for item wording are difficult to make because each questionnaire is potentially unique in important ways. Four recommendations that serve as general guidelines follow:

1. *Keep the respondent in mind.* This is perhaps the most important recommendation. It is easy to overestimate participants' knowledge and interest in a topic because of your knowledge and interest. Who will be responding to the questionnaire? What knowledge will they have? What knowledge will they be willing to share? Do not ask for information that participants cannot or will not provide.

2. *Make it simple.* Make sure the words in each item are understandable to respondents. It is nearly always reasonable to suppose that verbal understanding levels of at least some respondents are low. Thus, regardless of whether you use a written questionnaire or an interview, keep the words and questions simple. Construct items so demands on respondents' knowledge, attention, and memory are reasonable. Use technical words and jargon reluctantly even if respondents are technical specialists.

3. *Be specific.* It is dangerous to assume that respondents will share your frame of reference; at least some will not. As a consequence, it is important to be explicit about relevant contextual features such as who, what, when, where, and how.

4. *Be honest.* It is easy to manipulate results in one direction or another, because questionnaire responses are so sensitive to item wording. Thus, guard against leading respondents

to the answers you believe or hope will occur. An examination of your own assumptions and values can help you evaluate question wording for potential implicit biases.

Item Sequence

The way items are ordered in a questionnaire is constrained by the type of items included. For example, order is of little consequence if items are all similar. However, order can influence responses and response rates when items vary in content.

Research respondents are often hesitant to begin a questionnaire. They may be anxious about whether they can answer the questions. Or they may be reluctant to provide information. As a consequence, it is helpful to start a questionnaire with items that participants find interesting and that are easy to complete.

Ask for demographic information last. People are often reluctant to provide personal information. Asking for it last increases the likelihood that it will be provided because respondents have already made a commitment by completing the earlier part of the questionnaire. Furthermore, you will have obtained useful information even if the respondents do not provide personal information.

Scaling

There are many ways questionnaire item responses can be recorded. An ***open-ended response format*** permits respondents to answer questions in their own words. They are sometimes used on small groups early in the questionnaire development process to make sure the full range of potential responses is captured. They also are sometimes used in interviews, particularly when the questions are designed to elicit complex responses.

However, most questionnaire items are provided with ***closed-ended response formats*** in which respondents are asked to choose the one category that most closely applies to them. Closed-ended responses are easy to complete; they are also easy to code reliably. The MSQ and JDI pay scales shown in Exhibit 4.1 illustrate closed-ended response formats.

Constructs measured by items calling for self-reports or observer ratings are often scaled using closed-ended categories. When these categories are arranged in order, such as positive

---

RESEARCH HIGHLIGHT 4.1

Words to Avoid in Questionnaires

Absolutes. Words expressing absolutes such as *always, never, everyone,* and *all* create logical problems because statements including them are almost always false.

And. The word *and* usually signals that the item is getting at two ideas not one—a double-barreled question. Double-barreled questions are problematic because responses may differ depending on which "barrel" is considered.

You. You is problematic if there can be any question about whether it refers to the respondent or to a group the respondent represents (e.g., an organization).

Adjectives to describe quantity. Words such as *occasionally, sometimes, frequently,* and *often* mean different things to different people. One person's occasionally may be equivalent, numerically, to another person's frequently. Use numerical values when you want to obtain numerical information.

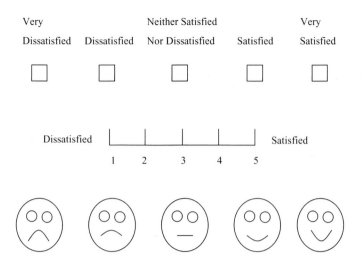

EXHIBIT 4.2. Equal appearing response formats for scaling satisfaction.

to negative or satisfied to dissatisfied, response categories are usually designed to yield equal-appearing intervals between categories. Researchers typically assign numerical values to these categories although these values may or may not be shown on the questionnaire. Exhibit 4.2 shows three equal-appearing scales for measuring satisfaction with some object.

Categories with equal intervals are attractive for conducting statistical analyses on scores, as discussed in part IV. As a consequence, there is a large body of research on methods for constructing scales that have equal intervals between response categories; these methods are often complex and laborious to carry out. Fortunately, there is evidence to suggest that rating scales with equal-appearing categories, such as those shown in Exhibit 4.2, perform about the same as more elegantly derived scale formats.

QUESTIONNAIRE RESPONSE STYLES

Chapter 3 noted that scores are critical for establishing the construct validity of measures. This is a reminder that the value of information obtained from questionnaires is determined by the quality of scores obtained. Items and scaling formats alone, no matter how elegant, do not guarantee successful questionnaire outcomes.

Research has established that characteristics of the individuals completing questionnaires and the environments in which they complete them often affect the scores obtained. Some of these characteristics have been studied in situations involving self-reports; others have been studied on observational ratings.

Self-Reports

Two tendencies that influence self-report responses have received substantial attention. *Social desirability* refers to the tendency to present oneself in a publicly favorable light. For example, a socially desirable response expresses approval for a public policy (e.g., the Supreme Court's decision on abortion) because the respondent believes others approve. *Response acquiescence* or *yea-saying* is a tendency to agree with a statement regardless of its content. Of the two, social desirability appears to be a more general problem for questionnaire responses.

RESEARCH HIGHLIGHT 4.2

Named Scaling Formats

Researchers have developed a wide variety of formats to scale questionnaire items. You may see reference to the following in organizational studies:

Thurstone scale. This is an attitude scale that is designed to generate items with equal intervals between them. The procedure uses judges to identify the degree to which items represent favorability or unfavorability toward some object (e.g., birth control). Twenty items are retained that cover the range of favorability or unfavorability from the subset of items that judges agree have the same favorability or unfavorability value. Respondents check whether they agree or disagree with each of the retained items. Their scores are based on the average numerical values assigned to each item by the judges.

Behaviorally anchored observation or rating scales. A procedure similar to the Thurstone method, this format is used to develop scales to measure behavior rather than attitudes. The scales have been used frequently in organizational research in which observers (e.g., supervisors) are asked to rate the performance behavior of employees.

Likert scale. This scale is designed to measure attitudes with equal intervals between categories, like the Thurstone scale. Participants in the development stage are asked to indicate their own agreement or disagreement with a large number of items about an attitude on a 5-point scale. Item analysis is then used to compare scores on each item with the total score made up from the sum of all items. Items are retained for the questionnaire if scores correspond closely with the total scores. Scales are often referred to as Likert scales even if the developer does not evaluate the items by the item analysis procedure recommended.

Semantic differential scale. This scale is designed to measure the meaning participants attribute to some object using 7-point bipolar adjectives such as good–bad, strong–weak, and active–passive. Most adjective pairs measure participants' evaluation of the object; the sum of these evaluations is often taken to represent an individual's attitude toward the object.

Observations

A number of response styles have also been identified when individuals are asked to make observations about some object. These include **leniency error**, a tendency to systematically provide a more favorable response than is warranted. **Severity error**, a tendency to systematically provide less favorable responses than warranted, is less frequent. Alternatively, **central tendency error** is present if an observer clusters responses in the middle of a scale when more variable responses should be recorded. **Halo error** is present when an observer evaluates an object in an undifferentiated manner. For example, a student may provide favorable evaluations to an instructor on all dimensions of teaching effectiveness because the instructor is effective on one dimension of teaching.

Implications for Questionnaire Construction and Use

Self-report and observer errors are difficult to identify in practice. For example, leniency error cannot necessarily be inferred because an observer provides high evaluations of all cases rated. All cases may deserve high evaluations; in this case, high evaluations are valid, not evidence of leniency error.

Furthermore, attempts to control for either self-report response styles or observational errors through questionnaire construction have only limited success. For example, researchers have attempted to reduce social desirability and leniency errors through the choice of response categories. **Forced-choice scales** are designed to provide respondents with choices that appear to be equal in social desirability or equal in favorability. Behaviorally anchored observation or rating scales (see Research Highlight 4.2) are designed to yield more accurate ratings by providing respondents with meaningful scale anchors to help generate scores that are less susceptible to rating errors. Unfortunately, research investigations comparing formats on common self-report and observational problems have not found one format to be systematically better than others.

Errors introduced by response styles can be reduced by ensuring that respondents have the ability and are motivated to complete the questionnaire task. For example, errors such as central tendency or leniency are more likely when observers do not have sufficient information to complete a questionnaire accurately. Improperly motivated respondents are also problematic.

PILOT TESTING

No matter how much care is used, questionnaire construction remains an imprecise research procedure. Before using a questionnaire for substantive research, it is essential to obtain information by pilot testing the questionnaire on individuals similar to those who will be asked to complete it as a part of the substantive research. Two types of pilot tests are desirable.

One type asks individuals, preferably like those who will complete the final questionnaire, to provide their interpretation and understanding of each item. This assessment will help identify errors in assumptions about participants' frames of reference. It also helps identify items that are difficult to understand. Pilot tests of this sort will almost always lead to changes in the design of a research questionnaire. These changes may help increase response rates, reduce missing data, and obtain more valid responses on the final questionnaire.

A second type of pilot test is more like a regular research study; a large number of respondents are desirable. Data from this type of pilot test are used to see if scores behave as expected. Are average scores reasonable? Do scores on items vary as expected? Analyses assessing relationships among items are also useful in this type of pilot test. For example, internal consistency reliability of multi-item measures can be assessed by a procedure described in chapter 17. Indeed, this second type of pilot test can be viewed as an important step in construct validation as described in the last chapter. However, its preliminary nature must be emphasized. Changes in items will almost always be suggested the first time scores from a new questionnaire are analyzed.

SUMMARY

Questionnaires, measuring instruments that ask research participants to respond to questions, are often used in research. Questionnaires may ask for **self-reports**, in which respondents provide information about themselves. They are also used to ask observers to describe or evaluate some externally visible characteristic (e.g., a behavior) of individuals or organizations. Getting information through observers often leads to more systematic measurement when there is a choice of methods.

Researchers should first see whether the research question of interest can be addressed in some other way before developing a questionnaire. *Secondary data*, information collected for some other purpose, are often available for research use or another researcher may have already developed a questionnaire that is satisfactory for your purposes.

Questionnaires may be administered in written form or they may be administered as *interviews* where an *interviewer* asks questions verbally. Interviews are useful early in the research process to help refine questions and possible responses. Alternatively, written questionnaires are typically more efficient to administer when the final research study is conducted. The choice between interviews and written questionnaires also depends on the accessibility of research participants and their language proficiency.

Questionnaire construction begins by defining the domain of information to be obtained. In developing questions, researchers need to attend to the ability and motivation of the individuals who will be asked to respond. Words and questions should be simple and specific, and researchers need to be honest in their efforts to obtain accurate information.

When possible, questionnaires should be designed so that participants are drawn in with interesting questions. Questions asking for personal information are best saved until the end of the questionnaire.

Questionnaires sometimes use *open-ended response formats* in which respondents provide their own answers. Alternatively, respondents are asked to choose a fixed category when questions have *closed-ended response formats*. Questions with closed-ended response formats are attractive because they are easy to complete and because they are easy to code. When response categories are arranged in order (e.g., from more to less), equal-appearing closed-ended response formats are typically constructed.

The quality of results provided by questionnaires depends largely on the care and attention participants give them. Self-reporting errors that can be problematic include *social desirability*, in which respondents attempt to present themselves in a favorable light, and *acquiescence* (or *yea-saying*), in which respondents tend to agree with a questionnaire item regardless of its content. Errors made by observers include *leniency* (*severity*), in which scores are systematically inflated (deflated); *central tendency*, in which scores have insufficient variability; and *halo*, in which evaluations of an object are made in an undifferentiated fashion.

Questionnaires need to be pilot tested before they are used for research purposes no matter how carefully constructed. It is useful to have individuals evaluate each question for interpretation and understanding. It is also useful to obtain information from a large number of individuals so statistical properties of the scores can be examined. Results from pilot testing invariably suggest questionnaire modifications.

FOR REVIEW

Terms to Know

Questionnaires: Measuring instruments that ask individuals to respond to a set of questions in verbal or written form.

Self-report questionnaires: Questionnaires that ask respondents to provide information about themselves.

Interviews: Measuring instruments in which another individual (the interviewer) asks the questions verbally and is responsible for recording responses.

Secondary data: Information used for research purposes but that has been collected for other purposes.

Open-ended response format: Questionnaire scaling that has participants respond in their own words.

Closed-ended response format: Questionnaire scaling in which the researcher provides participants with fixed response categories.

Social desirability: A self-report response style designed to present the respondent in a publicly favorable light.

Response acquiescence (also *yea-saying*): A self-report response style in which the respondent tends to agree with a questionnaire item regardless of its content.

Leniency error: Present when an observer systematically inflates ratings of a group of objects.

Severity error: Present when an observer systematically deflates ratings of a group of objects.

Central tendency error: Present when an observer clusters responses in the middle of a scale when more variable responses should be recorded.

Halo error: Present when an observer evaluates an object in an undifferentiated manner.

Forced choice scales: Scales in which response categories are equated on favorability or other characteristics to control for response styles.

Things to Know

1. Under what circumstances would you consider self-reports over observations? Observations over self-reports?
2. Under what circumstances would you consider using written questionnaires rather than interviews? Interviews rather than written questionnaires?
3. Are there any advantages to using an open-ended response format over a closed-ended response format?
4. What are characteristics of good questionnaire items?
5. How should questionnaire items be sequenced?
6. How do social desirability and response acquiescence differ?
7. Compare and contrast social desirability and leniency.
8. What types of pilot testing should be performed on new questionnaires?

PART II SUGGESTED READINGS

Many books are available on measurement methods for the social sciences; many of these are quite demanding in terms of the statistical knowledge required for understanding. I recommend any edition of Nunnally (1967; 1978; Nunnally & Bernstein, 1994). All are excellent yet understandable treatments of many measurement issues. Ghiselli, Campbell, and Zedeck's (1981) book is also good, and it too is accessible.

There are also more specific treatments of construct validity and related topics. Although a challenge to understand, Cronbach and Meehl (1955) wrote a seminal paper on construct validity. Barrett (1992), Blalock (1968), and Schwab (1980) provide useful elaborations on the topic. Schwab uses the general model of this book to frame his discussion. Although their methodology is now challenged, Campbell and Fiske (1959) present an understandable description of the logic of convergent and discriminant validity. For readings on reliability see chapter 17.

Sudman and Bradburn's (1982) book on questionnaire items is useful. Payne's (1951) book, *The Art of Asking Questions*, is a classic. There are also specialized volumes on particular types of questions, such as Schwarz and Sudman's (1994) book on obtaining retrospective reports from respondents. Price and Mueller (1986) provide a compilation of measures available for organizational research. White (1986) provides a bibliography of material on questionnaire construction.

III

Design: Addressing Internal Validity

5

Research Design Foundations

Chapter Outline

- *Causal Challenges*
  - *Causal Direction*
  - *Specification: Uncontrolled Variables and the Danger of Bias*
    - *Bias*
    - *Spurious Relationships*
    - *Suppressor Variables*
    - *Noise*
    - *Mediators*
    - *Moderators*
- *Using Design to Address Causal Challenges*
  - *Sampling: Selecting Cases to Study*
    - *Restriction of Range*
    - *Comparison Groups*
  - *Measurement Decisions*
    - *Control Over Independent Variables*
    - *Measurement and Statistical Control*
  - *Administering Measures to Cases*
    - *Matching*
    - *Random Assignment*
- *Design Types*
  - *Experiments*
  - *Quasi-Experiments*
  - *Field Studies and Surveys*
- *Summary*
- *For Review*

- *Terms to Know*
- *Questions for Review*
- *Issues to Discuss*

Movie and television portrayals of violence by humans to humans have increased, as has the perpetuation of violence in real life. There is a relationship between the depiction of violence and actual violence.

Does the portrayal of violence lead to violence in society? Or, does societal violence lead to its depiction? Or, are the two reciprocal? Or, are they only coincidental? These questions illustrate the greatest challenge for research. It is not whether relationships can be found between variables, but why? What are the reasons for the observed relationships?

Researchers use two sources to help draw causal inferences from relationships observed among variables. First, they draw on conceptual models formulated to explain relationships in causal terms. Second, they use research designs to assist in causal understanding.

This chapter is concerned with the second issue, with contributions of research design to causal understanding. It begins with a discussion of challenges to causal understanding. It then explores decisions researchers make to confront these challenges through research design. Finally, the chapter describes how these decisions combine into four common research design types. These designs are developed more fully in the following two chapters.

CAUSAL CHALLENGES

Internal validity is present when variation in an independent variable is responsible for variation in a dependent variable. Exhibit 5.1 summarizes the three criteria introduced in chapter 2 that help establish internal validity.

The first criterion refers to an empirical relationship, the association between the independent (X) and dependent (Y) variables. Such relationships typically are investigated by using statistical procedures described in parts IV and V of this book. In this chapter, assume that an empirical relationship between X and Y is established.

Thus, this chapter focuses on the latter two criteria. Does variation in the independent variable occur with, or before, variation in the dependent variable? And, particularly, are there other plausible explanations for the observed relationship?

These criteria suggest two general problems for concluding that an observed relationship means an independent variable causes a dependent variable ($X \rightarrow Y$). One involves the direction of causation; the other involves possible consequences of uncontrolled variables that may be responsible for the relationship observed between the independent and the dependent

---

1. Independent and dependent variables are meaningfully related

2. Variation in the independent variable is contemporaneous with, or precedes,

   variation in the dependent variable

3. There is a reasonable causal explanation for the observed relationship and

   there are no plausible alternative explanations for it

EXHIBIT 5.1. Internal causal criteria.

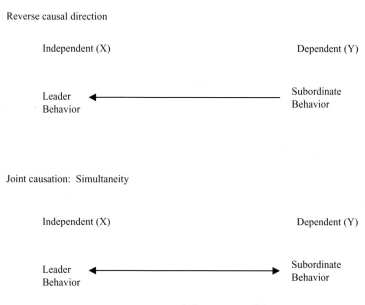

Reverse causal direction

Independent (X)   Dependent (Y)

Leader   ◄————————————————   Subordinate
Behavior   Behavior

Joint causation: Simultaneity

Independent (X)   Dependent (Y)

Leader   ◄————————————————►   Subordinate
Behavior   Behavior

EXHIBIT 5.2.   Causal direction problems.

variable. Different research designs offer different degrees of protection against these challenges to internal validity.

Causal Direction

A conceptual model states that there is a causal conceptual relationship between an independent variable and dependent variable ($X' \rightarrow Y'$). Suppose also that a relationship between X and Y is observed on a set of scores. Exhibit 5.2 shows two alternative explanations that involve causal direction. The top panel illustrates a possibility that $Y \rightarrow X$, not $X \rightarrow Y$.

For example, it is often assumed that a supervisor's leadership style (X') influences subordinate work behavior (Y'). However, one study obtained evidence suggesting that cause goes from Y' to X' (Lowin & Craig, 1968). In the study, a ***research confederate*** (given the pseudonym Charlie) was used to act as a subordinate for participants who role-played as supervisors. (A research confederate is, unknown to the research participants, a member of the research team.) Charlie engaged in systematically different work behaviors for different supervisor participants. He worked efficiently for some of the participants and inefficiently for others.

Research participants who supervised an efficient Charlie used different leadership styles than participants who supervised an inefficient Charlie. Subordinate behavior thus influenced supervisory behavior. This causal direction is illustrated in the top panel of Exhibit 5.2.

This study is causally persuasive for two reasons. First, Charlie's behavior occurred before the supervisors' behavior was recorded; the second criterion for causality was satisfied. More important, Charlie's behavior was controlled by the researchers. It was carefully scripted so that any causal influence could only go from Charlie to the participant supervisor, not the reverse.

The lower panel in Exhibit 5.2 illustrates another difficulty in reaching causal conclusions; it shows causation going both ways. Economists use the term ***simultaneity*** to describe a situation in which causation is reciprocal. The relationship between leadership style and subordinate behavior may be reciprocal. That is, supervisors' leadership styles may influence subordinate behavior and subordinates' behavior may also influence supervisory style. (Lowin and Craig did not rule out the possibility that leaders influence subordinates generally. They simply ruled out that possibility in their study; thus, they could concentrate on subordinates' roles in the influence process.)

Specification: Uncontrolled Variables and the Danger of Bias

Causal models are typically more complex than the models researchers actually study. A causal model includes variables and relationships that are not of interest and may not be accounted for in a study. For example, a researcher may measure and study a relationship between education level and subsequent employment income. Other variables that also influence income, such as years of work experience and type of occupation, may not be of interest.

However, the nature of any causal relationship between education and income may be misrepresented if these other causal variables are not considered. ***Misspecification*** occurs if variables that operate in the causal model are not included in the model studied. These variables if uncontrolled are called ***nuisance variables***. They provide potential alternative explanations for the relationship(s) of interest.

Consequences for causal understanding resulting from uncontrolled (nuisance) variables depend on how they are related to the independent and dependent variables studied. Several types are described here using the consumer computer satisfaction example introduced in chapter 3. As in chapter 3, relationships described are offered to illustrate research issues and not to explain consumer satisfaction.

Bias

The most serious result of misspecification is ***bias***, when the causal relationship between an independent and dependent variable is under- or overstated. A biased relationship may occur for several reasons. Often an uncontrolled variable is causally related to the dependent variable and is related to the independent variable(s), causally or otherwise. To illustrate, suppose a researcher believes consumer satisfaction depends on computer speed. Greater speed is expected to lead to higher satisfaction. However, the researcher does not account for computer memory, which also influences satisfaction. The larger the memory, the greater the satisfaction. Furthermore, computer speed and memory are positively related. Manufacturers make computers faster as they increase computer memory. These relationships are shown in the top panel of Exhibit 5.3.

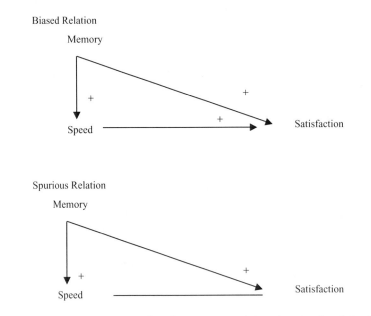

EXHIBIT 5.3.   Computer speed and memory as determinants of satisfaction.

RESEARCH HIGHLIGHT 5.1

Other Sources of Bias

This chapter focuses on bias generated from misspecification. Misspecification is not the only reason for biased relationships. Unreliability of measures introduced in chapter 3 is another source of bias. Chapter 17 explains in detail how unreliability can introduce bias and describes steps that can be used to alleviate it. Chapter 20 describes additional sources of bias in research models.

In this example the relationship between computer speed and satisfaction that is observed will overstate the causal relationship if computer memory is not controlled. Part of the observed speed–satisfaction relationship results because computer memory is positively related to both satisfaction and speed. Memory thus biases the relationship between speed and satisfaction; it must be controlled to remove the bias.

Spurious Relationships

A **spurious relationship** is a special case of bias. It occurs when an uncontrolled variable accounts for all the observed relationship between a dependent and independent variable(s). Assume, as stated previously, that memory influences satisfaction and is related to speed. However, now assume the improbable—that there is no causal relation between speed and satisfaction. A study that investigates only speed and satisfaction nevertheless will find the two related. They are related spuriously because of their joint relationships with memory. These relationships are shown in the bottom panel of Exhibit 5.3.

Biased relationships are often inflated. An observed relationship overstates the true causal relationship between an independent and a dependent variable because a nuisance variable(s) is not taken into account.

Suppressor Variables

Suppressor variables represent biasing variables that lead to an understatement of the true causal relationship. Suppressor variables most commonly have a positive relationship with the independent variable and no relationship or a small negative relationship with the dependent variable. For example, memory would suppress rather than inflate the relationship between speed and satisfaction in the top panel of Exhibit 5.3 if it is positively related to speed but has no relationship with satisfaction. In this case, failure to control for computer memory leads to an understatement of the relationship between speed and satisfaction. (This result may seem counter intuitive. Chapter 11 shows how suppressor variables operate with formulas for multiple correlation and regression.)

Uncontrolled variables related to the independent variable(s) under study thus seriously challenge causal interpretation. Depending on the strength and direction of their relationships, they may bias by inflating, deflating (suppressing), or even making spurious the observed relationship between independent and dependent variables.

Noise

A **noisy relationship** is more benign; a noise variable is related to the dependent variable but unrelated to the independent variable(s). Consumer affability illustrates such a possibility.

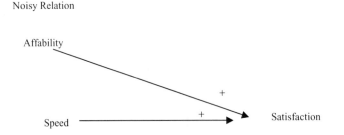

EXHIBIT 5.4.   Computer speed and consumer affability as determinants of satisfaction.

More affable consumers report higher satisfaction with their computers because they are more satisfied generally than are less affable consumers. However, there is no reason to suppose that affability is related to computer speed. The relationships are shown in Exhibit 5.4.

Noise variables do not misrepresent the strength of relationship between a dependent and an independent variable(s); they are benign in that sense. However, they do influence the dependent variable. They introduce variability in the dependent variable that is not accounted for by the independent variable(s) of interest. As a consequence, researchers are unable to explain as much of the variability in the dependent variable as is true if the noise variables are controlled. This is especially problematic for internal statistical and statistical generalization validation (see part V).

Mediators

Independent variables are ordinarily thought to influence dependent variables directly: variability in *X* leads immediately to variability in *Y*. **Mediator** or **intervening variables** come between an independent and a dependent variable in a causal chain. If a mediator is present, then some or all the influence of the independent variable operates indirectly on the dependent variable through the mediator.

Consider a conceptual model in which a researcher expects satisfaction with computers to be negatively influenced by computer weight. However, unknown to the researcher, weight influences price (lower weight is achieved only at a price). Price also influences satisfaction negatively.

The top panel of Exhibit 5.5 shows a case in which price *fully mediates* the relationship between weight and satisfaction. A relationship is observed if only weight and satisfaction are studied. However, if price is also included in the model studied, weight is found to have no direct effect on satisfaction. Its effect is only indirect because of its effect on price.

The bottom panel of Exhibit 5.5 shows a case in which price *partially mediates* the weight–satisfaction relationship. Weight has a direct effect on satisfaction and an indirect effect (through price). If price is uncontrolled, the influence of weight erroneously will appear to be only a direct effect.

Mediator variables are ubiquitous in research. Relationships between independent and dependent variables typically have variables that intervene. Indeed, mediator variables are often used to help explain why an independent variable influences a dependent variable. For example, the impact of weight on price can help explain the impact of weight on satisfaction.

Researchers choose to include or exclude mediator variables based on the type of understanding they seek. For example, a researcher likely would include price in a model explaining satisfaction, because price is important to consumers. Alternatively, computer manufacturing

Fully Mediated Relation

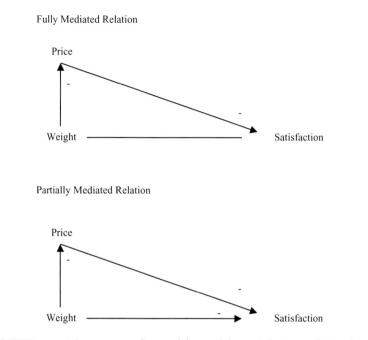

Partially Mediated Relation

EXHIBIT 5.5.   Price as a mediator of the weight–satisfaction relationship.

cost probably would not be included in a study of consumer satisfaction. Although cost mediates weight and price from a manufacturer's perspective, manufacturer's cost, per se, probably is not considered by consumers.

Moderators

Moderator variables have values that are associated with different relationships between an independent and a dependent variable. (In psychology, moderator variables are often also called **interaction variables**. In sociology, moderators are sometimes called **boundary conditions**.) The strength and/or direction of relationships between independent and dependent variables depend on values of a moderator variable.

Consider again a model in which weight is expected to have a negative influence on computer satisfaction. Such a relationship may exist only among owners of laptop computers; there may be no relationship between weight and satisfaction for desktop computer owners. If so, type of computer (laptop or desktop) moderates the relationship between computer weight and computer satisfaction.

Failure to control for a moderator variable misrepresents (biases) the observed causal relationship between weight and satisfaction for both computer types. The relationship will be overstated for desktop computer owners and understated for laptop computer owners.

The top panel of Exhibit 5.6 illustrates the scenario just described. The bottom panel of Exhibit 5.6 illustrates a case in which type of computer serves as both a moderator and an independent variable. Type of computer may moderate the relationship between weight and satisfaction as described above. However, in addition, type of computer may have a direct effect on satisfaction. Laptop computer owners may be more (or less) satisfied with their computers, regardless of weight.

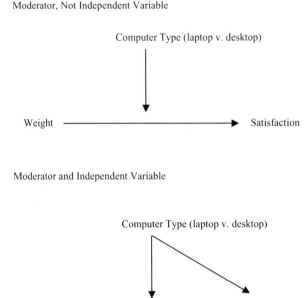

Moderator, Not Independent Variable

Computer Type (laptop v. desktop)

Weight ⟶ Satisfaction

Moderator and Independent Variable

Computer Type (laptop v. desktop)

Weight ⟶ Satisfaction

EXHIBIT 5.6. Computer type as a moderator of the weight–satisfaction relationship.

RESEARCH HIGHLIGHT 5.2

Difficulties Identifying Causally Problematic Variables

Empirical relationships among the variables of central interest and potential nuisance variables tell little about causal roles the latter variables may serve. For example, there is no way to decide whether a variable acts as a moderator from its relationships with the independent or the dependent variables. A moderator may be related to an independent and/or dependent variable, or it may not be related to either. The only way to identify a moderator variable is to test it directly. For example, a moderator can be investigated by subgrouping, as illustrated in the discussion of Exhibit 5.6. Moderator variables also can be assessed statistically as described in chapter 19.

As another example, relationships observed do not allow one to distinguish between a mediator variable and a nuisance variable that biases the relationship between an independent and a dependent variable. The distinction between these two variables hinges on the causal direction of their relationship with the independent variable. The independent variable is a cause of the mediator, but it is a consequence of the biasing nuisance variable.

Thus, by themselves, relationships observed among a set of variables provide little causal information. Conceptual models and design decisions described in this chapter are essential for causal clarification in most instances.

USING DESIGN TO ADDRESS CAUSAL CHALLENGES

The examples described all involve an observed relationship between independent and dependent variables. However, the examples also show that interpreting these relationships may be causally problematic. The causal relation between the variables may not be in the expected direction. Or, an additional variable(s) that operates in the causal model may result in a misrepresentation of the causal relationship(s) of interest if not controlled.

The examples also suggest how important strong conceptual models are for addressing causal concerns. A good conceptual model can make a compelling case for the direction of causation. It also can help identify potential nuisance variables that require control.

Research design also may help meet causal challenges, especially when coupled with strong conceptualization. This section identifies three key characteristics of research design: sampling cases, measurement, and administration of measures to cases. The section emphasizes how decisions about these design characteristics can contribute to causal clarity.

Sampling: Selecting Cases to Study

Decisions about samples to study often emphasize generalization of research results. Part V describes how statistical generalization procedures are used to generalize sample findings to cases in a larger population when probability rules are used to select the samples. *Probability sampling* of this sort is contrasted with other types, typically called *convenience* or *judgment sampling*. Probability sampling permits valid statistical generalization; convenience sampling does not.

Sampling decisions also have implications for causal inferences. These apply to both probability and convenience samples. Two sampling decisions that bear on the control of nuisance variables are discussed here.

Restriction of Range

Cases may be selected so that variation in an otherwise uncontrolled (nuisance) variable(s) is restricted or eliminated. *Restriction of range* reduces or eliminates relationships between nuisance and other variables.

To illustrate, consider the example in which computer memory is a nuisance variable affecting the relationship between speed and satisfaction (top panel in Exhibit 5.3). One way to control the nuisance variable memory is to restrict its variability. For example, a researcher includes only consumers with computers of one memory size. Eliminating the variation in computer memory through sample selection eliminates its effect on the speed–satisfaction relationship.

Despite this advantage, restricting the range of a nuisance variable is not recommended when, as is usually the case, generalization of a relationship is of interest. Except for moderator variables, nuisance variables by definition are related to either the independent or the dependent variable or both. Consequently, restricting the range of an otherwise uncontrolled (nuisance) variable necessarily also restricts the range of the independent variable, the dependent variable, or both. In turn, this means the relationship observed after the restriction takes place likely does not represent the relationship that would be observed over the entire range of the independent and dependent variables.

Restricting range is a more justifiable method of control when a moderator variable represents the nuisance and when it is unrelated to either the independent or the dependent variable. Computer type as shown in the top half (but not the bottom half) of Exhibit 5.6 is illustrative. For example, only participants with laptop (or desktop) computers may be studied. Even here, however, there is a down side to restricting the range of a moderator nuisance; generalization of research results again is limited. For example, if only laptop owners are studied, then generalization of the speed–satisfaction relationship cannot be made to owners of desktop computers.

Comparison Groups

Some research designs compare dependent variable scores across comparison groups—two or more groups of cases. The groups are chosen to represent different levels of an independent variable. However, efforts are made to ensure that the groups are similar on potential nuisance variables.

For example, a researcher is again interested in the effect of computer speed on consumer satisfaction. An organization is found that purchased computers for its office employees. Employees in some departments were provided faster computers than employees in other departments. If the researcher can assume that employees and computers are otherwise similar, computer satisfaction of the two employee groups can be compared to investigate the effect of computer speed. The value of this procedure hinges on the ability to identify groups that are truly comparable except for the levels of the independent variable of interest.

Measurement Decisions

Part II described how measurement decisions influence construct validity. Decisions in this realm are designed to enhance the correspondence between scores on a measure and the underlying construct of conceptual interest. Measurement decisions also have causal implications. Decisions about independent variables and variables to control are especially important in the latter context.

Control Over Independent Variables

The purpose of causally motivated research is to determine how independent variables influence dependent variable responses. Thus, values of the dependent variable are always a characteristic of the cases studied; the cases control or determine values of the dependent variable. Indeed, researchers must take care so that dependent variables are not influenced by the procedures used to measure them.

However, there is more latitude about measures of independent variables. Sometimes independent variables represent responses from cases much as dependent variables. Consider a study of the relationship between education (X') and income (Y'). A researcher likely would have participants report both their level of educational achievement and the amount of their income.

In such cases, measurement of the independent variable contributes little to internal validity. There is nothing about this design to rule out the possibility that $Y' \to X'$, because values of both variables are obtained from the cases investigated. Furthermore, nuisance variables (e.g., occupation level) also are likely to be problematical in this design, because often they are related to educational achievement.

Two alternative forms of measurement remove control of the independent variable from the cases studied; levels of the independent variable are established externally. First, this control may be exercised by some exogenous event. For example, a researcher may study property insurance purchases (Y) in two communities, one having recently experienced a hurricane and the other not. In this instance, the exogenous determination of values of the independent variable (hurricane or no hurricane) rules out the possibility that $Y \to X$.

Second, a researcher may exercise direct control over levels of an independent variable. The leadership study described early in this chapter is illustrative. In that study, researchers established two levels of subordinate behavior carried out by their research confederate; these levels represent the operationalization of the independent variable. The research participants who role-played supervisors had no control over the confederate and hence no control over the levels of the independent variable they experienced. Although any relationship between subordinate behavior and leadership behavior still might be biased by other uncontrolled variables, the design does rule out the possibility that a relationship resulted because the dependent variable influenced the independent variable.

Measurement and Statistical Control

Measurement combined with data analysis procedures also can contribute to the control of nuisance, mediator, and moderator variables. Specifically, when researchers measure variables that require control, they can include them in statistical models designed to deal with more than one causal variable. For example, a researcher studies the relationship between education level and income but recognizes that, if uncontrolled, occupation level may bias the relationship. In such instances, multiple correlation or regression (chapter 11) may be used to investigate the relationship between income and education, controlling for occupation level. Statistical models for addressing causal issues are discussed in chapter 19.

Administering Measures to Cases

Powerful causal designs can be built when researchers not only control levels of an independent variable(s) but also determine what cases experience each level. Such designs address both directional challenges and most nuisance variables.

The objective of these designs is to assign cases in a way that equalizes values of nuisance variables across levels of the independent variable. In the leadership study, for example, suppose leader assertiveness is a potential nuisance variable. Suppose further that cases are assigned to the two levels of subordinate behavior so they are on average equal in assertiveness. Subsequent differences across the two subordinate behaviors cannot be due to differences in assertiveness. Even though assertiveness may influence leader behavior, its effect will be the same in the two groups. There are two general procedures to equate values of nuisance variables across different levels of an independent variable.

Matching

One procedure involves **matching** (equating) cases that receive different levels of the independent variable on a nuisance variable(s). For example, assume a researcher is interested in the relationship between computer type (laptop or desktop) and satisfaction; computer speed and memory are recognized to be nuisance variables. The researcher sorts among a group of computer owners matching each laptop owner with a desktop owner whose computer has the same speed and memory. Subsequent satisfaction differences between laptop and desktop owners cannot be due to differences in these two nuisance variables, because each group has a similar mix of computer speed and computer memory.

Matching is a powerful form of control, but it is often difficult to achieve. The number of potential cases in the group to be matched may have to be large. It may be difficult, for example, to find desktop and laptop participants who have computers with the same speed and memory. Further, as the number of nuisance variables increases, so too does the difficulty of finding cases that meet the matching criteria.

Random Assignment

Another way to equalize groups on nuisance variables is through *random assignment*; cases are randomly assigned to different levels of an independent variable(s). This was the procedure used in the leadership study. Participants who role-played leaders were randomly assigned to the two levels of subordinate behavior carried out by the research confederate.

Random assignment of supervisor participants to subordinate behavior is attractive because it should average out the effect of personal characteristics that may serve as nuisance variables. Average assertiveness of those participants who were exposed to the efficient subordinate should be about the same as for those who experienced the inefficient subordinate. Other supervisor differences also should be equated approximately across the two subordinate behavior levels.

Random assignment has two potential and powerful advantages over matching. First, when successful, it controls for nuisance variables whether or not researchers are aware of them. Second, because random assignment does not require knowledge of specific nuisance variables, researchers do not have to measure them.

Nevertheless, measurement of nuisance variables is still desirable to determine whether randomization is successful. It is not always successful in equating groups on nuisance variables. Just as 10 flips of a coin occasionally may lead to 8, 9, or even 10 heads (instead of the expected 5), random assignment of cases to levels of an independent variable may not equate the resulting groups on nuisance variables. The larger the groups formed by random assignment, the more likely they will be equivalent on nuisance variables (see part V).

DESIGN TYPES

The characteristics outlined call for decisions in all research designs. Researchers must make decisions about cases to study, measures, and administration of measures to cases.

Exhibit 5.7 shows how these decisions combine to describe four common types of research. These four are introduced here and are developed more fully in the next two chapters.

Experiments

Experiments are characterized by random assignment of cases to levels of an independent variable(s). Researchers must be able to control (manipulate) levels of the independent variable(s) in experiments. The leadership study illustrates an experiment; the researchers randomly assigned supervisor participants to the two levels of subordinate behavior. Cases in experiments

Design	Assignment of Cases	Sample	Independent Variable Control
Experiment	Random	Probability/ Convenience	Researcher
Quasi-experiment	Nonrandom	Probability/ Convenience	Researcher/ Exogenous event
Survey	Nonrandom	Probability	Cases
Field study	Nonrandom	Convenience	Cases

EXHIBIT 5.7.   Typology of research designs.

may be from some intact group (e.g., all members of a department in an organization). Or cases may be obtained with a sample from some larger population.

Quasi-Experiments

Quasi-experiments share several characteristics of experiments. They also use an independent variable(s) that is not controlled by the cases studied. Also as in experiments, cases to study may be obtained by probability or convenience sampling.

Quasi-experiments differ from experiments with regard to the assignment of cases to levels of an independent variable. In quasi-experiments, assignment is not done randomly. Thus, researchers can try to match cases on a nuisance variable(s), or they can try to obtain comparable groups of cases for each level of the independent variable.

Field Studies and Surveys

Field studies and ***surveys*** differ from experiments and quasi-experiments with regard to the independent variable. In both, responses on the independent variable are provided by the cases studied and not by the researcher.

What differentiates field studies from surveys is how cases are sampled. Field studies obtain cases through a convenience sampling procedure. Surveys use probability sampling to obtain cases from a larger population. This is done so statistical inferences can be made from the sample to that larger population.

Experiments and quasi-experiments are potentially strong designs when causal direction is a concern, because values of the independent variable are determined outside the cases studied in both. Experiments are also strong for ruling out alternative explanations involving nuisance variables. Quasi-experiments can also be good in this regard, although they are generally less powerful than experiments.

Surveys and field studies are not strong designs for addressing causal direction. However, researchers who use the latter designs often measure variables that otherwise would obscure causal relationships if uncontrolled. They then couple these designs with statistical analysis procedures to control for potential biasing variables (see chapter 19).

SUMMARY

Research design is the main empirical research activity to attain internal validity. Internal validity addresses the causal relationship between scores on measures of an independent and a dependent variable.

RESEARCH HIGHLIGHT 5.3

Don't Confuse Research Design with Research Setting

Types of research design are to be thought of in terms of the characteristics in Exhibit 5.7. The four designs differ in sampling, in measurement of the independent variables, and in the assignment of cases to measurement. They do not necessarily differ in where they are conducted. Thus, field studies do not have to be carried out in the "field"; experiments do not have to be conducted in laboratories.

Given an observed relationship between independent and dependent variables, internal validity is challenged in two ways. One involves the direction of causality. Does an observed relationship warrant the conclusion that variation in the independent variable leads to variation in the dependent variable?

A second challenge results from *misspecification* when a variable(s) operating in the underlying causal model is not accounted for in the research model investigated. Such variables are called *nuisance variables*. Nuisance variables may *bias* relationships, typically by inflating the observed relationship between an independent and a dependent variable. But nuisance variables also may *suppress* observed relationships or even make them *spurious*. A nuisance variable that results in *noise* makes it more difficult to identify a relationship between an independent and a dependent variable. However, it does not bias the expected size of the observed relationship.

Mediator variables (also called *intervening variables*) come between independent and dependent variables. *Full mediation* occurs when an independent variable causes the mediator, and the mediator causes the dependent variable. *Partial mediation* occurs when an independent variable causes the mediator and the dependent variable, and the mediator causes the dependent variable.

Moderator variables (also called *interactions* and *boundary conditions*) may or may not be independent variables. However, they do influence the relationship between the dependent and some other independent variable. The relationship (direction and/or magnitude) between the dependent and an independent variable depends on values of a moderator variable.

A research design involves three sets of decisions. Each set has implications for causal direction and/or control of variables not accounted for in the research model investigated.

1. Decisions about the cases studied can help control nuisance variables. One way is to *restrict the range* of such variables through the group studied. However, range restriction will bias the relationship between the independent and the dependent variables if, as is usually the case, the restricted variable is related to the independent or the dependent variable. Nuisance variables also can be controlled if they are equated among *comparison groups* that experience each value of the independent variable.

2. Decisions about how an independent variable is measured can help make the causal direction between an independent and dependent variable unambiguous. Greater understanding of causal direction is possible when values of the independent variable are not determined by the cases studied. Measuring potential problematic variables also can contribute to internal validity when combined with statistical analysis procedures.

3. Decisions about how measures are administered to cases can help control both directional and nuisance variable challenges. This can be achieved through *matching* or *random assignment*.

Characteristics of these three sets of decisions are useful to identify four common types of research design. In *experiments*, researchers control the levels of independent variables and randomly assign participants to those levels. They provide researchers the greatest control over the research environment. Experiments thus may provide high internal validity. Although *quasi-experiments* do not include random assignment, researchers nevertheless maintain substantial control over the research process. Quasi-experiments also can provide strong internal validity if a researcher can successfully match participants on nuisance variables or can find comparable comparison groups. *Field studies* and *surveys* do not provide strong evidence for causal direction. However, they may be designed to control for potential nuisance, mediator, and moderator variables by using statistical procedures.

FOR REVIEW

Terms to Know

Research confederate: A member of the research team who interacts with participants but is not known by participants to be a member of the research team.

Simultaneity: When causal influence between the independent and the dependent variable is reciprocal, it goes in both directions.

Misspecification: Occurs if variables that operate in the causal model are not included in the model studied.

Nuisance variable: A variable in the causal model that is not controlled in a research study.

Biased relationship: An observed relationship between an independent and a dependent variable that under- or overstates the causal relationship.

Spurious relationship: An observed relationship between an independent and a dependent variable but no causal relationship. Occurs when a nuisance variable accounts for all the observed relationship between a dependent and an independent variable(s).

Suppressor variable: A nuisance variable that biases an observed relationship between an independent and a dependent variable downward; usually occurs when a nuisance variable has a positive relationship with the independent variable and a small negative relationship with the dependent variable.

Noisy relationship: Occurs when a nuisance variable is related to the dependent variable but not to the independent variable(s).

Mediator variable: Also *intervening variable*; comes between an independent and a dependent variable in a causal chain.

Full mediation: The relationship between an independent and dependent variable operates only through a mediator variable. The independent variable has no direct effect on the dependent variable.

Partial mediation: The relationship between an independent and dependent variable operates partially through a mediator variable. The independent variable has a direct effect on the dependent variable and an indirect effect through the mediator.

Moderator variable: A variable whose values are associated with different relationships between an independent and a dependent variable. It may or may not be an independent variable.

Interaction variable: Synonym for *moderator variable*. A relationship between an independent and a dependent variable depends on the value of another variable.

Boundary condition: Synonym for *moderator variable*. A relationship between an independent and a dependent variable depends on the value (boundary) of another variable.

Probability sampling: The selection of a subset of cases obtained from a larger population of cases by using rules of probability.

Convenience sampling (also *judgment sampling*): The selection of cases (usually an intact group) to study by using nonprobability methods.

Restriction of range: A reduction in the variance of a variable through selection of cases.

Comparison groups: Groups of research cases thought to be comparable on levels of potential nuisance variables.

Matching: Cases are selected for research so those who experience different levels of an independent variable(s) are equated on levels of nuisance variables.

Random assignment: Allocation of cases to levels of an independent variable(s) without order; a procedure designed to equate cases on nuisance variables at each level of an independent variable(s).

Experiments: A research design in which cases are randomly assigned to levels of an independent variable(s).

Quasi-experiments: A research design in which cases do not control the levels of the independent variable(s) they experience; cases are not randomly assigned to levels of the independent variable(s).

Field study: A research design in which values of the independent variable(s) are characteristics of the cases studied and in which cases are not randomly selected from some larger population.

Survey study: A research design in which values of the independent variable(s) are characteristics of the cases studied and in which cases are randomly selected from some larger population.

Questions for Review

1. Be able to differentiate between spurious and biased relationships brought about by nuisance variables.
2. How are mediator and moderator variables similar? How do they differ?
3. What key characteristics (e.g., sampling) differentiate between experiments, quasi-experiments, surveys, and field studies?
4. How can sampling be used to control for nuisance variables? What limitations does sampling have as a method of control?
5. How are matching and comparison groups as forms of control similar? How do they differ? Which would you prefer to use as a form of control for nuisance variables? Why?
6. What design(s) would you recommend if you were concerned about causal direction but not nuisance variables? Why?

Issues to Discuss

1. How does random assignment of cases to levels of some independent variable operate to control for bias or spuriousness?
2. Does random assignment of cases to levels of some independent variable control for moderator and mediator variables? Why or why not?
3. From a design perspective, why is it attractive that cases not provide responses to the independent variable?

6

Design Applications: Experiments and Quasi-Experiments

Chapter Outline

- *Basic Designs*
  - *Design A1: Cross-Sectional Between-Cases Design*
  - *Design B1: Longitudinal Within-Cases Design*
- *Threats to Internal Validity*
  - *Threats From the Research Environment*
    - *Demands on Participants*
    - *Researcher Expectations*
  - *Threats in Between-Cases Designs*
  - *Threats in Longitudinal Designs*
- *Additional Designs*
  - *Design C1: Longitudinal Between-Cases*
  - *Design D: Cross-Sectional Factorial Design*
  - *Design E: Cross-Sectional Design with Covariate*
  - *Design Extensions*
- *Summary*
- *For Review*
  - *Terms to Know*
  - *Questions for Review*
  - *Issues to Discuss*

Quasi-experiments, and especially experiments, are attractive when researchers seek to address causal issues through research design. These designs establish values of an independent variable (X) outside the control of the cases studied; a researcher or an exogenous event is responsible for levels of X that cases experience. As a consequence, variation in the dependent variable

(Y) cannot be responsible for variation in X. Causal influence, if it exists, must go from the X to Y.

Furthermore, quasi-experiments and experiments may provide opportunities to assign cases to different levels of X. In experiments, researchers randomly assign cases to levels of X. In quasi-experiments, cases are allocated to levels of X by a method other than random assignment. In either case, opportunities to assign cases to different levels of X may help control alternative explanations due to nuisance variables.

Nevertheless, both quasi-experiments and experiments are subject to internal validity challenges. Both experience *threats to internal validity,* characteristics of research studies that make causal claims vulnerable to alternative explanations.

Chapter 6 describes several experimental and quasi-experimental designs. It also evaluates these designs for threats to internal validity.

BASIC DESIGNS

There are two broad categories of experimental and quasi-experimental designs. *Between-cases designs* involve two or more groups of cases. These *designs* are typically *cross-sectional* in which X and Y are measured only once. Causal inferences are drawn by comparing scores on Y across two or more groups of cases that experience different levels of X.

Within-case designs involve only one group of cases. They must also be *longitudinal designs* in which Y (and perhaps X) is measured more than once. Within-case designs address causal relationships by measuring Y both before and after a change in values on X. Evidence consistent with a causal relationship is obtained if values of Y change systematically as values of X change.

The two designs described next illustrate major differences between longitudinal within-case designs and cross-sectional between-cases designs. More complicated designs are discussed later in the chapter.

Design A1: Cross-Sectional Between-Cases Design

Design A1 in Exhibit 6.1 illustrates the simplest form of between-cases design; it is cross-sectional. It has one independent variable, X, with two values ($X = 0$ and $X = 1$). Each value is assigned to a group of cases represented by the vertical boxes. The effect of the independent variable is determined by whether Y scores differ between the two groups, if $\mu_{Y|0}$ (read as, mean of Y given that $X = 0$) $\neq \mu_{Y|1}$.

For example, an organization may be interested in evaluating a training program aimed at providing employees with skills to diagnose and repair production problems that arise in the manufacture of a product. Y is a measure of product quality.

One group of employees receives training, $X = 1$; the other serves as a control group, $X = 0$. The effect of training on product quality is observed by comparing subsequent average (mean) scores on product quality between the two groups.

Design B1: Longitudinal Within-Cases Design

Design B1, shown in Exhibit 6.2, illustrates a simple longitudinal within-cases design. The results of a change in an independent variable is studied on a single group. The dependent variable is measured before, Y^b, and after, Y^a, the independent variable value $X = 1$ is introduced. An effect of X is concluded if $\mu_{Y^a} \neq \mu_{Y^b}$.

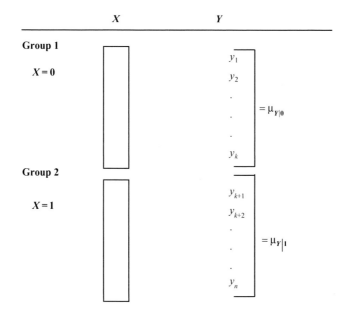

EXHIBIT 6.1. Design A1: Cross-sectional between-subjects experimental or quasi-experimental design.

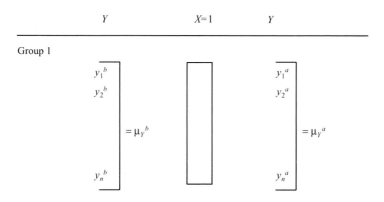

EXHIBIT 6.2. Design B1: Longitudinal within-subject design.

A longitudinal within-cases design also could be used to assess the influence of training. The organization measures product quality among a group of employees before training is introduced. It then trains all employees ($X = 1$) followed by another measurement of product quality at a later date. The effect of training is assessed by a comparison of μ_{Y^a} with μ_{Y^b}.

Both Designs A1 and B1 contrast one level of an independent variable with another. In Design A1, the contrast is explicit between two groups; in Design B1, it is made implicitly on a single group.

Design A1 may be either an experiment or a quasi-experiment. It is an experiment if cases are randomly assigned to the two X groups. It is a quasi-experiment if cases are assigned to the two levels of X in some other way, such as matching. Design B1 must be a quasi-experiment because only one group is studied. Cases cannot be randomly assigned to different levels of X.

THREATS TO INTERNAL VALIDITY

This section describes three classes of threats to internal validity that potentially trouble experiments and/or quasi-experiments of the type described. These threats are summarized in Exhibit 6.3 and are discussed next.

Threats from the Research Environment

Ironically, the very control that makes experiments and quasi-experiments attractive for addressing some threats to internal validity makes them vulnerable to others. Briefly, control over the research environment risks inadvertently influencing scores on Y. The greater the control, the greater the danger that the research environment influences Y scores. This results in part because greater control means the research study intervenes more explicitly on cases. It also results because greater control provides researchers more opportunity to influence Y scores in ways other than through X. Although these two threats work together, they are discussed separately.

Demands on Participants

When humans serve as cases, they typically know that they are involved in a research study. They have some knowledge before they participate in a study. They acquire additional knowledge based on its stated purposes, instructions, interactions with researchers, and information they are asked to provide as a part of the study.

Research Environment Threats

    Demand characteristics

    Expectancy effects

Between-Cases Threats

    Selection

    Intragroup history

    Treatment contamination

Longitudinal Threats

    History

    Maturation

    Mortality

    Testing

    Instrumentation

    Regression

EXHIBIT 6.3.   Summary: Threats to internal validity.

These cues may serve as ***demand characteristics***; they provide cases with expectations about what is being investigated. These, coupled with motivation (e.g., to be a good or a bad participant), may lead to Y scores that depend on expectations and motivation instead of, or along with, the level of X experienced. These influences threaten the internal validity of the relationship observed between X and Y. In the language of chapter 5, these expectations and motivations serve as potential nuisance variables.

Researcher Expectations

Researchers are also influenced by environmental characteristics. These shape researchers' attitudes and behaviors and may affect the research study and research outcomes. Of particular concern are unintended effects researchers may have on the dependent variable. For example, a researcher who treats participants in a warm and friendly manner may obtain different responses than one who is cool and aloof.

An ***expectancy effect*** occurs when researchers treat participants in ways that increase the likelihood of obtaining a desired result. For example, participants experiencing one form of training may perform better on some task than those who receive another form of training. These differences may be the result of a researcher's belief that one form of training is better; the researcher inadvertently treats the two groups differently in ways not related to the training itself. Such differences may involve subtle psychological processes that even the researcher is unaware of, such as various forms of nonverbal communication (e.g., body language).

Differential treatment of this type illustrates a form of nuisance variable. Furthermore, nuisance variables of this type serve to bias, or potentially make spurious, an observed relationship between X and Y, because they are related to levels of the independent variable.

Threats from the research environment can never be eliminated entirely. However, they can be minimized through design activities aimed at their control. For example, researcher expectancy may be controlled if confederates, who are not aware of a researcher's expectations, administer the independent variable treatments.

Threats in Between-Cases Designs

There are additional threats to internal validity that apply specifically to between-cases designs. First, ***selection*** is a threat to internal validity when there are preexisting differences between groups experiencing different levels of X. These differences, rather than different levels of X, may account for Y differences.

In the previous employee training in production diagnostics and repair illustration, one group of employees is trained and one untrained group serves as a control. Preexisting group differences, such as in motivation or ability levels, are possible alternative explanations for differences in average product quality measured after the training.

Selection is a serious threat, because there are many ways groups of cases may differ. These differences can produce the entire gauntlet of nuisance variable(s) possibilities involving bias, spuriousness, or suppression.

A second potential threat to between-cases designs, ***intragroup history***, represents an exogenous event(s) that has a different impact on one group than on another. For example, the trained group may work with better or poorer materials or equipment; it may have better or poorer supervision. These intragroup history effects are nuisance variables that appear to represent an effect of X if uncontrolled.

Third, between-cases designs may be subject to ***treatment contamination*** that occurs when a level of X assigned to one group is communicated to another. For example, an untrained control group of employees may reduce or increase product quality through greater or less

---

RESEARCH HIGHLIGHT 6.1

Selection Threats and Omitted Variables

The concept of an omitted variable represents another way to think about the selection problem. An ***omitted variable*** is an independent variable that operates in the causal system studied but is not, as the name implies, included in it.

Selection is typically discussed when there is concern that cases that experience alternative levels of an independent variable systematically differ in some way that may influence the relationship observed between that independent variable and Y. Alternatively, omitted variables are usually discussed when there is a concern that a research study does not include all the variables warranted by the conceptual model being tested. The two concepts address the same issue. A potential independent variable(s) serves as a nuisance, because it is not accounted for in a research study. The omission of this variable may result in a misinterpretation of the relationship between X and Y.

It is also the case that selection threats are discussed more frequently in the literature of experiments and quasi-experiments. Omitted variables are often discussed in survey and field study literatures.

---

effort if they learn another group is receiving training. Or, trained employees may transfer their learning to the untrained employees.

Threats in Longitudinal Designs

Longitudinal designs are also subject to internal validity threats. One is called ***history***, an outside event that occurs between measurements of the dependent variable; the historical event occurs along with the change in X. For example, the quality of the material used to produce the product in the training example is illustrative of a potential history effect. Any change in material quality between measurements of the dependent variable will appear to be a result of the training.

Another threat to longitudinal designs, ***maturation***, refers to changes in the cases investigated that occur between the measurements of the dependent variable. For example, suppose training is implemented among a group of new employees. Changes in product quality may then result simply because employees acquire experience with their jobs and not because of the training.

Still another potential threat is ***mortality***, which occurs when some cases leave between measurements of Y. Cases that leave before a study is completed often differ from those that stay. If so, an alternative explanation is provided for changes in Y. For example, if low-performing employees disproportionately leave the organization, average product quality may increase, because employees remaining are more effective performers.

Additional longitudinal threats involve measurement of the dependent variable. ***Testing*** is a threat if the initial measurement of Y influences scores when it is measured again. For example, human participants may remember how they responded to an initial questionnaire measuring Y when they are asked to complete it a second time. They may then try to "improve" (change) their scores independent of the research treatment.

Instrumentation refers to changes in the measure of Y. For example, the procedures used to measure product quality may become more sophisticated over time. Product quality may thus appear to be decreasing. The training is seen as unsuccessful when the measuring system is simply getting more discriminating at identifying quality.

One additional threat to longitudinal designs is called *regression*; it depends on two circumstances. First, it depends on unreliable measurement of the dependent variable. Unreliability results in scores that are sometimes too high, sometimes too low. Repeated measurements tend to average out these highs and lows (see chapter 17).

Second, regression as a threat requires that cases be chosen for extreme (high or low) Y scores on the first measurement. If both conditions hold, regression results in scores moving from the extreme toward average on a subsequent measurement.

For example, suppose the organization measures product quality on several groups of employees. It then chooses the group with the lowest average quality for training. Quality may increase on a second measurement. However, this increase may be due to regression, not training.

Although threats to internal validity are ubiquitous, different designs are more or less vulnerable to different threats. Skilled researchers capitalize on this knowledge. They choose designs that are least vulnerable to those threats that are likely given the conceptual model investigated.

ADDITIONAL DESIGNS

Designs A1 and B1 are elementary; both have only one independent variable with just two levels. The cross-sectional Design A1 has only two groups and the longitudinal Design B1 has only one.

These characteristics can be extended to make more sophisticated designs. By doing so, researchers often can accomplish two important objectives: they can study more complicated conceptual models, and they can control some of the previously identified threats to internal validity.

Three alternatives are described to provide a sample of ways experiments and quasi-experiments can be designed. The first shows how cross-sectional designs can be combined with longitudinal designs. The last two illustrate how additional independent variables can be added to experimental and quasi-experimental designs.

Design C1: Longitudinal Between-Cases

Exhibit 6.4 illustrates a design (C1) that is made from between-cases characteristics of Design A1 and longitudinal characteristics of Design B1. Y is measured before and after two groups of cases experience either of the two levels of an independent variable.

Design C1 potentially adds threats of longitudinal designs (e.g., testing) to threats of cross-sectional designs (e.g., treatment contamination). So why use it? The term *potentially* is the key word; Design C1 is attractive when selection is a likely threat and potential threats of longitudinal designs are less likely.

The first measurement of Y serves to identify whether groups are comparable before X is introduced. This is particularly advantageous in quasi-experiments in which intact comparison groups are used. Selection as a threat is probable if $\mu_{Y^b|0} \neq \mu_{Y^b|1}$.

Exhibit 6.5 shows two possible outcomes from a longitudinal between-cases design. In each example, $X = 1$ represents a treatment condition such as training, and $X = 0$ represents a control. Also, in each example, the control group experiences an increase in average Y scores of $5 - 3 = 2$. These score increases may reflect maturation or other threats associated with

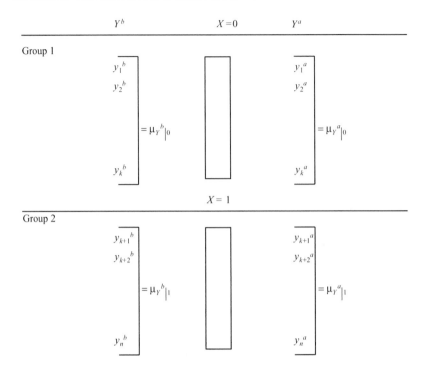

EXHIBIT 6.4.   Design C1: Longitudinal between-subjects experimental and quasi-experimental design.

longitudinal designs. Also, the treatment group in each example appears to increase Y scores more than the control.

The top panel of Exhibit 6.5 reports results that suggest no selection threat, $\mu_{Y^b|0} \cong \mu_{Y^b|1}$. This is an expected result if cases are randomly assigned to $X = 0$ and $X = 1$. In that case, the effect of X on Y can be assessed by looking at the difference between $\mu_{Y^a|1}$ and $\mu_{Y^a|0}$, $7 - 5 = 2$.

If cases are randomly assigned to groups, it is doubtful whether Y should be measured before the introduction of the levels of X. Randomization should equalize the groups on Y before X levels are introduced. The benefit of knowing whether Y scores are equal is likely more than offset by the potential threats introduced by a longitudinal design.

The bottom panel of Exhibit 6.5 shows results where a selection threat is probable. $\mu_{Y^b|0} \neq \mu_{Y^b|1}$. In this case, an effect of X can be assessed by calculating the difference of differences $[(\mu_{Y^a|1} - \mu_{Y^a|0}) - (\mu_{Y^b|1} - \mu_{Y^b|0})]$. The group experiencing $X = 1$ has an average Y score of 5 before and 9 after. The control group has corresponding scores of 3 and 5. The difference of differences, $[(9 - 5) - (5 - 3)] = 2$, suggests an effect of training on Y relative to the control.

Regrettably, results as shown in the bottom panel of Exhibit 6.5 may present internal validity problems not necessarily overcome by taking the difference of differences. Whatever leads to the pretest differences in Y scores may work in combination with X to influence post-test Y scores.

For example, the trained group may be more motivated to perform well. This accounts for its higher average Y scores in the first time period. Furthermore, this group may take greater advantage of the training because of its higher motivation. The improvement in Y scores for the (motivated) trained group is thus greater than would be the case if the control group experienced the training. Motivation moderates the relationships between X and Y.

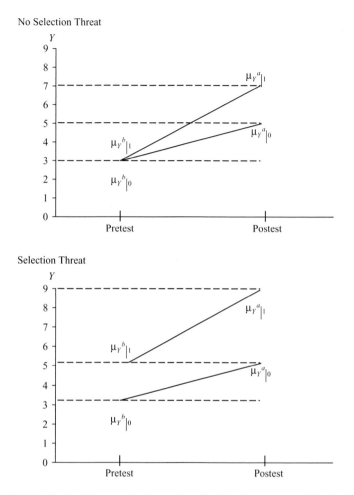

EXHIBIT 6.5.   Illustrative results from a longitudinal between-subjects design.

Design D: Cross-Sectional Factorial Design

The designs discussed to this point describe only one independent variable; yet, dependent variables typically are influenced by several independent variables. Researchers often seek to account for several independent variables in their research designs.

One form of this design occurs when researchers control the assignment of cases to levels of two or more independent variables. Designs with two or more independent variables that are manipulated by a researcher are called *factorial designs*; factor is a synonym for an independent variable that is under the control of a researcher.

Exhibit 6.6 illustrates such a design. It has two independent variables (XA and XB), and each has two levels. The dependent variable is measured once, making this a cross-sectional design.

For example, an organization may want to know if employee performance (Y) is influenced by training (XA) and monetary incentives (XB). $XA = XB = 0$ represents a control condition in each case. $XA = XB = 1$ represents training and monetary incentive conditions, respectively.

Two studies using Design A1 could be used to investigate the effects of training and monetary incentives separately. However, studying the variables in a factorial design has two important advantages.

(Training)

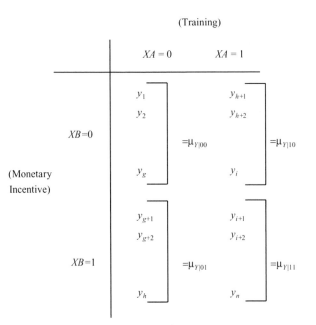

XA = 0   XA = 1

$XB=0$

y_1 y_{h+1}
y_2 y_{h+2}

$=\mu_{Y|00}$ $=\mu_{Y|10}$

(Monetary y_g y_i
Incentive)

y_{g+1} y_{i+1}
y_{g+2} y_{i+2}

$XB=1$

$=\mu_{Y|01}$ $=\mu_{Y|11}$

y_h y_n

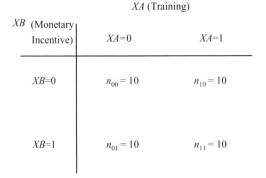
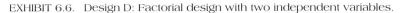

EXHIBIT 6.6.   Design D: Factorial design with two independent variables.

XA (Training)

XB (Monetary Incentive)	$XA=0$	$XA=1$
$XB=0$	$n_{00} = 10$	$n_{10} = 10$
$XB=1$	$n_{01} = 10$	$n_{11} = 10$

EXHIBIT 6.7.   Subjects in a factorial design of training and monetary incentives.

First, a study using Design D is more efficient than two studies using Design A1. To illustrate, assume a researcher wants to include 20 cases in each group. A study of training requires 40 cases (20 in a treatment condition, 20 in a control). A study of monetary incentives also requires 40 cases. Eighty cases are required to do the two studies separately.

Alternatively, a single factorial design of both training and monetary incentives requires just 40 cases as illustrated in Exhibit 6.7. Twenty cases who receive training (n_{10} plus n_{11}) can be contrasted with 20 training controls (n_{00} plus n_{01}). Analogously, 20 cases who experience monetary incentives (n_{01} plus n_{11}) can be contrasted with 20 controls (n_{00} plus n_{10}).

Second, one study using Design D provides more information than two studies using Design A. This is a beauty of factorial designs; it allows researchers to investigate moderator variables (interactions) directly. The term *interaction* is frequently used in the language of experiments and quasi-experiments.

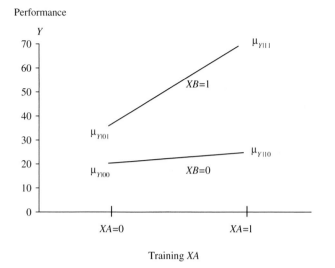

EXHIBIT 6.8.   Effects of training (XA) and monetary incentives (XB) on performance (Y).

Exhibit 6.8 shows a graph of how training and a monetary incentive might influence performance. $\mu_{Y|11}(=70)$ and $\mu_{Y|10}(=25)$ are greater than $\mu_{Y|01}(=35)$ and $\mu_{Y|00}(=20)$. These indicate a training effect. Similarly, $\mu_{Y|01}$ and $\mu_{Y|11}$ are greater than $\mu_{Y|00}$ and $\mu_{Y|10}$ indicating an effect of monetary incentives. A moderating or interaction effect is shown because $\mu_{Y|11}$ (representing the performance of the group experiencing both training and monetary incentives) is greater than the effects of training and monetary incentives added together. The effect is shown by the lack of parallelism between the solid lines in Exhibit 6.8.

Moderator variables (interactions) indicate that effects of one independent variable on Y depend on the values of another independent variable. In the example, the effect of monetary incentives on performance is greater when training is present than when it is not. It works either way. The effect of training is greater when monetary incentives are present than when they are not.

Design E: Cross-Sectional Design with Covariate

Another cross-sectional design combines independent variables that are assigned to cases with variables that represent cases' responses. The latter independent variables are called **covariates**.

Exhibit 6.9 illustrates the simplest case. It shows an independent variable (XA) that is assigned to cases at one of two levels ($XA = 0$ or $XA = 1$). It also shows a covariate (XB). Covariates are often continuously scaled variables (e.g., age, income). A unique subscript is given in each case on XB to acknowledge that each may have a unique value.

For example, a wholesaler may be interested in sales of designer sunglasses as a function of the way the item is displayed in retail stores. Stores represent cases and sunglasses sales per store represent the dependent variable. The glasses are displayed one way in half the stores studied ($XA = 0$) and another way in the other half ($XA = 1$). The firm also believes that sales of designer sunglasses depend on customer income. Thus, average customer income per store is treated as a covariate (XB). Income might be estimated from a questionnaire survey of a sample of customers.

The value of a covariate design depends on how XB is related to Y and XA. If XB is only a noise variable (related to Y but not XA), covariate analysis makes the assessment of the

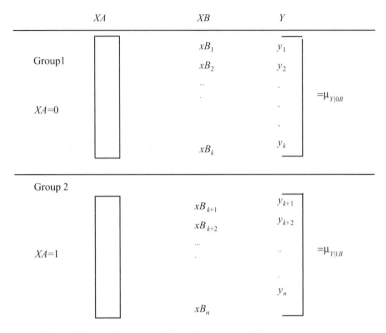

Note: Each case has a potentially unique score on *XB*.

EXHIBIT 6.9.   Design E: Cross-sectional design with a covariate.

effect of the independent variable more precise by reducing the amount of unexplained *Y* variation.

Covariate design and analysis may also be useful if *XB* is a biasing variable (related to *Y* and *XA*). In this case, the analysis adjusts *Y* for *XB* differences in *XA*. In the example, an adjustment in *Y* is made if customer income averages differ between stores with the two different displays. This adjustment is analogous to taking the difference of differences in Design C; it holds the same dangers. Covariate analysis does control for a selection threat to internal validity insofar as *XB* is concerned. However, if groups differ on a measured covariate, they may also differ on potential covariates not measured and hence not controlled by this analysis. Furthermore, as in the case of the difference of differences in Design C, covariate analysis does not control for the possibility that *XB* moderates the relationship between *Y* and *XA*. An analysis method described in chapter 19 accounts for a moderating effect of *XB*.

Design Extensions

The designs introduced here only scratch the surface. Each can be extended, usually in straightforward ways. For example, more levels of the independent variable can be added to Designs A1 through E. The dependent variable can be measured additional times before and/or after the introduction of *X* in the longitudinal Designs B1 and C1. More independent variables can be added to Design D. Independent variables and/or covariates can be added to Design E.

The choice of a particular design depends on the research issue investigated, tempered by constraints placed on the study; compromises are always required. The objective for researchers is to develop a satisfactory design, not an ideal design. Satisfactory designs help rule out plausible alternative explanations, not all alternative explanations.

SUMMARY

Experiments and quasi-experiments are designed to investigate systematic differences in a dependent variable between groups that experience different levels of an independent variable. Design A1 illustrates *cross-sectional between-cases design.* It is cross-sectional because X and Y scores are obtained from cases only once. Changes in Y scores as levels of X change can also be studied in *longitudinal within-cases designs* as illustrated by Design B1. Y scores are measured before and after some change in X is introduced.

Experiments and quasi-experiments are subject to *internal validity threats* regardless of specific design type. *Demands* placed on cases by virtue of their participation in a research study potentially can alter the relationships observed among the variables investigated. *Researcher expectations* can also threaten the internal validity of any study.

Additional threats are associated with specific types of research designs. *Selection* is a threat to between-cases designs when the cases that experience different levels of X are different in some other way(s). A selection threat is similar to an *omitted variable* threat. In both cases, there is a danger that the XY relationship studied is misrepresented because some independent variable(s) has not been taken into account.

Intragroup history effects also threaten between-cases designs. They refer to exogenous events that influence groups experiencing different levels of an independent variable differently. Between-cases designs are also threatened by the possibility of communication between groups experiencing different levels of X that may lead to *treatment contamination.*

Longitudinal designs are subject to a different set of threats. *History* or *maturation effects* may occur between measurements of Y and thus appear as an effect due to the introduction of an independent variable. *Mortality* is a threat if cases drop out of the study between measurements of the dependent variable.

Measurement issues also serve as potential threats in longitudinal designs. *Testing* is a threat if cases respond differently on repeated measurements of Y. *Instrumentation* is a threat if the procedure for measuring Y changes over time. *Regression* occurs if a group is chosen for study because it has extreme (high or low) scores on Y and Y is unreliably measured. In that case, a second measurement of Y will move (regress) toward average, suggesting an effect of the change in the independent variable.

Many alternative experimental and quasi-experimental designs are available. These designs can address more complex research issues than are possible with Designs A1 and B1. These alternatives also can be useful in ruling out certain threats to internal validity.

A longitudinal between-cases design, C1, adds a longitudinal dimension to a between-cases design. Y scores are obtained before as well as after the introduction of X. Design C1 is potentially useful when selection is a threat. Selection as a threat is suggested if groups differ on the measure of Y taken before the introduction of X.

Design D illustrates how cross-sectional designs can be extended when researchers control values on more than one independent variable. *Factorial designs* are more efficient than studies of each independent variable separately. They also provide more information because they permit investigation of interactions among the X variables. Interactions, like moderators, indicate that the effect of one X on Y depends on the level of another X.

Design E also describes an experiment or quasi-experiment with a second independent variable. However, in this case, the second X variable is a *covariate,* a case response on some variable. In quasi-experiments, inclusion of a covariate may help control for a selection effect. However, inclusion of a covariate that is related to Y can help more precisely identify the effect of the manipulated X variable even if the covariate does not serve as a selection threat.

The designs described are all simple. They can be extended in many ways to address more complex research topics.

FOR REVIEW

Terms to Know

Threats to internal validity: Characteristics of research studies that make a causal claim that an independent variable leads to a dependent variable vulnerable to alternative explanations.

Between-cases design: Design that uses two or more cases or groups of cases; each case or group experiences different levels of an independent variable. Effect of an independent variable is assessed by comparing dependent variable scores across the cases or groups of cases.

Cross-sectional design: Design in which the independent and dependent variables are measured only once. The relationship between the variables is taken as evidence of the influence of X on Y.

Within-cases design: Design that uses one case or one group of cases. Effect of an independent variable is assessed by measuring the dependent variable before and after a change in the level of the independent variable.

Longitudinal design: Design in which the dependent (and perhaps, independent) variable is measured more than once.

Demand characteristics: Characteristics of a research study that motivate participants' expectations about what is investigated; a threat to internal validity.

Expectancy effects: A nuisance variable that influences the dependent variable because a researcher treats some cases differently than others based on assumptions made about expected research results; a threat to internal validity.

Selection: A threat to internal validity when there are preexisting differences between groups experiencing different levels of an independent variable. These differences may account for differences observed on the dependent variable.

Omitted variable: An independent variable that operates in the causal system studied but that is not included in the model studied. Serves as a threat to internal validity in the same way selection is a threat.

Intragoup history: An exogenous event(s) that has an impact on a group of cases that experience one level of an independent variable differently than the event influences groups experiencing other levels of the independent variable; a threat to internal validity.

Treatment contamination: Occurs when a level of an independent variable assigned to one group of participants is communicated to another; a threat to internal validity.

History: An exogenous event that occurs between measurements of the dependent variable; a threat to internal validity in longitudinal designs.

Maturation: Changes in cases between measurements of the dependent variable; a threat to internal validity in longitudinal designs.

Mortality: Occurs when some cases leave between measurements of the dependent variable; a threat to internal validity in longitudinal designs.

Testing: A threat to internal validity in longitudinal designs when the initial measurement of a dependent variable influences participants' responses to the dependent variable on a subsequent measurement of it.

Instrumentation: A threat to internal validity in longitudinal designs when the measure of the dependent variable changes over time.

Regression: A threat to internal validity in longitudinal designs when (a) groups are chosen for levels of the independent variable based on dependent variable performance on a first measurement, and (b) there is unreliability in the dependent variable measure.

Factorial design: Studies with two or more independent variables. *Factor* is a synonym for *independent variable*, which is under the control of a researcher.

Covariate: A synonym for an independent variable that is not manipulated by a researcher in experiments and quasi-experiments.

Questions for Review

1. Explain how experiments and quasi-experiments rule out the threat that a relationship between an independent and a dependent variable is due to the influence of the latter on the former.
2. Compare and contrast testing and instrumentation as threats to internal validity in longitudinal designs.
3. Compare and contrast intragroup history and history as threats to internal validity.
4. Under what conditions would you consider using Design C1 instead of Design A1?
5. Explain why taking the difference of differences in Design C1 may not account for a selection threat when the pretest scores on Y differ across levels of the independent variable studied.
6. In what way(s) is a factorial design attractive relative to doing separate studies of each factor?

Issues to Discuss

1. Cross-sectional between-cases Design A1 may be experimental or quasi-experimental. What threat(s) does an experimental design reduce or rule out relative to a quasi-experimental design of this sort? Why? What threats to this design are present regardless of whether experimentation is used?
2. A covariate, if unaccounted for, is a potential nuisance variable. What is the effect of covariate analysis if the covariate is a noise variable? What problems remain for covariate analysis if the covariate is a biasing variable?
3. A researcher believes observing violent television programs leads to violent behavior. A quasi-experiment is chosen to address this expectation. Two levels of violent television will be investigated, and violent behavior will subsequently be measured by using official records (e.g., reports of school rule infractions, police arrest records).
   a. What group(s) of participants would you try to obtain for your study and how would you motivate this group to participate in the study? Would you try to match participants across the two levels, or would you seek comparison groups? In either case, what variables would you seek to control through matching or comparison groups?
   b. How would you make the two levels of television violence operational?
   c. What are the major threats to internal validity of your design decisions? Can you change your design decisions in any way to reduce these threats?
   d. How could you change your design to make it an experiment rather than a quasi-experiment? Are there any threats that would be reduced or eliminated by this change? Are there remaining threats or new threats?

7

Design Applications: Field Studies and Surveys

Chapter Outline

- *Basic Designs*
  - *Design A2: Between-Cases Design*
  - *Design B2: Within-Cases Time Series*
  - *Design C2: Longitudinal Between-Cases Panel Studies*
  - *Design Extensions*
- *Threats to Internal Validity*
  - *Concerns About Causal Direction*
  - *Biases Introduced by a Single Source and Similar Method*
- *Praise for Surveys and Field Studies*
  - *Internal Validity May Not Be a Concern*
  - *Causation May Not Be a Concern*
  - *Design Constraints*
- *Summary*
- *For Review*
  - *Terms to Know*
  - *Questions for Review*
  - *Issues to Discuss*
- *Part III Suggested Readings*

Unlike experiments and quasi-experiments, field and survey studies obtain scores on independent variables from the cases studied. On human participants, these may be biographical characteristics, such as age; variables representing ability, such as intelligence; and attitudes, such as satisfaction. Examples when organizations represent cases are size, such as number of employees; success, such as market value; and longevity, such as years since founding.

Surveys differ from field studies by how cases are chosen. Surveys use probability samples to obtain cases from a larger population (see part V). Field studies obtain cases some other way; typically, some intact group of cases is studied. For example, a study of student absenteeism may include all students from some elementary school. This procedure to obtain cases to study is called *judgment* or *convenience sampling.*

The two types of studies often also differ in conceptual complexity. Surveys usually focus on relatively simple research issues, such as voter or consumer opinions. Such studies usually investigate one or a few independent variables in straightforward ways. For example, a survey of political opinion may compare proportions of likely voters who prefer one candidate to others by their political affiliation, race, or gender.

Field studies are often more complex. They are frequently used to test conceptual models with a number of independent variables. These variables may be combined in complex (e.g., nonlinear) ways. For example, field studies are often used to investigate consumer, client, employee, student, or investor motivations to behave in various ways.

This chapter introduces three basic designs used in survey and field studies. Similarities and differences between these and quasi-experimental or experimental designs are noted. Also noted are ways these designs can be extended to address more complicated issues.

The second part of the chapter addresses threats to the internal validity of surveys and field studies. Many of these threats are also present in experiments and quasi-experiments as discussed in chapter 6. Threats that are more specifically associated with surveys and field studies are emphasized.

The discussion shows that surveys and field studies are generally more susceptible to internal validity threats than experiments or quasi-experiments. Of course, internal validity is not the sole criterion for evaluating research designs. The chapter closes with a discussion of situations in which surveys and field studies are attractive designs.

BASIC DESIGNS

Survey and field study designs can be classified as between-case or within-case, just as experiments and quasi-experiments. A between-case field or survey study involves a group of cases. A within-case field or survey study refers literally to one case in contrast to longitudinal quasi-experiments that typically study a group of cases. Surveys and field studies focus on relationships between *individual* cases, whereas experiments and quasi-experiments focus on differences between *groups* of cases.

These designs also can be classified as cross-sectional or longitudinal. Cross-sectional field or survey studies measure independent and dependent variables only once. Both independent and dependent variables typically are measured more than once in longitudinal surveys or field studies.

Design A2: Between-Cases Design

The most common form of field or survey study uses a cross-sectional between-cases design. Scores on measures of X and Y are obtained once.

The design, A2, is shown in Exhibit 7.1; it is a straightforward adaptation of the cross-sectional between-cases Design A1 shown in chapter 6 as Exhibit 6.1. Design A2 is modified to account for the measurement of X at an individual case level. Subscripts $1, \ldots, i, \ldots, n$ refer to individual cases to acknowledge that each case may have a unique score on X. For example, a survey might be conducted to estimate citizen opinion on a local government bonding referendum (Y). Information on participants' age serves as an independent variable (X).

X	Y
x_1	y_1
x_2	y_2
$\vdots$	$\vdots$
x_i	y_i
$\vdots$	$\vdots$
x_n	y_n

Note: Subscripts refer to individual cases.

EXHIBIT 7.1.   Design A2: Cross-sectional between-cases design.

Time 1		Time j		Time t	
x^1_1	y^1_1	x^j_1	y^j_1	x^t_1	y^t_1

Note: Superscripts refer to time periods; subscripts refer to the case.

EXHIBIT 7.2.   Design B2: Time series.

Design B2: Within-Cases Time Series

Time series studies provide information about how a dependent variable, Y, changes over time. It does so by obtaining scores from a case at several regular intervals, such as each month or year. A design with one independent, X, and one dependent, Y, variable is illustrated in Exhibit 7.2. Superscripts $1, \ldots, j, \ldots, t$ refer to time periods.

Time series are field study analogs to longitudinal within-cases designs. Y is measured in more than one time period, often many time periods. However, time series typically differ from quasi-experimental within-cases designs by also measuring an independent variable(s) each time Y is measured.

Time series can be performed on individuals as cases. However, in organizational research, time series studies commonly use an institutional case. For example, a time series might be performed on the relationship between a hospital's occupancy rate (Y) and the number of medical doctors affiliated with it (X); the hospital represents the case. Or, a time series might be conducted to determine whether changes in unionization rates (X) in an industry are associated with changes in real salary levels (Y); the industry represents the case.

Time series can be constructed to look at instantaneous changes between Y and X or lagged changes. In **instantaneous models** a change is studied within each time period. **Lagged models** are motivated by an assumption that it takes some time for a change in X to result in a change in Y. For example, changes in the number of doctors affiliated with a hospital may take several time periods before they are translated into changes in hospital occupancy.

Time series analyses are ordinarily performed on data that have been generated in the past. For example, historical data for a study of the relationship between the United States unemployment rate (X) and average wage rates in the United States can be obtained from Department of Labor sources.

Design C2: Longitudinal Between-Cases Panel Studies

Panel studies add a cross-sectional dimension to the time series design just described. X and Y scores are obtained on a group of cases in two or more time periods. As in time series, however, interest is in how Y scores change as X scores change over time.

A simple panel design is diagrammed in Exhibit 7.3. Scores on one independent and one dependent variable are obtained from several cases at two times. Subscripts refer to cases, and superscripts refer to time periods.

To illustrate, a sample of full-time employees in a geographical area may be surveyed twice with a year's separation. Y is hourly wage and X is union membership ($X_i^t = 0$, not a member; $X_i^t = 1$, a member). Analysis that investigates the relationship between the difference in wage ($Y_i^2 - Y_i^1$) and the difference in union membership status ($X_i^2 - X_i^1$) provides information about how changes in union membership influence wage levels.

Panel studies are attractive because they control for between-cases differences that do not change over time. For example, research has established that men obtain higher wages than women, on average. However, gender should influence income similarly in both time periods. Thus, an analysis of difference scores accounts for gender effects by "differencing" them away.

Time 1		Time 2	
$x^1{}_1$	$y^1{}_1$	$x^2{}_1$	$y^2{}_1$
$x^1{}_2$	$y^1{}_2$	$x^2{}_2$	$y^2{}_2$
.	.	.	.
$x^1{}_i$	$y^1{}_i$	$x^2{}_i$	$y^2{}_i$
:	:	:	:
$x^1{}_n$	$y^1{}_n$	$x^2{}_n$	$y^2{}_n$

Note: Subscripts refer to individual cases; superscripts refer to time periods.

EXHIBIT 7.3.   Design C2: Two-time-period panel study.

By contrast, a cross-sectional survey or field study may provide an erroneous estimate of the effects of union membership on wages if it does not explicitly account for gender. The union membership estimate will be biased if gender and union status are related.

Design Extensions

Modifications and extensions of all three of these designs are common. These changes typically are straightforward, as is also true of the experimental and quasi-experimental designs described in the previous chapter.

In particular, all three designs can account for more than one independent variable. Except in the simplest cross-sectional surveys, Design A2 is usually extended to include several independent variables. This is nearly always true in field study investigations of conceptual models. For example, a study of personal income may include measures of education and work experience as major independent variables. It may also measure biographical variables such as age, race and gender, and work environment variables such as union membership status and type of industry to serve as control variables.

Panel studies (Design C2) also often include more than two time periods. Analysis issues are somewhat complicated when more than two time periods are involved. However, data obtained from more than two time periods generally help reduce alternative explanations.

THREATS TO INTERNAL VALIDITY

Surveys and field studies are generally vulnerable to the same internal validity threats that challenge experiments and quasi-experiments. All the major threats to the internal validity of experiments and quasi-experiments described in chapter 6 apply; that discussion may be useful as a review.

Threats from the research environment exist. Although a field study or survey may not be as intrusive as an experiment or quasi-experiment, human participants nevertheless know they are participating in a research study. Demands on participants thus remain. Indeed, this problem may be exacerbated in field and survey studies when participants provide responses on measures of both independent and dependent variables.

Researcher effects also threaten surveys and field studies; they bring expectations to surveys and field studies just as they do to experiments and quasi-experiments. It is true that researchers do not intentionally manipulate levels of some independent variable in surveys and field studies. However, when designs use measures involving interaction between researchers and participants, such as interviews, surveys and field studies are potentially as vulnerable to researcher effects as studies involving more active manipulation of an independent variable.

Time series and panel studies are also susceptible to the threats associated with longitudinal designs described in the previous chapter. These threats are sometimes greater in time series and panel studies when more measurements of the variables are taken. In such situations, instrumentation is a likely threat because measures often change over time. Even when instrumentation is not a threat, repeated measurement may lead to testing effects.

History and maturation also pose problems for panels and time series. For example, a study may be performed to see how changes in income (X) influence buying behavior (Y). A panel of consumers is studied several years to investigate this issue. Over that time, historical events such as the amount and type of television advertising, and possibly maturation, may vary with changes in income.

The internal validity of time series and panel studies is also threatened by systematic trends in scores obtained on the variables. These trends may represent long-term increases or decreases in scores, such as yearly changes in wage rates, or repeating variations, such as seasonal changes in retail clothing sales. Trends and repeating variations bias estimates of the effect of X variables on Y. Fortunately, these threats can often be statistically removed before a relationship between X and Y is estimated.

Mortality is also a serious threat to panel studies. (Because time series are usually constructed on historical data and only involve one case, mortality is generally not a threat.) Mortality may result because cases literally expire (e.g., people die, organizations cease operations). It also may result because cases move and can no longer be located or they tire of participation and drop out of the research study. The longer a panel study obtains scores, the greater the threat of mortality.

Surveys and field studies are also vulnerable to internal validity threats not present in experiments and quasi-experiments. Two are of particular concern.

Concerns About Causal Direction

Levels of independent variables are established outside of cases in experiments and quasi-experiments. This exogenous determination of X levels is advantageous for causal statements, because such designs preclude the possibility that a relationship results because Y leads to X. Sometimes the nature of the X variable in surveys or field studies is also obviously exogenous to the causal system of interest. For example, an observed relationship between chronological age (X) and political party affiliation (Y) does not plausibly result because Y leads to X.

However, the direction of a causal relationship is often uncertain in surveys and field studies. Investigation of relationships between attitudes and behaviors is illustrative. Consider a field study that measures employee satisfaction and employee performance. A relationship obtained between these two variables contributes little to causal understanding. Satisfaction may cause performance, or the reverse; or, the relationship may be biased or even spurious.

Does the temporal sequence of measurement address the causal issue? The second causal criterion, which was summarized in Exhibit 5.1, states that X should occur with or before Y. What are the causal implications if job satisfaction is measured before job performance in a field study?

It is desirable design practice to measure the presumed causal variable before or with the presumed consequence, certainly not after. However, temporal sequence often adds little to the internal validity of surveys or field studies. A relationship may be observed regardless of measurement order when participant responses serve as both independent and dependent variables. For example, both employee satisfaction and performance are likely to be relatively stable over time. A high performer in one time period is likely to be a high performer in subsequent time periods. Satisfaction too tends to be stable. Thus, any relationship between the two probably does not depend on which variable is measured first.

Biases Introduced by a Single Source and Similar Method

Additional threats to internal validity are common when human cases provide scores on both X and Y variables. One is a form of demand effects introduced in the last chapter. It occurs when participants believe they see an expected relationship between the independent and dependent variables being measured and respond accordingly. For example, a participant believes perceived product quality (X) leads to purchasing intentions (Y). The participant completes a questionnaire stating a belief that a particular product is high quality. The questionnaire then asks about purchasing intentions. To be consistent with the belief stated previously, the participant indicates an intention to buy the product, whether or not this reflects a true intention.

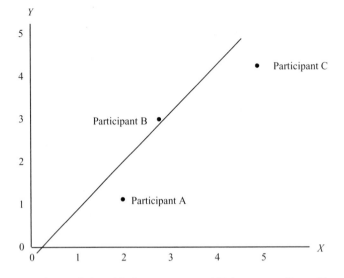

EXHIBIT 7.4.   Spurious relationship between X and Y due to predisposition differences.

Another threat involves differences in predispositions that participants bring to any social situation. For example, participants likely differ in their inclination to be agreeable or disagreeable. A study in which both X and Y call for degrees of agreement may obtain a relationship that reflects only differences in participants' predispositions.

Exhibit 7.4 illustrates the problem. Three participants—A, B, and C—are asked to evaluate X and Y statements that call for responses on a 5-point scale ranging from 1 (strongly disagree) to 5 (strongly agree).

Assume all three participants are neutral on both variables. They "neither agree nor disagree" (scale point 3) with the constructs X' and Y'. However, Participant A is inherently critical and reports scores of $X = 2, Y = 1$. C is inherently agreeable (scores of 5 and 4), and B is neither agreeable nor disagreeable (scores of 3 and 3). As Exhibit 7.4 shows, a relationship between X and Y is observed. Given the assumption, this relationship results from differences in participants' predispositions to agree or disagree; there is no relationship between X' and Y' at the construct level.

The threat illustrated in Exhibit 7.4 can be viewed as a measurement problem, a problem of construct invalidity. Measures that capture general predispositions rather than true construct variance are contaminated. The issue is raised here because the contamination operates on both the independent and the dependent variable. Contamination operates to suggest an empirical relationship between variables when none exists; thus, it illustrates a threat to internal validity.

A related problem is also suggested by this example. The similarity of measurement procedures for X and Y variables can contribute to inflated or even spurious relationships. In the example, both X and Y are measured with a common 5-point scale of agreement and disagreement. Similarity in the format (e.g., wording) of items used to measure independent and dependent constructs can also contribute to inflated relationships.

PRAISE FOR SURVEYS AND FIELD STUDIES

It is clear that design characteristics of surveys and field studies make them more vulnerable to internal validity threats than experiments and quasi-experiments. Simply stated, surveys and field studies, especially when cross-sectional, are not attractive for addressing causal concerns. However, that does not mean surveys and field studies are unattractive research designs.

Internal Validity May Not Be a Concern

There are times when causation is important, but a design providing high internal validity is not. These situations occur when researchers are confident that causal relationships are not in question. This confidence is often based on a well-accepted conceptual explanation.

For example, human capital theory predicts that investments, such as education and training, influence success in subsequent life experience, such as financial attainment. Field studies and surveys are conducted to estimate the strength of relationships; questions about causality are answered conceptually.

Causation May Not Be a Concern

In other situations, noncausal relationships are of interest. Often these involve information about people's opinions, expectations, or preferences. For example, surveys are conducted to identify voter opinions or consumer product preferences. Statistical generalization is more important in such situations than are causal issues.

As another example, a researcher develops a short inexpensive alternative to a time-consuming and expensive test of some ability. The time-consuming and expensive test is known to be valuable in predicting important behaviors (e.g., educational performance). The short form may serve as a substitute for the more involved form if a strong relationship between the two is demonstrated. The researcher is interested in the strength of the relationship between the two test forms and not whether one causes the other. A field study can effectively address the issue.

Design Constraints

There are still other situations in which experimentation is desirable but impractical. For example, there is great personal and public policy interest in whether smoking causes cancer. Experimentation could clearly inform this issue. Random assignment of a large group of individuals to smoking and nonsmoking conditions would answer many of the criticisms raised by the tobacco industry of research using other types of designs. Of course, an experiment in this context is illegal (people cannot be required to smoke or not smoke) and unethical. Knowledge about the relationship between smoking and cancer must be made from nonexperimental research.

These illustrations suggest that designs cannot be arranged in a single hierarchy; one is not uniformly superior to others. The appropriate design for any situation depends on validity issues taking the conceptual state of the model investigated into account. Practically speaking, it also depends on the constraints imposed on the research environment.

SUMMARY

Surveys and field studies can use between-cases or within-cases designs. They can also be cross-sectional where X and Y are measured only once. Or, they can be longitudinal involving several measurements of X and Y over time.

Variations of Design A2, between-cases design, are widely used for both surveys and field studies. X and Y scores are obtained from cases once. In practice, cross-sectional between-cases field studies and surveys usually obtain scores on a variety of independent variables.

Time series are less widely used. They obtain repeated scores from a single case, often on an organization or larger unit such as an industry. Frequently scores are obtained over a long time period. The time series described here, Design B2, included one independent and one dependent variable. The design is used to show how changes in values of X correspond to changes in values of Y.

Panel studies combine multiple cases with multiple time periods. Like time series, they are typically used to study within-case changes in Y values as X values change. Panel studies control for stable between-cases variables that can serve as selection (or omitted variable) threats in cross-sectional studies.

Surveys and field studies are subject to the same internal validity threats present in quasi-experiments and experiments. Researcher and participant effects brought about through the research environment are present in surveys and field studies as they are in experiments and quasi-experiments. Experiments and quasi-experiments may be intrusive through their manipulation of levels of the independent variable. However, the measurement procedures of surveys and field studies may also be intrusive.

Surveys and field studies that obtain multiple measurements of independent and dependent variables are also prone to the longitudinal threats identified in experiments and quasi-experiments. History, maturation, instrumentation, and testing are frequent possibilities. These threats may be more serious for longitudinal survey and field studies, because often more measurements are taken.

Additional internal validity threats are present in surveys and field studies, because independent variables are measured with participant responses. Even the causal direction of a relationship between X and Y is in doubt in these situations. Participants' responses also raise concerns, because nuisance variables represented by case demand effects and predispositions can produce misleading relationships between independent and dependent variables. These difficulties are especially likely when similar instruments are used to measure X and Y.

Surveys and field studies are often attractive designs despite their many difficulties for causal inference. They are attractive in many situations in which causation is not a concern. They are also useful when alternative designs are impractical or cannot be used.

FOR REVIEW

Terms to Know

Time series: Design to investigate longitudinal changes in a dependent variable; independent and dependent variables are measured more than once over time.

> *Instantaneous models*: Time series model in which changes in the independent and dependent variables are assumed to occur without an intervening time interval.

> *Lagged models*: Time series model in which changes in the independent variable are assumed to take some time to influence the dependent variable.

Panel studies: Independent and dependent variables are measured two or more times on a group of cases; design to measure changes in the dependent variable as a function of changes in an independent variable(s).

Questions for Review

1. Compare and contrast field studies and surveys.
2. Distinguish between lagged and instantaneous time series models.
3. Be able to describe internal validity threats to surveys and field studies not present in experiments or quasi-experiments.

Issues to Discuss

1. How are panel study designs potentially superior to cross-sectional between-cases designs? Are they less advantageous in any way(s)?
2. Identify a research topic in which a field study would be more attractive than an experiment or quasi-experiment. Why is a field study the most attractive way to address this topic? Which specific Design—A2, B2, or C2—would you recommend to carry out this field study?

PART III SUGGESTED READINGS

Cook and Campbell's (1979) book on quasi-experimentation is probably the most influential work on design in the social sciences. In particular, their discussions of causal evidence and threats to internal validity are broadly accepted. The volume also contains chapters on quasi-experimental designs and analysis methods. An article by Cook and Shadish (1994) provides an update on many of the issues in the original volume. An earlier volume by Campbell and Stanley (1963) offers a less technical discussion of threats to internal validity.

Many books that purport to be on research design actually focus more on statistical analysis, given a design, than they do on design itself. Fortunately, there are several excellent exceptions. I like Keppel's (1982) book on experiments; it offers a readable treatment of experimental design and analysis. Design issues are not slighted; Keppel also gives more attention to within-cases designs than some other books of this type.

Cochran (1982) and Kish (1987) are two excellent treatments of research design generally. Quasi-experiments and field studies are emphasized, although both use experiments as a point of departure. Kish also has things to say about the design of survey research. Both Cochran and Kish emphasize design issues over analysis, although at least an intermediate level of statistical knowledge makes these books more understandable.

IV

Analysis: Investigating Empirical Relationships

8

Data Analysis Foundations

Chapter Outline

- *Data Analysis and Statistics*
  - *Statistical Information*
  - *Statistical Purposes*
- *Properties of Scores*
  - *Levels of Measurement*
  - *Discrete and Continuous Variables*
- *Conventions*
- *Summary*
- *For Review*
  - *Terms to Know*
  - *Questions for Review*
- *Appendix 8A: On Clean Data*
  - *Errors Made on Measuring Instruments*
  - *Data File Errors*
  - *Missing Values*
  - *Evaluating Secondary Data Sets*

- At most colleges and universities, students' first (or only) exposure to research method activities is a course in statistics.
- Statistics courses are typically taught by statisticians.

These unremarkable observations nevertheless may be important for your mindset about research. If your introduction to research methods was as described, you probably started this book believing statistics represents the main empirical research activity.

Hopefully that idea was dispelled in part I, where it was argued that empirical research is aimed at enhancing conceptual understanding. It does so by providing information about probable relationships between scores that validly represent the constructs at issue. Statistics are helpful in this process; but statistics are far from sufficient. Causal relationships and relationships that correspond to conceptual meanings also require sound design and measurement.

But why the observation—statisticians teach statistics? It's a matter of perspective. Statisticians are understandably most interested in advancing knowledge about the field of statistics. Alternatively, empirical researchers are interested in statistics as a tool for advancing knowledge about conceptual relationships. These differences lead to different concerns and emphases.

An important difference has to do with the way scores are viewed. To statisticians, scores illustrate how statistical procedures operate. Hypothetical scores are as good as scores from real cases for their purposes.

Not so for empirical researchers; information provided by scores from real cases are central empirical ingredients. Moreover, these scores typically do not satisfy statistical assumptions; they frequently are in error, or even missing. Empirical researchers must seek to make appropriate inferences to the conceptual level from an operational environment of fallible scores. (Appendix 8A discusses errors in data sets and methods to minimize them. Chapter 16 describes additional procedures that are available to address missing data.)

DATA ANALYSIS AND STATISTICS

Data is another term for *scores*. Data often refer to a set of scores on two or more variables. (**Datum** is singular and refers to one score.) For researchers, the data are as challenging as the statistical procedures used to analyze them. This book adopts a research orientation to analysis; it emphasizes data analysis, not statistical analysis per se.

The chapter begins with a definition of statistics and describes how statistics contribute to research. It then describes characteristics of scores for research purposes. These characteristics have implications for decisions about using statistical procedures. It concludes with a description of conventions for statistical operations on scores used in the remainder of this book.

The term *statistic* is used in several ways. Sometimes it refers to a field of study. Sometimes it describes procedures developed by statisticians or procedures researchers use to analyze data. Sometimes the term is used to characterize outcomes of statistical procedures.

In this book, the term *statistic* is used to designate a summary characteristic of scores. For example, a mean is a statistic whose values describe the central tendency of a set of scores on some measure. A simple correlation coefficient is a statistic whose values describe the degree of relationship between scores on two variables.

Statistical Information

There are many statistics and many ways to summarize data. Means and correlation coefficients are just examples. However, statistics almost always provide information about just one of two issues. First, some statistics provide summary information on scores obtained on a single variable. The mean, which identifies the weighted middle of a set of cases' scores, is one example. Chapter 9 discusses statistics that describe scores on a single variable.

Second, statistics provide information about how values on two or more variables vary together. In this role, statistics are used to address the central issue in research—namely, relationships between variables. Chapters 10 and 11 discuss statistics that describe relationships.

Statistical Purposes

Statistics also serve two purposes. First, they are used to summarize scores and empirical relationships among the cases studied. This section describes statistics for this purpose.

Second, statistical procedures are used to address two types of validity introduced in chapter 2. One of these involves the contribution of statistics to causal analysis—internal statistical validity and validation. The other applies when statistics are used in generalization—statistical generalization validity and validation. Both procedures rely heavily on probability, and their discussion is postponed to part V.

PROPERTIES OF SCORES

An operational variable has a measure that is used to obtain scores on the cases studied. These scores are numerical, and there are several ways to classify them. Two such ways have implications for data analyses and interpretation.

Levels of Measurement

Numerical values assigned in measurement refer to characteristics of cases on some variable of interest. However, the amount of information conveyed by the numerical values can vary. Four *levels of measurement* representing different amounts of information are commonly identified. Examples of each level are shown in Exhibit 8.1.

Nominal

    Branches of Government   **Legislative, Executive, Judicial**

    Computer Ownership   **Yes, No**

Ordinal

    Job Level   **Professor, Associate Professor, Assistant Professor**

    Theatre Popcorn Sizes   **Small, Large, Jumbo**

Interval

    Temperature (Celsius or Fahrenheit)

    Calendar Time

Ratio

    Salary

    Age

EXHIBIT 8.1. Examples of levels of measurement.

Nominal (or *categorical*) *variables* signify that different numbers mean only that values represent different things. No order is implied by the numerical values assigned. For example, numbers can be assigned to a nominal variable that identifies members of the three branches of government; it has the values legislative, judicial, and executive. Legislative members can be assigned 1s, judicial 2s, and executive 3s. All members with values of 1 are different than members with values of 2, and so forth.

But the assignment of numbers is arbitrary. Members of the legislature may be assigned a value of 3 and executive branch members a value of 1. In fact, any number can be assigned to members of any branch of government as long as it is not the same number assigned to another branch. The numbers convey only similarity (same number) and differences (different number).

Three additional measurement levels connote increasingly sophisticated degrees of order. Numerical values of *ordinal variables* imply only order—"most" to "least" and vice versa. For example, job titles often represent ordinal variables. A professor has a higher job level than an associate professor who has a higher level than an assistant professor. However, only order is implied, not magnitude of difference between the titles; any numbers that preserve the order are thus permissible. Professors can be assigned 1, associates 2, and assistants 3. Assigning professors 3, Associates 7, and assistants 10 also suffices because the same order is implied (although it is reversed).

Interval variables have ordinal characteristics, and the distance between them is meaningful. However, interval variables do not provide information about the absolute level of a variable.

Temperature measured by Celsius or Fahrenheit illustrates an interval variable. Temperature differences of 10 degrees Celsius are the same anywhere on the variable. The difference between 10 and 20 degrees is the same as the difference between 35 and 45 degrees. However, neither Celsius nor Fahrenheit variables provide information about the absolute temperature level; zero temperature is arbitrary in both cases. Consequently, one cannot say that a Fahrenheit temperature of 50 degrees is twice as warm as a temperature of 25 degrees.

Finally, *ratio variables* have interval characteristics and a true zero point. Salary is an example. The difference between a yearly salary of $25,000 and $35,000 is the same as a difference between $90,000 and $100,000. Furthermore, a yearly salary of $100,000 is twice as large as a salary of $50,000.

Recognizing differences between these levels of measurement is important for the choice of statistics in some instances; it is also important for the interpretation of statistical output. Statistics that provide information about relationships between variables, in particular, are sometimes sensitive to levels of measurement.

RESEARCH HIGHLIGHT 8.1

Nearly Interval Measurement

Researchers disagree about whether certain widely used types of measures such as attitude questionnaires meet interval measurement requirements. For example, are the intervals on a response scale that ask people to indicate 1 (strongly disagree), 2 (disagree), 3 (neither disagree nor agree), 4 (agree), or 5 (strongly agree) really equal? Or, do they satisfy only ordinal requirements? Further, there is disagreement about whether statistics that rely on meaningful intervals can be used for these types of measures.

This book takes the view that such measures, if not strictly interval, are nearly interval. Furthermore, statistics that require meaningful intervals can be used without serious difficulty as long as measures are nearly interval.

Discrete and Continuous Variables

Another measurement distinction is between discrete and continuous variables. ***Discrete variables*** have a countable number of values. For example, gender is a discrete variable that can assume two values, male and female.

Alternatively, ***continuous variables*** are infinitely divisible between any two values. For example, age can be scaled in years, but it can be divided into months, weeks, days, hours, and so forth.

The distinction between discrete and continuous variables is important for some types of statistical validation procedures (see part V) and for reporting scores in research reports (see chapter 9). For simplicity, researchers report continuous variables as discrete. For example, they may round continuous age values to the nearest whole year.

CONVENTIONS

Mathematical formulae and operations in part IV are modest; symbols used are shown in Exhibit 8.2. Letters are used to designate the meaning to be attached to variables. These conventions are shown in Exhibit 8.3.

Symbol	Interpretation
+	add.
-	subtract.
$\pm$	add and subtract, or plus and minus.
$\times$	multiply.
/	divide.
=	equal.
$\approx$	approximately equal.
$\neq$	not equal.
>	greater than.
$\geq$	greater than or equal.
<	less than.
$\leq$	less than or equal.
$\sum_{i=1}^{N}(y_i)$	$= y_1 + y_2 + ... + y_i + ... + y_N$, where i designates the ith case, $i = 1$ indicates that the summing begins with the first case, and N designates that the summing continues through the Nth case. The complete representation is shortened to, $\Sigma(y_i)$, because in this book the summing always begins with the first case and continues through all cases.
x^2	$x \times x$
$\sqrt{}$	take the square root

EXHIBIT 8.2. Math symbol conventions.

Letter	Interpretation

One variable. If only one variable is considered, it is designated X. An independent variable is also designated X and a dependent variable is designated Y.

X	variable or independent variable.
x_i	value of the ith case on X where i goes from 1 to N cases.
N	total number of cases.
Y	dependent variable.
y_i	value of the ith case on Y where i goes from 1 to N cases.

Two or more variables. When two or more independent variables are considered (or when independent/dependent variable status is not an issue) variables are designated X with a subscript:

X_j	jth variable where j goes from 1 to k variables.
k	total number of X variables.
X_{ji}	value of the ith case on the jth variable.

EXHIBIT 8.3.   Letter conventions.

Cases	Y	X1	X2	$\cdots$	Xj	$\ldots$	Xk
				Variables			
1	y_1	$x1_1$	$x2_1$		xj_1		xk_1
2	y_2	$x1_2$	$x2_2$		xj_2		xk_2
3	y_3	$x1_3$	$x2_3$		xj_3		xk_3
.							
.							
.							
i	y_i	$x1_i$			xj_i		xk_i
.							
.							
N	y_N	$x1_N$	$x2_N$		xj_N		xk_N

EXHIBIT 8.4.   A data matrix.

When shown, scores are placed in a ***data matrix***. A data matrix is a rectangular array of scores with cases in the rows and variables in the columns as represented in Exhibit 8.4. This representation can help you understand formulae and other statistical operations. Create a mental picture of rows (cases) and columns (variables).

SUMMARY

Data analysis contributes to conceptual understanding along with design and measurement. Statistics are often calculated as a part of this activity. A ***statistic*** is a characteristic of scores. It describes scores on single measures or relationships between scores among two or more measures.

Scores representing variables differ in ways that have consequences for types of statistics calculated on them and their interpretation. Numbers identify only similarity and dissimilarity among ***nominal variables***. Numbers additionally imply order (more than, less than) among ***ordinal variables***. ***Interval variables*** have the added property that the differences between values are meaningful. Finally, ***ratio variables*** have the characteristics of an interval variable plus a true zero point.

Discrete variables have a countable number of values. ***Continuous variables*** are infinitely divisible between values.

FOR REVIEW

Terms to Know

Data: Scores characterizing cases obtained on measures. ***Datum*** refers to one score.
Statistics: Refers to a field of study, procedures to analyze data, or a term to describe outcomes of statistical procedures. It also refers to a summary characteristic of scores.
Level of measurement: Refers to the amount of information provided by scores.
   Nominal (categorical) variable: Variable in which similar values signal the same thing; different values signal different things.
   Ordinal variable: Variable with nominal properties, and values signal order from highest to lowest (or lowest to highest).
   Interval variable: Variable with ordinal properties, and the distance between values is meaningful.
   Ratio variable: Variable with interval properties, and there is a true zero point.
Discrete variable: Variable with a countable number of values.
Continuous variable: Variable that is infinitely divisible between any two values.
Data matrix: A rectangular array of scores with cases in the rows and variables in the columns.

Questions for Review

1. You learn the values of the following variables that apply to an individual:

   Gender
   Age
   Whether the individual owns an automobile
   Years of work experience
   Number of books the individual owns
   Political party affiliation

Whether the individual is a union member

How many telephones the individual has at home

  Specify the level of measurement for each of these variables. Classify each variable as discrete or continuous.

2. A student takes four college classes: Economics 100, a 3-credit course that meets 3 times a week; Psychology 100, a 3-credit course that meets 3 times a week; Algebra 100, a 5-credit course that meets 4 times a week; Golf 100, a 1-credit course that meets once a week. Arrange this information in a data matrix in which classes represent the cases, and the two variables are the number of credits and the number of days classes meet.

3. Professors rank higher than associate professors who rank higher than assistant professors. Assign numbers to these three ranks that satisfy a nominal scale but violate an ordinal scale.

Rank	*Number*
Professors	
Associate Professors	
Assistant Professors	

APPENDIX 8A: ON CLEAN DATA

Computers and statistical software are a great help to research and data analysis. Many analyses now performed quickly and easily are virtually impossible without a computer because of the number of calculations required. Even analyses that can be done by hand or on a calculator are greatly speeded with a computer. Once data are entered, a computer can perform calculations with unerring accuracy.

But there is a rub; data must be correctly entered. This appendix identifies data error sources. It also makes recommendations for minimizing errors when creating data sets and for locating them in existing data files.

Errors Made on Measuring Instruments

Most serious errors occur when information is recorded on the original measuring instrument, such as a self-report questionnaire or an interview form. Participants completing self-report questionnaires may generate errors. For example, they may respond incorrectly because they do not understand a question. Errors are also likely when research observers complete measurement instruments. For example, an observer may not have access to correct information or may misinterpret information provided.

Errors by participants and observers are difficult to correct. They are best minimized before data are collected. Two precautions help. First, the measuring instrument should be constructed with a concern for missing data in mind. Keep it simple to complete; make questions unambiguous. Second, do not assume participants or observers have your knowledge or motivation. Provide training to obtain knowledge and incentives to obtain motivation.

Data File Errors

A second source for errors occurs when data are transcribed from the original measuring instruments into a file for subsequent analysis. Such errors can be minimized at the outset. Three things can help. First, use a rectangular format for data sets. Maintain a separate row for scores on each case and a separate column for each variable. Missing responses are much easier to account for if this suggestion is followed.

Second, make the job of recording original data simple. For example, suppose you want to record gender by making male equal 1 and female equal 0. However, participants are asked to circle *M* if male and, *F* if female on a questionnaire. *M*s and *F*s should be entered in the computer file. The letters *M* and *F* can be transformed to the numbers 1 and 0 by the software program in the computer without errors.

Finally, if resources permit, all data should be recorded twice. The two data files can then be compared; any differences can be resolved by an examination of the original data source.

Missing Values

Research studies are almost always plagued by missing data; these present a serious problem (chapter 16 discusses ways to address missing data at the analysis stage of a research study). Two recommendations are made here for recording information about missing data. First, record a specific value to identify all missing data rather than leaving cells in the data set blank. This helps the individuals transcribing the data maintain values in the correct rows and columns. Second, if possible, assign the same value to missing responses across all variables. This is another way to help transcribers minimize errors. In doing so, however, make sure the values to identify missing values cannot be legitimate responses for any of the variables.

Evaluating Secondary Data Sets

Research is often conducted on data that have been collected and recorded by someone else. Although you can never be certain about the accuracy of such data, you can evaluate them for values that are impossible, improbable, or inconsistent.

Suppose a variable is measured with a 5-point rating scale that ranges from 1 (low) to 5 (high). Any numerical value outside this range is impossible; it must be incorrect. Similarly, some values are possible but improbable. For example, it is improbable that an employee is 94 years old.

Impossible and improbable values can be identified one variable at a time. Inconsistent values must be examined in the context of two or more variables. For example, it is inconsistent for a student to be younger than the number of years of education.

Sometimes you can correct impossible, improbable, or inconsistent data by using responses to other variables measured. Often, however, such values must be treated as missing.

9

Analysis Applications: Describing Scores on a Single Variable

Chapter Outline

- *A Data Matrix*
- *Tables and Graphs*
  - *Tables*
  - *Graphs*
- *Statistical Representation of Scores*
  - *Central Tendency*
  - *Variability*
  - *Shape*
    - *Skew*
    - *Kurtosis*
- *Relationships Between Statistics*
  - *Skew and Central Tendency*
  - *Skew and Variability*
- *Summary*
- *For Review*
  - *Terms to Know*
  - *Formulae to Use*
  - *Questions for Review*
  - *Issues to Discuss*

Statistics describe scores on a variable or describe relationships between scores obtained on two or more variables. This chapter presents a selective review of statistics and other methods to describe scores on a single variable.

There are at least three reasons to investigate scores on single variables before looking at relationships between variables:

1. Investigation is needed to decide whether the scores are ready, or can be made ready, for analyses of relationships between variables. Such investigation is needed because data files usually contain errors after initial construction (see chapter 8, appendix 8A, and chapter 16).
2. Statistics that summarize scores on single variables can aid in understanding the cases studied and generalizations that may follow from a study. For example, knowledge of biographical information about research participants—such as age, education, and gender—suggest how research findings may generalize to other persons.
3. Knowledge about how scores are distributed on each variable also helps researchers understand statistics of relationships among variables. Subsequent chapters show that both the variability and the shape of score distributions on single variables influence relationships that may be obtained between variables.

The chapter begins by describing ways to summarize scores on a measure using tables and graphs. Statistics that describe three characteristics of score distributions—central tendency, variability, and symmetry or asymmetry—are then defined. Relationships between these statistics are also discussed.

A DATA MATRIX

Exhibit 9.1 shows a data matrix of scores on four variables obtained from 19 cases. The first two, $X1$ and $X2$, are discrete and range from 1 to 7. They are ordered interval (or nearly interval) scales and may represent, for example, levels of satisfaction ranging from 1, "very

	7-Point Rating Scales		Age	Weight
Case	$X1$	$X2$	$X3$	$X4$
1	3	4	38.6	126. 1
2	5	7	54.5	147. 1
3	6	7	63.8	163. 7
4	2	3	26.2	116. 5
5	1	1	28.4	110. 5
6	4	6	46.0	135. 6
7	4	6	45.2	138. 1
8	5	6	51.3	143. 3
9	6	7	62.7	155. 1
10	7	7	68.9	174. 8
11	3	5	39.7	128. 9
12	3	4	35.5	124. 6
13	5	7	56.6	150. 9
14	3	3	32.1	121. 2
15	2	2	25.3	112. 3
16	4	5	44.9	132. 4
17	4	6	48.1	137. 8
18	5	6	53.4	146. 5
19	4	5	42.8	129. 0

EXHIBIT 9.1.   Data matrix: Scores from 19 cases on four variables.

dissatisfied," to 7, "very satisfied." $X3$ is age and $X4$ is weight. These are ordered continuous scales rounded to the first decimal place.

It is difficult to obtain much information from a visual inspection of Exhibit 9.1 even though there are only 19 cases. Summarizing scores in frequency tables, in graphs, and/or statistically, can aid interpretation and understanding.

TABLES AND GRAPHS

Researchers sometimes do not appreciate how useful tables and graphs can be for summarizing scores.

Tables

A *frequency table* provides a summary of scores from a data matrix by reporting the number (and/or percentage or proportion) of cases at each level of a discrete variable or within each interval of a continuous variable. Exhibit 9.2 shows a frequency table for $X1$, a discrete 7-value variable from the data matrix shown in Exhibit 9.1. Exhibit 9.3 shows a frequency table for age, $X3$, from Exhibit 9.1. Age is a continuous variable. Intervals have been created in Exhibit 9.3 and cases with ages that fall within each interval are grouped together.

Graphs

A graph of scores on a variable provides a picture of the data that often is more informative than a frequency table. A **bar chart** reports the values of a discrete variable on one axis and the frequency (number and/or proportion or percentage) of cases with scores at each value on the other. Exhibit 9.4 shows a bar chart for $X1$; the values are on the horizontal axis and the frequency is on the vertical axis.

Histograms graph continuous variables. A histogram reports values of a continuous variable placed in intervals as illustrated for age, $X3$, in Exhibit 9.5.

Value	Frequency	Percent
1	1	5.3
2	2	10.5
3	4	21.1
4	5	26.3
5	4	21.0
6	2	10.5
7	1	5.3
Total	19	100.0

EXHIBIT 9.2.   Frequency table for $X1$, a 7-point ordered scale.

Age Intervals	Frequency	Percent
20 < 30	3	15.8
30 < 40	4	21.1
40 < 50	5	26.3
50 < 60	4	21.0
60 < 70	3	15.8
Total	19	100.0

EXHIBIT 9.3.   Frequency table for $X3$, age, a continuous scale.

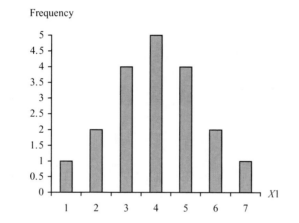

EXHIBIT 9.4.   Bar chart of scores on $X1$, a 7-value ordered scale.

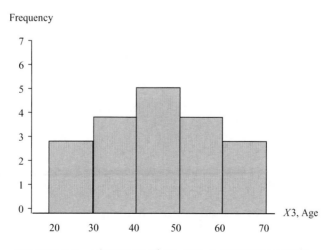

EXHIBIT 9.5.   Histogram of $X3$, age, a continuous scale.

STATISTICAL REPRESENTATION OF SCORES

Statistics are also available to describe characteristics of distributions, such as those shown in Exhibits 9.2 and 9.3.

Central Tendency

The middle of a distribution of scores is called its **central tendency**. Three statistics are often used to describe central tendency. The **median** is the middle score (or if there is an even number of scores, the sum of the two middle scores divided by 2).

The **mean** is the sum of the values of each score divided by the number of scores:

$$\mu_X = \sum x_i/N = (x_1 + x_2 + \dots x_i + \dots + x_N)/N \tag{9.1}$$

where μ_X = mean of X
$\quad x_i$ = score of the ith case on X
$\quad N$ = number of cases

The **mode** is the most frequent score in a distribution. It is sometimes of interest in describing the central tendency of nominal variables. Further, it is of interest to know whether a distribution has one (unimodal) or more modes. For example, a bimodal distribution might have peaks at the extremes instead of one peak in the middle.

In most cases, however, the median or mean is of more interest. Hereafter, the mode is used only to distinguish distributions that have one or more peaks.

Variability

Variability refers to the spread in the distribution of scores. A useful and intuitively meaningful statistic indicating variability is the **standard deviation**, the average variability of scores around the mean:

$$\sigma_X = \sqrt{\frac{\sum (x_i - \mu_X)^2}{N}} \tag{9.2}$$

where σ_X = standard deviation of X.

Formula 9.2 is worth study. When calculations are completed, the square and square root leave the values of the deviations between each x_i and the mean unchanged but with a positive number. Dividing by N is analogous to dividing by N in Formula 9.1. It creates an average. However, the average now refers to the deviations around the mean of the distribution.

Exhibit 9.6 summarizes steps to calculate the standard deviation of $X1$ from Exhibit 9.1. The mean is calculated first from Formula 9.1, $\mu_{X1} = 76/19 = 4.00$. The mean is then subtracted from each value of $X1$ in the column $(X1 - \mu_{X1})$; this column must sum to 0.0. The deviations are squared in the last column. The sum of this column is divided by N, and its square root is taken. The standard deviation, $\sigma_{X1} = \sqrt{42/19} = \sqrt{2.21} = 1.49$. The average variability of $X1$ scores about its mean is 1.49.

Although not as intuitively meaningful, variance is useful for certain mathematical operations involving statistics. **Variance** is the standard deviation squared.

$$\sigma_X^2 = \sum (X_i - \mu_X)^2/N \tag{9.3}$$

where σ_X^2 = variance of X.

Case	$X1$	$(X1 - \mu_{X1})$	$(X1 - \mu_{X1})^2$
1	3	-1	1
2	5	1	1
3	6	2	4
4	2	-2	4
5	1	-3	9
6	4	0	0
7	4	0	0
8	5	1	1
9	6	2	4
10	7	3	9
11	3	-1	1
12	3	-1	1
13	5	1	1
14	3	-1	1
15	2	-2	4
16	4	0	0
17	4	0	0
18	5	1	1
19	4	0	0
Σ	76	0	42
μ	4		

EXHIBIT 9.6.   Calculation of the standard deviation: $X1$ from Exhibit 9.1.

RESEARCH HIGHLIGHT 9.1

Another Standard Deviation Statistic

You may see Formula 9.2 with $n - 1$ in the denominator instead of N. The denominator $n - 1$ is appropriate when estimating a population standard deviation from a sample (where n refers to the sample size) that has been randomly drawn from it. In this section, the cases studied are assumed to represent the population of cases N; thus, Formula 9.2 is appropriate.

Shape

The *shape of a distribution* of scores is described by its symmetry around the central tendency and by its peakedness or flatness. The reference point for shape is a *normal distribution*. It describes a continuously scaled unimodal variable that has 68.3% of scores falling within ±one standard deviation of the mean, 95.5% of scores falling within ±two standard deviations of the mean, and 99.7% of scores falling within ±three standard deviations of the mean.

Exhibit 9.7 shows a normal distribution. The distribution is shown under a smooth curve to illustrate a continuous variable. Because a continuous variable is infinitely divisible between values, it is not appropriate to assign a frequency to any particular value. Thus, areas under the

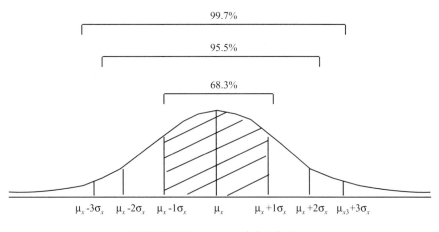

EXHIBIT 9.7.   A normal distribution.

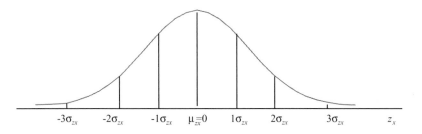

EXHIBIT 9.8.   A standard normal distribution: $\mu_{ZX} = 0, \sigma_{ZX} = 1$.

curve are identified to represent proportions or percentages of scores that are contained in the total distribution of scores. The cross-hatched area between negative and positive one standard deviations in Exhibit 9.7 contain 68.3% of the scores.

A normal distribution can have any mean or standard deviation; hence, there are many normal distributions. However, all are symmetrical as described; all have the same percentages of scores falling within the sets of standard deviations as described. A **standard normal distribution** has mean $= 0.00$ and standard deviation $= 1.00$. Exhibit 9.8 shows a standard normal distribution.

Distributions of scores on many variables approximate the normal distribution. For example, physical characteristics of human and other animal populations often approximate a normal distribution. Part V shows that a normal distribution is also often approximated in many sampling situations in which generalizations from a sample to a population are desired. Thus, normal distributions are widely used in statistical work and have become a standard for judging other types of distributions.

Skew

Skew describes the symmetry or asymmetry of a distribution relative to a normal distribution. When a distribution is symmetrical, as the normal distribution, skew $= 0.0$. When the distribution is asymmetrical and the tail is toward the right, skew > 0.0. Exhibit 9.9 shows a histogram of $X4$ from the data in Exhibit 9.1. It is an asymmetrical distribution with a positive skew > 0.0. Exhibit 9.10 shows a bar chart of $X2$ in Exhibit 9.1. The tail is to the left, skew < 0.0.

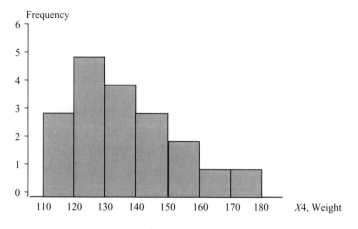

EXHIBIT 9.9.   Histogram of scores on $X4$, weight, positive skew.

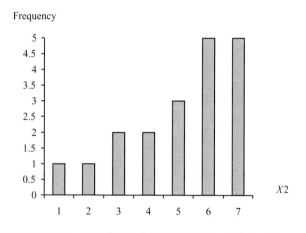

EXHIBIT 9.10.   Bar chart of scores on $X2$, negative skew.

Kurtosis

Kurtosis shows the peakedness or flatness of a distribution relative to a normal distribution. Kurtosis = 0.0 signifies a distribution that is similar to a normal distribution in height. When a distribution is more peaked than a normal distribution, kurtosis > 0.0; when less peaked, kurtosis < 0.0. Kurtosis generally is not as important for describing distributions as other statistics, and hence it is not emphasized here.

RELATIONSHIPS BETWEEN STATISTICS

Skew and Central Tendency

The mean and median are equal when a distribution of scores is symmetrical. When skew > 0.0, the mean > median. The mean < median when skew < 0.0.

Distributions of individual income often have skew > 0.0. Relatively few individuals have very large incomes, and these "pull" the mean above the median. In contrast, distributions of employee performance evaluations in organizations often have skew < 0.0. Most employees

---

RESEARCH HIGHLIGHT 9.2

Percentiles: Locating Scores in a Distribution

It is often of interest to know the location of a score relative to other scores in a distribution. For example, as a student you may want to know how your test score compares with test scores of other students in a class.

Percentiles provide this information. A percentile reports a score in percentage terms relative to the lowest score in the distribution. Thus, if your test score is at the 90th percentile, only 10% of students scored higher than you. Percentiles are especially useful with asymmetrical distributions because standard deviations provide equivocal information about location of scores.

---

obtain middle or high evaluations. The few employees who receive low evaluations "pull" the mean below the median. When a distribution is markedly skewed, it is informative to report both the mean and median.

Skew and Variability

When a distribution is symmetrical, the number or percentage of scores one standard deviation above the mean is the same as the number or percentage of scores one standard deviation below. Thus, 34% of scores are between the mean and +1 standard deviations and 34% of scores are between the mean and −1 standard deviations in normal distributions.

Not so when the distribution is skewed. To illustrate, visual inspection of Exhibit 9.9 (skew > 0.0) suggests that a larger percentage of scores falls in a given negative area close to the mean (=136.55 pounds). However, as one gets further from the mean, a greater percentage falls within positive standard deviation intervals. The process is reversed if skew < 0.0 (see Exhibit 9.10, where $\mu_{X2} = 5.11$).

Thus, the standard deviation (and variance) provide more equivocal information as a distribution becomes more asymmetrical.

SUMMARY

Understanding characteristics of scores on single variables is a valuable first step in data analysis. A *frequency table* showing variable scores at different levels, or level intervals, is one way to obtain information about single variables. Another way is to graph score distributions. Graphs of discrete variables are called *bar charts*; graphs of continuous variables are called *histograms*.

Statistics can also summarize distributions of scores on single variables. The *median* and *mean* are two ways to describe *central tendency*. *Standard deviations* and *variances* represent *variability*.

Scores often approximate a *normal distribution*, which is symmetrical and has a known proportion of scores falling within any specified distance on a continuous scale (e.g., ±1 standard deviations). *Distribution shapes* that are not normal may be symmetrical or asymmetrical. *Skew* is a statistic that indicates a distribution's symmetry or asymmetry. *Kurtosis* is a statistic that indicates a distribution's degree of peakedness or flatness relative to a normal distribution.

When distributions are asymmetrical, the mean and median no longer provide the same central tendency value. Further, standard deviations and variance statistics provide ambiguous information when distributions are asymmetrical because the numbers of scores above and below the mean are no longer equal.

FOR REVIEW

Terms to Know

Frequency table: Provides a summary of cases' scores from a data matrix by reporting the number (and/or percentage) of cases at each level of a discrete variable or within each interval of a continuous variable.

Bar chart: A graph that reports the values of a discrete variable on one axis and the frequency (number and/or percentage) of cases on the other.

Histogram: A graph that reports values of a continuous variable placed in intervals on one axis with the frequency (number and/or percentage of cases) on the other.

Central tendency: The middle of a distribution of scores.

  Mean: The sum of the values of each score divided by the number of scores.

  Median: The middle score in a distribution (or if there are an even number of scores, the sum of the two middle scores divided by 2).

  Mode: The most frequent score in a distribution of discrete values.

Variability: The spread in a distribution of scores.

  Standard deviation: The average variability of scores around the mean.

  Variance: The standard deviation squared.

Distribution shape: The degree to which a distribution is symmetrical or asymmetrical and the degree to which it is peaked or flat. These characteristics are defined by *skew* and *kurtosis*.

Normal distribution: A distribution of a continuous variable that is unimodal, is symmetrical around its middle, and has 68.3% of scores falling within ±one standard deviation of the mean, 95.5% of scores falling within ±two standard deviations, and 99.7% of scores falling within ±three standard deviations.

Standard normal distribution: A normal distribution with mean = 0.0 and standard deviation = 1.0.

Skew: Describes the symmetry or asymmetry of a distribution relative to a normal distribution. When a distribution is symmetrical, skew = 0.0. When the distribution is asymmetrical and the tail is toward the right, skew > 0.0; when the tail is to the left, skew < 0.0.

Kurtosis: Describes the flatness or peakedness of a distribution relative to a normal distribution. Kurtosis > 0.0 when a distribution is more peaked than a normal distribution. Kurtosis < 0.0 when a distribution is less peaked than a normal distribution.

Percentile: Reports a score in percentage terms relative to the lowest score in the distribution.

Formulae to Use

Mean

$$\mu_X = \sum x_i/N = (x_1 + x_2 + \ldots x_i + \ldots + x_N)/N \qquad (9.1)$$

where x_i = score of the ith subject
  N = number of subjects

Standard deviation

$$\sigma_X = \sqrt{\frac{\sum (x_i - \mu_x)^2}{N}} \tag{9.2}$$

Variance

$$\sigma_X^2 = \sum (x_i - \mu_x)^2 / N \tag{9.3}$$

Questions for Review

1. Explain why it is important to study characteristics of scores on single distributions even though as a researcher you are more interested in relationships between variables.
2. For what types of variables are bar charts appropriate? Histograms?
3. Using Formulas 9.1 and 9.2, calculate the mean and standard deviation for the variable X.

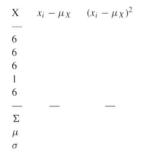

X	$x_i - \mu_X$	$(x_i - \mu_X)^2$
6		
6		
6		
1		
6		
—	—	—
Σ		
μ		
σ		

4. How does a standard normal distribution differ from other normal distributions? How is it the same?

Issues to Discuss

1. Be prepared to discuss whether skew and kurtosis are related to the relationship between the mean and median, and, if so, how.
2. Be prepared to discuss what implications skew has for interpretation of the standard deviation.

10

Analysis Applications: Simple Correlation and Regression

Chapter Outline

- *Graphical Representation*
- *Simple Correlation*
  - *Correlation Formulae*
    - *Covariance*
    - *Standard Scores*
  - *Variance Explained*
- *Simple Regression*
  - *Regression Model*
  - *Regression Formulae*
- *Nominal Independent Variables*
- *Summary*
- *For Review*
  - *Terms to Know*
  - *Formulae to Use*
  - *Questions for Review*
  - *Issue to Discuss*

Empirical research investigates relationships between scores on operational variables. This chapter begins the "good stuff" from a data analysis perspective. It introduces two procedures that generate statistics to describe relationships among variables: correlation and regression.

Correlation and regression are attractive because they are appropriate any time a research problem involves a dependent variable that is measured at a nearly interval level or better and has one or more independent variables. This is a sweeping claim—intendedly so. Consider the following illustrative studies:

- A large clinic sends a questionnaire to all recent patients to investigate, among other things, whether patients' satisfaction with medical services depends on the time they must wait before obtaining an appointment.
- A manufacturing firm conducts a study to see whether employees who are trained perform at higher levels than a comparable (control) group of employees who are not trained.
- A college graduate program reviews its records to determine whether student grade point average (GPA) is related to undergraduate GPA and residence status in the state.
- A state human services office randomly samples from census data to see if residents' income levels differ by county.
- A foundation research team performs a study expecting to learn that participants' behavior on computer tasks depends on a multiplicative relation between participants' motivation and ability to do the task.

All these studies have a dependent variable that is measured at a nearly interval to ratio level. However, as Exhibit 10.1 summarizes, the studies differ widely with regard to independent variables. The clinic, business firm, and state services office studies have just one independent variable. The graduate program and foundation studies have two. Independent variables are

Study	Number	Scale	Other
Large clinic	1	Interval	
Manufacturing firm	1	Nominal	Two levels
Graduate program	2	Interval and nominal	
State services office	1	Nominal	Many levels
Foundation research team	2	Interval	Nonlinear relation

EXHIBIT 10.1. Independent variables in the hypothetical studies.

RESEARCH HIGHLIGHT 10.1

The Designs Also Differ

If you have read part III, you'll recognize that the design of the studies also differs. The clinic and college graduate program are field studies; the state human services office is a survey. The business firm study is an experiment or quasi-experiment, depending on how employees are assigned to training and control groups. Finally, the foundation study may be a field study if both ability and motivation are measured as characteristics of the participants. On the other hand, it is an experiment or quasi-experiment if levels of motivation participants experience are established by the research team.

By itself, research design has few implications for the type of data analysis method used.

measured at an interval level in the clinic and foundation studies; they are nominal in the business firm and state services studies. The graduate program has both an interval (GPA) and a nominal (residence) variable. Finally, a nonlinear relationship is expected in the foundation research team study.

There are correlation and regression procedures to analyze the data in all the studies described. (The examples actually understate the generality of correlation and regression. In particular, if the number of cases warrants, there can be any number of independent variables.) This and the next chapter describe many of these procedures.

This chapter focuses on **simple linear** correlation and regression. Simple means that only two variables are involved—one dependent and one independent. Linear means that only a relationship that conforms to a straight line is identified. Hereafter, *correlation* and *regression* mean *simple linear correlation and regression*, unless otherwise stated.

Most of the chapter deals with relationships in which both the dependent and independent variables are measured at a nearly interval, interval, or ratio level. It begins by showing how such relationships can be demonstrated graphically. It then describes correlation followed by regression. The chapter also describes correlation and regression when the independent variable is measured at a nominal level.

GRAPHICAL REPRESENTATION

Exhibit 10.2 shows scores and descriptive statistics from seven participants on a dependent (Y) and five independent (X_j) variables. All are measured at a nearly interval level and are summarized as discrete variables. For example, they might represent an opinion scale ranging from 1 (strongly disagree) to 7 (strongly agree).

It is often informative to begin an investigation of a relationship between two variables by plotting their scores in two dimensions. Exhibits 10.3 and 10.4 show plots of scores on Y and $X1$ and $X2$ (from Exhibit 10.2), respectively. It is conventional to represent the dependent variable on the vertical axis and the independent variable on the horizontal axis as shown.

Case	Y	$X1$	$X2$	$X3$	$X4$	$X5$
1	2	2	6	4	1	1
2	2	3	3	2	7	1
3	2	4	5	1	4	1
4	4	4	5	7	4	4
5	6	3	4	6	1	7
6	6	4	2	4	4	7
7	6	6	3	4	7	7
μ	4.00	3.71	4.00	4.00	4.00	4.00
σ	1.85	1.16	1.31	1.93	2.27	2.78

EXHIBIT 10.2.   Scores and descriptive statistics on six interval variables.

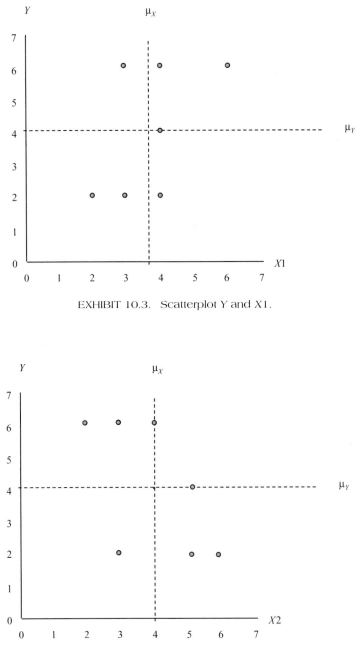

EXHIBIT 10.3.   Scatterplot Y and $X1$.

EXHIBIT 10.4.   Scatterplot Y and $X2$.

Visual inspection suggests that scores on $X1$ are positively related to scores on Y in Exhibit 10.3. Scores on Y are larger as scores on $X1$ are larger. Alternatively, the relationship is negative in Exhibit 10.4; scores on Y are smaller as scores on $X2$ are larger.

Correlation and regression provide statistics that add to visual inspection by describing such relationships quantitatively.

SIMPLE CORRELATION

It is often attractive to study relationships between scores on variables without concern for the scale values or variability of the scores involved. For example, one may want to know whether the relationship between individuals' age and income is larger or smaller than the relationship between their height and weight. Time, dollars, height, and weight all represent different scales that must be accounted for if a comparison is to be made.

It is also often desirable to obtain the same relationship regardless of how any one variable is scaled. For example, one may want a measure of relationship between age and income that does not change whether age is recorded in years, months, or some other time unit.

A ***product moment (PM) correlation coefficient*** provides such information; it is a statistic that describes the degree of relationship or association between two variables in *standardized* ($\mu = 0.0, \sigma = 1.0$) form. It can range between -1.00 and $+1.00$. ***Correlation*** hereafter means ***PM correlation***.

The sign of the PM correlation coefficient signals the *direction* of the relationship between the two variables. A positive sign means that as values of one variable increase, so do values of the other. A negative sign means that as values of one variable get larger, values of the other get smaller.

The size of the coefficient signals the *strength* of relationship. A perfect linear relationship has a value of ± 1.00. Scores on the two variables (after standardization) are identical. A correlation coefficient of 0.00 indicates no linear relationship between the two variables. The strength of relationship increases as correlation coefficients move from 0.00 toward ± 1.00.

Correlation Formulae

There are several algebraically equivalent ways to calculate correlation coefficients. Two are shown here to help you understand what is accomplished.

RESEARCH HIGHLIGHT 10.2

Other Correlation Coefficients

There are other correlation coefficients. Three of these provide PM correlation coefficients using different computational procedures. A ***phi coefficient*** is sometimes calculated when both Y and X are dichotomous variables—variables that can take on only two values. A ***point-biserial correlation*** may be calculated when Y or X is dichotomous and the other is not. A ***rho coefficient*** may be calculated when variables are measured at an ordinal level.

The computational formulae for these correlation coefficients are less demanding than for the PM coefficient, which may explain their use before the widespread availability of statistical software on computers. With statistical software, there is little need for these coefficients, because they are all variations on the basic PM formula (Formula 10.2a or 10.2b).

Covariance

One way to think about correlation coefficients extends the notion of variability discussed in chapter 9. **Covariance** is a statistic that provides information about how values of two variables go together. It is given as follows:

$$\text{CoVar}_{YX} = \sum [(Y_i - \mu_Y) \times (X_i - \mu_X)]/N \qquad (10.1)$$

where CoVar_{YX} = covariance of Y and X, the average cross-product of the deviations about
their respective means of Y and X
μ_Y and μ_X = means (Formula 9.1) of Y and X, respectively
N = number of cases

Covariance provides information about a relationship in the original units of the variables; it must be standardized to provide a correlation coefficient. This is accomplished by dividing the covariance by the product of the respective standard deviations.

$$\rho_{YX} = \text{CoVar}_{YX}/(\sigma_Y \times \sigma_X) \qquad (10.2a)$$

where ρ_{YX} = simple linear correlation coefficient between scores on Y and X
σ_Y and σ_X = standard deviations (Formula 9.2) of Y and X, respectively

Exhibit 10.5 summarizes steps to calculate the simple correlation coefficient of Y and $X1$ using Formulae 10.1 and 10.2a. Deviation scores are first calculated for both Y and $X1$. Then, in the last column, each case's deviation scores are multiplied together and divided by N. The sum of this column is the covariance ($\text{CoVar} = 1.14$) from Formula 10.1. The correlation coefficient is then obtained by using Formula 10.2a ($\rho_{YX1} = .53$).

Case	Y	X1	$(Y - \mu_Y)$	$(X1 - \mu_{X1})$	$(Y - \mu_Y) \times (X1 - \mu_{X1})/N$
1	2	2	-2	-1.71	0.49
2	2	3	-2	-0.71	0.20
3	2	4	-2	0.29	-0.08
4	4	4	0	0.29	0.00
5	6	3	2	-0.71	-0.20
6	6	4	2	0.29	0.08
7	6	6	2	2.29	0.65
Σ					1.14
μ	4.00	3.71			
σ	1.85	1.16			

$\rho_{YX1} = \text{CoVar}/(\sigma_Y \times \sigma_{X1}) = 1.14 / (1.85 \times 1.16) = .53.$

EXHIBIT 10.5. Covariance method to calculate a simple correlation coefficient: Y and $X1$ (Exhibit 10.2).

Standard Scores

Another way to obtain correlation coefficients is to work with scores that are already standardized. A *standard score* is the deviation of a score from its mean divided by the standard deviation. It is given by

$$z_{Xi} = (x_i - \mu_X)/\sigma_X \qquad (10.3)$$

where z_{Xi} = standard score of the *i*th case on variable X

Exhibit 10.6 illustrates how standard scores are generated from the Y scores in Exhibit 10.2. A deviation score distribution is calculated by subtracting the mean of the Y scores from each case score $(y_i - \mu_Y)$. This creates a distribution with $\mu_Y = 0.00$ and a standard deviation of the original distribution. The deviation score distribution is then transformed to a standard score distribution by dividing each deviation score by the original standard deviation σ_Y. A *standard score distribution* thus has a transformed mean, $\mu_{zY} = 0.00$, and a transformed standard deviation, $\sigma_{zY} = 1.00$. (Standard scores do not change the symmetry or asymmetry of the original distribution.)

Standard scores create a scale in standard deviation units. Case 1 has a score 1.08 standard deviations below the mean; Case 7 has a score 1.08 standard deviations above the mean. A correlation coefficient can be obtained from standard scores by:

$$\rho_{YX} = \sum (z_{Yi} \times z_{Xi})/N \qquad (10.2b)$$

where ρ_{YX} = simple linear correlation coefficient between Y and X
z_{Yi} and z_{Xi} = standard scores of the *i*th case on Y and X, respectively
N = number of cases

Exhibit 10.7 shows correlation computations for the variables Y and $X1$ in Exhibit 10.2 by using the standard score formulas. The means and standard deviations of Y and $X1$ are first standardized. The product of each pair of standardized score, is summed and divided by

Case	Y	$Y - \mu_Y$	z_y
1	2	-2	-1.08
2	2	-2	-1.08
3	2	-2	-1.08
4	4	0	0
5	6	2	1.08
6	6	2	1.08
7	6	2	1.08
μ	4.00	0	0
σ	1.85	1.85	1.00

EXHIBIT 10.6.   Transformation of Y scores (Exhibit 10.2) to standard scores.

Case	Y	X1	z_Y	z_x	$z_Y \times z_x$
1	2	2	-1.08	-1.47	1.59
2	2	3	-1.08	-.61	.66
3	2	4	-1.08	.25	-.27
4	4	4	0.00	.25	.00
5	6	3	1.08	-.61	-.66
6	6	4	1.08	.25	.27
7	6	6	1.08	1.97	2.13
Sum	28.0	26.0	0.0	0.0	3.72
μ	4.00	3.71	0.00	0.00	.53
σ	1.85	1.16	1.00	1.00	

$\rho_{YX1} = 3.72 / 7 = .53$

EXHIBIT 10.7.   Calculation of correlation coefficient: Y and X1 (Exhibit 10.2).

the number of cases. The resulting correlation coefficient from Formula 10.2b, the average product of the standardized scores, is $\rho_{YX1} = .53$. This is identical to the result obtained from Formula 10.2a.

Variance Explained

The PM correlation coefficient is attractive for the reasons specified. Nevertheless, the definition, standardized degree of relationship, may lack intuitive meaning. A closely related statistic provides greater intuitive understanding. The **coefficient of determination** represents the proportion of variance in Y that is accounted for (explained) by some X variable. It can range from 0.00 to 1.00 and is given by:

$$\rho_{YX}^2 = \left[\sum (z_{Yi} \times z_{Xi}) / N \right]^2 \tag{10.4}$$

where ρ_{YX}^2 = coefficient of determination
The coefficient of determination for Y and X1 is $.53^2 = .28$.

One way to think about ρ_{YX}^2 (usually called *r square*) is to understand that a relationship between variables indicates that scores on one variable provide information about scores on the other. The coefficient of determination provides such information in terms of proportions. The extreme values of ρ_{YX}^2 are shown in Exhibits 10.8a and 10.8b, where Y is plotted with X4 and X5 from Exhibit 10.2. Because Y is the same in both cases, its variability is the same in both. Y ranges from 2 to 6 and has a standard deviation of 1.85.

In Exhibit 10.8a information about X4 scores provides no information about Y scores. The entire range of Y scores occurs with every X4 score. For example, if X4 = 1, Y ranges from

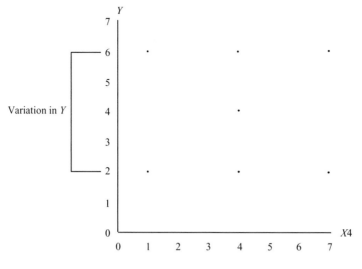

EXHIBIT 10.8a.   Scatterplot Y and X4.

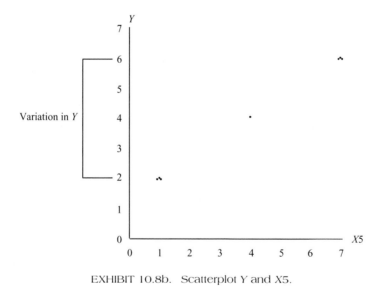

EXHIBIT 10.8b.   Scatterplot Y and X5.

2 to 6. It also ranges from 2 to 6 if $X4 = 7$. The coefficient of determination is $\rho^2_{YX4} = 0.00$. Alternatively, knowledge of $X5$ scores in Exhibit 10.8b provides exact information on Y scores. If $X5 = 1$, $Y = 2$; if $X5 = 7$, $Y = 6$. All Y variation is accounted for by knowing the values of $X5$; the coefficient of determination is $\rho^2_{YX5} = 1.00$.

Another way to think about the coefficient of determination is to represent the variability in Y and X with circles. Exhibit 10.9 illustrates this using Y and $X1$ from Exhibit 10.2. Each circle represents 100% of the variability in the scores for that variable. The overlap shows $\rho^2_{YX1} = .28$, the proportion of variance that is common to the two variables.

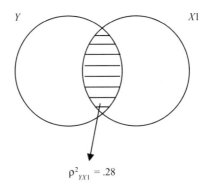

$$\rho^2_{YX1} = .28$$

EXHIBIT 10.9. ρ^2_{YX} explained with circles.

SIMPLE REGRESSION

The correlation coefficient and its informative relative, the coefficient of determination, provide information about a relationship in *standardized* form. It is also often useful to describe a relationship in the original units of the variables.

Suppose an interest in a relationship between annual income (Y) and years of education (X). Among many participant groups, this relationship is positive, ρ_{YX} and $\rho^2_{YX} > 0.0$. However, one also may want to know how changes in years of education relate to changes in level of annual income. For example, what is the average effect of an additional year of education on level of income?

Regression Model

Regression statistics answer questions of the latter sort. Regression describes relationships between a dependent and independent variable in the scale values of the variables. It does so by expressing Y scores as a straight line (linear) function of X scores. This is called the regression line. Y scores can be determined by:

$$Y_i = \alpha + \beta_{YX} X_i + \varepsilon_i$$

where α = regression intercept, where the regression line intersects the vertical line describing Y when $X = 0$

β_{YX} = regression coefficient, the slope of the line representing the change in Y for a unit change in X

ε_i = $\pm$ error in Y predicted by the regression line and the actual Y value for the ith case

The ***regression prediction model*** is:

$$\hat{Y} = \alpha + \beta_{YX} X \qquad (10.5)$$

where $\hat{Y}$ = predicted value of Y given X

Formula 10.5 has no subscripts because it applies to all scores obtained jointly on Y and X. It has no error term, although it will be in error unless $\rho_{YX} = \pm 1.00$. The dependent variable Y thus includes a superscript, $\hat{}$, to denote it is predicted, not actual. The ***regression intercept***,

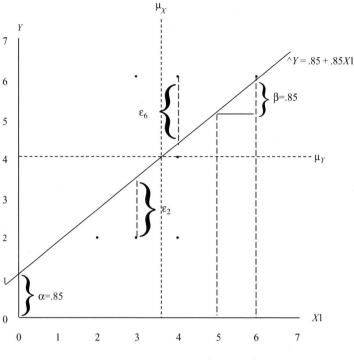

EXHIBIT 10.10.   Scatterplot Y and X1.

α, in the prediction model refers to the predicted value of Y when $X = 0$. The *regression coefficient*, β_{YX}, refers to the predicted change in Y for a unit change in X.

Exhibit 10.10 (as Exhibit 10.3) shows a plot of Y and $X1$ scores from Exhibit 10.2. Exhibit 10.10 adds a regression prediction line with an intercept, α, and regression coefficient, β_{YX}. Errors ε_i in the prediction of Y scores for Cases 2 and 6 are also shown.

The intercept and regression coefficient are identified by using the *least squares criterion*, which establishes α and β_{YX} so that the sum of the squared deviations (errors) between actual Y_i and the value predicted from the regression line $\hat{Y}_i$ is minimized. The value of the PM correlation coefficient is established with this same criterion.

$$\sum(\varepsilon_i)^2 = \sum(y_i - \hat{Y}_i)^2 = \text{minimum}$$

Thus, the least squares criterion provides an estimated regression line that provides the best linear fit between Y and X overall—taking all scores into account.

Regression Formulae

One formula for β_{YX} is obtained by transforming the standardized correlation coefficient into a slope coefficient with the original score variability of both Y and X.

$$\beta_{YX} = (\rho_{YX} \times \sigma_Y)/\sigma_X \tag{10.6}$$

where β_{YX} = simple regression coefficient for X

A formula for α is:

$$\alpha = \mu_Y - \mu_X \times \beta_{YX} \qquad (10.7)$$

where α = regression intercept

NOMINAL INDEPENDENT VARIABLES

So far correlation and regression have been described in situations in which Y and X represent at least nearly interval variables. However, the procedures are equally appropriate when X represents a nominal variable. Values of nominal variables mean that cases with identical values are similar, and cases with different values are dissimilar; no order is implied by the numbers.

The case in which a nominal independent variable has just two values (a dichotomy) is considered here. (Situations in which an independent variable has three or more nominal categories, or in which there are two or more nominal variables, are considered in the next chapter.) Many variables are dichotomous or can be made dichotomous. Examples include responses to a test question (correct or incorrect), gender (female or male), production sector (manufacturing or other), race (majority or minority), type of educational institution (public or private), and assignment in a training intervention (trained group or control group).

Although any two numerical values are permissible, it is convenient to create ***dummy variables*** for dichotomous variables. Dummy variables are two-level nominal variables assigned values of 1 or 0. Thus, correct responses might be assigned 1 and incorrect responses might be assigned 0 for a test question.

RESEARCH HIGHLIGHT 10.3

Nominal Dependent Variables

PM correlation and regression are not appropriate when the dependent variable is nominal and has three or more values. Meaningful interpretation of correlation and regression coefficients is not possible unless such dependent variables have values that are ordered. There are alternative statistical techniques, such as discriminant analysis, that may be appropriate when the dependent variable has more than two nominal values.

PM correlation and regression are conditionally acceptable when the dependent variable is a nominal dichotomy. There are no problems with the use of correlation when the purpose is to describe a set of scores as emphasized in this chapter. There are some problems for both correlation and regression when used to make statistical inferences (see part V and chapter 19).

Regression with a dichotomous nominal Y variable also can be used to describe a set of scores. However, Y values predicted by the regression equation may be outside the dummy variable range of 0 and 1. Logit and probit regression models are more appropriate than PM regression in this situation. They predict values within the 0 and 1 range and are more suitable when statistical inferences are desired.

Case	Y	X
1	6.00	1
2	4.00	1
3	5.00	0
4	4.00	0
5	3.00	0
6	5.00	1
7	4.00	0
μ	4.43	.43
σ	.90	.49
ρ_{YX}		.55
α		4.00
B		1.00
$\mu_{Y|x=0}$		4.00
$\mu_{Y|X=1}$		5.00

EXHIBIT 10.11.   Scores and descriptive statistics on an ordered Y and a two-value nominal variable X.

Exhibit 10.11 shows a data matrix with an ordered Y variable and a dummy coded nominal X variable. Descriptive, correlation, and regression statistics are also shown.

Nominal coding of an independent variable does not change how the correlation and regression statistics are computed or how they are interpreted. Thus, the correlation coefficient tells that the mean product of standard scores for Y and X is .55. The coefficient of determination ($.55^2 = .30$) means that 30% of the variability in Y is explained by variability in X. The intercept shows that the predicted value of Y when $X = 0$ is 4.00, and the regression coefficient signals that a unit change in X is associated with a predicted increase of 1.00 in predicted Y.

However, the intercept and the regression coefficient have additional meaning because X is dummy coded. Not only do they provide information about *predicted* Y values, they also provide information about *average* (mean) Y values. Specifically, the intercept is also equal to mean Y when $X = 0$.

$$\alpha = \mu_{Y|X=0}$$

Furthermore, the intercept plus the regression coefficient is equal to mean Y when $X = 1$.

$$\alpha + \beta_{YX} = \mu_{Y|X=1}$$

Exhibit 10.12 shows the plot of Y and X scores from Exhibit 10.11. The regression prediction line is also shown. This line intersects the Y axis at 4.00, $\mu_{Y|X=0}$. It increases by 1.00 as X goes from 0 to 1 (a unit change) and thus goes through a line drawn perpendicular to $X = 1$ at $Y = 5$, $\mu_{Y|X=1}$. Thus, dummy coding of independent variables provides bonus information.

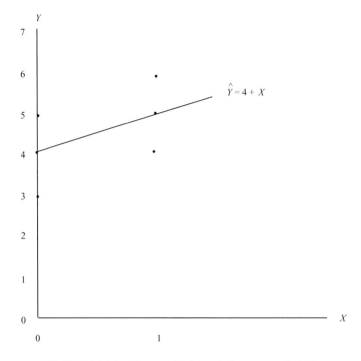

EXHIBIT 10.12. Scatterplot Y and dummy coded X.

<hr>

RESEARCH HIGHLIGHT 10.4

Correlation/Regression and Conceptual Relationships

Researchers hope that the strength of the relationship between X and Y constructs is the major influence on the size of the correlation and regression coefficients obtained from research studies. Further, this does not always imply that the coefficients should be large. The degree of relationship should conform to the conceptual model, large or modest, if the model is valid.

However, correlation or regression coefficients obtained may misrepresent the underlying conceptual relationships for several reasons. Unreliability and other sources of construct invalidity can seriously distort relationships observed from those that apply at a conceptual level (see chapter 17). The observed relationship also may be distorted if the research design has inadequate controls for other independent variables that influence the dependent variable (see chapters 5 and 20). Inappropriate sampling, in which variability among the participants studied does not reflect variability among the population of participants one wants to generalize to, is yet another problem for observed relationships (see part V).

In short, correlation, regression, and any other statistics of relationships can provide good estimates of conceptual relationships only when other characteristics of research design and measurement are also good. Statistics become increasingly necessary to identify relationships between scores on variables as the number of cases become large. However, statistics alone are never sufficient to establish relationships between constructs.

SUMMARY

Correlation and regression are statistical procedures appropriate for identifying relationships between a dependent variable and one or more independent variables. This chapter described correlation and regression methods to identify linear relations among one dependent and one independent variable (simple linear correlation and regression).

It is often useful to plot Y scores (on the vertical axis) and X scores (on the horizontal axis) before calculating correlation or regression statistics. Visual inspection can give insight to the relationship between the two variables.

A *product moment (PM) correlation coefficient* is a statistic that provides a standardized measure of a relationship between two variables. Its permissible limits range between -1.00 and $+1.00$. Values near the extremes indicate a strong positive $(+)$ or negative $(-)$ relationship. Values close to zero indicate little relationship.

The *coefficient of determination* is the square of the correlation coefficient. It is defined as the proportion of variance in the dependent variable that is explained by variation in the independent variable. It can range from 0.00, X scores provide no linear information about Y scores, to 1.00, X scores provide exact information about Y scores.

Regression statistics describe a relationship between Y and X in the original scores of the variables. Scores on Y are described as a linear function of scores in the regression prediction model. That model has an *intercept*, the predicted value of Y when $X = 0.0$; it also has a *regression coefficient*, the predicted change in Y for a unit change in X.

Product moment correlation and regression statistics are calculated using the *least squares criterion*. This criterion results in statistics that provide the best overall linear fit between Y and X. It does so by minimizing the sum of the squared deviations between predicted and actual Y values.

Simple correlation and regression are also appropriate when the independent variable represents a nominal variable with two values. *Dummy variables* are a convenient way to create such variables; one value is assigned 0, the other 1. When dummy coded, the correlation and regression statistics have the same definitions as when X represents an ordered variable. However, in addition, the intercept and regression coefficient can be used to obtain information about mean Y values for the two groups of cases being studied.

FOR REVIEW

Terms to Know

Product moment correlation coefficient: A statistic that describes the degree of linear relationship between two variables in a standardized form ranging between -1.00 and $+1.00$.

   Phi coefficient: A correlation coefficient, sometimes calculated when both variables are dichotomous.

   Point-biserial correlation coefficient: A correlation coefficient, sometimes calculated when one variable is ordered and the other has two values.

   Rho coefficient: A correlation coefficient, sometimes calculated when the variables represent only rank order.

Covariance: A statistic that provides information about how values of two variables go together. It is the average cross-product of the deviations of the values of each variable about its respective mean.

Standard score: A score that results by subtracting its distribution mean and dividing the result by the distribution standard deviation.

Standard score distribution: A distribution of scores on a variable that have been transformed to mean = 0.0 and standard deviation = 1.0.

Coefficient of determination: The square of the correlation coefficient. A statistic that reports the proportion of linear variance in one variable that is explained or associated with variance in another variable.

Regression: Describes relationships between a dependent and an independent variable in the scale values of the variables.

Regression intercept: A statistic that reports the predicted value of the dependent variable when the independent variable is equal to 0.0.

Regression coefficient: A statistic that reports the predicted change in the value of the dependent variable for a unit change (change of 1.0) in the independent variable.

Least squares criterion: A rule that establishes the regression line so that the sum of the squared deviations between the actual dependent variable values and the values predicted are minimized.

Dummy variable: A nominal variable with two values coded 0 and 1.

Formulae to Use

Covariance

$$\text{CoVar}_{YX} = \sum [(Y_i - \mu_Y) \times (X_i - \mu_X)]/N \tag{10.1}$$

where μ_Y and μ_X = means (Formula 9.1) of Y and X, respectively
N = number of cases

Standard score

$$z_{Xi} = (x_i - \mu_X)/\sigma_X \tag{10.3}$$

where σ_X = is the standard deviation of X

Correlation coefficient

$$\rho_{YX} = \text{CoVar}_{YX}/(\sigma_Y \times \sigma_X) \tag{10.2a}$$

where σ_Y is the standard deviation of Y

$$\rho_{YX} = \sum (z_{Yi} \times z_{Xi})/N \tag{10.2b}$$

Coefficient of determination

$$\rho_{YX}^2 = \left[\sum (z_{Yi} \times z_{Xi})/N \right]^2 \tag{10.4}$$

Regression prediction model

$$\hat{Y} = \alpha + B_{YX} X \tag{10.5}$$

where $\hat{Y}$ is the predicted value of Y
α is the intercept, $\hat{Y}$ when $X = 0.0$
β_{YX} is the regression coefficient, the predicted change in Y for a unit change in X
Regression coefficient

$$\beta_{YX} = (\rho_{YX} \times \sigma_Y)/\sigma_X \qquad (10.6)$$

Regression intercept

$$\alpha = \mu_Y - \mu_X \times \beta_{YX} \qquad (10.7)$$

Questions for Review

1. Contrast a standard normal distribution (chapter 9) with a standard score distribution (chapter 10). How are they similar? How do they differ?
2. Use Formula 10.2a to calculate a correlation coefficient between Y and $X2$. Now, use Formula 10.2b to calculate the same coefficient. Your answers should be the same.
3. Assume that the variable gender (female or male) is dummy coded, that females earn less than males and that the correlation between gender and income is positive. How has gender been coded?
4. State verbally how the slope of the regression line, β_{YX}, can be increased when ρ_{YX} is held constant.
5. Assume the regression coefficient is 1.0 and the correlation coefficient is .25 when years of experience is regressed on age in years. What can you say about the regression coefficient if age was coded in months instead of years? What about the correlation coefficient?
6. Use Formulas 10.6 and 10.7 to calculate the estimated regression prediction model (Formula 10.5) with Y as the dependent variable and $X2$ as the independent variable. Repeat, only this time treat $X2$ as the dependent variable and Y as the independent variable. Does it matter which variable is treated as the dependent variable in regression? Why?
7. Other things equal, what happens to the regression intercept α when there is an increase in μ_Y? What happens to the intercept, other things equal, if there is an increase in the regression coefficient β_{YX}?
8. In the matrix below, Y is dependent and X is a dummy coded independent variable. From your knowledge of the bonus information provided by regression in this situation, what is μ_Y for the group coded zero? What is the intercept? What is the regression coefficient?

Y	X
12	0
14	0
13	1
09	1
11	1

Issue to Discuss

1. Simple linear correlation and regression both address relationships between two variables. If you can use one, you can use the other. What conditions would lead you to recommend using correlation instead of regression? Regression instead of correlation?

11

Analysis Applications: Multiple Correlation and Regression

Chapter Outline

- *Graphical Representation*
- *Multiple Correlation*
  - *Multiple Coefficient of Determination*
  - *Examples of the Multiple Coefficient of Determination*
- *Multiple Regression*
  - *Intercept and Partial Regression Coefficients*
  - *Partial Beta Coefficients*
  - *Examples of Multiple Regression*
- *More Than Two Independent Variables*
- *Nominal Independent Variables*
  - *One Nominal Variable With More Than Two Values*
  - *Other Independent Variables*
- *Summary*
- *For Review*
  - *Terms to Know*
  - *Formulae to Use (Text)*
  - *Formulae to Use (Appendix A)*
  - *Questions for Review*
- *Appendix 11A: Contributions of Single Independent Variables in Multiple Correlation*
  - *Squared Semipartial Correlation Coefficient*
  - *Squared Partial Correlation Coefficient*
  - *Examples*
- *Appendix 11B: Another Way to Think About Partial Coefficients*
- *Part IV Suggested Readings*

Chapter 10 characterized simple correlation and regression as "good stuff," because it addresses relationships between variables. In that spirit, this chapter addresses "really good stuff." "Really good" because researchers believe that variation in a dependent variable usually depends on more than one independent variable. Multiple correlation and regression are designed to address just such research issues.

Both are straightforward extensions of simple correlation and regression. This chapter focuses on linear (straight line) relationships between a dependent variable, Y, and two or more independent variables, $X1, X2, \ldots, Xk$. Most of the chapter emphasizes cases in which there are just two independent variables; multiple correlation and regression are easiest to understand when only two independent variables are involved. Fortunately, the logic extends intuitively to more than two independent variables.

The chapter first introduces multiple correlation and regression graphically for two ordered independent variables. More detail is then provided on the two independent variable multiple correlation case. Emphasis is placed on how multiple correlation can be thought of in variance explained terms. This is followed by a description of multiple regression with two independent variables.

The chapter then discusses issues in extending multiple correlation and regression to situations in which there are more than two independent variables. Generalization of multiple correlation and regression to independent variables that are measured at a nominal level is also described.

Two appendixes follow the chapter. The first provides information on ways contributions of individual independent variables can be assessed in a multiple correlation framework. The second describes an alternative way to think about coefficients in multiple correlation and regression.

GRAPHICAL REPRESENTATION

Data introduced in the last chapter (Exhibit 10.2) are repeated at the top of Exhibit 11.1. The bottom of the exhibit reports means, standard deviations, and simple correlation coefficients between these variables. Only the latter statistics are needed to calculate multiple correlation and regression output.

A relationship between a dependent (Y) and two independent (X) variables can be graphed as illustrated in Exhibit 11.2. It shows a scatterplot of the Y and $X1$ and $X2$ from Exhibit 11.1. A linear relationship among these three variables is expressed by a plane that originates at Y. Exhibit 11.2 shows that the plane increases as $X1$ increases and decreases as $X2$ increases.

The general problem for multiple correlation and regression is to establish a plane to best "fit" Y scores from the two X variable scores. The least squares criterion is used for this purpose just as in simple correlation and regression. Multiple correlation and regression statistics are established so the sum of the squared deviations of actual Y minus Y values predicted by the plane is minimized, $\Sigma(y_i - \hat{Y})^2 = \text{minimum}$. Furthermore, just as in the simple case, multiple correlation provides statistics that describe the relationship in standardized form; multiple regression describes the relationship in numerical units of the dependent variable Y.

MULTIPLE CORRELATION

A multiple correlation coefficient, P, describes the degree of linear relationship between one ordered dependent variable and two or more independent variables in standardized form. It

Case	Y	X1	X2	X3	X4	X5
1	2	2	6	4	1	1
2	2	3	3	2	7	1
3	2	4	5	1	4	1
4	4	4	5	7	4	4
5	6	3	4	6	1	7
6	6	4	2	4	4	7
7	6	6	3	4	7	7

Simple Correlations

	μ	σ	Y	X1	X2	X3	X4	X5
Y	4.00	1.85	1.00					
X1	3.71	1.16	.53	1.00				
X2	4.00	1.31	-.59	-.47	1.00			
X3	4.00	1.93	.56	.00	.11	1.00		
X4	4.00	2.27	.00	.65	-.58	-.39	1.00	
X5	4.00	2.78	1.00	.53	-.59	.56	.00	1.00

EXHIBIT 11.1. Scores and statistics of six ordered variables.

ranges from 0.0, indicating no linear relationship, to 1.0, indicating a perfect linear relationship. P is always as large or larger than the absolute value of the largest simple correlation between the dependent and any independent variable.

P is always positive even though one or more simple correlation coefficients with Y may be negative. Think of a multiple correlation coefficient as a simple correlation coefficient between the actual Y values and the Y values predicted by the regression equation. This simple correlation coefficient must be positive if not zero.

Multiple Coefficient of Determination

The square of P, the *multiple coefficient of determination*, P^2, represents the proportion of variance in Y that is jointly accounted for by the independent variables. The multiple coefficient of determination also ranges from 0.0 (no linear variance in Y is explained by the X variables) to 1.0 (all linear variance in Y is explained jointly by the X variables).

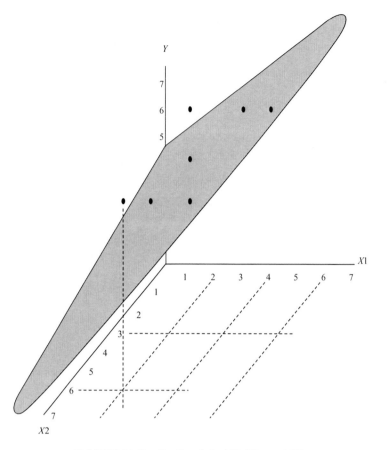

EXHIBIT 11.2.   Scatterplot of Y, X1, and X2.

Researchers usually report and discuss P^2 rather than P; the explanation here focuses on P^2, which is usually called *R square*. Where there are two independent variables, one formula for P^2 is:

$$P^2_{Y \cdot X1X2} = \left(\rho^2_{YX1} + \rho^2_{YX2} - 2 \times \rho_{YX1} \times \rho_{YX2} \times \rho_{X1X2}\right) / \left(1 - \rho^2_{X1X2}\right) \qquad (11.1)$$

where $P^2_{Y \cdot X1X2}$ = multiple coefficient of determination of Y and two independent variables, $X1$ and $X2$

ρ^2_{YX1} = simple coefficient of determination between Y and $X1$ (and likewise for the other variables)

ρ_{YX1} = simple correlation coefficient between Y and $X1$ (and likewise for the other variables)

The simple coefficients of determination between Y and each X contribute to $P^2_{Y \cdot X1X2}$ through the first two terms in the numerator. Other things equal, the higher the simple coefficients of determination between each X and Y, the higher $P^2_{Y \cdot X1X2}$.

However, if $X1$ and $X2$ are also correlated, the second part of the numerator generally reduces $P^2_{Y \cdot X1X2}$. The larger the correlation coefficient between the independent variables, the smaller $P^2_{Y \cdot X1X2}$, other things equal.

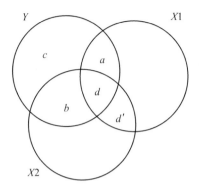

EXHIBIT 11.3.   Variance in Y explained by $X1$ and $X2$.

It is possible that the signs of the coefficients can lead the second part of the numerator to increase $P^2_{Y \cdot X1X2}$. For example, this would occur if ρ_{YX1} and $\rho_{YX2} > 0.0$ and $\rho_{X1X2} < 0.0$. This is an unlikely empirical outcome.

A simple correlation between independent variables is called **multicollinearity**. Some of the variance that each independent variable explains in Y is redundant when there is multicollinearity. The redundant portion must be removed so that the amount of Y variance explained jointly by $X1$ and $X2$ is not overstated. (See appendix 11A for a description of the contribution of single independent variables to the explanation of Y variance and chapter 18 for more detail on multicollinearity.)

Examples of the Multiple Coefficient of Determination

Formula 11.1 can be used to calculate $P^2_{Y \cdot XiXj}$ between Y and any two independent variables. For example, use $X1$ and $X2$ from Exhibit 11.1:

$$P^2_{Y \cdot X1X2} = (.53^2 + -.59^2 - 2 \times .53 \times -.59 \times -.47)/(1 - -.47^2) = .43$$

Forty-three percent of the variance in Y is explained jointly by $X1$ and $X2$. This is less than the sum of the simple coefficients of determination, $(.53^2 + -.59^2 = .63)$, because some of the Y variance that $X1$ and $X2$ explain separately is redundant.

Exhibit 11.3 illustrates the outcome of Formula 11.2 with circles to show variance in the variables as introduced in the last chapter. Each circle represents 100% of the variability in the scores of its variable.

The area designated by a shows the proportion of Y variance explained by $X1$ that is not redundant with $X2$; the area b shows the analogous proportion of Y variance explained by $X2$. The area d shows the proportion of Y explained by both $X1$ and $X2$. (The square of the multicollinearity between $X1$ and $X2$ is shown by $d + d'$.) $P^2_{Y \cdot X1X2}$ is shown in Exhibit 11.3 as:

$$(a + b + d)/(a + b + c + d), \quad \text{or} \quad (1 - c)/(a + b + c + d).$$

Another example from Exhibit 11.1 uses $X1$ and $X3$,

$$P^2_{Y \cdot X1X3} = (.53^2 + .56^2 - 2 \times .53 \times .56 \times .00)/(1 - .00^2) = .59$$

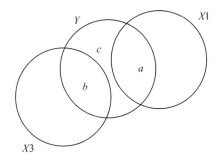

EXHIBIT 11.4.   Variance in Y explained by $X1$ and $X3$.

Fifty-nine percent of the variance in Y is explained jointly by $X1$ and $X3$. This is greater than the Y variance explained by $X1$ and $X2$, even though the simple correlation coefficient of Y and $X2$ is greater than of Y and $X3$. Why is this so?

The explanation can be found in multicollinearity. $X1$ and $X2$ are correlated (multicollinear), but $X1$ and $X3$ are not. Exhibit 11.4 shows the linear variance in Y explained by $X1$ and $X3$; there is no redundant explanation:

$$P^2_{Y \cdot X1X3} = (a+b)/(a+b+c), \quad \text{or} \quad (1-c)/(a+b+c)$$

In field and survey research, independent variables are usually correlated not only with Y but with each other. Thus, typically, $P^2_{Y \cdot X_i X_j} < \rho^2_{Y X_i} + \rho^2_{Y X_j}$ because of multicollinearity. However, in experiments and in some quasi-experiments, researchers may assign cases to levels of independent variables so that there is no multicollinearity. In such cases, Formula 11.1 shows that $P^2_{Y \cdot X_i X_j}$ simplifies to $\rho^2_{Y X_i} + \rho^2_{Y X_j}$.

MULTIPLE REGRESSION

Multiple regression describes relationships between Y and two or more X variables in units of Y. Where there are two independent variables, $X1$ and $X2$, the dependent variable scores can be determined by:

$$Y_i = \alpha + \beta_{Y X1 \cdot X2} \times X1_i + \beta_{Y X2 \cdot X1} \times X2_i + \varepsilon_i$$

where α = regression intercept, where the regression plane intersects the vertical line
describing Y when $X1 = X2 = 0.0$
$\beta_{Y X1 \cdot X2}$ = partial regression coefficient, the change in Y for a unit change in $X1$ controlling
for $X2$, and analogously for $\beta_{Y X2 \cdot X1}$
ε_i = error, the deviation between the Y score predicted by the regression plane and the
actual Y value for the ith case

The multiple regression prediction model for these two independent variables is:

$$\hat{Y}_{X1X2} = \alpha + \beta_{Y X1 \cdot X2} \times X1 + \beta_{Y X2 \cdot X1} \times X2 \qquad (11.2)$$

where $\hat{Y}_{X1X2}$ = predicted value of Y given $X1$ and $X2$

As with the prediction model for simple regression (Formula 10.5), Formula 11.2 has no subscripts, because it applies to all scores obtained jointly on Y, $X1$, and $X2$. It has no error

RESEARCH HIGHLIGHT 11.1

Suppressor Variables

Occasionally a researcher finds a suppressor variable as defined in chapter 5; it is a collinear independent variable that has only a small (often negative) or no relationship with the dependent variable. $X4$ is a suppressor variable in Exhibit 11.1. Use data from Exhibit 11.1 to show:

$$P^2_{Y \cdot X1X4} = (.53^2 + .00^2 - 2 \times .53 \times .00 \times .65)/(1 - .65^2) = .48.$$

Only Y variance explained by $X1$ contributes to the numerator $.53^2 = .28$. The latter part of the numerator drops out because $\rho_{YX4} = 0.00$. However, the denominator is less than 1.0 by virtue of the multicollinearity. Consequently, $P^2_{Y \cdot X1X4} = .48 >$ $.28$. The suppressor variable takes away irrelevant variance from an independent variable ($X1$ in this case) and thus increases the proportion of the remaining $X1$ variance that explains Y. In the language of chapter 5, $X4$ serves as a noise variable not with respect to Y but with $X1$.

term, although it will be in error unless $P^2_{Y \cdot X1X2} = 1.0$. The dependent variable Y_{X1X2} again includes a superscript, ^, to denote it is predicted, not actual.

The ***multiple regression intercept***, α, is now the predicted value of Y when both $X1$ and $X2 = 0.0$. A ***partial regression coefficient***, $\beta_{YX1 \cdot X2}$ ($\beta_{YX2 \cdot X1}$) refers to the predicted change in Y for a unit change in $X1$ ($X2$), holding $X2$ ($X1$) constant. (See appendix 11B for another interpretation of partial regression coefficients.)

Intercept and Partial Regression Coefficients

Formulas for partial regression coefficients for the two independent variables are:

$$\beta_{YX1 \cdot X2} = (\sigma_Y/\sigma_{X1}) \times \left[(\rho_{YX1} - \rho_{YX2} \times \rho_{X1X2})/\left(1 - \rho^2_{X1X2}\right)\right] \qquad (11.3a)$$

$$\beta_{YX2 \cdot X1} = (\sigma_Y/\sigma_{X2}) \times \left[(\rho_{YX2} - \rho_{YX1} \times \rho_{X1X2})/\left(1 - \rho^2_{X1X2}\right)\right] \qquad (11.3b)$$

where $\beta_{YX1 \cdot X2}$ and $\beta_{YX2 \cdot X1}$ = the partial regression coefficient of X1 and X2, respectively
σ_Y and σ_{Xj} = standard deviation of Y and Xj, respectively

A formula for the intercept when there are two independent variables is:

$$\alpha = \mu_Y - \beta_{YX1 \cdot X2} \times \mu_{X1} - \beta_{YX2 \cdot X1} \times \mu_{X2} \qquad (11.4)$$

where α = intercept
μ_Y and μ_{Xj} = mean of Y and Xj, respectively

Partial Beta Coefficients

$\beta_{YX1 \cdot X2}$ and $\beta_{YX2 \cdot X1}$ are unstandardized partial regression coefficients because they are expressed in the original units of the variables. They are attractive for just this reason.

However, researchers sometimes transform regression coefficients to a standardized form. **Beta coefficients** are regression coefficients standardized so that the means of Y and $Xj = 0.0$ and standard deviations $= 1.0$.

In simple regression, beta coefficients are identical to correlation coefficients. This is not true of partial beta coefficients in multiple regression if there is multicollinearity among the independent variables. Formulae for partial beta coefficients in the two independent variable case are:

$$\text{Beta}_{YX1\cdot X2} = \beta_{YX1\cdot X2} \times (\sigma_{X1}/\sigma_Y) \tag{11.5a}$$

$$\text{Beta}_{YX2\cdot X1} = \beta_{YX2\cdot X1} \times (\sigma_{X2}/\sigma_Y) \tag{11.5b}$$

where $\text{Beta}_{YX1\cdot X2}$ and $\text{Beta}_{YX2\cdot X1}$ = partial beta coefficients of $X1$ and $X2$, respectively

Partial beta coefficients are an attractive way to express multiple regression results when researchers are interested in assessing the relative contribution of different independent variables to the explanation of the dependent variable. Because they are standardized, beta coefficients can be compared directly to see which has the largest impact on Y, holding other independent variables constant.

Examples of Multiple Regression

From Exhibit 11.1, the partial regression coefficients when Y is regressed on $X1$ and $X2$ are (Formulae 11.3a and 11.3b):

$$\beta_{YX1\cdot X2} = (1.85/1.16) \times [(.53 - -.59 \times -.47)/(1 - .22)] = .52$$
$$\beta_{YX2\cdot X1} = (1.85/1.31) \times [(-.59 - .53 \times -.47)/(1 - .22)] = -.62$$

Y is predicted to increase .52 for a unit change in $X1$ when $X2$ is held constant; it is predicted to decrease .62 for a unit change in $X2$ when $X1$ is held constant.

The multiple regression intercept in this case is (Formula 11.4):

$$\alpha = 4.00 - (.52 \times 3.71) - (-.62 \times 4.00) = 4.55$$

The predicted Y value when $X1 = X2 = 0.0$ is 4.55.

Putting these together, the regression prediction model (Formula 11.2) for $X1$ and $X2$ is:

$$\hat{Y} = 4.55 + .52 \times X1 - .62 \times X2$$

The standardized partial (beta) coefficients are (Formulas 11.5a and 11.5b):

$$\text{Beta}_{YX1\cdot X2} = .52 \times (1.16/1.85) = .33$$
$$\text{Beta}_{YX2\cdot X1} = -.62 \times (1.31/1.85) = -.44$$

Use $X1$ and $X3$ as another example:

$$\beta_{YX1\cdot X3} = (1.85/1.16) \times [(.53 - .56 \times .00)/(1 - .00)] = .85$$
$$\beta_{YX3\cdot X1} = (1.85/1.93) \times [(.56 - .53 \times .00)/(1 - .00)] = .54$$
$$\alpha = 4.00 - (.85 \times 3.71) - (.54 \times 4.00) = -1.31$$

RESEARCH HIGHLIGHT 11.2

Simple and Partial Regression Coefficients

Y regressed on $X1$ to $X3$ in three separate simple equations, Formula 10.6 ($\beta_{YX} = \rho_{YX} \times \sigma_Y/\sigma_X$), yields simple regression coefficients $\beta_{YX1} = .85$, $\beta_{YX2} = -.83$, and $\beta_{YX3} = .54$. Compare these with the partial regression coefficients in the two example prediction models.

When Y is regressed on $X1$ and $X2$, the partial regression coefficients differ from their respective simple regression coefficients. This happens because of multi-collinearity. $X1$ and $X2$ are correlated; the coefficient resulting from a simple regression of Y on either X alone is biased (see chapter 5). However, if there is no correlation between the independent variables, as is true of $X1$ and $X3$, the partial and simple regression coefficients are identical.

and

$$\hat{Y} = -1.31 + .85 \times X1 + .54 \times X3$$

In this example the partial beta coefficients are:

$$\text{Beta}_{YX1 \cdot X3} = .85 \times (1.16/1.85) = .53$$
$$\text{Beta}_{YX3 \cdot X1} = .54 \times (1.93/1.85) = .56$$

Compare the relative size of the unstandardized and standardized partial regression coefficients of $X1$ and $X3$. The results using the standardized formulae 11.5a and 11.5b show $X3$ contributes more than $X1$ to the explanation of Y. The difference between the unstandardized and standardized results is found in the standard deviations of the independent variables. The standard deviation of $X3$ is greater than $X1$. When these are equalized by standardization, $X3$ contributes relatively more than $X1$ to the explanation of Y.

MORE THAN TWO INDEPENDENT VARIABLES

Multiple correlation and regression can be performed with any number of independent variables as long as there are more cases than independent variables. Although the formulae become more complex, the meaning of the statistics extends intuitively from the two independent variable case. An appeal to intuition is made with an example using Y and $X1$ to $X3$ from Exhibit 11.1.

Multiple correlation and regression statistics are shown in Exhibit 11.5. (SPSS for Windows, a statistical software package, was used to calculate all multiple correlation and regression statistics involving three or more independent variables here and elsewhere in the book.) The coefficient of determination $P^2_{Y \cdot X1X2X3} = .81$ indicates the proportion of Y variance that is jointly explained by $X1$, $X2$, and $X3$. Exhibit 11.6 shows this proportion as $(a + b + c + d1 + d2)/(a + b + c + d1 + d2 + e)$ or $(1 - e)/(a + b + c + d1 + d2 + e)$.

Variable	$B_{YXi \cdot XjXk}$	$\text{Beta}_{YXi \cdot XjXk}$
$X1$	.45	.28
$X2$	-.74	-.53
$X3$	.59	.62
α	2.90	
$P^2_{Y \cdot X1X2X3}$	.81	

EXHIBIT 11.5. Multiple correlation and regression output with three independent variables.

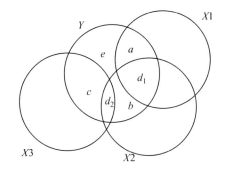

EXHIBIT 11.6. Variance in Y explained by $X1$, $X2$, and $X3$.

Area d_1 represents Y variance redundantly explained by $X1$ and $X2$; d_2 represents Y variance redundantly explained by $X2$ and $X3$. ($X1$ and $X3$ are not collinear, so their explanations of Y variance do not overlap.) The multicollinearity implied by those two areas signals that $P^2_{Y \cdot X1X2X3}$ is smaller than the sum of the simple coefficients of determination ($.53^2 + -.59^2 + .56^2 = .94$).

Exhibit 11.5 also shows regression output for the three independent variables. The intercept $\alpha = 2.90$ is the value of Y predicted when $X1$, $X2$, and $X3 = 0.0$. A partial regression coefficient represents the predicted change in Y for a unit change in one X, holding the other two X variables constant. For example, Y is predicted to change .45 for a unit change in $X1$ if $X2$ and $X3$ do not change. Standardized partial (beta) coefficients are also shown.

NOMINAL INDEPENDENT VARIABLES

Chapter 10 showed how a nominal independent variable with two values can be analyzed by simple correlation and regression. This is done by creating a dummy variable with value 0 or 1. This valuable procedure can be generalized several ways in multiple correlation and regression.

Case	Y	X	X1	X2	X'1	X'2
1	6.00	A	1	0	0	0
2	4.00	A	1	0	0	0
3	5.00	A	1	0	0	0
4	4.00	B	0	1	1	0
5	3.00	C	0	0	0	1
6	5.00	C	0	0	0	1
7	4.00	B	0	1	1	0

			Simple Correlations			Multiple Correlation/Regression Output
	μ	σ	Y	$X1$	$X2$	
						$P^2_{Y \cdot X1X2} = .30$
Y	4.43	.90	1.00			$\alpha = 4.00$
$X1$	.43	.49	.55	1.00		$B_{YX1 \cdot X2} = 1.00$
$X2$	.29	.45	-.30	-.55	1.00	$B_{YX2 \cdot X1} = 0.00$

Note: A = never married, B = currently married, C = formerly but not currently married.

EXHIBIT 11.7.   Scores and descriptive statistics on an ordered Y and a three-value nominal variable.

One Nominal Variable With More Than Two Values

When a nominal independent variable has more than two values, its information can be captured for multiple correlation and regression by creating more than one dummy variable. For example, Exhibit 11.7 shows the dependent variable Y used to illustrate simple correlation and regression. However, this time the independent variable has three values: A, B, and C. For example, these might represent three levels of marital status: A = never married, B = currently married, and C = formerly but not currently married.

Two dummy variables are needed to capture the information of a three-value nominal variable as shown by $X1$ and $X2$. In general, k values of a nominal variable are captured by $k - 1$ dummy variables. Thus, a two-value nominal variable is captured by one dummy variable, $k - 1 = 1$. $X1$ contrasts the never married group (A) with the other two groups (B and C); $X2$ contrasts the currently married group (B) with the other two. Group C (formerly but not currently married) is assigned zeros in both $X1$ and $X2$. The value assigned zeros to all dummy variables is called the ***omitted category*** in multiple regression and correlation.

Multiple correlation and regression can be performed on these two independent variables in the usual way with the calculating procedures already discussed. Thus, from Formula 11.1, the simple correlation coefficients and their squares can be used to obtain $P^2_{Y \cdot X1X2} = .30$. Thirty percent of Y variance is accounted for by the two dummy variables; the three categories of marital status account for 30% of the variance in Y.

Regression output can be calculated with Formulae 11.2 to 11.4. Statistical values from these formulae are shown at the bottom of Exhibit 11.7. The predicted value of Y when $X1$ and $X2 = 0.00$ is $\alpha = 4.00$. The predicted change in Y for a unit change in $X1$ is $\beta_{YX1 \cdot X2} = 1.00$ holding $X2$ constant; the predicted change in Y for a unit change in $X2$ is $\beta_{YX2 \cdot X1} = 0.00$ holding $X1$ constant. These are the standard interpretations of regression statistics.

However, because the two dummy variables are mutually exclusive and exhaustive, bonus information of the sort described in chapter 10 is also provided. Specifically, the intercept $\alpha = 4.00$ is also the mean Y value for the omitted Group C (formerly but not currently married). Mean Y for Group A (never married) is given by the sum of $\alpha + \beta_{YX1 \cdot X2}$, $4.00 + 1.00 = 5.00$; mean Y for Group B (currently married) is given by the sum of $\alpha + \beta_{YX2 \cdot X1}$, $4.00 + 0.00 = 4.00$.

The coding of the nominal variable is arbitrary; any value can serve for the omitted category. For example, $X'1$ and $X'2$ in Exhibit 11.7 show an alternative way to capture information about marital status with two dummy variables. In this case, Group A constitutes the omitted category. Group B is assigned ones in $X'1$ and Group C is assigned ones in $X'2$.

Which value one chooses for the omitted category depends on the group comparisons of greatest interest. The coding of $X1$ and $X2$ provides a contrast between the mean of Y for Group C (formerly married) with the Y means of Groups A ($\beta_{YX1 \cdot X2}$) and B ($\beta_{YX2 \cdot X1}$). Alternatively, the coding of $X'1$ and $X'2$ provides a contrast between the mean of Y for Group A (never married) and the Y means of Groups B ($\beta_{YX' \cdot 1 X'2}$) and C ($\beta_{YX'2 \cdot X'1}$). Contrasts between the mean Y value of the currently married and the other two groups could be obtained by making B the omitted category.

Other Independent Variables

A group of dummy variables representing one nominal independent variable can be included in multiple correlation and regression along with other independent variables. These other independent variables may be ordered, nominal, or a mixture of both.

Exhibit 11.8 illustrates all possibilities. The variables, Y, $X1$, and $X2$ are repeated from Exhibit 11.7. $X3$ is an ordered variable, participants' age. Finally, $X4$ is another nominal variable, gender, dummy coded so males $= 1$, females $= 0$.

Multiple correlation and regression output from data in Exhibit 11.8 are shown in Exhibit 11.9. Results from four regression models are shown. The first repeats the model shown in Exhibit 11.7. It shows the intercept, partial regression coefficients, and multiple coefficient of determination when Y is regressed on just $X1$ and $X2$. As noted, the intercept and partial regression coefficients have the standard interpretation. They also provide bonus information about group means on Y, because $X1$ and $X2$ account for marital status in a mutually exclusive and (when combined in a multiple regression model) exhaustive fashion.

The intercept and partial regression coefficients have only the standard meaning once other independent variables are included with the two variables defining marital status. For example, Model 2 shows results of Y regressed on $X1$ through $X3$ (the ordered independent variable, age). The coefficient for $X1$, 2.31, represents the predicted change in Y for a unit change in $X1$ holding $X2$ and $X3$ constant. It no longer necessarily or typically reflects the mean Y value for the group coded 1 on $X1$ (never married), because $X3$ is also in the model. Age values and marital status values are not mutually exclusive. The intercept is now the predicted Y value for formerly married participants age 0.0, which is a nonexistent group in this data set.

The intercept and partial regression coefficients of $X1$ and $X2$ also refer only to predicted Y values if another dummy variable is added. Model 3 shows results when Y is regressed on $X1$, $X2$, and $X4$. Again, the intercept and coefficients cannot be interpreted in terms of mean Y values for marital status groups, because they are not mutually exclusive with gender. The intercept is now the predicted Y value for formerly married females.

Case	Y	X1	X2	X3	X4
1	6.00	1	0	32	0
2	4.00	1	0	28	1
3	5.00	1	0	40	1
4	4.00	0	1	43	0
5	3.00	0	0	40	0
6	5.00	0	0	51	1
7	4.00	0	1	46	1

Simple Correlations

	μ	σ	Y	X1	X2	X3	X4
Y	4.43	.90	1.00				
X1	.43	.49	.55	1.00			
X2	.29	.45	-.30	-.55	1.00		
X3	40.00	7.31	-.11	-.79	.39	1.00	
X4	.57	.49	.09	.17	-.09	.20	1.00

Note: $X1 = 1$ if never married, $X2 = 1$ if currently married; $X4 = 1$ if male.

EXHIBIT 11.8.   Scores and statistics on an ordered Y and several types of independent variables.

Finally, Exhibit 11.9 also shows the model when all four independent variables are entered in Model 4. In each instance, partial regression coefficients represent predicted changes in Y values for a unit change in the X variable when (now) three other independent variables are held constant. The intercept is the predicted Y value for formerly married females age 0.0.

SUMMARY

Multiple correlation and *regression* generalize simple correlation and regression to cases in which there are an ordered dependent variable and two or more independent variables. The present chapter describes linear multiple correlation and regression and emphasizes situations in which there are just two independent variables.

A *multiple correlation coefficient* describes the degree of linear relationship between one dependent variable and two or more independent variables in a standardized form ranging from

Multiple Regression Models

Variable	(1)	(2)	(3)	(4)
		(Partial Regression Coefficients)		
$X1$	1.00	2.31	1.00	2.99
$X2$	.00	.11	.00	.15
$X3$		.11		.15
$X4$			.00	-.76
α	4.00	-.89	4.00	-2.58
$P^2_{Y \cdot X1X2}$	.30	.58	.30	.70

EXHIBIT 11.9. Multiple correlation and regression output from Exhibit 11.8.

0.0 to 1.0. Its square, the *multiple coefficient of determination*, represents the proportion of Y variance that is jointly accounted for by the X variables. It ranges from 1.0 (all Y variance is explained by the X variables) to 0.0 (no Y variance is explained by the X variables).

A *multiple regression* equation describes relationships between Y and two or more X variables in units of Y. The *multiple regression intercept* of this equation is the predicted value of Y when all X variables have a value of zero. A *partial regression coefficient* refers to the predicted change in Y for a unit change in one X variable, holding the other X variables constant. A *beta coefficient* is a standardized regression coefficient.

Multicollinearity is represented by a nonzero correlation among independent variables in a multiple correlation or regression model. Interpretation of multiple correlation and regression output becomes more complex when there is multicollinearity.

As with simple correlation and regression, multiple correlation and regression can be performed on independent variables that are measured at a nominal level. When a nominal X variable has more than two values, a set of dummy variables can be created for use in multiple correlation and regression; $k - 1$ dummy variables are needed to account for k values of a nominal X variable. The nominal value that is scored zero for all the dummy variables is called the *omitted category*. Mean values of Y can be obtained from regression coefficients when only the dummy variables representing one nominal variable are included in a multiple regression model. Multiple correlation and regression statistics have standard interpretations when a nominal variable is dummy coded and included with other independent variables.

FOR REVIEW

Terms to Know

Multiple correlation coefficient: Describes the degree of linear relationship between one ordered dependent variable and two or more independent variables. It describes the relationship in standardized form and ranges from 0.0 to 1.0.

Multiple coefficient of determination: Describes the proportion of linear variance in one ordered dependent variable that is accounted for jointly by two or more independent variables. It ranges from 0.0 to 1.0.

Multiple regression: Describes relationships between a dependent and two or more independent variables in units of the dependent variable.

 Multiple regression intercept: The predicted change in Y when all independent variables $= 0.0$.

 Partial regression coefficient: The predicted change in Y for a unit change in one independent variable when all other independent variables in the equation are held constant.

 Beta coefficient: A standardized (mean $= 0.0$, standard deviation $= 1.0$ of all variables in the model) regression coefficient. In simple regression, the beta coefficient is identical to the simple correlation coefficient.

Multicollinearity: Nonzero correlation among independent variables in a multiple correlation or regression context.

Omitted category: The value of a nominal variable assigned zeros to all dummy variables established to account for the nominal variable in multiple correlation and regression.

Squared semipartial (or *part*) *correlation coefficient*: Represents the proportion of the total variance in Y that is uniquely (nonredundantly) explained by an independent variable (see appendix 11A).

Squared partial correlation coefficient: Represents the proportion of Y variance explained by an independent variable that is not otherwise explained (see appendix 11A).

Formulae to Use (Text)

Multiple coefficient of determination for two independent variables

$$P^2_{Y \cdot X1X2} = \left(\rho^2_{YX1} + \rho^2_{YX2} - 2 \times \rho_{YX1} \times \rho_{YX2} \times \rho_{X1X2} \right) / \left(1 - \rho^2_{X1X2} \right) \tag{11.1}$$

where $P^2_{Y \cdot X1X2}$ = multiple coefficient of determination of Y and two independent variables, $X1$ and $X2$

  ρ^2_{YX1} = simple coefficient of determination between Y and $X1$ (and likewise for the other variables)

  ρ_{YX1} = simple correlation coefficient between Y and $X1$ (and likewise for the other variables)

Multiple regression prediction model for two independent variables

$$\hat{Y}_{X1X2} = \alpha + \beta_{YX1 \cdot X2} \times X1 + \beta_{YX2 \cdot X1} \times X2 \tag{11.2}$$

Partial regression coefficients for two independent variables

$$\beta_{YX1 \cdot X2} = (\sigma_Y / \sigma_{X1}) \times \left[(\rho_{YX1} - \rho_{YX2} \times \rho_{X1X2}) / \left(1 - \rho^2_{X1X2} \right) \right] \tag{11.3a}$$

$$\beta_{YX2 \cdot X1} = (\sigma_Y / \sigma_{X2}) \times \left[(\rho_{YX2} - \rho_{YX1} \times \rho_{X1X2}) / \left(1 - \rho^2_{X1X2} \right) \right] \tag{11.3b}$$

where σ_Y and σ_{Xj} = standard deviation of Y and Xj, respectively

Intercept when there are two independent variables

$$\alpha = \mu_Y - \beta_{YX1 \cdot X2} \times \mu_{X1} - \beta_{YX2 \cdot X1} \times \mu_{X2} \tag{11.4}$$

where μ_Y and μ_{Xi} = mean of Y and Xi, respectively

Beta coefficients when there are two independent variables

$$\text{Beta}_{YX1\cdot X2} = \beta_{YX1\cdot X2} \times (\sigma_{X1}/\sigma_Y) \qquad (11.5a)$$

$$\text{Beta}_{YX2\cdot X1} = \beta_{YX2\cdot X1} \times (\sigma_{X2}/\sigma_Y) \qquad (11.5b)$$

Formulae to Use (Appendix A)

Squared semipartial correlation coefficients when there are two independent variables (see appendix 11A)

$$sp^2_{YX1\cdot X2} = P^2_{Y\cdot X1X2} - \rho^2_{YX2} \qquad (11A.1a)$$

$$sp^2_{YX2\cdot X1} = P^2_{Y\cdot X1X2} - \rho^2_{YX1} \qquad (11A.1b)$$

Squared partial correlation coefficients for two independent variables (see appendix 11A)

$$pp^2_{YX1\cdot X2} = \left(P^2_{Y\cdot X1X2} - \rho^2_{YX2}\right) / \left(1 - \rho^2_{YX2}\right) \qquad (11A.2a)$$

$$pp^2_{YX2\cdot X1} = \left(P^2_{Y\cdot X1X2} - \rho^2_{YX1}\right) / \left(1 - \rho^2_{YX1}\right) \qquad (11A.2b)$$

Questions for Review

1. Use the descriptive and simple correlation results below to answer the following questions.

	Mean	SD	Y	X1	X2	X3	X4	X5	X6	X7
			Simple Correlation Coefficients							
Y	100	10	1.00							
X1	5	1	.50	1.00						
X2	10	4	.40	.40	1.00					
X3	7	2	−.30	−.20	−.10	1.00				
X4	8	3	.30	.30	.30	−.30	1.00			
X5	11	5	.20	.10	.00	−.15	.05	1.00		
X6	10	2	.50	1.00	.40	−.20	.30	.10	1.00	
X7	4	1	.00	.30	.20	−.30	.20	.20	.30	1.00

a. How much variance in Y is explained by $X1$ and $X2$?
b. How much variance in Y is explained by $X1$ and $X3$?
c. Consider a regression of Y on $X1$ and $X4$. What is the intercept? What is the partial regression coefficient and partial beta coefficient for $X1$?
d. Consider a regression of Y on $X6$ and $X4$. What is the intercept? What is the partial regression coefficient and partial beta coefficient for $X6$?
e. Explain the similarities and differences for the coefficients $X1$ and $X6$ in Answers c and d.

f. Calculate P^2_{YX1X7}. Explain why this result explains more variance than the simple sum of ρ^2_{YX1} and ρ^2_{YX7}.

g. From appendix A, what is $s\rho^2_{YX1 \cdot X2}$?

h. In words, what does your answer to question g mean?

2. Compare and contrast a partial regression coefficient with a partial beta coefficient.

3. Explain what the least squares criterion accomplishes in multiple regression.

4. From appendix 11A, compare and contrast a squared semipartial correlation coefficient with a squared partial correlation coefficient. When would they be equal? Which one will generally be larger?

5. Be prepared to recognize the implications, if any, of changes in N, the number of observations, the mean of Y, $X1$, and/or $X2$, the standard deviation of Y, $X1$, and/or $X2$, the simple (zero-order) correlation coefficients among any of the three pairs (r_{YX1}, r_{YX2}, and r_{X1X2}) for the following outcomes:

a. The raw or standardized (Beta) regression coefficients,

b. The corrected or uncorrected multiple coefficient of determination, and

c. The partial or semipartial correlation coefficients (from appendix 11A).

For example, other things equal, what outcomes (a through c) change as N (the number of observations) changes? As another example, does an increase in the standard deviation of $X1$, other things equal, change the regression coefficient for $X1$? the standardized (beta) regression coefficient for $X1$? If the answer is yes in either case, will the coefficient increase or decrease? What are your answers to the preceding three questions if the standard deviation of Y were to increase?

6. A nominal independent variable with three mutually exclusive and exhaustive values (A, B and C) has been recorded into two dummy variables (with C omitted). The resulting regression equation is:

$$\hat{Y} = 10 + 3 \times XA - 4 \times XB$$

Write the regression equation (with the appropriate numbers for the intercept and partial regression coefficients) if A were the omitted category instead of C.

7. An investigator makes three mutually exclusive dummy variables out of race (majority, minority) and gender (female, male) by creating the variables majority males $= 1$, else 0; majority females $= 1$, else 0, and minority males $= 1$, else 0. (Minority females serve as the omitted category.) These variables serve as independent variables in a regression equation.

a. Are the independent variables collinear?

b. The dependent variable is income and the coefficient for majority males is positive. In words, what does that partial coefficient mean?

APPENDIX 11A: CONTRIBUTIONS OF SINGLE INDEPENDENT VARIABLES IN MULTIPLE CORRELATION

Multiple correlation coefficients and multiple coefficients of determination provide information about the relationship between Y and the independent variables combined. It sometimes is also of interest to know how each independent variable contributes to the relationship with Y in correlational terms.

The issue is not straightforward because of multicollinearity. There is no way to adequately partition the collinear variance among the independent variables. Thus, the two standard methods for addressing the contributions of each independent variable ignore Y variance, which is explained jointly by the independent variables (e.g., d in Exhibit 11.3). Again, the focus is on the square of the coefficients to cast the discussion in variance explained terms.

Squared Semipartial Correlation Coefficient

A *squared semipartial* (or *part*) *correlation coefficient* represents the proportion of the total variance in Y that is uniquely (nonredundantly) explained by an independent variable. In the case of $X1$ and $X2$, $sp^2_{YX1 \cdot X2}$ is shown by area $a/(a + b + c + d)$ in Exhibit 11.3; $sp^2_{YX2 \cdot X1}$ is shown by area $b/(a + b + c + d)$.

Formulae for a two independent variable case are:

$$sp^2_{YX1 \cdot X2} = P^2_{Y \cdot X1X2} - \rho^2_{YX2} \tag{11A.1a}$$

$$sp^2_{YX2 \cdot X1} = P^2_{Y \cdot X1X2} - \rho^2_{YX1} \tag{11A.1b}$$

where $sp^2_{YX1 \cdot X2}$ and $sp^2_{YX2 \cdot X1}$ = the squared semipartial correlation coefficient of $X1$ and $X2$, respectively

Squared Partial Correlation Coefficient

A *squared partial correlation coefficient* represents the proportion of Y variance explained by an independent variable that is not otherwise explained. In the case of $X1$ and $X2$, $p\rho^2_{YX1 \cdot X2}$ is shown by area $a/(a + c)$ in Exhibit 11.3. $p\rho^2_{YX2 \cdot X1}$ is shown by area $b/(b + c)$.

Formulae for a two independent variable case are:

$$p\rho^2_{YX1 \cdot X2} = \left(P^2_{Y \cdot X1X2} - \rho^2_{YX2}\right) / \left(1 - \rho^2_{YX2}\right) \tag{11A.2a}$$

$$p\rho^2_{YX2 \cdot X1} = \left(P^2_{Y \cdot X1X2} - \rho^2_{YX1}\right) / \left(1 - \rho^2_{YX1}\right) \tag{11A.2b}$$

where $p\rho^2_{YX1 \cdot X2}$ and $p\rho^2_{YX2 \cdot X1}$ = the squared partial correlation coefficient of $X1$ and $X2$, respectively

The numerator of 11A.2a (11A.2b) is the same as for the squared semipartial correlation coefficient, 11A.1a (11A.1b). The difference is in the denominators. In 11A.1a (11A.1b) the denominator is (implied) 1.0. Variance accounted for by $X1$ ($X2$) is the proportion of *all* Y variance.

In Formula 11A.2a (11A.2b) the denominator is 1.0 minus the variance accounted for uniquely and redundantly by $X2$ ($X1$). Thus, the square of the partial correlation coefficient tells how much of the *otherwise unexplained* Y variance is accounted for by $X1$ ($X2$). Because the denominator of 11A.2a (11A.2b) is smaller than 11A.1a (11A.1b), the squared partial correlation of $X1$ ($X2$) is larger than the squared semipartial correlation coefficient of $X1$ ($X2$). [This is true unless $X2$ ($X1$) is uncorrelated with Y. Then $sp^2_{YX1} = p\rho^2_{YX1}(sp^2_{YX2} = p\rho^2_{YX2})$.]

Examples

Consider again the scores on the variables in Exhibit 11.1. The squared semipartial correlation coefficients for $X1$ and $X2$ are,

$$sp^2_{YX1 \cdot X2} = .43 - .35 = .08$$

$$sp^2_{YX2 \cdot X1} = .43 - .28 = .15$$

Eight percent of Y variance is uniquely explained by $X1$; 15 percent is explained by $X2$. The unique contributions of the two do not sum to the total variance explained in Y by $X1$ and $X2$ because of multicollinearity.

The square of the partial correlation coefficients for $X1$ and $X2$ are:

$$pp_{YX1 \cdot X2}^2 = (.43 - .35)/(1 - .35) = .13$$

$$pp_{YX2 \cdot X1}^2 = (.43 - .28)/(1 - .28) = .21$$

Thirteen percent of Y variance that is unexplained by $X2$ is explained by $X1$. Twenty-one percent of Y variance that is unexplained by $X1$ is explained by $X2$. The square of the partial correlation coefficient of $X1$ ($X2$) is greater than the square of the semipartial correlation coefficient of $X1$ ($X2$) because $\rho_{YX2}^2 > 0.0$ ($\rho_{YX1}^2 > 0.0$).

Consider $X1$ and $X3$ as another example from Exhibit 11.1.

$$sp_{YX1 \cdot X3}^2 = .59 - .31 = .28$$

$$sp_{YX3 \cdot X1}^2 = .59 - .28 = .31$$

In this case, the squared semipartial correlation coefficients equal their corresponding simple coefficients of determination, because there is no collinearity between $X1$ and $X3$. The sum of the squared semipartial correlation coefficients also sum to $P_{Y \cdot X1X3}^2 = .59$.

The square of the partial correlation coefficients in this example are:

$$pp_{YX1 \cdot X3}^2 = (.59 - .31)/(1 - .31) = .41$$

$$pp_{YX3 \cdot X1}^2 = (.59 - .28)/(1 - .28) = .43$$

Forty-one percent of Y variance not explained by $X3$ is explained by $X1$. Forty-three percent of Y variance not explained by $X1$ is explained by $X3$.

Neither of these two methods of expressing the effect of a single independent variable on Y is inherently superior. Squared semipartial correlation coefficients are used more frequently in organizational research.

APPENDIX 11B: ANOTHER WAY TO THINK ABOUT PARTIAL COEFFICIENTS

In general, partial regression or correlation coefficients are defined as showing the contribution of one independent variable holding other independent variables in the model constant. For example, a partial regression coefficient is the predicted change in Y for a unit change in an independent variable holding other independent variables constant. This is useful because it correctly indicates the predicted change in Y for a unit change in an independent variable if there were no changes in other independent variables in the multiple regression model.

However, if there is multicollinearity, a change in values on one independent variable means that values of collinear independent variables also must change. Thus, although the definition is technically correct, it is of limited value unless the independent variables are uncorrelated.

There is another way to think about partial regression and correlation coefficients. This alternative is illustrated with a partial regression coefficient, although it also can be applied to the partial or semipartial correlation coefficient and their squares. Specifically, a partial regression coefficient also approximates the weighted average simple regression coefficient across all values of other independent variables in the model.

To illustrate, consider a case in which Y scores are regressed on $X1$ and $X2$ as shown in Exhibit 11B.1. Y and $X1$ are ordered variables, $X2$ is a dummy variable. A regression of Y on $X1$ and $X2$ produces (from Formula 11.2):

$$\hat{Y}_{X1X2} = 1.62 + .77X1 - .13X2$$

A unit change in $X1$ leads to a predicted change of .77 in Y holding $X2$ constant.

Now subgroup on $X2$ and calculate simple regressions of Y on $X1$ for each subgroup. From Formula 10.6, $\beta_{YX1|X2=0} = .50$ and $\beta_{YX1|X2=1} = 1.20$. The weighted (by the number of cases) average of these simple regression coefficients approximates the partial regression coefficient $[(10 \times .50 + 5 \times 1.2)/15 = .73]$.

Thinking of a partial regression coefficient as a weighted average of simple regression coefficients helps to understand its limited value when a relationship between Y and Xi is moderated by Xj (chapter 5). For example, consider the regression of Y on $X3$ and the dummy

Case	Y	$X1$	$X2$	$X3$	$X4$
01	3	5	0	1	0
02	7	4	0	5	0
03	2	1	0	3	0
04	7	2	0	5	0
05	6	2	0	2	0
06	4	4	0	3	0
07	1	1	0	3	0
08	2	3	0	1	0
09	1	2	0	1	0
10	4	3	0	2	0
11	4	3	1	3	1
12	2	1	1	5	1
13	5	5	1	1	1
14	7	4	1	2	1
15	1	2	1	3	1

				Simple Correlations			
	μ	σ	Y	$X1$	$X2$	$X3$	$X4$
Y	3.73	2.17	1.00				
$X1$	2.80	1.32	.47	1.00			
$X2$	.33	.47	.02	.11	1.00		
$X3$	2.67	1.40	.27	-.40	.07	1.00	
$X4$	.33	.47	.02	.11	1.00	.07	1.00

EXHIBIT 11B.1. Scores and statistics for partial regression coefficient examples.

variable $X4$ from Exhibit 11B.1. The multiple regression prediction model is:

$$\hat{Y}_{X3X4} = 2.67 + .40 \times X3 + .02 \times X4$$

The partial regression coefficient indicates a predicted increase in Y of .40 for a unit increase in $X3$ holding $X4$ constant. Subgrouping on $X4$ provides a different picture. The simple regression coefficients are $\beta_{YX3|X4=0} = 1.02$, while $\beta_{YX3|X4=1} = -1.04$. The $YX3$ relationship is positive when $X4 = 0$, but negative when $X4 = 1$. The weighted average ($10 \times 1.02 + 5 \times -1.04 = .33$) approximates the partial regression coefficient of .40. However, neither is informative about the relationship within each $X4$ subgroup. (Chapter 19 shows another way multiple regression can be performed to account for moderator variables.)

PART IV SUGGESTED READINGS

The topics covered in part IV in no way exhaust basic statistics. If you have used a basic statistics book you are probably best off returning to it for issues not covered here. Cryer and Miller (1993) and Hays (1988) are my personal favorites. Both are a little demanding as introductory books, but both are very competent.

There are also many books available just on multiple regression and correlation (e.g., Bobko, 1995; Cohen, Cohen, West and Aiken, 2003; Frees, 1996; Pedhazur, 1982). I especially like two of these. Cohen et al.'s data analysis as opposed to a statistical approach parallels the viewpoint taken here. They do an especially good job explaining the use of multiple regression and correlation for testing different kinds of conceptual models (see also chapters 19 and 20). I also like Frees's treatment of multiple regression for causal analysis and his coverage of the use of regression for time series analyses.

V
Statistical Validation

12

Statistical Inference
Foundations

Chapter Outline

- *Probability*
  - *Random Variables*
  - *Independent Random Variables*
- *Probability Distributions*
  - *Discrete Probability Distributions*
  - *Continuous Probability Distributions*
- *Sampling Distributions*
  - *Statistics and Parameters*
  - *Sampling Distribution of the Mean*
  - *Other Sampling Distributions*
- *Summary*
- *For Review*
  - *Terms to Know*
  - *Formulae to Use*
  - *Questions for Review*
  - *Issues to Discuss*

Part IV discussed the use of statistics to describe scores on variables and to identify the strength and direction of relationships between variables. Statistics applied in this way help describe characteristics of cases studied in research. In terms of the research model introduced in chapter 2, statistics used this way help establish empirical relationships linking scores on independent and dependent variables.

But chapter 2 also pointed out that statistics are used to help make two types of inference. ***Statistical inference*** uses probability theory to draw conclusions that transcend the relationships between variables per se. One of these involves inferences about whether an observed relationship is due to chance or to coincidence. For example, a study is conducted in which a group of young students are randomly assigned to one of two reading programs. One program includes explicit parental involvement including scheduled sessions in which parents read to their children at home. The other group is taught reading at school in the standard way with no special effort to obtain parental participation. Reading achievement test scores are administered at the end of the school year, and it is found that the students whose parents participated score higher, on average, than students taught in the standard way.

Chapter 2 introduced and defined *internal statistical validation* procedures as those used to infer whether a difference between the two groups is large enough to conclude that it is due to the difference in reading programs rather than to chance differences in reading achievement that might be expected between any two groups of randomly selected students. Statistical inferences of this sort are most appropriately made in experimental studies in which cases (students in the example) are randomly assigned to levels of an independent variable (reading program).

A second type of statistical inference introduced in chapter 2 is made in survey research in which a probability sample is drawn from some identifiable population. For example, a polling agency conducts a probability sample of adult citizens in a metropolitan area. Sample members are asked to state preferences between two mayoral candidates. Candidate A is preferred to Candidate B among sample members. *Statistical generalization validation* procedures are used to infer whether it is reasonable to also conclude that Candidate A is preferred in the population from which the sample was drawn.

Exhibit 12.1 illustrates these two types of inference. Internal statistical inference refers to conclusions made about differences or relationships observed in the cases studied. Statistical

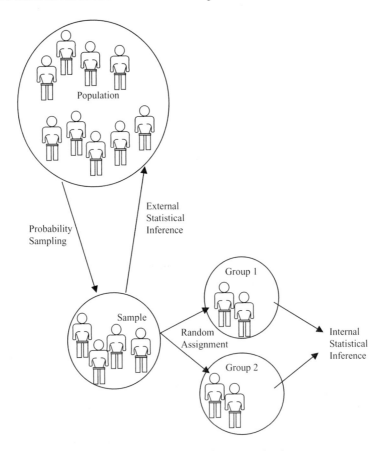

EXHIBIT 12.1.   Two types of statistical inference.

generalization validity refers to conclusions made about a probable population statistic based on a sample statistic.

Exhibit 12.1 also indicates that both types of inference use procedures that rely on knowledge developed about chance phenomena. In the first example, it is possible that the group of students attaining higher reading achievement scores would have done so regardless of whether they had been assigned to the parental involvement group. By the luck of the draw, students that form this group may simply have greater reading aptitude than the other group. Analogously, the sample of citizens drawn from the population may not be representative of that population. Sample preferences for Candidate A may not reflect citizen opinions in the population where Candidate B may be preferred.

Thus, the validity of both internal and external statistical inference is uncertain. Validation procedures that account for such uncertainty are described in chapter 13. These procedures allow researchers to quantify the risks they confront when making statistical inferences.

However, use of these procedures requires that you first understand how uncertainty operates in statistical validation contexts. This chapter introduces issues that underlie statistical validation. Briefly, statistical validation requires knowledge of probability distributions and sampling distributions. These, in turn, require knowledge of random variables and probability. Accordingly, the chapter begins with a discussion of probability and random variables; it then describes probability distributions and sampling distributions.

It turns out that these probability issues and distributions play the same role for both internal and external statistical validity. Thus, to simplify the discussion, examples and illustrations focus only on external statistical validation. Implications of the ideas developed in this chapter for internal statistical validation are explained in chapter 13.

PROBABILITY

The basic building block for statistical validation is probability. **Probability** (P_r) specifies the likelihood that a particular value of a variable will be obtained. Probability can range from 0.0 (the value is certain not to occur) to 1.0 (the value is certain to occur). When P_r is greater than (>) 0.0 but less than (<) 1.0, there is uncertainty about whether the value will occur.

There are many types of probability and interesting issues associated with them. However, only the probability topics needed to understand basic statistical inference issues are addressed here.

Random Variables

Statistical inferences are made about values of variables. For example, an inference is made about the proportion of citizens preferring Candidate A in the population. A proportion is a variable that can take on different values. The population proportion cannot be known exactly based on a sample proportion. However, when a sample is chosen in particular ways the population proportion can be known probabilistically. In such cases, the population proportion becomes a *random variable*. The values of the variable are not known exactly, but they are described by probability.

Consider an illustration. The outcome of a coin toss is a random variable that can take on two values: heads or tails. It is a random variable because each value is determined by its probability. If the coin is tossed many times it will land heads about half the time, P_r (heads) = .50, and tails about half the time, P_r (tails) = $1.00 - .50$. Although the outcome of any one toss is unknown, the probability is known. Statistical inference capitalizes on this type of probabilistic knowledge.

Values of random variables are **mutually exclusive**, meaning that if one value occurs then another value cannot, and vice versa. For example, one toss of a coin can produce either a head or a tail, but not both. They are also **exhaustive**, meaning that one value must occur. A toss of a coin must produce a head or a tail. When values of a random variable are mutually exclusive and exhaustive, they must sum to $P_r = 1.0$. For example, the probability of a head or tail following a coin toss:

$$P_r(\text{head or tail}) = P_r(\text{head}) + P_r(\text{tail}) = (.5) + (1.0 - .5) = 1.0$$

Independent Random Variables

One additional property of probability, **independence**, is needed to understand how probability and sampling distributions are developed. Two different random variables are independent if the probabilities associated with values of one provide no information about the probabilities of values of the other. Consider the outcome of each of two coin tosses as variables. The variables are independent if the probabilities of the values obtained on the second toss remain the same regardless of the value obtained on the first toss. Probabilities of values of two or more random variables that are independent are multiplicative. For example:

$$P_r(\text{toss 1} = \text{head and toss 2} = \text{head}) = P_r(\text{toss 1} = \text{head}) \times P_r(\text{toss 2} = \text{head})$$
$$= (.5) \times (.5) = .25$$

PROBABILITY DISTRIBUTIONS

A **probability distribution** summarizes probabilities associated with values of a random variable. Characteristics of these distributions depend on whether the probability distribution is of a discrete or continuous variable (chapter 8).

Discrete Probability Distributions

Discrete random variables have a countable number of identifiable values. Accordingly, a **discrete probability distribution** has a probability associated with each value of the random variable. To illustrate, create a random variable by counting the number of heads after three tosses of a coin. Four discrete values of this random variable are possible: 0, 1, 2, or 3 heads.

RESEARCH HIGHLIGHT 12.1

Variables That Are Independent and Independent Variables

Researchers use the term "independent" in two distinctly different ways. Independent means two variables have no connection in probability theory. The expected correlation coefficient between two variables that are independent is 0.00. Alternatively, in causal models as described in chapter 2, independent variables are assumed to influence dependent variables; there is an expected relationship. The correlation coefficient between an independent and a dependent variable in the latter context is assumed to be greater or less than 0.00.

These four values are mutually exclusive (only one value can occur after three tosses) and exhaustive (one of the values must occur).

Exhibit 12.2 shows all possible outcomes of this variable in a probability tree. For example, the first toss might result in a tail ($P_r = 1.0 - .5$), the second a head ($P_r = .5$), and the third a head ($P_r = .5$). Because outcomes of each toss are independent, the probability of this sequence of values (t, h, h) is:

$$P_r(\text{tails}) \times P_r(\text{heads}) \times P_r(\text{heads}) = (1.0 - .5) \times (.5) \times (.5) = .125.$$

Exhibit 12.2 shows that there are eight possible outcome sequences. Because the probability of a head or tail on each toss is equal, each outcome after three tosses has an equal probability of occurring.

The results shown in the probability tree of Exhibit 12.2 can be combined and summarized in a discrete probability distribution, a bar chart, as shown in Exhibit 12.3. This distribution shows each value of a random variable on the horizontal axis and the probability of each value on the vertical axis.

In the example, $P_r(0 \text{ heads}) = .125$, there is only one combination of values that leads to zero heads, all tails (the leftmost set of branches in Exhibit 12.2). Alternatively, there are three combinations that lead to one head:

$$P_r(\text{toss } 1 = \text{head, toss } 2 = \text{tail, toss } 3 = \text{tail}) +$$
$$P_r(\text{toss } 1 = \text{tail, toss } 2 = \text{head, toss } 3 = \text{tail}) +$$
$$P_r(\text{toss } 1 = \text{tail, toss } 2 = \text{tail, toss } 3 = \text{head}) = .125 + .125 + .125 = .375$$

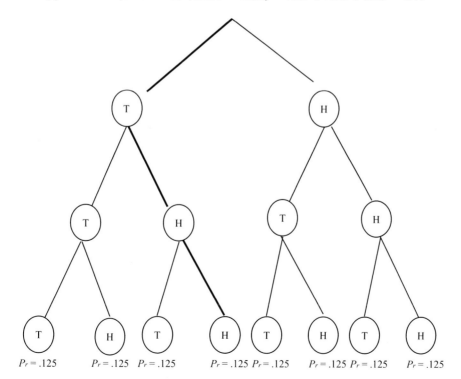

EXHIBIT 12.2. Probability tree.

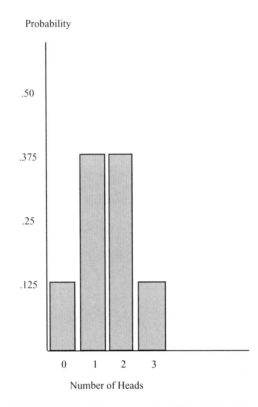

EXHIBIT 12.3.   Discrete probability distribution.

This discrete probability distribution illustrates a ***binomial probability distribution***, a distribution of values from a set of trials in which:

1. The values of trials are independent.
2. Each trial can lead to one of two values.
3. The probability of each value is constant across trials.

In the example, each coin toss represents a trial. Each toss can lead to one of two values: heads or tails. Finally, the probability remains constant across tosses.

Binomial probability distributions are widely applicable in research, because many situations approximate a binomial probability process. For example, transactions recorded by a discount store scanning device can be characterized as correct or incorrect. Job applicants can be characterized as having prior work experience or not. Products coming off an assembly line can be characterized as satisfactory or unsatisfactory. All these examples illustrate a binomial probability process as long as the probabilities remain constant from trial to trial.

Continuous Probability Distributions

Continuous variables and continuous random variables are infinitely divisible between any two values. For example, chronological age can be reported in years. But years can be subdivided into months, days, hours, and so forth. Age values can be infinitely divided into smaller values.

Continuous probability distributions summarize probabilities associated with continuous random variables. However, the infinite divisibility of continuous random variables presents a small problem for continuous probability distributions. Because continuous variables are infinitely divisible between any two values, a probability cannot be assigned to specific values. As a consequence, probabilities are assigned to *regions* of a continuous probability distribution, just as frequencies are assigned to regions of histograms when distributions of continuous variables are described generally (chapter 9).

A *normal probability distribution* that shows probabilities associated with a normal distribution is shown in Exhibit 12.4 to illustrate a continuous probability distribution. Probabilities are assigned to regions under the normal probability curve. In a normal distribution, 68.3% of the cases fall between ±1.0 standard deviations of the mean. Consequently, the probability distribution shows that 68.3% of cases fall between ±1.0 standard deviations of the mean.

Normal probability distributions are widely useful in research. Many processes, natural and otherwise, produce continuous probability distributions that approximate a normal distribution. Furthermore, some discrete distributions, such as the binomial, also approximate a normal distribution as the number of trials becomes large.

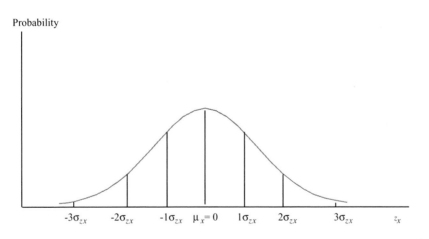

EXHIBIT 12.4. A normal probability distribution.

RESEARCH HIGHLIGHT 12.2

Probabilities Are Conceptual Constructions

A probability distribution reports the proportion of values to expect in an infinitely long series of trials; in the example, there is an infinitely long series of three coin tosses. If one were to actually toss three coins many times, recording the number of heads that appeared each time, an empirical frequency distribution could be obtained. This frequency distribution shows outcomes of tossing actual coins. Although frequencies of values in this distribution are expected to converge on the probabilities associated with each value as the number of tosses increases, they may never match the probabilities exactly.

SAMPLING DISTRIBUTIONS

Sampling distributions are probability distributions with two special characteristics:

1. They apply to random variables that are sample statistics. For example, the variable may be a mean or a regression coefficient.
2. The probabilities assigned values (discrete variables) or regions (continuous variables) are those that occur from the calculation of a statistic on all possible probability samples of a given size (n) that have been drawn from a population.

In ***probability samples*** the likelihood that each case in the population is chosen for the sample is known. There are several ways to obtain probability samples. Explanations of statistical validation typically use a simple random sample to illustrate probability sampling. In a ***simple random sample***, each unique sample (of some given size) in a population has an equal chance of being selected. Randomness depends solely on the process for selecting cases; the actual probability of being selected in the sample may be large or small. A simple random sample requires only that the probability of one unique sample being selected is the same as the probability for any other unique sample.

Statistics and Parameters

In part IV, statistics were described assuming that the data at hand exhausted a researcher's interest; cases were treated as a population, and no inferences were involved. Now it is useful to distinguish between statistics calculated on the scores investigated in a study from statistics representing the inferences one wants to make. Accordingly, the term *statistic* is now reserved to summarize numerical information about the scores studied. When a statistic is used to make an inference it is called a ***parameter***. Different symbols are also used to distinguish statistics that are calculated from parameters estimated. These are summarized in Exhibit 12.5.

Sampling Distribution of the Mean

Issues associated with sampling distributions are illustrated with a sampling distribution of the mean. A sampling distribution of the mean is a distribution created by calculating means for all

---

RESEARCH HIGHLIGHT 12.3

Sampling Distributions Are Also Conceptual Constructions

Sampling distributions are conceptual just as probability distributions. Researchers do not actually draw all possible probability samples from a population. To do so would be far more laborious than including all population cases in a study.

Rather, researchers estimate key characteristics of sampling distributions from statistics obtained on the sample drawn and from knowledge of what sampling distribution applies to a particular sample statistic. They use such information to estimate characteristics of the sampling distribution. These estimated characteristics of sampling distributions, in turn, are used to make statistical inferences.

Variable	Statistic	Parameter
Number of cases	n	N
Mean	X_{Bar}	μ_X
Standard deviation	SD_X	σ_X
Variance	SD^2_X	σ^2_X
Correlation coefficient	r_{YX}	ρ_{YX}
Coefficient of determination	r^2_{YX}	ρ^2_{YX}
Regression coefficient	b_{YX}	β_{YX}
Regression intercept	a	α
Multiple correlation coefficient	$R_{Y \cdot X1X2}$	$P_{Y \cdot X1X2}$
Multiple coefficient of determination	$R^2_{Y \cdot X1X2}$	$P^2_{Y \cdot X1X2}$
Partial regression coefficient	$b_{YX1 \cdot X2}$	$\beta_{YX1 \cdot X2}$
Partial beta coefficient	$beta_{YX1 \cdot X2}$	$Beta_{YX1 \cdot X2}$

Note: Multiple correlation and regression statistics are illustrated with two independent variables.

EXHIBIT 12.5.   Symbols for statistics and parameters.

possible probability samples of a given size. Suppose a researcher is interested in the average height of adult males in a metropolitan area. (Height is a continuous variable requiring a continuous sampling distribution.) Although unknown to the researcher, the population distribution of height (as shown in Exhibit 12.6a) is near normally distributed with mean, $\mu_X = 5.70$ feet, and standard deviation, $\sigma_X = .25$ feet.

The researcher draws one simple random sample of five male participants from the population. Each sample member's height is measured, and the sample mean height X_{Bar} and standard deviation SD_X are calculated.

The researcher's best estimate of the population mean μ_X is the sample mean X_{Bar}. But it is unlikely that the two are equal. X_{Bar} is probably greater or smaller than μ_X because of sampling error. **Sampling error** is the deviation between a sample statistic and a population parameter that results because the sample size n is smaller than the population N. Most random samples of five participants also yield means above or below μ_X because of sampling error.

Think now of drawing all possible random samples ($n = 5$) from the population, measuring participants' height in each sample and calculating X_{Bar}. These means represent values of a new variable, sample means of height. It is a random variable, because mean values of the samples result from a random sampling process. The probability of any region of this distribution is given under the curve of the sampling distribution of the mean as illustrated in Exhibit 12.6b.

(a) Distribution of Height in the Population

Frequency

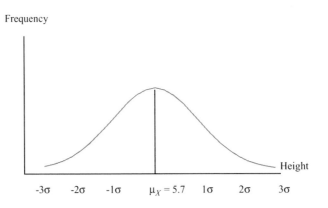

Height

-3σ   -2σ   -1σ $\mu_X = 5.7$ 1σ   2σ   3σ

(b) Sampling Distribution of Mean Height: $n = 5$

Probability

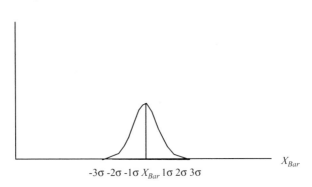

X_{Bar}

-3σ -2σ -1σ X_{Bar} 1σ 2σ 3σ

EXHIBIT 12.6.   Population and sampling distributions.

This distribution has several noteworthy characteristics. First, the mean of the sampling distribution (the mean of the sample means of all samples, $n = 5$) is equal to μ_X.

Second, there is variability in this distribution, because there is variation in the amount of sampling error from sample to sample. Some samples consist of cases that mirror the population height distribution and hence produce means close to μ_X. Some, however, consist of a disproportionate number of cases with height values at the high or low end of the population height distribution. Such samples result in means that deviate from μ_X to a greater or lesser degree.

Nevertheless, there is less variability in the sampling distribution of the means than there is in the population distribution of cases. This is illustrated with an example. Suppose a population of male adults is rank ordered by height and the 10 tallest are shown in Exhibit 12.7. The largest sample value in the population is 7.30 feet. However, in the sampling distribution ($n = 5$), the sample with the tallest adults must include the first five tallest participants. Thus, the largest mean value in the sampling distribution is only 6.89 feet.

Finally, as the sample size increases, variability in the sampling distribution of the mean decreases. Exhibit 12.7 also illustrates this characteristic. If the sample size is 10, the largest

Participant	Height
1	7.30 feet
2	7.05
3	6.81
4	6.73
5	6.54
6	6.46
7	6.35
8	6.33
9	6.28
10	6.21

EXHIBIT 12.7.   Ten tallest participants in the population.

sample mean must include all participants in Exhibit 12.7. The largest sampling distribution value ($n = 10$) is 6.61 feet.

Variability can be addressed for sampling distributions just as it can be addressed for any other distribution. The standard deviation of sampling distributions is an especially important measure of variability, because it is needed to make statistical inferences. The standard deviation of a sampling distribution of the mean is:

$$SE_{X Bar} = \frac{\sigma_X}{\sqrt{n}} \qquad (12.1a)$$

where $SE_{X Bar}$ = standard deviation of a sampling distribution of the mean
$\qquad \sigma_X$ = standard deviation of X in the population
$\qquad n$ = number of cases in the sample

Because the population standard deviation typically is unknown, $SE_{X Bar}$ typically is estimated by using the sample standard deviation:

$$SE_{X Bar} = \frac{SD_x}{\sqrt{n}} \qquad (12.2b)$$

where SD_X = standard deviation of X in the sample

Standard deviations of sampling distributions are called **standard errors**. The **standard error of the mean** is the standard deviation of a sampling distribution of the mean, sample size = n. (The **standard error of the correlation coefficient** is the standard deviation of the sampling distribution of the correlation coefficient, and so on for other statistics.)

The formula for $SE_{X Bar}$ has sample size in the denominator. This indicates that a sampling distribution of the mean has less variability than the population distribution, as suggested by the examples using Exhibit 12.7. Furthermore, the larger the size of the sample, the smaller the standard error. The relationship between sample size and standard error is important for statistical inference, because it correctly suggests that estimates of parameters improve as sample sizes become larger.

The sampling distribution of the mean shown in Exhibit 12.6b is symmetrical and is approximately normal. When the population is normally distributed, the sampling distribution of the mean is normally distributed. Moreover, even if the population is not normally distributed, the sampling distribution of the mean will approach the normal distribution as the sample becomes large. This follows from the **central limit theorem**; it states that, as sample sizes randomly obtained become larger, the sampling distribution of the mean becomes less variable and more normally distributed.

Other Sampling Distributions

The shape of a particular sampling distribution depends on the probability sampling procedure and the statistic under consideration. A normal distribution represents the sampling distribution for some, but not all, statistics. Indeed, two other distributions better characterize the sampling distributions for most statistics used in research.

Students' t Distributions

Students' t distributions are symmetrical (skew = 0.0), have mean = 0.0, and have standard deviation = 1.0, just as a standard normal distribution. However, they have greater variability than the standard normal distribution (kurtosis < 0.0). A t distribution, rather than a standard normal distribution, is usually appropriate when making inferences about simple correlation coefficients and simple and partial regression coefficients. It is also appropriate for inferences about a mean when the standard deviation of the population must be estimated from the sample.

F Distributions

Students' t distributions were developed to address inferential problems involving the mean of a distribution. Other distributions are applicable to inferential issues involving variability in distributions. **F distributions** are sampling distributions designed to make inferences about the equality of two variances. These are important for statistical inference using either multiple regression or multiple correlation. Researchers make statistical inferences in multiple regression and correlation by comparing the variance in the dependent variable that is explained by the independent variables to the total variance in the dependent variable using F distributions.

SUMMARY

Researchers use statistical validation procedures to make inferences about population parameters and to make inferences about whether relationships observed are meaningfully greater than what might be expected by chance or coincidence. Inferences appropriately made require that statistics be combined with probabilistic processes. These are probability sampling for statistical generalization validity or random assignment for internal statistical validity.

Probabilities range from 0.0 to 1.0 and indicate the likelihood that a particular value of a variable will be obtained. Probabilities are characteristics of **random variables**, variables whose values are not known exactly but are described by probability. Random variables possess **mutual exclusivity** when the occurrence of one value precludes the occurrence of other values and vice versa. A random variable is *exhaustive* when one value must occur. The probability of mutually exclusive and exhaustive values must sum to 1.0.

Two or more random variables are independent when the values of one variable provide no information about the probabilities of the values of the other(s). The probability that specific values will occur among two or more independent variables is multiplicative.

Probability distributions are formed with values from random variables. Such distributions may be *discrete*, if there are a countable number of mutually exclusive values, or *continuous*, if the values are infinitely divisible into smaller values.

Sampling distributions are probability distributions that describe statistics obtained from probability sampling. The standard deviations of such distributions are called *standard errors*. For example, the standard error of the mean is the standard deviation of the sampling distribution of the mean for a given sample size.

Three distributions that describe probability distributions and sampling distributions are *normal probability distributions, Students' t distributions*, and *F distributions*. Student's *t* distributions are similar to a standard normal distribution but are more variable. Normal probability and *t* distributions are used to make inferences about means. Students' *t* distributions are also used to make inferences about simple and partial regression and correlation coefficients. *F* distributions address the equality of variances and are used to make inferences in multiple correlation and regression.

FOR REVIEW

Terms to Know

Statistical inference: Use of statistics and probability theory to draw conclusions about population parameters or the likelihood that observed relationships (differences) are due to chance.

Probability (P_r): Specifies the likelihood that a particular value of a variable will be obtained. It can range from 0.0 to 1.0.

Random variable: A variable whose values are not known exactly but are described by probability.

Mutually exclusive values: When the presence of one value precludes the presence of another value and vice versa.

Exhaustive values: When one of the values on a variable must result.

Independence: Two variables are independent when information about the value on one variable provides no information about the probability of values on the other variable.

Probability distribution: A distribution that summarizes probabilities associated with values of a random variable.

 Discrete probability distribution: Probability distribution has a probability associated with each value of the discrete random variable.

 Binomial probability distribution: Discrete probability distribution that results from a set of trials where the value of each trial is independent, the probability remains constant from trial to trial, and each trial can lead to one of two values.

 Continuous probability distribution: Probability distribution where probabilities are assigned to regions of the continuous random variable.

 Normal probability distribution: Continuous probability distribution where probabilities assigned to regions conform to a normal distribution.

 Sampling distribution: A probability distribution of a sample statistic obtained on all possible probability samples of a given sample size.

Probability sample: Obtained when the likelihood of each case chosen for the sample is known.

Simple random sample: A probability sample where every unique sample of a given size from a population has an equal chance of being selected.

Parameter: Statistic that describes a statistical inference drawn by a researcher.

Sampling distribution of the mean: A sampling distribution created by calculating means for all possible probability samples of a given size.

Sampling error: The difference between a sample statistic and population parameter brought about because the sample size is smaller than the population. The size of this error can be estimated when probability sampling is used.

Standard error: Standard deviation of a sampling distribution.

Standard error of the mean: Standard deviation of a sampling distribution of the mean.

Standard error of the correlation coefficient: Standard deviation of a sampling distribution of the correlation coefficient.

Central limit theorem: States that as sample sizes randomly obtained become larger, the sampling distribution becomes less variable and more normally distributed. Applies to several, but not all, sampling distributions.

Students' t distributions: A set of symmetrical sampling distributions that are shaped as a standard normal distribution but more variable. Students' t distributions become more like a standard normal distribution as the sample size gets larger.

F distributions: A set of asymmetrical sampling distributions with positive skew. F distributions are designed to test the equality of variances from two populations.

Formulae to Use

Standard error of the mean

$$SE_{X Bar} = \frac{\sigma_X}{\sqrt{n}} \qquad (12.2a)$$

$$SE_{X Bar} = \frac{SD_x}{\sqrt{n}} \qquad (12.2b)$$

where σ_x and SD_x = the standard deviation of the population and sample, respectively

Questions for Review

1. How do the objectives of statistical generalization validity differ from internal statistical validity?
2. How are standard deviations and standard errors similar? How are they dissimilar?
3. Compare and contrast statistics and parameters.
4. Compare and contrast the t distribution with the standard normal distribution.
5. A coin is biased so that $P_r(\text{head}) = .60$ and $P_r(\text{tail}) = .40$. Create a probability tree resulting from three tosses of this biased coin. Given the bias, develop the probability distribution for the possible values 0, 1, 2, or 3 heads.
6. Political party affiliation is a random variable that has four mutually exclusive values. Assign a probability (P_r) to "other" to make this variable exhaustive.

$P_r(\text{Republican}) = .25$; $P_r(\text{Democrat}) = .30$; $P_r(\text{Independent}) = .30$; $P_r(\text{Other}) = \underline{\quad}$?

Issues to Discuss

1. Explain why the sample mean in a sampling distribution of the mean is a random variable.
2. What is the parameter when statistical inference is used to make an external statistical inference? An internal statistical inference?
3. What characteristic(s) of the sampling distribution of the mean are influenced by sample size? What characteristic(s) are not?

13

Statistical Inference Applications

Chapter Outline

- *Statistical Hypothesis Testing*
  - *Hypothesis Testing Logic and Procedures*
    - *Specify Statistical Hypotheses and Significance Levels*
    - *Draw a Probability Sample*
    - *Estimate the Sampling Distribution If the Null Hypothesis Is True*
    - *Identify Critical Region(s) of the Null Sampling Distribution*
    - *Use Sample Statistic to Decide If the Null Sampling Distribution Is False*
  - *Hypothesis Testing Example*
  - *Hypothesis Testing Outcomes*
  - *Statistical Power*
    - *Statistical Power Conventions*
    - *Other Power Determinants*
- *Confidence Intervals*
  - *Confidence Interval Logic and Procedures*
    - *Set Confidence Level*
    - *Draw a Probability Sample and Calculate Sample Statistic*
    - *Estimate Sampling Distribution Assuming the Statistic Represents the Parameter*
    - *Identify Probable Region of the Sampling Distribution*
    - *Infer That the Population Parameter Falls Within the Probable Region*
  - *Confidence Interval Example*
- *Confidence Intervals Versus Hypothesis Testing and Power*
- *Internal Statistical Validity*
  - *Randomization Tests*
  - *Concluding Cautions*
- *Summary*
- *For Review*

- *Terms to Know*
- *Formulae to use*
- *Questions for Review*
- *Issues to Discuss*
- *Appendix 13A: Formulae for Statistical Inference*
  - *Sampling Distributions*
  - *Statistical Inference Tests*
    - *Simple Correlation Coefficient*
    - *Simple Regression Coefficient*
    - *Multiple Coefficient of Determination*
    - *Partial Beta Coefficients*
    - *Incremental R^2*
  - *Part V Suggested Readings*

The probability and sampling distributions described in chapter 12 provide a foundation for making external and internal statistical inferences. This chapter describes two procedures researchers use to make such inferences. These two, statistical hypothesis testing and confidence intervals, are intimately related; they are simply different ways of addressing the same objectives.

However, the objectives differ depending on whether a researcher is interested in statistical generalization validity or in internal statistical validity. When statistical generalization validity is of interest, hypothesis testing and confidence intervals are used to estimate a population parameter from a statistic calculated on a sample that has been drawn from the population. When internal statistical validity is of interest, the two procedures are used to estimate whether a statistic observed on cases is large enough to rule out chance as its explanation.

Both types of inference use probability and sampling distributions. In statistical generalization, this requires that a probability sample be drawn from the population. Internal statistical validation requires that cases be randomly assigned to levels of an independent variable.

However, except for the way probability is used to produce statistics that meet probability distribution assumptions, hypothesis testing and confidence interval procedures are identical. Thus, to simplify the presentation, hypothesis testing and confidence intervals are first described only for statistical generalization validity. Internal statistical validity is discussed later in the chapter.

The chapter also contains an appendix. It identifies procedures to calculate statistical hypothesis tests and confidence intervals on the statistics described in this book.

STATISTICAL HYPOTHESIS TESTING

Statistical hypothesis testing estimates whether a relationship (or difference) observed on the cases studied suggests there is a relationship (or difference) among the population from which the sample was drawn. It may address whether the sample results suggest there is any population relationship or difference. For example, a sample correlation coefficient may be assessed to decide whether any relationship exists among cases in the population. Alternatively, the research hypothesis may address a directional issue, whether a relationship is positive or negative, or whether a difference favors one group over another. For example, a sample correlation coefficient may be assessed to decide whether it suggests the population relationship is positive.

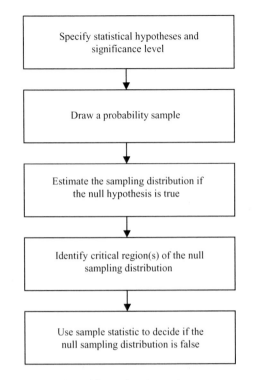

EXHIBIT 13.1.   Statistical hypothesis testing sequence of steps.

Hypothesis Testing Logic and Procedures

Hypothesis testing involves five steps. These steps are summarized in Exhibit 13.1; each is explained below.

Specify Statistical Hypotheses and Significance Levels

Hypothesis testing has two statistical hypotheses. The ***research hypothesis*** (H_1) represents an investigator's expectation about what is true of the population parameter. For example, a research hypothesis may be that salary level is positively related to years of work experience, or it may be that the average age of women in a population differs from the average age of men.

Research hypotheses are evaluated against a ***null hypothesis*** (H_0), the hypothesis of no association or no difference. [The null hypothesis does not have to specify there is literally no relationship (or difference) in the population. However, it is unlikely that you will see the null hypothesis stated any other way.] The null hypothesis for the salary level-years of work experience example is that there is no relationship between the two or that the relationship is negative. If the research and null hypotheses are tested by regressing salary level (Y) on years of work experience (X) then:

$$\text{research hypothesis, } H_1 \beta_{YX} > 0.0$$

$$\text{null hypothesis, } H_0 \beta_{YX} \leq 0.0$$

The research hypothesis is directional because it anticipates a positive relationship between salary level and years of work experience. A directional research hypothesis is called ***one-tailed***.

In the second example, the research hypothesis is that the average age of women (W) is different than that of men (M). The null hypothesis is that the average age of women and men are the same:

$$\text{research hypothesis, } H_1 \mu_W \neq \mu_M$$

$$\text{null hypothesis, } H_0 \mu_W = \mu_M$$

In this example, the research hypothesis is nondirectional. It does not suggest that women are younger or older than men, only that the average age of the two groups differs. A nondirectional research hypothesis is called ***two-tailed***.

At this stage, researchers should also establish a ***statistical significance level***, which refers to the risk they take of accepting the research hypothesis (H_1) when the null hypothesis (H_0) is true. Probability sampling involves uncertainty. The probability sample drawn from a population may not be representative of that population. The conclusion drawn from the sample may thus be in error. For example, the sample regression coefficient may support the research hypothesis that salary level is related to the years of work experience. Yet in the population no such relationship may exist.

Researchers set a statistical significance level so that the risk of erroneously concluding H_1, when H_0 is true, is small. Typically, researchers use significance levels of $p < .05$ or $p < .01$. In the salary example, a significance level of $p < .05$ means the researcher has established a risk of erroneously concluding a relationship between salary and years of work experience less than 5% when the null hypothesis is true in the population.

The choice of a significance level is arbitrary in the absence of information about the costs and benefits of incorrect and correct decisions. The levels of .05 and .01 are merely conventions widely used by researchers. As Rosnow and Rosenthal (1989) said, "surely, God loves the .06 nearly as much as the .05" (p. 1277).

Draw a Probability Sample

The researcher next draws a sample from the population. This must be a probability sample so that the sampling distribution estimated in the next step has the shape, variability, and central tendency assumed for it. A researcher has no way of knowing these sampling distribution characteristics unless a probability sample is used. The procedures described here assume the probability sample is a simple random sample.

Estimate the Sampling Distribution If the Null Hypothesis Is True

Here is a critical point of hypothesis testing: Researchers estimate a sampling distribution assuming the null (H_0) hypothesis is true. Of course, a researcher doesn't really believe this; the researcher believes that H_1 is true. The null distribution is created only to serve as a criterion against which the research hypothesis (H_1) is evaluated. This criterion distribution is used to protect researchers from erroneously concluding support for the research hypothesis in the event that the null hypothesis is really true.

A sampling distribution contains sample statistics from all possible samples of a given sample size. It thus must follow that the sample statistic calculated in a research study comes from the null sample distribution if the null hypothesis is true in the population. H_0 is rejected in favor of H_1 only if it is unlikely ($p < .05$ or $p < .01$) that the sample statistic obtained comes from the null sampling distribution. Alternatively, H_0 is not rejected if the sample plausibly comes from the null distribution. It is in this sense that statistical hypothesis testing establishes a low risk of erroneously concluding H_1 when H_0 is true.

The null sampling distribution must be estimated because a researcher draws one sample of a given sample size, not all possible samples of that size. Because a distribution is defined by its central tendency, variability, and shape, researchers must estimate these three characteristics of null sampling distributions.

1. **Central tendency**. The central tendency of the distribution is established assuming the null hypothesis is true. Thus, the sampling distribution is assumed to have a mean of zero.
2. **Variability**. The variability in the sampling distribution is usually estimated with information obtained from the sample. Formulae for sample estimates of variability (sampling errors) differ by parameter estimated but typically include the sample size and/or the variability in the sample. For example, the standard error of the mean is estimated using both (see Formula 12.2).
3. **Shape**. Researchers draw on knowledge provided by statisticians to decide the shape of the sampling distribution for a given statistic. As noted in chapter 12, the standard normal distribution, Students' t distributions, and F distributions frequently approximate the shape of sampling distributions for the statistics used in research.

Identify Critical Region(s) of the Null Sampling Distribution

Information about the sampling distribution estimated given the null and the significance level established are combined to identify the region(s) of the distribution where a sample statistic is unlikely if the null hypothesis is true. Exhibit 13.2 shows values identifying several critical regions for one- and two-tailed tests involving t distributions with various degrees of freedom. **Degrees of freedom** (**d.f.**) refer to the amount of information available to estimate population parameters from sample statistics. They are more accurate for this purpose than is sample size, although the two are closely connected. The number of degrees of freedom available to conduct tests of statistical inference has been identified by statisticians.

To identify the critical value(s) in Exhibit 13.2 you must know whether the research hypothesis is one- or two-tailed, the significance level, and the degrees of freedom. For example, suppose the test is one-tailed, $p < .05$, and the degrees of freedom equal 25. Exhibit 13.2 shows that the critical t distribution value is 1.71. Less than 5% of the sample statistics drawn from a population if the null hypothesis is true will have t distribution values greater than 1.71.

Use Sample Statistic to Decide If the Null Sampling Distribution Is False

In the last step, a researcher transforms the sample statistic to a scale value on the null sampling distribution and compares it with the critical value established in the previous step. If the transformed sample statistic falls in the critical region, the researcher concludes the sample drawn actually comes from a distribution other than the null distribution. The researcher rejects H_0 and accepts H_1. In the example just given, a researcher concludes H_1 if the transformed sample statistic is greater than 1.71. The researcher does not reject H_0 if the transformed sample statistic is 1.71 or less.

Two-Tail   One-Tail

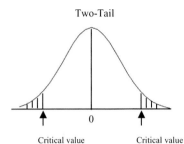
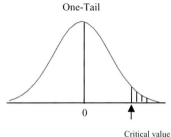

	Two-Tail	.100	.050	.020	.010
	One-Tail	.050	.025	.010	.005
d.f.					
1		6.31	12.70	31.80	63.70
2		2.92	4.30	6.96	9.92
3		2.35	3.18	4.54	5.84
4		2.13	2.78	3.75	4.60
5		2.02	2.57	3.36	4.03
10		1.81	2.23	2.76	3.17
15		1.75	2.13	2.60	2.95
20		1.72	2.09	2.53	2.85
25		1.71	2.06	2.49	2.79
30		1.70	2.04	2.46	2.75
40		1.68	2.02	2.42	2.70
60		1.67	2.00	2.39	2.66
120		1.66	1.98	2.36	2.62
∞ Standard Normal		1.64	1.96	2.33	2.58

EXHIBIT 13.2.   Values identifying critical regions of *t* distributions.

Hypothesis Testing Example

The steps in statistical hypothesis testing are illustrated with the example of the research hypothesis that salary level (Y) is positively related to years of work experience (X) among a population of working adults. The research hypothesis is one-tailed. The researcher establishes a significance level of .01 and intends to test the hypothesis by calculating a simple correlation coefficient on salary and work experience scores from a simple random sample of 27 adults chosen from the population. The research and null hypotheses are:

$$\text{research hypothesis, } H_1\, p_{YX} > .0$$

$$\text{null hypothesis, } H_0\, p_{YX} \leq .0.$$

In this situation the null sampling distribution has a mean equal to zero, $p_{YX} = .0$, a shape approximated by a t distribution with $n - 2$ degrees of freedom, and a standard

RESEARCH HIGHLIGHT 13.1

A Legal Analogy

Hypothesis testing logic is analogous to the logic for determining a defendant's guilt or innocence in the American judicial system. The null hypothesis is accepted as provisionally true; the defendant is provisionally assumed to be innocent. The null hypothesis is rejected and the research hypothesis accepted only if it is improbable that the null hypothesis is true; the assumption of innocence is rejected and a decision of guilt is accepted only if the defendant is found guilty beyond a reasonable doubt.

Both decision rules are asymmetrical and for the same general reason. The cost of erroneously concluding a relationship when none exists is seen as greater than the cost of erroneously missing a relationship that does exist. The cost of erroneously convicting an innocent defendant is seen as greater than the cost of erroneously letting a guilty defendant go free.

error:

$$SEr_{YX} = \frac{1}{\sqrt{n-1}} \tag{13.1}$$

where SEr_{YX} = standard error of the correlation coefficient when $p_{YX} = .0$

The standard error of the correlation coefficient depends only on the sample size when $p_{YX} = .0$. The larger the sample size, the more tightly clustered are the sample correlation coefficients around the population correlation coefficient. When $p_{YX} \neq .0$, the sampling distribution is no longer symmetrical; hence, it no longer assumes the shape of a t distribution and the appropriate statistical test is a little more complicated.

The critical region for this null sampling distribution is found in Exhibit 13.2. It shows that a critical region for a one-tailed test, $p < .01$, with $n - 2 = 25$ d.f. begins at 2.49.

The researcher draws a sample, obtains salary and years of experience scores, and calculates a simple correlation coefficient, $r_{YX} = .55$. This correlation coefficient is transformed to a t distribution value by:

$$t_{cc} = r_{YX} \times \frac{\sqrt{n-2}}{\sqrt{1 - r_{YX^2}}} \tag{13.2}$$

where t_{cc} = location of the sample correlation coefficient on a t distribution with $n - 2$ degrees of freedom

From the example:

$$t_{cc} = .55 \times \sqrt{(27-2)}/\sqrt{1 - .55^2} = 3.29.$$

This value, 3.29, is greater than the value of 2.49 that identifies the beginning of the critical region. Consequently, H_0 is rejected and H_1 is accepted. The sample correlation coefficient of .55 suggests there is a positive relationship between salary level and work experience in the population as hypothesized.

Inference	Parameter	
	H_0	H_1
H_0	Correct	B (Type II)
H_1	α (Type I)	Correct

EXHIBIT 13.3.   Outcomes of statistical hypothesis tests.

This conclusion is modest because of the way it is tested. The null hypothesis states that there is a negative or no (zero) relationship in the population. Thus, to reject H_0 and accept H_1, given a directional one-tailed test, only permits a conclusion that some positive relationship probably exists in the population. The actual population relation may be less than $r_{YX} = .55$ or greater.

Hypothesis Testing Outcomes

Research and null hypotheses pertain to parameters. A researcher draws inferences about these parameters based on evidence obtained from a sample. These inferences and parameters are shown in Exhibit 13.3.

Exhibit 13.3 shows that a researcher can make two correct inferences. A correct inference is drawn when H_1 is accepted and H_1 is true of the parameter. A correct inference is also made when a researcher fails to reject H_0 and H_0 is the true parameter value.

Two errors are also possible. An α or *Type I error* is made if a researcher concludes H_1 based on sample evidence but H_0 is true in the population. Alternatively, a β or *Type II error* is made if H_1 is true in the population but a researcher fails to reject H_0.

Hypothesis testing is designed to protect against Type I error, an error of concluding a relationship in the population when none exists. As noted, it does so by specifying the likelihood that a sample statistic comes from a population with no relationship. This likelihood is usually set low ($p < .05$ or $p < .01$) so it is unlikely that H_1 is accepted from the sample when H_0 is true in the population.

While unlikely, it is not impossible. For example, suppose a significance level, $p < .05$, is established, and H_0 is true in the population. Further, suppose many, many samples are drawn and a sample statistic is calculated on each. About 5% of the time, these statistics will fall in the improbable region of the null sampling distribution, leading to the erroneous conclusion that a relationship exists in the population when it does not. This illustrates how hypothesis testing controls the risk of a Type I error but doesn't eliminate its possibility.

Further, hypothesis testing does not protect against Type II error, an error of failing to accept H_1 from a sample statistic when H_1 is true of the population parameter. The latter issue is addressed by statistical power.

Statistical Power

Statistical power refers to the likelihood of concluding H_1 from a sample statistic when H_1 is true of the population parameter. It is equal to 1-Type II error. Power thus addresses the second error that can be made in statistical hypothesis testing. Statistical hypothesis testing addresses Type I error—the error of erroneously concluding a relationship (difference) when there is none. Statistical power addresses Type II error—the error of failing to detect a relationship (difference) in the population when it exists. The two procedures are best used together.

RESEARCH HIGHLIGHT 13.2

Don't Accept the Null Hypothesis

Only the risk of erroneously accepting the research hypothesis is known in hypothesis testing. The risk of erroneously accepting the null hypothesis is not known (i.e., the risk of erroneously concluding there is no relation in the population). Consequently, in hypothesis testing H_0 should never be accepted unless one also knows the power of a statistical test.

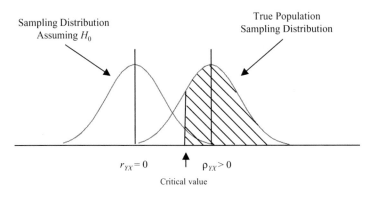

EXHIBIT 13.4.   Power of a test of a simple correlation coefficient.

Exhibit 13.4 illustrates statistical power using a one-tailed directional hypothesis test for a correlation coefficient. The null sampling distribution on the left assumes $\rho_{YX} = .0$, a critical value ($p < .01$), and a particular sample size.

However, assume now that the null hypothesis is really false. H_1 is true, $\rho_{YX} > .0$, as represented by the distribution to the right in Exhibit 13.4. Any sample a researcher draws must be from the sampling distribution centered over the true parameter ($\rho_{YX} > .0$). Statistical power is shown by the proportion of this distribution that is to the right of the critical value established for the null distribution. It is the proportion of the total population sampling distribution with diagonal lines. This follows because a researcher concludes H_1 (correctly in this case) for any sample drawn that results in a sample correlation coefficient to the right of the critical value. Any sample from the distribution around the population parameter resulting in a correlation coefficient to the left of the critical value results in a Type II error.

Statistical Power Conventions

Statistical treatments of power usually emphasize four factors. One is whether the research hypothesis is one- or two-tailed. Exhibit 13.2 shows that a one-tailed test locates the critical region farther to the left (right if a negative relationship is hypothesized) than a two-tailed test, other things equal. This means the critical region of the null distribution does not reach as far into the true sampling distribution. Statistical power is thus higher given a one-tailed hypothesis test than with a two-tailed hypothesis test.

A second factor is the statistical significance level established as illustrated in Exhibit 13.5. For example, as the significance level is relaxed from .01 (top panel) to .05 (bottom panel), power increases. The proportion of sample correlation coefficients in the sampling distribution

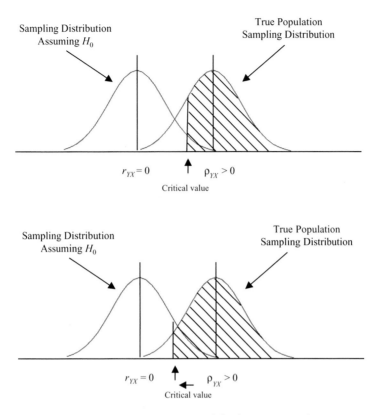

EXHIBIT 13.5.   Power increases as risk of Type I error increases.

around the population parameter that fall to the right of the critical value increases as statistical significance is relaxed from .01 to .05. Thus, increases in the risk of Type I error decrease the risk of Type II error (and vice versa).

A third factor influencing power is the sample size. Exhibit 13.6 shows that power increases as sample size increases. An increase in the sample size has two effects; both increase power (compare the top and bottom panels). First, the larger sample size decreases the variability (standard error) in the sampling distribution given H_0. This pulls the critical value closer to the mean of the null sampling distribution and further from the mean of the sampling distribution around the population parameter. Second, the increase in sample size also decreases the standard error of the sampling distribution around the population parameter, pulling more sample correlation coefficients away from the null distribution.

Finally, the power of a statistical test increases as the population relationship increases. The bottom panel in Exhibit 13.7 shows that the entire population sampling distribution is shifted to the right (compared to the top panel) as ρ_{YX} increases. This pulls more of the population sampling distribution above the critical value established for the null sampling distribution.

The relative contribution of the latter three factors is illustrated in Exhibit 13.8. It shows the power of two-tailed statistical tests of sample correlation coefficients for two population relationships ($\rho_{YX} = .10$, and $\rho_{YX} = .40$) and two levels of significance ($p < .05$, and $p < .01$) across sample sizes ranging to 500.

Exhibit 13.8 shows that power is low, even for large sample sizes, when the relationship in the population is small. The statistical power ($p < .05$, two-tailed) to detect $\rho_{YX} = .10$ is less than 0.50 until a sample size reaches almost 400. Alternatively, power quickly becomes high

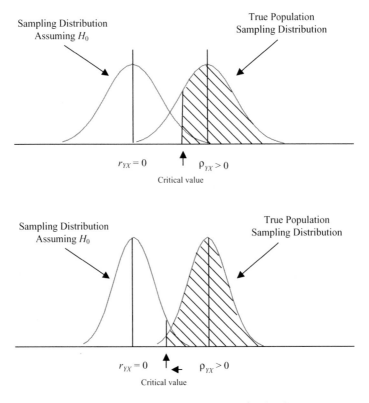

Sampling Distribution
Assuming H_0

True Population
Sampling Distribution

$r_{YX} = 0$

Critical value

$\rho_{YX} > 0$

Sampling Distribution
Assuming H_0

True Population
Sampling Distribution

$r_{YX} = 0$

Critical value

$\rho_{YX} > 0$

EXHIBIT 13.6. Power increases as sample size increases.

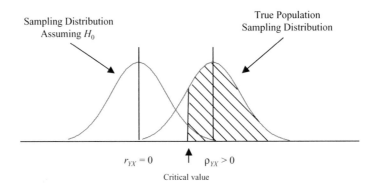

Sampling Distribution
Assuming H_0

True Population
Sampling Distribution

$r_{YX} = 0$

Critical value

$\rho_{YX} > 0$

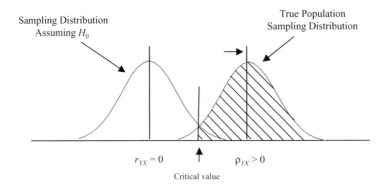

Sampling Distribution
Assuming H_0

True Population
Sampling Distribution

$r_{YX} = 0$

Critical value

$\rho_{YX} > 0$

EXHIBIT 13.7. Power increases as relationship in population increases.

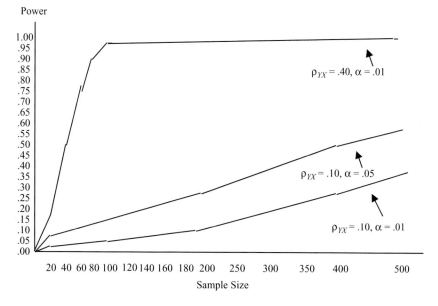

EXHIBIT 13.8. Statistical power as a function of α, n, and ρ_{YX}.

RESEARCH HIGHLIGHT 13.3

When Statistical Power Analysis Is Essential

There are times when researchers want to claim that a relationship (difference) in the population does not exist. For example, a researcher wishes to combine two samples into one for purposes of analysis. The researcher performs a statistical hypothesis test to determine whether the two samples differ on some characteristic(s) of the cases; for example, age. If H_0 is not rejected at some level of significance the researcher reasons that the two samples do not differ and hence combines them.

There are several problems with such a procedure. Here note only the problem for statistical inference. Hypothesis testing protects against Type I error—the risk of concluding there is a relationship or difference in the population when there is none. However, in this example, the researcher should be concerned with Type II error—the risk of not finding a relationship (difference) when it exists. Statistical power, not hypothesis testing, addresses Type II risk.

---

as the sample size increases when $\rho_{YX} = .40$. A sample of 100 has statistical power of 0.95 to detect $\rho_{YX} = .40$ ($p < .01$, two-tailed).

Other Power Determinants

The power determinants just identified receive most attention. However, the utility of such knowledge for improving power is limited. A researcher has no control over the size of the relationship that exists in the population. Increasing power by relaxing statistical significance levels pits one desirable feature (low Type II error) against another (low Type I error). Of the determinants identified, only increases in sample size are unambiguously attractive and potentially within a researcher's control.

However, there are other ways to increase the power of statistical tests. One involves measurement. Chapter 17 shows that unreliability tends to attenuate (reduce) observed relationships compared with relationships obtained with reliable measurement. Increasing the reliability of measures serves to increase statistical power.

Good research designs can also help improve the power of statistical tests. Design activities that serve to control nuisance variables (see chapters 5 and 19), in particular, can help strengthen the power to detect population relationships or differences.

CONFIDENCE INTERVALS

Statistical hypothesis testing begins with an assumption that the null (no relationship or difference) hypothesis is the true parameter. This is the hypothesis that a researcher expects to reject in favor of a research hypothesis that there is a relationship (difference). Researchers using confidence intervals take a different perspective. They assume that the best estimate of the parameter is the sample statistic. Thus, the sampling distribution estimated is not centered over 0.0, it is centered over the value of the sample statistic. Researchers estimate this sampling distribution to create a ***confidence interval*** representing a range around a sample statistic that likely includes its population parameter. The probabilistic logic underlying confidence intervals parallels that of hypothesis testing. However, the logic is used differently, and the procedure is carried out using different steps as summarized in Exhibit 13.9 and developed more fully below.

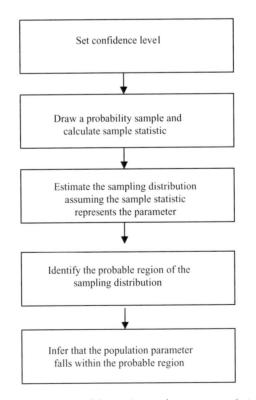

Set confidence level

Draw a probability sample and
calculate sample statistic

Estimate the sampling distribution
assuming the sample statistic
represents the parameter

Identify the probable region of the
sampling distribution

Infer that the population parameter
falls within the probable region

EXHIBIT 13.9.   Confidence interval sequence of steps.

Confidence Interval Logic and Procedures

Set Confidence Level

A **confidence level** refers to the likelihood that a range created around a sample statistic includes the population parameter. Any level may be established, but researchers usually set confidence levels at 95% or 99%. These are the inverse of statistical significance levels of .05 and .01, respectively. Like statistical significance levels, confidence levels refer to the process being used and not to a specific interval created based on one sample. A confidence interval based on one sample either includes the population parameter or it does not. Likelihood refers to the process, not to the outcome from any one sample.

Draw a Probability Sample and Calculate Sample Statistic

The second step, as in statistical hypothesis testing, is to draw a sample. This must also be a probability sample so that a sampling distribution can appropriately be estimated. The sample statistic of interest is then calculated.

Estimate Sampling Distribution Assuming the Statistic Represents the Parameter

Here is where confidence intervals and hypothesis testing differ most dramatically. As noted, the sampling distribution for confidence intervals is centered over the sample statistic. In hypothesis testing, it is centered over the null hypothesis value. The other characteristics of the sampling distribution do not differ between hypothesis testing and confidence intervals. The shape of the distribution is again determined by knowledge provided by statisticians. The variability in the sampling distribution typically is estimated from the sample as in hypothesis testing.

Identify Probable Region of the Sampling Distribution

Because it is assumed that the sample statistic estimates the population parameter, the sampling distribution is now centered over the sample statistic. The most probable region of this sampling distribution is identified. As noted, this is typically the most probable 95% or 99% of this distribution.

Infer That the Population Parameter Falls Within the Probable Region

The researcher concludes that the population parameter falls within the most probable region from the procedure above. In doing so, the researcher runs a risk that is exactly analogous to the risk of a Type I error in hypothesis testing. In this case, the risk is that the parameter may not actually fall within the interval created.

Confidence Interval Example

Consider again the example in which a researcher is interested in the relationship between salary level (Y) and years of work experience (X). However, instead of testing a hypothesis that the relationship between these variables is greater than zero, the researcher now develops a 95% confidence interval around the sample regression coefficient, b_{YX}, calculated on a probability sample of 27 participants.

The top of Exhibit 13.10 shows the true but unknown population sampling distribution. Assume its mean (which is equal to the population regression coefficient B_{YX}) equals $800.00.

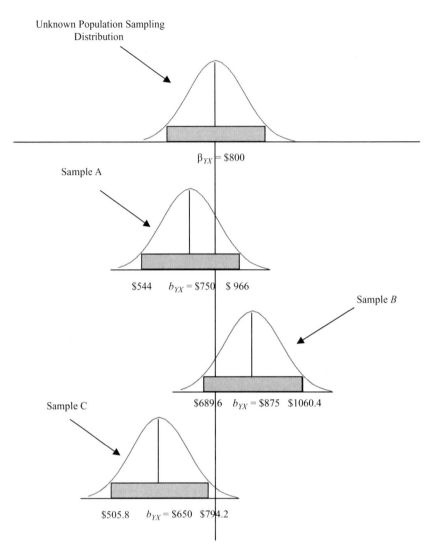

EXHIBIT 13.10.   Population sampling distribution of β_{YX} and three sample confidence interval estimates.

In the population, there is a positive relationship between income and years of experience. Each additional year of work experience leads to a predicted increase in income of $800.00. Assume the standard error of this distribution, $SEB_{YX} = \$80.00$, for $n = 27$.

The researcher draws a probability sample, calculates the sample regression coefficient, $b_{YX} = \$750$, and estimates the standard error of the regression coefficient, $SEb_{YX} = \$100$, from:

$$SEb_{YX} = \frac{SD_{Y \cdot X}}{SD_X \sqrt{n - 1}} \tag{13.3}$$

where SEb_{YX} = standard error of the regression coefficient, and

$$SD_{Y \cdot X} = \sqrt{\frac{n - 1}{n - 2} \times SD_Y^2 \left(1 - r_{YX}^2\right)} \tag{13.4}$$

where $SD_{Y \cdot X}$ = standard error of estimate of Y on X, estimate of the standard deviation of the residual errors in the population

The standard error of the regression coefficient has a t distribution with $n - 2$ degrees of freedom. The 95% confidence interval is found from:

$$CI = b_{YX} \pm SEb_{YX} \times t_{95} \tag{13.5}$$

where $t_{95} = 2.06$ when $d.f. = 25$ (see Exhibit 13.2).

Thus, from Sample A:

$$CI = 750.00 \pm 100.00 \times 2.06 = 750.00 \pm 206.00 = 544.00 \leftrightarrow 956.00$$

The researcher concludes the population regression coefficient likely falls within the range $544.00 to $956.00. Given the assumption about the population parameter in this illustration, $B_{YX} = \$800.00$, the researcher's conclusion is correct.

Suppose instead that the researcher had drawn probability Sample B shown in Exhibit 13.10. The sample regression coefficient $b_{YX} = \$875.00$ and $SEb_{YX} = \$90.00$. Given these values,

$$CI = 875.00 \pm 90.00 \times 2.06 = 875.00 \pm 185.40 = 689.60 \leftrightarrow 1060.40$$

Given this sample, the researcher concludes the population regression coefficient likely falls within the range $689.60 to $1,060.40. Again the conclusion is correct.

Finally, suppose the researcher draws Sample C shown at the bottom of Exhibit 13.10. The sample regression coefficient $b_{YX} = \$650.00$ and $SEb_{YX} = \$70.00$. Given these values:

$$CI = 650.00 \pm 70.00 \times 2.06 = 650.00 \pm 144.20 = 505.80 \leftrightarrow 794.20$$

Given Sample C, the researcher concludes that the population regression coefficient likely falls within the range $505.80 to $794.20. This time the researcher is incorrect, as is expected about 5% of the time if many, many samples are drawn and 95% confidence intervals are established each time.

CONFIDENCE INTERVALS VERSUS HYPOTHESIS TESTING AND POWER

Confidence intervals and statistical hypothesis testing are two ways to make statistical inferences from a sample statistic. Both rely on exactly the same probability processes and logic to generate inferences. Both share risks that inferences made are incorrect. However, because the probability processes are known, the likelihood of the risks is known and can be controlled.

The procedures differ in the type of inference made and hence the form the risks take. Statistical hypothesis testing is set up to identify the risks of erroneously concluding there is a parameter relationship or difference if none exists. Statistical hypothesis testing does not provide information about the risk of missing a parameter relationship or difference. Statistical power analysis must be performed to assess that risk.

Alternatively, confidence intervals begin with the assumption that the sample statistic is the best estimate of a parameter. Thus, an interval is created around the sample statistic that likely includes the parameter. The risk here is that the interval may not include the parameter relationship or difference.

Researchers who conduct organizational research overwhelmingly report inferential results in statistical hypothesis testing form. Research reporting conventions clearly favor statistical hypothesis testing. Furthermore, it is not conventional to report power analyses with statistical hypothesis testing. The risk of failing to recognize a parameter relationship or difference thus is typically unknown.

Although less used, confidence intervals are attractive relative to statistical hypothesis testing in several respects. First, they focus attention on the sample statistic; it is usually a better estimate of the parameter than the null hypothesis value of no relationship or difference. They thus focus attention on the probable strength of the relationship or difference, not just whether a relationship or difference exists as assessed by statistical hypothesis tests.

Second, confidence intervals provide information about statistical power without actually requiring power analysis. Specifically, the narrower the confidence interval, the greater the statistical power. Although confidence intervals do not provide a quantitative estimate of power as is available from formal power analysis, neither does it require that one specify a parameter value to obtain the power estimate.

Finally, confidence intervals can be interpreted so that they provide the same information as a two-tailed hypothesis test. When a confidence interval of 95% (99%) does not include zero, a two-tailed hypothesis test on the same data set will reject the null hypothesis at $p < .05 (p < .01)$. If the confidence interval includes zero, a statistical hypothesis test will not reject the null hypothesis. These outcomes follow because the underlying probability logic of the two procedures is identical.

INTERNAL STATISTICAL VALIDITY

Hypothesis testing, statistical power, and confidence interval procedures so far have been described for statistical generalization validity, for generalizing from a sample statistic to a population parameter after drawing a probability sample from that population. However, the same procedures are also used to make internal statistical inferences when cases are randomly assigned to levels of an independent variable. This inference is of a different sort. Internal statistical validation addresses whether a particular relationship or difference is potentially the result of assignment error. **Assignment errors** lead to group differences in values of a dependent variable because of the uncertain outcomes of random assignment.

Consider an example to illustrate assignment error when cases are randomly assigned to two levels of an independent variable. A researcher randomly assigns six students to one of two training methods; three are assigned to Method A and three are assigned to Method B. A standardized achievement test is administered to all students after the training.

Outcomes are shown in Exhibit 13.11. It shows that Individuals C, E, and F are assigned to Method A and that their average achievement score is 17.33. Individuals A, B, and D are assigned to Method B and their average achievement score is 12.67. The difference is 4.67. Should the researcher conclude that Method A results in higher achievement scores than Method B?

Randomization Tests

Statistical hypothesis testing can be used to address this question. Begin with a null hypothesis that there is no difference in the average achievement test performance resulting from the two training methods. A null probability distribution can be developed by using a randomization test. A **randomization test** generates a distribution of mean differences from all possible ways that the six students can be assigned to the two training methods in groups of three.

Training Type	Method A	Method B
Individual		
A		10.00
B		12.00
C	14.00	
D		16.00
E	18.00	
F	20.00	
	———	———
Group Mean	17.33	12.67

EXHIBIT 13.11.   Training example outcomes.

In the example, there are 20 such combinations, as shown in Exhibit 13.12. Also shown are the average achievement test scores and the mean differences in test scores between groups. Exhibit 13.13 shows the distribution created by the mean differences. This distribution has a mean of zero (consistent with the null hypothesis) and is symmetrical. The variability in this distribution reflects assignment error, because it shows differences in results due to different ways random assignment can combine the six individuals into two groups.

Hypothesis testing can now proceed by the same logic described for statistical generalization. The researcher asks whether the mean difference observed is improbable given the null hypothesis. In the example, the mean difference of 4.67 is the second largest difference favoring Method A. If the null hypothesis is true, there are $2/20 = 0.10$ differences as large as those obtained in the study. A probability of .10 is larger than the p values .05 and .01 that are ordinarily regarded as statistically significant. Thus, the researcher likely would be reluctant to conclude that Method A was superior to Method B in this example.

Randomization tests are laborious to construct, the more so as sample sizes increase. Fortunately, as sample sizes increase, internal statistical inference tests can be approximated by using the same probability and sampling distributions used for statistical generalization tests. In the example, a t test of mean differences can be used to perform the statistical hypothesis test. Conducting that test on the data in Exhibit 13.11 produces a probability value of .13.

Concluding Cautions

The similarity of methods used to conduct statistical hypothesis testing, confidence intervals, and statistical power calculations in both internal statistical inference and statistical generalization inferences is a source of potential confusion. Because the methods are similar, there may be a temptation to conclude that the inferences drawn are similar. They are not.

Statistical generalization is appropriate when a probability sample is drawn from a population. Sample statistics are used to make inferences about population parameters subject to sampling error. Internal statistical inference is appropriate when cases are randomly assigned to levels of an independent variable. Statistics generated in such studies are used to make inferences that the results are not due to assignment error.

Method A	Mean	Method B	Mean	Mean Difference
ABC	12.00	DEF	18.00	-6.00
ABD	12.67	CEF	17.33	-4.67
ABE	13.33	CDF	16.67	-3.33
ABF	14.00	CDE	16.00	-2.00
ACD	13.33	BEF	16.67	-3.33
ACE	14.00	BDF	16.00	-2.00
ACF	14.67	BDE	15.33	-0.67
ADE	14.67	BCF	15.33	-0.67
ADF	15.33	BCE	14.67	0.67
AEF	16.00	BCD	14.00	2.00
BCD	14.00	AEF	16.00	-2.00
BCE	14.67	ADF	15.33	-0.67
BCF	15.33	ADE	14.67	0.67
BDE	15.33	ACF	14.67	0.67
BDF	16.00	ACE	14.00	2.00
BEF	16.67	ACD	13.33	3.33
CDE	16.00	ABF	14.00	2.00
CDF	16.67	ABE	13.33	3.33
CEF	17.33	ABD	12.67	4.67
DEF	18.00	ABC	12.00	6.00

EXHIBIT 13.12.   Possible random assignments and outcomes: Six individuals to two groups.

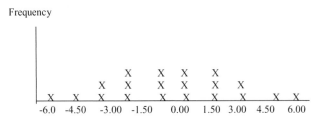

EXHIBIT 13.13.   Distribution of mean training differences given the null hypothesis.

Sometimes researchers misinterpret their use of internal statistical validation procedures. They obtain statistically significant results by using random assignment and then discuss implications of the results as if statistical generalization were addressed. This is an error.

There is a further, more widespread danger. Researchers often use statistical inference techniques without benefit of either probability sampling or random assignment. Field studies and quasi-experiments (part III) are illustrative. In such designs use of statistical inference to draw conclusions is more problematic. Chapter 20 discusses issues associated with the use of statistical inference when probability procedures are not used.

SUMMARY

There are three closely related methods for using sampling distributions to make inferences about population parameters from statistics calculated on sample cases. ***Hypothesis testing*** addresses whether a relationship (or difference) observed in a sample suggests a relationship (difference) in the population. Hypothesis testing pits a ***research hypothesis*** (H_1) against a ***null hypothesis*** (H_0). The research hypothesis is the hypothesis of a relationship (difference); the null hypothesis is the hypothesis of no relationship (difference). The research hypothesis is ***two-tailed*** when only a relationship is hypothesized; it is ***one-tailed*** when the direction of the relationship (difference) is specified as well.

Hypothesis testing begins by specifying the research and null hypotheses and a significance level. A probability sample is then drawn. Information from this sample is used to estimate the null hypothesis sampling distribution and to calculate the sample statistic. A critical region of the null sampling distribution is identified that serves as the criterion for the researcher's conclusion. Finally, the sample statistic is compared with this critical region that leads to a decision to either reject or not reject the null hypothesis.

Hypothesis testing may lead to two incorrect decisions. A ***Type I error*** is made if a researcher concludes H_1, but H_0 is true in the population. This is the error that is specified in hypothesis testing and generally kept low (5% or 1%). Alternatively, a ***Type II error*** is made if the researcher fails to conclude H_1 when H_1 is true in the population. Hypothesis testing does not provide information about Type II error.

Statistical power refers to the likelihood of correctly concluding H_1 from a sample statistic when H_1 is true in the population. Thus, statistical power provides information about the likelihood of making a Type II error. The power of a statistical test generally increases (likelihood of a Type II error decreases) as the (a) sample size increases, (b) likelihood of a Type I error increases, and (c) relationship (difference) in the population increases. The power of one-tailed tests is also higher than the power of two-tailed tests. Measurement reliability and research design also can contribute to more powerful statistical tests.

Confidence intervals use a sample statistic and information about sampling distributions to create a range of values that likely includes the population parameter. Unlike hypothesis testing, confidence intervals are created on the assumption that the sample statistic is the best estimate of the population parameter. The intervals created around this sample statistic are likely to include the population parameter.

Statistical hypothesis testing, typically without power analyses, is reported by researchers more often than confidence intervals. However, confidence intervals are attractive relative to hypothesis testing because they: (a) focus on the strength of the relationship between the variables, (b) provide indirect information on statistical power, and (c) provide the same information as a two-tailed hypothesis test.

These inferential procedures can be used to make internal statistical inferences as well as external generalizations. Internal statistical inference addresses whether a statistic obtained on a group of cases studied is potentially a result of ***assignment error***. Assignment errors result because random assignment procedures may not equalize scores on the dependent variable across the groups studied.

Internal statistical validity can be assessed by using ***randomization tests*** that create null probability distributions from all possible combinations of ways cases can be assigned to levels of an independent variable. However, as sample sizes get larger, results of randomization tests are approximated by distributions used to perform statistical generalization tests. Although the procedures are identical, internal statistical inferences and statistical generalization inferences are different. Researchers should not confuse these inferences when interpreting research results.

FOR REVIEW

Terms to Know

Statistical hypothesis test: Estimates whether a relationship (or difference) observed on a sample of cases suggests there is a relationship (difference) in the population from which the sample was drawn.

Research hypothesis (H_1): Represents a researcher's expectation about what is true of the population parameter.

> **One-tailed hypothesis**: A research hypothesis that is directional; the researcher believes a relationship is positive or negative.

> **Two-tailed hypothesis**: A research hypothesis that is not directional; the researcher believes there is a relationship but does not speculate on whether it is positive or negative.

Null hypothesis (H_0): The hypothesis of no relationship (or no difference) in the population.

Statistical significance level: Level of risk a researcher takes when rejecting the null hypothesis.

Degrees of freedom (d.f.): The amount of information available to estimate population parameters from sample statistics. Are used to identify the appropriate sampling distribution for statistical hypothesis tests and confidence intervals.

Type I error, also α **error**: In hypothesis testing, the error of concluding a relationship exists in the population when it does not.

Type II error, also β **error**: In hypothesis testing, the error of failing to conclude a relationship exists in the population when it does.

Statistical power: The likelihood that a statistical hypothesis test will lead to the rejection of the null hypothesis when the research hypothesis is true in the population.

Confidence intervals: A range of statistical values that likely includes the population parameter.

Confidence level: The likelihood that a confidence interval includes the population parameter.

Assignment error: Results because the random allocation of cases to levels of an independent variable typically does not exactly equalize scores on the dependent variable across groups.

Randomization test: Used to develop a null probability distribution by generating all possible ways cases may be assigned to levels of the independent variable.

Formulae to Use

Standard error of the correlation coefficient

$$SEr_{YX} = \frac{1}{\sqrt{n-1}} \tag{13.1}$$

where n = sample size

Location of the sample correlation coefficient on a t distribution with $n - 2$ d.f.

$$t_{cc} = r_{YX} \times \frac{\sqrt{n-2}}{\sqrt{1 - r_{YX}^2}} \tag{13.2}$$

Standard error of the regression coefficient

$$SEb_{YX} = \frac{SD_{Y \cdot X}}{SD_X \sqrt{n-1}} \tag{13.3}$$

where SD_{YX} = standard error of estimate of Y on X, estimate of the standard deviation of the residual errors in the population

Standard error of estimate of Y on X

$$SD_{Y \cdot X} = \sqrt{\frac{n-1}{n-2} \times SD_Y^2 (1 - r_{YX}^2)} \tag{13.4}$$

Regression coefficient confidence interval (95%), n − 2 d.f.

$$CI = b_{YX} \pm SEb_{YX} \times t_{95} \tag{13.5}$$

where t_{95} is the t distribution value for a 95% confidence interval.

Questions for Review

1. Use the formulae provided to test a research hypothesis that a simple correlation coefficient between Y and X is not equal to zero in the population. A simple random sample of 62 cases has been drawn from a population and a sample correlation, $r_{YX} = 0.20$, has been calculated. Exhibit 13.2 has needed t distribution information. What conclusion do you reach?

2. Use the formulae provided to develop a 95% confidence interval around a sample regression coefficient, $b_{YX} = 5.00$, obtained on a random sample of 122 cases. Other sample statistics are $SD_Y = 150.00$, $SD_X = 9.00$, and $r_{YX} = .30$. Exhibit 13.2 has needed t distribution information. What conclusion would you reach if instead of confidence intervals you had tested a two-tailed statistical hypothesis test, $p < .05$?

3. A researcher conducts a statistical hypothesis test in the usual way and concludes that a sample correlation coefficient ($r = .25$) is statistically significant ($p < .05$). What does this statement say about the population correlation coefficient?

4. A researcher conducts a two-tailed statistical hypothesis test in the usual way and makes a Type II error. What can you say about the population parameter, and what can you say about the sample statistic?

5. Be able to discuss how the statistical power of a test is influenced by the strength of the relationship in the population, the significance level, and the sample size.

6. A researcher conducts an experiment by randomly assigning cases to two levels (A or B) of an independent variable. The researcher tests a research hypothesis that the dependent variable is larger on average in Group A than B against a null hypothesis of no difference. The test is correctly performed, and the researcher rejects the null hypothesis at $p < .05$.

In this case, the researcher may make a Type I error. In words, what does a Type I error mean in this situation?

Assume instead that the statistical test provides a correct outcome. What conclusion should the researcher draw from the statistical test?

7. Compare and contrast sampling error with assignment error.

Issues to Discuss

1. Type I errors have been described in the context of hypothesis testing. Think about them in the context of confidence intervals. Using a simple regression coefficient, describe a population parameter, sample statistic, and confidence intervals that would be comparable to making a Type I error in hypothesis testing.
2. For a given sample statistic, sample size, and so forth, what assumption(s) about the sampling distribution differs in hypothesis testing compared with confidence intervals? What assumption(s) remains the same?
3. Statistical hypothesis testing and confidence intervals both use probability theory to make internal and external statistical inferences. Researchers usually report one or the other but not both. Discuss your preferences. Why would you prefer one method to the other?

APPENDIX 13A: FORMULAE FOR STATISTICAL INFERENCE[1]

This appendix provides procedures to compute tests of statistical inference for simple and multiple correlation and regression. Computer programs that calculate statistics usually calculate some, but not all, of the statistical inference values reported here.

Sampling Distributions

Three sampling distributions are needed to perform statistical inference tests for statistics described in this book. These are the standard normal, t, and F distributions.

Exhibit 13.2 (in the body of the chapter) shows values that identify conventional critical regions of the t and standard normal distributions. There are separate t distributions for each number of degrees of freedom ($d.f.$). Inference tests described next that use t distributions report the number of $d.f.$ to use.

Exhibit 13A.1 shows critical values for F distributions. These distributions are used to make statistical inferences about overall multiple correlation and regression statistics. For example, an F distribution can be used to estimate whether a sample multiple coefficient of determination obtained from a set of independent variables suggests that they collectively explain variance in a dependent variable among the population of cases.

F distributions are formed from the ratio of two variances. They thus involve two sets of $d.f.$, one that applies to the numerator, the other to the denominator. There is a separate F distribution for each combination of numerator and denominator $d.f.$ Unlike t and standard normal distribution inferential tests that can be one- or two-tailed, F distribution tests for the statistical significance of multiple correlation and regression are always one-tailed.

Statistical Inference Tests

Simple Correlation Coefficient

Test H_1, $\rho_{YX} \neq 0.0$ (two-tailed) or $\rho_{YX} > 0.0$ (one-tailed) against H_0, $\rho_{YX} = 0.0$

$$t_{cc} = \frac{r_{YX}\sqrt{n-2}}{\sqrt{1-r_{YX}^2}} \tag{13A.1}$$

---

[1]Linda Brothers's contribution to this appendix is gratefully acknowledged.

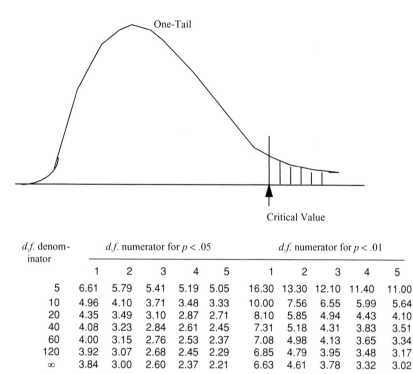

d.f. denom- inator	d.f. numerator for $p < .05$					d.f. numerator for $p < .01$				
	1	2	3	4	5	1	2	3	4	5
5	6.61	5.79	5.41	5.19	5.05	16.30	13.30	12.10	11.40	11.00
10	4.96	4.10	3.71	3.48	3.33	10.00	7.56	6.55	5.99	5.64
20	4.35	3.49	3.10	2.87	2.71	8.10	5.85	4.94	4.43	4.10
40	4.08	3.23	2.84	2.61	2.45	7.31	5.18	4.31	3.83	3.51
60	4.00	3.15	2.76	2.53	2.37	7.08	4.98	4.13	3.65	3.34
120	3.92	3.07	2.68	2.45	2.29	6.85	4.79	3.95	3.48	3.17
∞	3.84	3.00	2.60	2.37	2.21	6.63	4.61	3.78	3.32	3.02

EXHIBIT 13A.1.   Values identifying critical regions of the F distributions.

where t_{cc} is the sample correlation coefficient transformed to a value on a t distribution with $(n-2)$ d.f.

The hypothesis is tested by comparing the computed value of t_{cc} with the critical value on the t distribution determined by the significance level, test of a two-tailed or a one-tailed hypothesis, and the d.f.

Example.   A researcher sets a statistical significance criterion of $p < .05$ for a test of whether a sample correlation coefficient obtained on a sample of 122 participants signals that a relationship in the population is greater than 0.0 (a one-tailed hypothesis). Exhibit 13.2 shows that the value on the t distribution, d.f. $= 120$, is 1.66. The correlation coefficient obtained on the sample is $r_{YX} = .24$. From Formula 13A.1, $t_{cc} = 2.71$, the researcher concludes H_1, the relationship in the population is greater than 0.0.

Confidence Interval for ρ_{YX}.   Confidence intervals for simple correlation coefficients require a new statistic, z_r; it is created because the sampling distribution of r_{YX} is symmetrical only when $\rho_{YX} = 0.0$. The sampling distribution of z_r, alternatively, is approximately normal for any value of ρ_{YX} and has a standard error of:

$$SE_{z_r} = \frac{1}{\sqrt{n-3}}$$

(13A.2)

To obtain a confidence interval for ρ_{YX}, first establish the confidence level (e.g., 95% or 99% corresponding to significance levels of $p < .05$ or $p < .01$, respectively). Second, find

r	Z_r	r	Z_r	r	Z_r	r	Z_r
0.000	0.000	0.300	0.310	0.600	0.693	0.850	1.256
0.010	0.010	0.310	0.321	0.610	0.709	0.855	1.274
0.020	0.020	0.320	0.332	0.620	0.725	0.860	1.293
0.030	0.030	0.330	0.343	0.630	0.741	0.865	1.313
0.040	0.040	0.340	0.354	0.640	0.758	0.870	1.333
0.050	0.050	0.350	0.365	0.650	0.775	0.875	1.354
0.060	0.060	0.360	0.377	0.660	0.793	0.880	1.376
0.070	0.070	0.370	0.388	0.670	0.811	0.885	1.398
0.080	0.080	0.380	0.400	0.680	0.829	0.890	1.422
0.090	0.090	0.390	0.412	0.690	0.848	0.895	1.447
0.100	0.100	0.400	0.424	0.700	0.867	0.900	1.472
0.110	0.110	0.410	0.436	0.710	0.887	0.905	1.499
0.120	0.121	0.420	0.448	0.720	0.908	0.910	1.528
0.130	0.131	0.430	0.460	0.730	0.929	0.915	1.557
0.140	0.141	0.440	0.472	0.740	0.950	0.920	1.589
0.150	0.151	0.450	0.485	0.750	0.973	0.925	1.623
0.160	0.161	0.460	0.497	0.760	0.996	0.930	1.658
0.170	0.172	0.470	0.510	0.770	1.020	0.935	1.697
0.180	0.182	0.480	0.523	0.780	1.045	0.940	1.738
0.190	0.192	0.490	0.536	0.790	1.071	0.945	1.783
0.200	0.203	0.500	0.549	0.800	1.099	0.950	1.832
0.210	0.213	0.510	0.563	0.805	1.113	0.955	1.886
0.220	0.224	0.520	0.576	0.810	1.127	0.960	1.946
0.230	0.234	0.530	0.590	0.815	1.142	0.965	2.014
0.240	0.245	0.540	0.604	0.820	1.157	0.970	2.092
0.250	0.255	0.550	0.618	0.825	1.172	0.975	2.185
0.260	0.266	0.560	0.633	0.830	1.188	0.980	2.298
0.270	0.277	0.570	0.648	0.835	1.204	0.985	2.443
0.280	0.288	0.580	0.662	0.840	1.221	0.990	2.647
0.290	0.299	0.590	0.678	0.845	1.238	0.995	2.994

EXHIBIT 13A.2. Z_r transformations of r.

the value of z_r from Exhibit 13A.2 corresponding to the sample value of r_{YX}. Third, determine the confidence interval for z_r from:

$$CI_{zr} = z_r \pm (z_{sl} \times SE_{z_r}) \tag{13A.3}$$

where z_{sl} is the two-tailed value on the standard normal distribution corresponding to the significance level (see bottom of Exhibit 13.2).

Finally, set the confidence interval for ρ_{YX} by transforming the values of z_r back to correlation coefficient values.

Example.   A researcher wants to determine a confidence interval for the population's correlation coefficient at the 99% confidence level based on a sample correlation coefficient of $r_{YX} = .63$ obtained on a sample of 67 participants. From Exhibit 13A.2, $z_r = .741$, and by Formula 13A.2, $SE_{z_r} = .125$. Formula 13A.3 then shows that $.419 < CI_{zr} < 1.064$. Finally, after transforming the values of z_r back to correlation coefficient values (use Exhibit 13A.2), the researcher finds that $.40 < CI\rho_{YX} < .79$.

Test H_1, $\rho_{YXa} \neq \rho_{YXb}$ (two-tailed), or $\rho_{YXa} > \rho_{YXb}$ (one-tailed) against $H_0\rho_{YXa} = \rho_{YXb}$, where a and b refer to two different populations. (This test also requires z_r.)

$$z_{cc} = \frac{z_{rYXa} - z_{rYXb}}{\sqrt{\dfrac{1}{n_a - 3} + \dfrac{1}{n_b - 3}}} \tag{13A.4}$$

where z_{cc} = a transformed value of the sample statistic on a standard normal distribution, z_{rYXa} and z_{rYXb} refer to the z_r transformations of r_{YXa} and r_{YXb} for samples from populations a and b, respectively, and n_a and n_b refer to the sample sizes selected from populations a and b, respectively

The hypothesis is tested by comparing the computed value of z_{cc} with the value on the standard normal distribution determined by the significance level and whether the test is of a two-tailed or a one-tailed hypothesis.

Example. A researcher hypothesizes that the relationship between income level and financial contributions to a political party is greater among the population of registered Democrats than among the population of registered Republicans. This is a one-tailed hypothesis and a significance level of $p < .05$ is established. Probability samples are obtained of 112 registered Democrats (Population A) and of 128 registered Republicans (Population B). The correlation coefficients obtained on these samples are $r_{YXa} = .36$ and $r_{YXb} = .29$. From Exhibit 13A.2, $z_{rYXa} = .377$ and $z_{rYXb} = .299$. From Formula 13A.4, $z_{cc} = .60$. Comparing this value to the value of 1.64 obtained from Exhibit 13.2 leads to the conclusion that the hypothesis test fails to reject the null hypothesis that $\rho_{YXa} = \rho_{YXb}$ at a significance level of $p < .05$.

Test $H_1, \rho_{YX1} \neq \rho_{YX2}$ (two-tailed), or $\rho_{YX1} > \rho_{YX2}$ (one-tailed) against $H_0, \rho_{YX1} = \rho_{YX2}$, when computed for the same population.

$$t_{cc} = (r_{YX1} - r_{YX2})\sqrt{\frac{(n-3)(1 + r_{X1X2})}{2 \times \left(1 - r_{X1X2}^2 - r_{YX1}^2 - r_{YX2}^2 + 2 \times r_{X1X2} \times r_{YX1} \times r_{YX2}\right)}} \tag{13A.5}$$

where t_{cc} is a transformed value of the sample statistic on a t distribution with $(n-3)$ d.f.

The hypothesis is tested by comparing the computed value of t_{cc} with the value on the t distribution determined by the significance level, test of a two-tailed or a one-tailed hypothesis, and the d.f.

Example. A researcher hypothesizes that the relationship between job pay (Y) and years of work experience ($X1$) is greater than the relationship between Y and age ($X2$) in a population of employees. This is a one-tailed hypothesis and the researcher establishes a statistical significance level of $p < .01$. An employee sample of 83 is obtained. The correlation coefficients determined for this sample are $r_{YX1} = .73$, $r_{YX2} = .57$, and $r_{X1X2} = .68$. From Formula 13A.5, $t_{cc} = 2.65$, the researcher concludes that $\rho_{YX1} > \rho_{YX2}$ at a significance level of $p < .01$ after comparing this value with the value of 2.38 obtained from Exhibit 13.2 ($d.f. = 80$).

Simple Regression Coefficient

Test $H_1 B_{YX} \neq 0.0$ (two-tailed) or that $B_{YX} > 0.0$ (one-tailed) against $H_0 B_{YX} = 0.0$

$$t_{cc} = \frac{b_{YX}}{SEb_{YX}} \tag{13A.6}$$

where t_{cc} is a transformed value of the sample statistic value on a t distribution with $(n-2)$ d.f. and SEb_{YX} is the standard error of the regression coefficient defined as:

$$SEb_{YX} = \frac{SD_{Y \cdot X}}{SD_X \sqrt{n-1}} \tag{13A.7}$$

and $SD_{Y \cdot X}$ is the standard error of estimate of Y on X, which is defined as:

$$SD_{Y \cdot X} = \sqrt{\frac{n-1}{n-2} \times SD_Y^2 \left(1 - r_{YX}^2\right)} \tag{13A.8}$$

The hypothesis is tested by comparing the computed value of t_{cc} with the value on the t distribution determined by the significance level, test of a two-tailed or a one-tailed hypothesis, and d.f. $(n-2)$.

Example. A researcher hypothesizes that changes in levels of job satisfaction predict changes in levels of absenteeism. This is a two-tailed hypothesis and a significance level of $p < .05$ is established. The researcher obtains a sample of 32 employees. Exhibit 13.2 shows that the value on the t distribution, d.f. $= 30$, is 2.04.

Sample statistics required to test H_1 are $SD_X = 0.5$, $SD_Y = 3.0$, $r_{YX} = 0.20$, and $b_{YX} = 1.20$. From Formula 13A.8, $SD_{Y \cdot X} = 2.99$; from Formula 13A.7, $SEb_{YX} = 1.07$; and from Formula 13A.6, $t_{cc} = 1.11$. The researcher concludes that the hypothesis test based on the sample regression coefficient fails to reject the null hypothesis that $B_{YX} = 0.0$.

Confidence Interval for B_{YX}.

$$CI = b_{YX} \pm (t_{sl} \times SEb_{YX}) \tag{13A.9}$$

where t_{sl} is the the t distribution value with $(n-2)$ d.f. corresponding to the two-tailed significance level

Example. From the preceding illustration, assume the researcher instead wants to determine the confidence interval for the regression coefficient of the population. As before, the researcher establishes a significance level of $p < .05$. From Formula 13A.9, $-0.98 < CIB_{YX} < 3.35$.

Multiple Coefficient of Determination

Test H_1, $P_{YXiXj}^2 > 0.0$ *(one-tailed only) against* H_0, $P_{YXiXj}^2 = 0.0$ (This is the same statistical test to determine whether $P_{YXiXj} > 0.0$.)

$$F_{cc} = \frac{R_{YXiXj}^2 / k}{\left(1 - R_{YXiXj}^2\right)/(n - k - 1)} \tag{13A.10}$$

where k is the number of independent variables (two shown in this case) and F_{cc} is a transformed value of the sample statistic on an F distribution with $[k$ and $(n-k-1)]$ d.f.

The hypothesis is tested by comparing the computed value of F_{cc} with the value on the F distribution determined by the significance level and the $[k$ and $(n-k-1)]$ d.f.

Example.   A researcher hypothesizes that variance in the rate of turnover of companies in the same industry will be explained by differences in average employee income level, level of employer-provided benefits, and perceived job alternatives. The researcher establishes a significance level of $p < .01$ for the test and obtains data on a sample of 24 companies. The multiple coefficient of determination obtained on the sample is $R^2_{YX1X2X3} = .45$. From Formula (13A.10), $F_{cc} = 5.45$. Comparing this with the value of 4.94 obtained from Exhibit 13A.1, the researcher concludes that $P^2_{YX1X2X3} > 0.0$ at a significance level of $p < .01$.

Partial Beta Coefficients[2]

Test hypothesis that Beta $_{YXi \cdot Xj} \neq 0.0$ (two-tailed) or that Beta$_{YXi \cdot Xj} > 0.0$ (one-tailed)

$$SEbeta_{YXi \cdot Xj} = \sqrt{\frac{1 - R^2_{YXiXj}}{n - k - 1}} \sqrt{\frac{1}{1 - r^2_{YXJ}}} \qquad (13A.11)$$

$$t_{cc} = \frac{(beta_{YXi \cdot Xj})}{SEbeta_{YXi \cdot Xj}} \qquad (13A.12)$$

where t_{cc} is a transformed value of the sample statistic value on a t distribution with $(n - k - 1)$ d.f., and k is the number of independent variables

The hypothesis is tested by comparing the computed value of t_{cc} with the value on the t distribution determined by the significance level, test of a two-tailed or a one-tailed hypothesis, and the d.f.

Example.   A researcher hypothesizes that satisfaction with life depends on job satisfaction ($X1$) and gender ($X2$). These are two-tailed hypotheses and significance levels of $p < .05$ are established for each independent variable. The researcher obtains a sample of 63 employees. Exhibit 13.2 shows that the value on the t distribution, $d.f. = 60$, is 2.00. The statistics obtained on the sample are $R^2_{YX1X2} = .49$; $r^2_{X1X2} = .20$; $beta_{YX1 \cdot X2} = .35$; $beta_{YX2 \cdot X1} = .27$; $SD_Y = .92$; $SD_{X1} = .85$; $SD_{X2} = .50$; and, by Formula 13A.11, $SEbeta_{YX1 \cdot X2} = .10 = SEbeta_{YX2 \cdot X1}$. From Formula 13A.12, $t_{cc} = 3.50$ and 2.70. Comparing these values to 2.00, the researcher concludes that $Beta_{YX1 \cdot X2} \neq 0.0$ (or $B_{YX1 \cdot X2} \neq 0.0$) and that $Beta_{YX2 \cdot X1} \neq 0.0$ (or $B_{YX2 \cdot X1} \neq 0.0$) at a significance level of $p < .05$.

Confidence Interval for Beta$_{YXi \cdot Xj}$($B_{YXi \cdot Xj}$).

$$CI = beta_{YXi \cdot Xj} \pm (t_{sl/2} \times SEbeta_{YXi \cdot Xj}) \qquad (13A.13a)$$

$$CI = b_{YXi \cdot Xj} \pm (t_{sl/2} \times SEb_{YXi \cdot Xj}) \qquad (13A.13b)$$

where $t_{sl/2}$ is the value on the t distribution with $(n - k - 1)$ d.f. corresponding to the significance level divided by two ($sl/2$).

---

[2]The same test establishes the statistical significance of the corresponding unstandardized partial regression coefficients.

Example.   Using information from the previous example, assume the researcher instead wants to determine the confidence intervals for the partial beta coefficients of the population. The researcher establishes a confidence level of 95%. From Formulas 13A.13a and 13A.13b, $.15 < CIBeta_{YX1 \cdot X2} < .55$ ($.16 < CIB_{YX1 \cdot X2} < .60$) and $.07 < CIBeta_{YX2 \cdot X1} < .47$ ($.13 < CIB_{YX2 \cdot X1} < .87$).

Incremental R^2

Test hypothesis that addition of an independent variable(s) adds to variance explained in Y

$$F_{cc} = \frac{\left(R_{YB}^2 - R_{YSA}^2\right)/(B - A)}{\left(1 - R_{YB}^2\right)/(n - B - 1)} \qquad (13A.14)$$

where F_{cc} is a transformed value of the sample statistic on a F distribution with $[(B - A)$ and $(n - B - 1)]$ d.f. B is the total number of independent variables, A is the number of initial independent variables, and $(B - A)$ is the number of independent variables added

The hypothesis is tested by comparing the computed value of F_{cc} with the value on the F distribution determined by the significance level and $[(B - A)$ and $(n - B - 1)]$ d.f.

Example.   A researcher hypothesizes that incremental variance in income will be explained by race and gender after controlling for age, years of work experience, and years of education; $A = 3$, $B = 5$, and $B - A = 2$. A statistical significance level of $p < .05$ is established. A probability sample of 126 participants is drawn from a population; $R_{YA}^2 = .25$ and $R_{YB}^2 = .28$. The addition of race and gender adds 3% to the explanation of income variance after the control variables are accounted for. F_{cc} from Formula 13A.14 equals 2.50. Comparing this value with the value of 3.07 obtained from Exhibit 13A.1, the researcher concludes that the hypothesis test based on the sample multiple coefficients of determination fails to reject the null hypothesis that $P_{YXB}^2 - P_{YXA}^2 = 0.0$ at a significance level of $p < .05$.

Part V Suggested Readings

A substantial number of statistical hypothesis testing and confidence interval procedures are provided in the Appendix to chapter 13 for correlation and regression. Standard statistics textbooks also typically include hypothesis testing and confidence interval procedures for other statistics such as means and proportions.

However, standard textbooks may not have much to say about statistical power. Cohen et al. (2003) have the most complete discussion of power regarding correlation and regression that I am familiar with. In addition, Cohen (1988) has a book devoted to statistical power issues and methods for calculating it.

Abelson (1995) offered an interesting perspective on statistics and especially statistical inference. He emphasized contributions that probability and statistics can make to the generalization of understandings from research; the book is easy to understand.

VI

Generalization: Addressing External Validity

14

External Validity

Chapter Outline

- *External Generalization Challenges*
- *Generalizing from Single Studies*
- *Replication*
  - *Replication Roles*
  - *Narrative Reviews of Replications*
- *Meta-Analysis*
  - *Example*
    - *Illustrative Data*
    - *Meta-Analysis Interpretations*
    - *External Statistical Inference*
    - *Internal Statistical Inference*
  - *Evaluation*
    - *Contributions of Meta-Analysis*
    - *Meta-Analysis Reservations*
    - *Closing Observations*
- *Summary*
- *For Review*
  - *Terms to Know*
  - *Questions for Review*
  - *Issues to Discuss*
- *Part VI Suggested Readings*

A training manager in an investment firm hypothesizes that knowledge about investment derivatives will help a firm's investment counselors recommend more profitable investment choices to clients. (An *investment derivative* is a security whose value depends on the price of some other security. A stock option is an example; the value of the option depends on the price of the stock.) A training program is developed, and a sample of investment counselors is trained. Client investment performance is then compared between the trained counselors and a sample of untrained counselors over a 12-month period after the training. As expected, the manager finds that clients of the trained counselors obtain a higher investment return.

No generalization issues are involved if the manager is simply curious about the relationship between counselor training and client investment performance in the group studied. However, research is seldom conducted for such a limited purpose; researchers and research consumers are almost always interested in generalizing research results.

The following questions illustrate ways a researcher may wish to generalize the observed relationship:

- Does the relationship found among sample counselors suggest a relationship in the firm's population of counselors?
- Does the relationship suggest that clients who worked with trained counselors will continue to obtain superior investment performance in the next 12 months?
- Should another firm conclude investment performance will improve if its counselors are given the same training?
- Will investment performance improve if the training program is modified to be less expensive?
- Will investment performance improve if the training focuses on another type of investment instrument?

The external statistical validation procedures described in part V provide information only on the first question. During the previous 12 months, was there a relationship between training and investment performance in the population of firm counselors? Furthermore, statistical generalization procedures address this question correctly only if the sample drawn is representative of the population of counselors in the firm.

External statistical validation receives separate status largely because there are elegant procedures available. It is not necessarily more important than the other kinds of generalization suggested by these questions; often it is not as important.

This chapter discusses issues associated with other types of research generalization that interest researchers and consumers who rely on research results. It begins by discussing challenges confronting such generalization. It then describes contributions of repeating research studies to address generalization. Finally, it discusses two procedures for evaluating research repetitions and generalizing from them.

EXTERNAL GENERALIZATION CHALLENGES

Empirical research studies are conducted on a specific group of cases at a particular moment in time. However, researchers are almost always interested in generalizing the findings beyond that group and time period. For example, it is almost certain that the investment training manager is not particularly interested in a relationship between training and client investment performance observed in the past. The manager wants to know if the relationship can be expected in the future. Is it reasonable to suppose future client investment performance will improve relative to untrained counselors if the same training were implemented with a group of counselors now?

This illustrates one of the greatest challenges facing research—change. Research findings obtained at one time often do not generalize to findings at another time. In the illustration, economic conditions change, so it is likely that successful investment strategies change. As a consequence, strategies involving investment derivatives that are successful during a time period studied may be more or less successful as economic conditions change in the future.

Research investigations that ask for opinions about topical issues are particularly susceptible to changes that may invalidate generalizations to other time periods. For example, survey studies designed to predict election outcomes are conducted before citizens actually vote. Questions to a probability sample of prospective voters are often prefaced with, "If the election were held today, . . ."

Results of such surveys often accurately reflect voter population sentiment at the time taken; sampling error as discussed in part V is small. Yet the sample estimate may not predict the election outcome. Voter opinions in the population change between the date the survey is conducted and the date the election is held. The research results, even though statistically valid, do not generalize to the relevant time period.

So, change resulting from the passage of time is one important dimension of external generalization. Another important dimension involves the cases in which research results are applicable. Researchers often are interested in generalizing results from a group(s) studied to groups not studied. For example, if the derivative training is successful among counselors in one investment firm, will it also be successful among counselors in other investment firms?

Statistical generalization procedures are not designed to address questions of this sort. Inferences using sampling distributions as described in the last chapter require that generalization be made only to the population from which the probability sample was drawn. Generalizations beyond that specific population transcend what statistical generalization can deliver.

GENERALIZING FROM SINGLE STUDIES

There is no systematic or verifiable method to conduct external validation based solely on a single investigation of a research relationship. By definition, external generalization is aimed at cases and environments that transcend the boundaries of a study and hence cannot be addressed within it. Nevertheless, researchers usually are interested in ways their results likely generalize as noted.

As a consequence, researchers usually address external validity in the discussion section of research reports. When done well, this section is the product of the thoughtful identification of similarities and potentially important differences between the cases and environment studied and other cases and environments in which the results also may apply. Simply put, results from any one study are most likely to generalize to similar cases and environments.

The quality of this type of generalization depends on a researcher's knowledge of important characteristics (variables) that may influence results from one research setting to another. In the language of chapter 5, researchers must be able to identify probable moderator variables (boundary conditions). Relationships generalize across research environments, such as time, as long as the new environments do not represent different values of moderator variables that change the nature of the relationship(s) observed.

To illustrate, under what conditions might the investment derivative training not generalize? One potential moderator may be the investment sophistication of the counselors trained. A group of counselors markedly less sophisticated than those studied may not acquire the necessary knowledge and hence not provide appropriate investment advice even though they are trained. Or, the counselor payment system may serve as a moderator. The counselors trained in

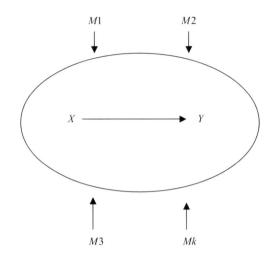

EXHIBIT 14.1.   Limits on generalization.

the illustration may be paid incentives for improving client investment returns. Training may be ineffective among counselors who are not paid in the same way.

Exhibit 14.1 shows a simple representation of the issues involved. Research investigates a relationship between X and Y. These variables are inside the ellipse to signal that their relationship is actually studied by a researcher. Outside the circle are potential moderator variables ($M1$ to Mk), potential limits or boundaries to generalization.

REPLICATION

Researchers conducting single studies can only speculate about conditions that may apply outside the domain of the variables studied. Judgmental claims of generalization, therefore, must be provisional. Whether results actually generalize across potential moderator variables to other cases or environments can be established only by **replication**. A *replication* is a research study that investigates an issue that has already been studied; it repeats a previous study.

Replication Roles

Replications permit external generalization of a more rigorous sort if they differ from previous research on values of potential moderator variables. Although neither the original study nor its replication has variation in a moderator variable (e.g., $M1$ in Exhibit 14.1), the two taken together may bring the moderator into the ellipse. For example, a comparison of the original training study with a replication using less sophisticated counselors provides information about whether the training generalizes across levels of counselor sophistication.

Some researchers argue that the word *replication* should be reserved for studies that are identical to a study replicated. In this view, replications are often seen as superior to *partial replications* or *constructive replications*, terms recommended if the studies are not identical.

This view misses the point that a replication always differs from a prior study. The time period must be different even in the unlikely event the cases and measures are identical. Subtle design characteristics typically also differ even when researchers seek to identically replicate a prior study. More important, it is desirable that replications differ, because the differences provide information about the generalizability of findings as noted.

This last observation may suggest that the more variability between an original study and a replication the better. For example, why not conduct a replication on counselors that are both less sophisticated and are paid with a different compensation system? One obtains evidence that the results generalize over both potential moderator variables if the results of the replication and the original results are similar. This strategy is often acceptable as long as the results from the replication mirror the results in the original study. However, when they do not, the replication provides little information about whether the difference is due to differences in counselor sophistication, differences in pay systems, or both.

As a consequence, researchers must seek a balance when designing replications. On the one hand, it is desirable to generalize as broadly as possible. This encourages varying replications along values of several potential moderators. On the other hand, it is also important to link replications to previous research. Cumulative knowledge is possible only when research studies share important characteristics, when they are similar enough so that results obtained in one study provide useful information for interpreting results from another.

How closely replications should mirror prior research depends largely on the strength of the conceptualization underlying the research and the "maturity" of the finding(s). Replications should closely approximate the design of original research when a research result is novel and has little conceptual support. Researchers conducting replications involving relationships that are supported in several prior studies, or by strong conceptual models, may be justified in testing the limits of generalization.

Replications serve as the best method for addressing external generalization. As more replications are conducted, more potential moderator variables can be drawn inside the ellipse shown in Exhibit 14.1. Replication is even desirable for external statistical validation because of the probabilistic, and hence potentially erroneous, conclusions that emerge from statistical inference procedures.

However, drawing valid external generalizations from replications is a challenging exercise. Challenges arise because results obtained on studies of the same conceptual relationship(s) are seldom identical. Two studies of the same relationship often obtain different results even though they use the same measures, are conducted at about the same time, and study cases that appear to be similar. The water is muddied further when another replication obtains results that are similar to one of the first two but differs from it on some important characteristic. Now, multiply these ambiguous outcomes across many replications, and you begin to appreciate the difficulties confronting external generalization.

Narrative Reviews of Replications

Until about three decades ago, most generalization of replications was performed through ***narrative research reviews***. A narrative research review reports a researcher's judgmental summary and evaluation of a body of research on some topic. The quality of the review depends on the reviewer's knowledge of the topic and research methods.

For example, a reviewer may wish to know what research says about the effectiveness of investment derivative training for improving investment performance. Such reviews begin with a search for studies of investment derivative training that have already been conducted and summarized in research reports. The studies found serve in the same role as cases in an empirical study; each study contains information that is analogous to information provided by research cases more generally.

Typically, reviewers next evaluate the studies and make decisions about which "cases" to include for analysis. Should all studies found be included, regardless of design characteristics? Or, should some studies be excluded because they do not meet standards for design (e.g., evidence of internal validity), sampling (e.g., sample size), or other characteristics? For example,

RESEARCH HIGHLIGHT 14.1

Triangulation As Replication

There are many challenges for studies investigating causal conceptual relationship as emphasized throughout this book. Seldom does a single study lead to great confidence that construct or internal validity is established, much less both. These reservations are raised in part because each research method has shortcomings. To illustrate, experiments potentially address certain threats to internal validity but may be problematic in other respects. For example, one may question whether a research manipulation of an independent variable properly captures the construct of interest in an experiment that is otherwise exemplary.

Researchers are encouraged to address this type of challenge by *triangulation*, by investigating a research question by using other methods of measurement, design, and even analysis. In triangulation, the concern is not so much substantive as it is methodological. Replications are designed to see if results hold up across different research methods for obtaining them.

should training studies be included only if they are true experiments, in which counselors are randomly assigned to training or control conditions? Or should quasi-experiments also be included? Reviewers using different evaluation standards often reach different conclusions about a body of research because they impose different standards in this stage.

Reviewers then analyze the studies; they make judgments about the findings obtained in each study reviewed. An assessment is made about whether, and to what degree, each study finds support for the investigated relationship(s) of interest. For example, to what degree does each study find evidence that investment derivative training improves subsequent investment performance?

Evaluations of specific studies, often combined with a description of noteworthy design characteristics, are followed by conclusions about the findings overall. For example, what can be concluded about the direction and strength of the relationship between investment derivative training and investment performance, and under what conditions does this relationship likely hold? In narrative reviews, judgments about findings, and the probable conditions over which these findings generalize, are made qualitatively by the reviewer.

Reviews of the type described can make valuable contributions. They are especially useful when combined with thoughtful suggestions for additional research and conceptual development.

But such reviews also face difficulties. As with discussions of generalization found in single studies, they depend heavily on the expertise and good judgment of the reviewer. Although these may be substantial, they cannot be articulated for public examination. Such reviews become increasingly problematic as the number of studies to review becomes large. As the number of studies increases, so do burdens on reviewers; it is an increasing challenge to apply consistent standards for the many decisions that must be made about each study.

META-ANALYSIS

Meta-analysis is a more recent procedure used to evaluate and generalize from research replications. It is designed to overcome some of the problems of traditional narrative reviews. It does

Research Elements	Elements in Meta-Analysis
Cases to study	Research studies, or results of research studies
Dependent variable	Direction and strength of relationships observed in the studies reviewed
Independent variables	Substantive and methodological characteristics of the studies reviewed

EXHIBIT 14.2. Special characteristics of meta-analysis.

so by using quantitative procedures developed for conducting original research. Meta-analysis is especially useful as the number of studies to review becomes large.

Meta-analysis techniques sprang up independently in several different academic disciplines. Researchers started to conduct reviews by using meta-analysis techniques before a methodology was codified and named; the techniques have been used in the social sciences beginning at least as early as the 1930s. Codification of meta-analysis procedures was reported beginning in the 1970s.

Meta-analysis is distinguished from narrative reviews by its use of additional empirical research methods. Indeed, a good way to understand meta-analysis is to think of it as a special form of field study research, as described in chapter 7. Exhibit 14.2 summarizes characteristics that differentiate meta-analysis from a typical original survey or field study.

As Exhibit 14.2 shows, "cases" in meta-analysis are studies, or results from studies, just as in narrative literature reviews. A feature that distinguishes meta-analysis techniques from both narrative reviews and conventional empirical research involves the dependent variable. In meta-analysis, the dependent variable is a statistic that describes the results of the studies reviewed. Preferred dependent variables describe the size and direction of a relationship(s) found in the studies reviewed. For example, a meta-analysis of investment derivative training studies might take the mean difference in client investment performance between groups receiving training versus control groups. This difference is standardized for each study so that comparisons can be made across studies.

Another characteristic that distinguishes meta-analysis from conventional empirical research involves independent variables. In meta-analysis, independent variables are study characteristics that may account for differences in the relationship (difference) that represents the dependent variable. For example, market conditions prevailing when the training was conducted may serve as an independent variable if a meta-analyst believes market conditions influence the effectiveness of investment training.

Independent variables may be either substantive or methodological. Substantive characteristics are specific to the conceptual issue researched (e.g., market conditions, in the investment training illustration). Methodological characteristics refer to design issues. For example, a meta-analysis of derivative training may differentiate between studies that used a control group to contrast with a training group (between-cases design) and studies that compared investment performance before and after a group of counselors have been trained (within-case design). Methodological variables are investigated to see whether results depend on the methods used to study the substantive issue.

RESEARCH HIGHLIGHT 14.2

An Inappropriate Dependent Variable for Meta-Analysis

Sometimes reviewers use statistical significance values reported in the studies reviewed as the dependent variable. For example, a review of investment derivative studies may calculate and then report the percentage of studies that found investment derivative groups to obtain statistically significantly greater client investment performance ($p < .05$) than control groups.

This ***box-score method*** has two related limitations and is generally to be avoided. First, what is statistically significant, at any level, depends only partly on the strength of the relationship between the variables. It also depends on sample size. Small sample sizes require larger relationships (differences) to be statistically significant. Thus, the statistical significance between two studies can differ, even though the strength of the relationship does not, because the studies used different sized samples. Second, the box-score method ignores valuable information about the strength of the relationships (differences). Studies with large samples may have statistically significant results even though the relationships, or differences, are small.

These substantive and methodological variables are thus investigated as potential moderator variables that may influence the generalizability of results. Meta-analysis evaluates these variables quantitatively. This represents an advantage of meta-analysis compared with narrative reviews that only provide judgmental evaluations of potential moderating conditions.

Example

Statistical analyses are carried out once the dependent variable and potential independent variables have been identified and coded. To some extent, the type of analyses recommended varies across different meta-analysis procedures. A hypothetical data set using the investment derivative training example is used here to illustrate major similarities and differences among different meta-analysis procedures.

Illustrative Data

Characteristics of 10 original studies investigating the relationship between investment derivative training and client investment performance have been created and are summarized in Exhibit 14.3. (An actual meta-analysis typically would not be conducted with so few studies.) These 10 studies involved a total of 510 counselors who were either trained or served as controls.

The dependent variable used by the meta-analyst is the simple correlation coefficient (chapter 10) between client investment performance measured after training and whether counselors experienced training. Training (versus control) is coded so that a positive coefficient indicates clients of trained counselors obtained greater returns than clients of untrained counselors. In Exhibit 14.3, the correlation coefficient of .28 in Study 1 signals that clients of trained counselors obtained a higher rate of investment return than the clients of untrained counselors. Exhibit 14.3 shows that investment performances of clients with trained counselors are greater in 8 of the 10 studies.

Study	Number of Counselors	Study Results[1]	Market Conditions	Study Design
01	12	0.28	<.15	Between
02	30	0.40	<.15	Between
03	20	0.36	>.20	Within
04	18	0.22	<.15	Between
05	22	-0.03	<.15	Between
06	30	0.32	>.20	Between
07	18	0.42	>.20	Between
08	24	0.44	>.20	Within
09	16	0.26	<.15	Within
10	20	-0.12	<.15	Between

[1]Correlation coefficient between investment derivative training (trained = 1; not trained = 0) and client investment performance.

EXHIBIT 14.3.   Summary characteristics from 10 studies on investment training.

The results shown in Exhibit 14.3 oversimplify a meta-analyst's coding task. Studies often report results using a variety of statistics. For example, some might report mean investment performance differences between trained and untrained counselors. Others might report results in correlation coefficients, and yet others may report results in still other ways. A meta-analyst must report results from all studies by using a common statistic, so that results can be summarized across the studies quantitatively. Fortunately, results reported by using one statistic often can be converted into others. For example, a simple transformation of Formula 10.6 could be performed to convert a simple regression coefficient into a simple correlation coefficient. A variety of conversion formulae are provided by Glass, McGaw, & Smith (1981, ch. 5) and Hunter & Schmidt (1990, ch. 7).

Exhibit 14.3 shows that the meta-analyst has also coded two independent variables, one substantive and one methodological. The substantive independent variable is the market conditions prevailing at the time of the study. The meta-analyst finds that all studies were conducted during times when average market returns were either less than 15% or more than 20%. The researcher hypothesizes that the benefits of investment derivative training are greater when market conditions are more favorable. Methodologically, the meta-analyst records whether the studies compared client investment performance with trained counselors or controls (between-cases studies) or whether they compared performance before and after training (within-cases studies). The researcher believes that within-cases studies often obtain more favorable results than between-cases studies.

Meta-Analysis Interpretations

Steps recommended for data collection and coding generally are not controversial among meta-analysts. Moreover, researchers agree that an important outcome from meta-analysis is an average value to characterize the dependent variable. In the illustration from Exhibit 14.3,

the average correlation coefficient is calculated ($r_{YX} = .26$).[1] This signals that whether counselors were trained accounts for about 7% of the variance in average investor returns across
the studies conducted ($r_{YX}^2 = .07$). Meta-analysis is attractive relative to traditional narrative
reviews, because it provides this type of quantitative summary of the results of previous research.

Controversy arises about the interpretation of such averages and recommendations for
additional analyses. This controversy centers on appropriate statistical inferences to be drawn
from meta-analysis. There are differences in viewpoints about both external statistical inference
and internal statistical inference.

External Statistical Inference

Some meta-analysts take the studies reviewed as a population.[2] From this perspective, meta-
analysis is a way to describe the studies in statistical terms and not to generalize to some
broader population. Proponents of this perspective question whether meta-analysis is more
useful than traditional narrative reviews for external generalization, statistical or otherwise.

Alternatively, other researchers argue that the studies reviewed represent a sample that
can be generalized to a broader population.[3] Although this broader population is not well
defined, advocates of this approach use external statistical inference procedures to test statistical
hypotheses or to create confidence intervals about these broader population parameters (see
chapter 13). This perspective thus claims more for meta-analysis than is claimed for traditional
narrative reviews.

Internal Statistical Inference

There are also different perspectives with regard to appropriate procedures to address internal statistical inference. These differences are related to differences in views about external
generalization.

Some researchers who see meta-analysis as a way of describing a population of studies
emphasize assignment error over sampling error. To illustrate, advocates of this perspective
might correlate the dependent variable in Exhibit 14.3 with the two independent variables,
market conditions and design type. Exhibit 14.4 shows the results of this procedure when
market conditions ($>.20 = 1$) and design type (within-case $= 1$) are dummy coded. Exhibit
14.4 shows that both independent variables are positively correlated with investment return;
market conditions are statistically significantly correlated with investment return ($p < .05$;
one-tailed). A meta-analyst using this perspective would conclude that market conditions
moderate the relationship between training and investment performance in the population of
studies performed. In the studies reviewed, investment derivative training results in higher
client performance when market conditions are more favorable.

Alternatively, those meta-analysts who view results from the studies as a sample to be
generalized to a population emphasize sampling error. One widely used procedure recommends
that variability in the study results first be adjusted for an estimate of sampling error (Hunter
& Schmidt, 1990). Possible moderator variables should be investigated only if substantial

---

[1] A technical disagreement involves whether summary statistics should be weighted (e.g., by sample size) when
averaging. In the example, the weighted and unweighted correlation coefficients are the same. There is also disagreement over whether the coefficients from each study should be transformed to a distribution that is more normal than a
distribution of correlation coefficients before averaging (see appendix 13A). Details of these disagreements go beyond
the purposes here.

[2] This approach is represented by Glass, McGaw, & Smith (1981).

[3] Hunter & Schmidt's (1990) approach to meta-analysis represents this perspective.

Correlation Coefficients

Variable	1	2	3
1. Study results	1.00		
2. Market conditions	.59*	1.00	
3. Study design	.36	.36	1.00

*$p < .05$ (one-tailed)

EXHIBIT 14.4.   Correlation coefficients between the training dependent variable and the substantive and methodological independent variables.

variability between results of studies remains after the estimated variability due to sampling error is removed. This procedure applied to the results summarized in Exhibit 14.3 leads to the conclusion that sampling error is responsible for most of the variation between the studies.[4] A researcher using this procedure concludes that the results all come from a single population; the results are not influenced by market conditions or by any other moderator variable.

Evaluation

One of the most serious shortcomings of empirical research has been a lack of trustworthy procedures to evaluate and make appropriate external generalizations from research once conducted. Traditionally, evaluations of and generalizations from previous research have been made after researchers conduct narrative reviews. These reviews depend primarily on the quality of judgments and decisions made by a reviewer. Conclusions reached by one reviewer are often challenged by another, even after examining the same body of literature.

Disagreements between narrative reviews often increase as the body of replications increases. More research findings, paradoxically, can lead to greater confusion about the internal and external validity of relationships. Standard narrative review procedures are increasingly vulnerable to errors as the number of studies reviewed becomes large.

Contributions of Meta-Analysis

Given the problems associated with narrative reviews, it is not surprising that meta-analysis has been embraced with great enthusiasm. Meta-analysis introduces quantitative and publicly replicable research methods to research literature reviews.

Some meta-analysis procedures are as applicable to narrative as to quantitative reviews. In particular, meta-analysis calls for systematic coding not only of a quantitative dependent variable but of independent variables as well. This practice can be emulated to improve narrative reviews.

For example, a narrative reviewer may focus on the sample size of one study in the review. The reviewer may conclude it is attractively large, or too small. The point? If sample size is a salient characteristic of one study, it is salient for all. A good narrative review will systematically code sample size for all studies, just as in a meta-analysis.

Meta-analysis also extends contributions made by narrative reviews. Quantifying study results and converting them to a common statistic (e.g., a correlation coefficient) allows reviewers to generate an average result across studies. This is useful summary information, even if you

---

[4]Calculations using procedures from Hunter & Schmidt (1990) are not shown here.

conclude that meta-analysis is best used only to describe prior research. If you conclude further that meta-analysis can be used for inference, the average may be extended more broadly.

The analysis of relationships between study results and coded independent variables is an especially attractive feature of meta-analysis. Relationships between the dependent variable and either substantive or methodological independent variables provide information about potential moderator variables. This feature of meta-analysis provides researchers with quantitative estimates about the external generalizability of research findings. As noted, however, there is still disagreement among meta-analysts about how best to address these potential moderator variables.

Meta-Analysis Reservations

Despite its promise, meta-analysis is not a panacea. In the first place, although meta-analysis may reduce controversy about findings from prior research, it does not eliminate it. The use of meta-analysis requires researcher skill and judgment, just as with any other empirical technique. Different meta-analysts will reach different conclusions about the most appropriate ways to carry out a meta-analysis. As a consequence, two researchers using the same meta-analysis procedure likely will arrive at somewhat different conclusions regarding a body of research.[5]

Furthermore, there is still disagreement about how best to think about and understand the variation between results of different studies. It is now generally agreed that variation between studies is due at least in part to sampling error and other sources of differences between studies (e.g., the reliability of measurement). The perspective that this variation can be viewed solely as a result of potential moderator variables and assignment error has fallen out of favor among most meta-analysts. However, the currently popular view that sampling error is likely responsible for all or most of the variation between studies is also increasingly challenged. Advances in meta-analysis require better methods for differentiating between sampling error within a single population and variation that is due to differences between populations.

Closing Observations

Meta-analysis is a method in process. However, the still-emerging character of the methodology should not discourage your use of meta-analysis. Meta-analysts have written books describing procedures they recommend. These will be understandable to those who understand the topics covered in this book.

SUMMARY

Many times researchers and research consumers are more interested in the generalization of research findings than they are in the original findings themselves. For example, do the findings that have been observed in one population apply in another? Will findings obtained in the past apply in the future? These questions illustrate challenges for external generalization. They go beyond external statistical generalization, which speaks only to the likelihood that statistics observed on a probability sample of cases apply to the population from which the sample was drawn.

Moderator variables serve as limits to external generalization. A relationship(s) observed in one context generalizes to another context as long as characteristics that differ between the two contexts do not act as moderator variables. Researchers who have studied a relationship

---

[5]For example, compare the conclusions of Scott & Taylor (1985) with Hackett & Guion (1985) regarding the relationship between satisfaction and absenteeism.

in only one context can only speculate on whether their results generalize. They do not have empirical evidence on variation in the moderator variables.

Evidence on external generalization must be obtained by *replication*. Replications are studies of the same research relationship(s) in another context. Replications that differ on values of potential moderator variables provide evidence on the generalizability of results across these potential moderators.

Until recently, interpretation of replications was confined to traditional *narrative research reviews*. A narrative review consists of a researcher's judgmental summary and evaluation of a body of research on a topic. Narrative reviews draw heavily on nonquantifiable skills and knowledge of the reviewer and hence are often subject to challenge.

Meta-analysis is a method for evaluating and generalizing research replications. Meta-analysts apply standard quantitative procedures to review and evaluate previous research. These include standardized measures to represent the results from previous studies. Standard measures of characteristics that may influence the results are also created. Results of previous studies are then analyzed statistically. Meta-analysis is especially attractive when the number of studies on a particular topic is large because results are coded and evaluated more systematically than is true of most narrative reviews.

There are still a number of contentious issues in meta-analysis. These issues hinge on how best to evaluate the differences in results found in the studies reviewed.

FOR REVIEW

Terms to Know

Replication: A research study that addresses the same research issue(s) as an earlier study.
Triangulation: In research, a form of replication that seeks to discover whether research findings generalize across different research methods.
Narrative research review: A review of prior research studies that depends largely on a reviewer's knowledge of the topic and research methods. The review typically includes a summary and an evaluation of the previous research.
Meta-analysis: Procedures to review and evaluate prior research studies that depend on quantitative research methods.
Box-score method: In meta-analysis, the use of statistical significance values as the dependent variable. Its use is not recommended.

Questions for Review

1. How do potential moderator variables limit external generalization?
2. What major meta-analysis procedures are also desirable in narrative research reviews?
3. How do replications contribute to external generalization?
4. What are advantages of meta-analysis compared with traditional narrative reviews?
5. What are major characteristics of meta-analysis that are still contentious among meta-analysts?

Issues to Discuss

1. Suppose it is established that Scholastic Achievement Tests (SATs) predict grade-point averages among freshmen enrolled in large public universities. What potential moderator variables would concern you about the likely predictive value of SAT scores in exclusive private universities?

2. Evaluate the following statement:

Researchers and research consumers are always interested in generalizing findings obtained in the past to findings expected in the future. For example, research evidence of a successful advertising campaign suggests that the advertising should continue only if you are still to assume that what applied in the past will apply in the future. As a result, external generalization over time is always essential to research. Furthermore, because the future is never known, research findings can never be confidently generalized.

PART VI SUGGESTED READINGS

A readable overview of meta-analysis is provided by Hunt (1997). In addition, there are a number of books describing meta-analysis procedures. These include Hedges & Olkin (1985), Hunter & Schmidt (1990), Glass, McGaw, & Smith (1981), and Rosenthal (1991). Rosenthal (1995) offers suggestions for summarizing meta-analysis studies in research reports.

Meta-analysis is now the standard way of reviewing and generalizing research in many social science disciplines. A few examples from substantive areas of interest to me include reviews of relationships between satisfaction and absenteeism (Hackett & Guion, 1985; Scott & Taylor, 1985, as mentioned in this chapter), satisfaction and job performance (Petty, McGee, & Cavender, 1984), motivation and job performance (Schwab, Gottlieb-Olian, & Heneman, 1979; Van Eerde & Thierry, 1996), perceived employment opportunity and turnover (Steel & Griffeth, 1989), job performance and turnover (McEvoy & Cascio, 1987), strategic planning and firm performance (Miller & Cardinal, 1994), applicant characteristics and interviewer evaluations (Olian, Schwab, & Haberfeld, 1988), and college grade-point average and subsequent employment success (Bretz, 1989; Roth, BeVier, Switzer, & Schippmann, 1996).

There are a very large number of studies on relationships between tests of mental ability and job performance. Many meta-analyses have been conducted on these studies. An article by Schmidt, Law, Hunter, Rothstein, Pearlman, & McDaniel (1993) has references to many of these meta-analyses.

VII

Research Reports

15

Research Report Writing

Chapter Outline

- *Research Report Format*
  - *Introduction*
  - *Methods*
    - *Cases*
    - *Measures*
    - *Procedure*
    - *Analyses*
  - *Results*
  - *Discussion*
- *Alternative Research Report Formats*
- *Additional Suggestions*
  - *Begin by Organizing*
  - *Rewrite, Then Rewrite*
  - *Draft a Critic*
  - *Take a Scout's Oath*
- *Summary*
- *Appendix 15A: On Table Construction*
  - *When to Use Tables*
  - *Table Characteristics*
  - *Integrate Tables and Text*
  - *An Example*
    - *Descriptive Results*
    - *Substantive Results*

Chapter 1 argued that empirical research, carried out appropriately, has two important advantages over other methods for understanding observable events. First, research is systematic. Measurement, design, and data analysis are all carried out in a methodical way. Previous parts of this book emphasize these systematic procedures to conduct research.

Second, it argued that good research is a public process; it is transparent. Research methods, as well as results, are made available by researchers so that others may critically evaluate the research. This second characteristic is important for research reports. It means researchers must do more than summarize research findings. They must also describe the methods that produced the results so that critical evaluation is possible.

This chapter is designed to help you write clear research reports. It describes a format that is suitable for most research reports. This format corresponds closely to one recommended in the *Publication manual of the American Psychological Association* (1994). The chapter also identifies an alternative research report format and concludes with additional recommendations for successful report writing. An appendix at the end of the chapter provides suggestions for using tables in research reports.

RESEARCH REPORT FORMAT

Introduction

Your introduction provides the best opportunity to grab the readers' interest in a study. Make it address three issues. First, state the research problem clearly and succinctly. Place this statement early in the paper so readers understand what to expect. From a research perspective, the trick here is to state the problem in a way that can be solved by the study conducted.

Second, link the research problem to prior conceptualization and research. Knowledge obtained from research is cumulative; no one study alone is very persuasive. In context, however, with conceptual models and findings from other research, results of a study can often be quite convincing. Make the introduction provide that context. Think of your study as one piece of a puzzle. Where does this piece fit in that puzzle?

Finally, state why the research problem is important. For example, will its solution advance understanding of a conceptual model? Will it answer a specific organizational question? Will the study speak to an important policy question? Stating why a research problem is important can help motivate reader interest.

Methods

The methods section describes the overall plan of the study and the steps taken to obtain and analyze scores. It reports on cases studied, measures, administrative procedures used to obtain scores, and the methods used to analyze scores. The order of these topics may vary within the section. The methods section differentiates research report writing most clearly from other types of writing. Thus, it is often a challenging section for fledgling researchers.

A good method section is key to providing the information needed for critical evaluation and potential replication. As a consequence, your objective should be to describe the methods so that another researcher could repeat (replicate) your study.

Cases

Research cases are the objects whose characteristics are measured and studied in a research project. Identify the number and type of cases and report how they were chosen. For example, all employees in an organization may serve as cases. Or, a sample of those employees may be studied. If the latter, also describe the sampling procedure used to obtain participants.

Here is an idea for deciding what participant information to report: Include information about cases that can be used to decide how the research results may generalize to other cases. In addition, describe the population if your study involves statistical generalization.

Report the size of the sample drawn and the sampling procedure used. Also report any attrition between sample cases chosen and those that actually participate (i.e., provide information about nonrespondents and missing data).

Measures

Provide several types of information about each measured variable used. Unless the study is very simple, remind the reader how each measure serves in the model investigated. Is it a dependent, independent, or control variable?

Always report whether a measure was constructed especially for the study or whether it came from another source. In either case, it is usually appropriate to include the item(s) that makes up the measure in the report. If there are only one or two of these, you may place them in the body of the report. Or, you may put them in an appendix.

Regardless of source, tell how each item(s) is scaled (i.e., how numerical values are assigned to responses). This is especially important when variables have no intuitively sensible numerical order. For example, a measure of gender is often scaled 0 and 1. To understand relationships between gender and any other variable it is essential to know whether female = 0 and male = 1, or female = 1 and male = 0.

Cite the source for measures that are borrowed. In addition, include information about the measure from prior research that speaks to its quality. For example, report evidence on characteristics of the measures that address reliability and construct validity.

Procedure

The procedure describes how measurement information was obtained from the cases studied. This should include a description of the methods and inducements used to obtain participation in the study.

Many organizational studies use designs that obtain scores with questionnaires or interviews. In such cases, questions to be answered in the procedures section include the following: How did participants obtain questionnaires (e.g., through the mail, at a meeting)? Where did they complete the questionnaire or interview (e.g., at home, at work)? When did participants complete them (e.g., during regular work hours)?

Experimental and quasi-experimental designs place cases in different circumstances representing different levels of the independent variable. For example, customers may be placed in one of two groups, each exposed to a different type of advertisement. Subsequent purchasing behavior may serve as the dependent variable. In such studies, describe the procedures used to assign participants to different levels of the independent variable. For example, were participants assigned to different levels of the independent variable by a random procedure? Or, were intact groups assigned different levels (e.g., groups located in different geographic regions)?

Research procedures used to obtain scores have important implications for most types of research validity. The way measures are administered to cases can influence construct validity. The way cases are assigned to levels of independent variables can influence internal validity. Procedures also influence conditions under which external validity can be expected. It is essential, therefore, that the research procedures used be thoroughly described for a reader's understanding.

Analyses

The *Publication manual of the American Psychological Association* (1994) does not include a description of the analyses conducted in the methods section. I nevertheless recommend you provide such a description. When included, the methods section contains a description of the entire research plan. If written well, another researcher can replicate a study by working from just your methods section.

Provide information about two types of analyses. First, describe methods used for any initial analyses performed to investigate, and perhaps to prepare, the data for the main analyses. These initial analyses include investigating the data set for missing values. They also include the calculation of descriptive statistics, such as means and standard deviations, on each of the variables measured. Assessments of reliability are also examples of preliminary analyses to describe.

Second, describe analysis methods used to investigate the main research question(s). These are usually statistics that address relationships between variables. Examples include correlation, regression, and analysis of variance.

Results

Your results section may be brief, especially if the methods section includes a description of the procedures used to perform analyses as recommended.

Begin with a description of the results from initial analyses. Report descriptive statistics on independent and dependent variables. Include any evidence addressing the quality of the measures. Follow results of these preliminary analyses with a summary of results from analyses investigating the main research issue(s).

Tables often help communicate results of both initial and main analyses. There are several tricks and conventions to successful table construction (see the appendix). Make the results section descriptive and concise. Just the facts, but all the facts! Save interpretation and editorializing for the discussion.

RESEARCH HIGHLIGHT 15.1

Reporting and Discussing Statistical Significance

Here are four conventions for reporting on statistical significance levels (see Part V):

1. Establish a significance level a priori, state it explicitly, and then use it faithfully. Do not report results that miss your stated level as "nearly significant," or the like. A sample statistic provides a correct estimate of the population parameter, or it does not. Use of terms such as *nearly significant* implies you do not understand what statistical significance means.

2. Always use the entire term: *statistical significance* when you mean to refer to results of an inferential test; *significance* by itself can refer to many things. Something can be statistically significant and yet not be significant in any practical sense.

3. Provide information on the magnitude of relationships, or differences, as well as whether a result is statistically significant. Information on variance explained by an independent variable is almost always helpful to the reader.

4. Do not use failure to reach statistical significance as evidence that there is no relationship, or difference, unless you also provide evidence on the statistical power of your inferential test.

Discussion

The discussion is the capstone of a research report. It is the place to summarize and interpret results, to speculate on generalizations to other contexts, and to identify limitations. In short, it is the section that pulls all parts of a study together, makes sense of them, and makes them interesting.

Although the organization of the discussion section may vary, it is often good to summarize findings first. Which of the hypothesized relationships obtained support? Was internal validity established? Do the measures used suggest that causal conceptual relationships are tenable among the cases studied? If sampling procedures warrant, you can also discuss external statistical validity at this point.

A discussion of the study's implications logically follows the summary of basic findings. If a conceptual model was tested, was support obtained? Do the findings suggest the model be modified? How?

If an applied issue was investigated, the summary can be followed by policy recommendations. For example, was the program tested (e.g., training, advertising) successful enough to recommend for implementation?

The discussion may then become more speculative. External validity, for example, may be discussed. For example, to what other contexts or populations are your findings likely to apply? Why do you think so?

Another issue to discuss involves implications of findings from the current study for additional research. During the course of a study, limitations in the methods used will likely surface. Some findings will be ambiguous. New questions will occur as the study is in progress. These can serve to formulate useful recommendations not only for additional research but for methods to effectively address them.

Finally, perhaps as part of other topics identified, include candid recognition of the study's limitations. Research studies always require compromises. Difficulties may include cost constraints, problems obtaining access to cases, and suboptimal measurement. Some research decisions thought to be ideal when made turn out to be less than satisfactory.

Communicate such limitations. The purpose of research is to learn about relationships between variables. The object of a research report is to communicate what was learned. Sometimes the primary knowledge obtained from a study may be that little was learned. It is ethical to report these research shortcomings in the discussion. Moreover, sophisticated readers will likely identify a study's shortcomings whether articulated in the discussion or not. Explicit identification of limitations signals that you are knowledgeable about research methods.

ALTERNATIVE RESEARCH REPORT FORMATS

The outline described here follows closely one recommended in the *Publication manual of the American Psychological Association* (1994). All original research journals sponsored by the American Psychological Association follow this format, as do many independent journals covering related topics (e.g., *Personnel Psychology*). This outline is also followed by the academic journals of the Academy of Management.

Other journals that publish original social science research follow similar, although not identical, outlines. The main difference between the outline described and the outlines used by journals in related fields, such as economics, sociology, and industrial relations, involves the results and discussion sections. The latter journals are more likely to include much of the discussion with the explanation of results. The last section in such journals usually contains a short summary and conclusions.

The advantage of combining results and discussion material is that it can make for more succinct presentation of the material. The disadvantage is that it does not clearly distinguish the objective results material from the more subjective discussion material.

When given a choice, I prefer to separate results from discussion. It helps me distinguish between what is supported by evidence generated from the study and how I interpret that evidence.

ADDITIONAL SUGGESTIONS

Novices often experience difficulty writing research reports. In part, this is because research writing is different from most other writing experiences. However, research report writing is simply difficult. A research study is a complicated enterprise involving measurement, design, and analysis. Communication of these complicated activities presents a challenge for anyone.

It is helpful for both writer and reader to keep the explanation as simple and as straightforward as possible.

Begin by Organizing

The outline presented in this chapter can serve as a start. Fill in details by arranging your story around the variables in the study. Start the variables off properly with conceptual definitions in the introduction. Report on how you believe they are connected (the conceptual model). In the methods section, describe how these variables are operationalized. Tell how the scores on the measured variables relate in the results section. Provide meaning to relationships between these variables in the discussion.

Daft (1985) offered an interesting metaphor. He recommended that variables in a research report be treated as characters in a novel. Don't bring variables into a study without a proper introduction. And don't let variables disappear from a study without a suitable burial. Exhibit 15.1 provides a summary of information to report on each variable in various sections of the research report.

Report Section		Provide Information About
Introduction	(1)	Define each variable at a construct level.
	(2)	Describe where each variable fits in the research model (e.g., dependent variable)
Methods	(1)	Describe how each variable is measured.
	(2)	Describe how scores are obtained on measures
	(3)	Describe how scores on the measures are analyzed.
Results	(1)	Describe results of scores on measures.
	(2)	Describe relationships between scores across measures.
Discussion	(1)	Summarize findings about measures.
	(2)	Discuss how measures address constructs (including shortcomings).

EXHIBIT 15.1. A tale for each variable.

Rewrite, Then Rewrite

Even the best authors rewrite drafts to obtain satisfactory results. Three or more major drafts of a report are typical. Schedule time so that a week or more can elapse between rewrites. Problems that aren't visible as you work on a report may become visible when you pick it up at a later time.

Draft a Critic

Motivate someone to read and make comments on your draft(s). A colleague, particularly if critical, can provide invaluable assistance in ferreting out inconsistencies, illogic, omissions, and other sins that invariably creep into writing projects.

Take a Scout's Oath

Your study probably will not be the greatest scientific achievement of the century. It will not be flawlessly conducted, nor will it generalize to all cases or to all time. Write your research report accordingly. Be honest, be descriptive, be modest.

SUMMARY

Research reporting holds a special place in the research process; it provides essential information for making research public. Research reports must include a detailed description of the method used as well as research findings. Exhibit 15.2 summarizes information that is important to include in research reports.

Section	Topics to Include
Introduction	Statement of the problem; relationships to other research; importance of problem.
Methods	
Cases	Number; characteristics relevant for generalization; sampling procedure; population.
Measures	Constructed (how?) or borrowed (source?)? Items; scaling formats; reliability and construct validity evidence.
Procedure	Methods to obtain participation; steps for administering measures; types of manipulations; methods to assign cases to levels of independent variables.
Analyses	Describe procedures to conduct preliminary analyses, analyses of measures, and tests of research hypotheses.
Results	Summary of results from descriptive and substantive analyses.
Discussion	Summary of findings; generalizability findings and/or policy recommendations; implications for future research; research limitations.

EXHIBIT 15.2. Research report outline and checklist of topics to include.

APPENDIX 15A: ON TABLE CONSTRUCTION[1]

Decisions about when to use tables and how to construct them are important for effective communication of research findings. Tables can help readers understand and they can help you communicate statistical findings efficiently.

When to Use Tables

Use tables to summarize quantitative information about results obtained on the measures used in a study. The more variables in a study, the more helpful are tables for summarizing results. Two types are often appropriate:

1. Table(s) to summarize descriptive information about the participants studied and the measures used.
2. Table(s) to summarize the results from the main statistical analyses performed to test the research expectations or to address the research questions.

Table Characteristics

Tables vary because table content varies. However, it is good practice to see that all tables have the following characteristics:

1. *Table numbers.* Number each table consecutively so that reference can easily be made to it in the body of the paper.
2. *Descriptive title.* A title should accurately, but briefly, describe the content reported in the body of the table.
3. *Table headings.* Title each column in the table.
4. *Abbreviations.* Avoid abbreviations except for common statistical symbols, such as M (for mean), SD (for standard deviation), and N (for number). Explain necessary abbreviations in a footnote to the table.

Integrate Tables and Text

Design each table so it is understandable without reference to the text. However, do not assume readers will understand a table. Thus, explain the content and summarize important information from the table in the text. This is essential and is often overlooked by beginning research report writers. Also, identify every table by number when referring to it in the body of the report.

An Example

Suppose you are interested in explaining variation in yearly income (Y) as a function of age (X_1), years of work experience (X_2), and years of education (X_3). The population consists of working adults in a metropolitan area, and you draw a random sample of participants from this population. Scores on measures of the four variables are obtained and analyses are performed. The following tables and descriptive information are appropriate.

---

[1]For details on table construction see *Publication manual of the American Psychological Association* (4th ed., pp. 120–141). (1994). Washington, DC: American Psychological Association.

Descriptive Results

One type of table, illustrated in Exhibit 15A.1, includes descriptive statistics that are generally useful in a research report. The mean shows central tendency, the standard deviation shows the average variability, and the simple correlation coefficients among the variables show how scores on the measures are related. Reporting the number of cases for each variable is useful when there are missing data. Otherwise, the sample size can be reported in a note at the end of the table. For ease of reading, place the dependent variable at either the head or the end of the list of variables.

In describing the contents of Exhibit 15A.1, call attention to any of the statistics that are unusual for samples of this sort. For example, correlation coefficients that are unusually high (or low) might be identified. Not all statistics should be discussed in the body of the report; to do so would make the table unnecessary.

Substantive Results

A second type of table(s) should ordinarily summarize the substantive results. For example, suppose you use multiple regression to test your hypotheses. Y is regressed on the X variables. A summary of results as reported in Exhibit 15A.2 is appropriate.

In describing the contents of Exhibit 15A.2, point out which independent variables are related to income as expected and which, if any, are not. The statistical significance of findings is appropriate for both the table and the discussion in the text, because you are interested in generalizing results from the probability sample of participants studied to the population they came from.

An explanation also could be given for one relationship to help readers interpret the results of the entire table. Given the results reported in Exhibit 15A.2, for example, you could say that a one-year increase in age results in an expected yearly income increase of $320, holding years of work experience and education constant.

Variables	N	M	SD	Correlation Coefficients			
				1	2	3	4
1. Yearly Income	281	34,631.21	7,211.40	1.00			
2. Age in years	283	41.68	13.12	.58*	1.00		
3. Years work experience	284	19.79	8.91	.58*	.68*	1.00	
4. Years education	282	13.13	2.78	.41*	-.15*	.19*	1.00

Note. The number for each variable is smaller than the 285 participants sampled because of missing data. Correlation coefficients were calculated by using listwise deletion.

*$p < .05$ (two-tailed).

EXHIBIT 15A.1.   Table of variable means, standard deviations, and intercorrelations among income, age, years of work experience, and education.

Variable	Regression Coefficient	Standard Error
Age in years	320.17*	31.64
Years work experience	79.39	46.06
Years education	1,143.39*	102.80
Constant	4,732.29*	1,753.19

Note. Adjusted R^2 = .48, $p < .05$. Missing data eliminated listwise, $N = 278$.

* $p < .05$ (one-tailed).

EXHIBIT 15A.2.   Table summarizing multiple regression predicting yearly income from age, years of work experience, and education.

Notice that the tables in both exhibits have several desirable characteristics:

1. Titles are descriptive.
2. Decimals are to the same number of places (two are almost always enough).
3. Asterisks are used to indicate statistically significant results (a common convention). The level of significance signified by the asterisk is reported in a footnote.
4. Notes are added at the end of each table to explain material that otherwise might leave readers with questions.

VIII

Extensions

16

On Incomplete Data

Chapter Outline

- *Avoid Incomplete Data*
- *Evaluate Nonresponse*
- *Address Missing Data*
  - *Dependent Variables*
  - *Independent Variables*
    - *Delete Variables*
    - *Delete Cases*
    - *Mean Substitution*
    - *Alternative Methods*
    - *Identify "Missingness"*
- *Reporting Incomplete Data*
  - *Current Reporting Practices*
  - *Recommended Practices*
- *Summary*
- *For Review*
  - *Terms to Know*
  - *Questions for Review*
- *Suggested Readings*

Consider a study conducted in an organization to see whether salary is related to age and evaluations of employee performance. Although this study is overly simple and deficient in sample size, it illustrates several pandemic challenges confronted in research.

An e-mail is sent to a random sample of 14 organizational employees. They are asked to report their current annual salary (Y), chronological age $(X1)$, and most recent performance

Individual	Salary (Y)	Age (X1)	Performance Rating (X2)	Missing Age
1	28,054	31	3	0
2	37,555	28	2	0
3	37,643	.	3	1
4	24,264	20	5	0
5	.	25	4	.
6	44,521	29	1	0
7	27,878	.	5	1
8	.	.	.	.
9	.	.	.	.
10	37,318	32	4	0
11	37,798	29	1	0
12	28,071	25	3	0
13	43,104	35	2	0
14	39,374	.	1	1
Mean	35,052.82	28.63	2.73	.27
Std Dev	6,814.56	4.57	1.49	
n	11	8	11	11

Note: Individual 5 removed from all analysis because of a missing datum on Y.

EXHIBIT 16.1.   Salary study data matrix with missing data.

evaluation score (X2), which ranges from 1 (low performance) to 5 (high performance). Two days elapse and responses obtained are recorded in a matrix where rows represent individuals and columns represent variables, as shown in Exhibit 16.1.

The researcher is eager to perform statistical analyses. But, wait! Not all cells in the matrix have values. Entire rows are without values. Employees 8 and 9 did not respond to the study— they are **nonrespondents**. In the example, they failed to respond to the e-mailed request. Exhibit 16.1 also shows that employees 3, 5, 7, and 14 are **missing data** for salary or age. They participated, but incompletely.

Nonresponse and missing data create two problems. First, lost cases reduce statistical power when internal or external statistical validity is an issue. The more cases lost, the more power lost.

More seriously, nonresponse and missing data usually lead to biased relationships that exist among the group of cases a researcher seeks to study. For example, the illustrative study is interested in the relationship between salary, age, and performance ratings. Suppose sample members at the high (or low) end of the income distribution are less likely to respond to a question about income. This may explain why employee 5 did not respond. If so, the range of salary values obtained is restricted compared with the range that exists in the entire sample. Consequently, the relationship between salary, age, and performance ratings observed will differ from the relationship that exists in the entire sample.

AVOID INCOMPLETE DATA

The best way to address nonresponse and missing data is to prevent them. A plan to elicit high levels of participation should be carefully developed as a part of any research design.

Whether participants respond or not depends on both their ability and their motivation. Ability issues include the opportunity (e.g., time) to participate. Another is participants' ability to respond to the requirements of the study. For example, missing data and nonresponses are almost certain if participants are asked for information they do not understand.

Participants may be motivated to participate for various reasons. Monetary incentives are often used when the time and location demands of a study are extensive, as is frequently true of experiments. Other motivators are the stated purpose(s) of the research and the research sponsor.

Participant groups differ in ability and motivation. Thus, decisions about participants studied should be made early in the design process. Reading levels of questionnaires constructed and motivational incentives used are examples of design issues that depend on the intended participants.

Great effort should be made to minimize nonresponses and missing data. However, it is unlikely that either will be eliminated. The next two sections describe procedures used when nonresponses and missing data are present.

EVALUATE NONRESPONSE

Sometimes it is possible to get information on the consequences of nonresponse by comparing respondents with nonrespondents on variables known for all intended participants. For example, suppose a charitable organization solicits contributions in December, just before the end of the tax year. A study is initiated to learn whether donors are willing to make contributions throughout the year. A questionnaire is developed and sent to a random sample drawn from the organization's database of December donors. This database contains donor names, addresses, and contributions. A 25% response rate is obtained.

The organization can compare the 25% who responded with the 75% who did not on information in its database: amount of contribution, location (from addresses), and gender (estimated from names). Differences between respondents and nonrespondents on any of these variables suggest that the questionnaire responses obtained may not apply to all contributors. Regrettably, the charitable organization cannot know that respondents and nonrespondents would provide similar answers even if the two groups are similar on all characteristics compared.

Consequently, comparing respondents and nonrespondents on variables available for both provides only limited information. Research information obtained from respondents may apply to nonrespondents if the groups are similar on the comparison variables, but it may not. However, it is likely that information provided by respondents does not generalize to nonrespondents when the two groups differ on comparison variables. Despite this gloomy outcome, a comparison is recommended. It will inform the researcher (and research consumers) of a potential research limitation.

ADDRESS MISSING DATA

Researchers have several options when confronted with missing data. The choice of these options depends on whether the missing data represent the dependent or independent variables.

Dependent Variables

Some participants may provide partial information but fail to provide information on the dependent variable(s). Employee 5 is an example in Exhibit 16.1. Such cases are best dropped from a study because research is aimed at explaining or predicting the dependent variable. Researchers cannot explain what they have no information on; participants with missing Y scores are effectively nonrespondents.

It is possible to see if participants who provide or do not provide Y scores differ on the independent variables. Relationships observed among Y score providers may apply to cases

---

Delete Variables

Delete Cases

Listwise

Pairwise

Estimate Scores

Mean substitution

Alternative methods

Identify "Missingness"

EXHIBIT 16.2.   Methods to account for missing independent variable values.

with missing Y scores in the unlikely event that scores do not differ between the two groups across independent variables. However, it is likely that independent variables will differ between those who provide and those who do not provide Y scores. Generalization of research results to participants with missing Y scores is then problematic.

Independent Variables

Exhibit 16.2 summarizes methods to deal with missing values on independent variables; each may be appropriate in certain circumstances. More than one method can be used in a single investigation when there are several independent variables.

Delete Variables

The amount of missing data may vary greatly from variable to variable. Variables may have missing data because some participants do not reveal certain information about themselves (e.g., age, income). In such situations, and if the variable is important to the conceptual model investigated, it may be useful to estimate missing values and identify "missingness" (more on this later).

Alternatively, a researcher may conclude the problem rests with the measure of the variable. For example, it may be a poorly worded item on a questionnaire. In such situations, it is probably best to drop the variable from the study. Responses from those answering are suspect (e.g., unreliable) if the wording kept other participants from answering.

Delete Cases

Cases can be dropped two ways when there are two or more independent variables; neither method is typically attractive. **Listwise deletion** drops an entire case if responses to any independent variable are missing. A participant with any missing data is treated as a nonrespondent.

Listwise deletion can result in a large loss of cases even though the total amount of missing information is small. This happens if the missing data are spread more or less evenly across cases. Listwise deletion is not recommended in such circumstances. Only if missing data are concentrated among a small proportion of cases is listwise deletion potentially attractive. (However, if concentrated, the missing data signal that these cases probably differ systematically from cases with complete data. Generalization of findings to all cases again becomes suspect.)

Pairwise deletion uses all data available for each statistic calculated. For example, the mean of $X2$ is calculated by using scores of employees 3, 7, and 14 in Exhibit 16.1 even though their values for $X1$ are missing. Pairwise deletion is thus attractive because all data that can be used are used.

However, there are problems that make the procedure generally unattractive as a research practice. First, different sample statistics are not generalizable to the same population unless missing data are randomly distributed among participants and variables.

Second, there is another generalization problem when relationships between more than two variables are examined in the same statistical model. For example, multiple correlation and regression account for relationships between two or more pairs of simple relationships. Each pair may have a different sample size when pairwise deletion is used. The appropriate sample size for multiple correlation and regression is thus ambiguous. To illustrate, Exhibit 16.1 shows that the pairwise sample size for r_{YX1} is 8, but for r_{YX2}, it is 11.

Mean Substitution

There are a variety of ways researchers estimate missing independent variable scores from scores available on respondents. *Mean substitution* is most common; it replaces missing independent variable values with the mean score obtained from responding cases. For example, the mean of $X1$ would be substituted for the missing values of Individuals 3, 7, and 14 in Exhibit 16.1.

Replacing missing values with the mean has two predictable statistical consequences for simple correlation and regression. First, the simple regression coefficient Y on X is the same whether missing X scores are replaced with the mean or whether cases with missing values are dropped from the analysis. Second, the simple correlation coefficient between Y and X is generally attenuated (made smaller) by the substitution of means for missing data.

Exhibit 16.3 illustrates these outcomes by using Y and $X1$ scores from Exhibit 16.1. Model 1 shows regression and correlation output when individuals with missing values on $X1$ are deleted; Model 2 shows results when missing $X1$ are replaced with the mean of $X1$.

RESEARCH HIGHLIGHT 16.1

Another Type of Mean Replacement

Researchers often seek to measure constructs with multiple items. The six-item computer satisfaction questionnaire described in chapter 3 is illustrative. For analysis purposes the sum (or mean) of the six items is used to represent the score for each respondent rather than scores from single items. This sum (mean) measures computer satisfaction more reliably than any single item.

Data collection using multiple item scales can result in three outcomes. Respondents answer (a) all items, (b) some items, or (c) no items. If the mean of the items to form the scale is used (rather than the sum) little error typically will be introduced by including the respondents in the (b) group along with those in the (a) group. Judgment must be exercised regarding this recommendation. It is probably unwise to replace five missing items with the score obtained on only one item. Nevertheless, the procedure is recommended if information is available on some but not all items using multiple item scales.

	Model					
Variable	(1)	(2)	(3)	(4)	(5)	(6)
Regression Coefficient $X1$	1,122.38	1,122.38*	1,122.38*	714.23	716.66	710.81
$X2$				-2,818.45	-2,801.63*	-2,842.07*
"Missing" dummy			-120.63			945.15
Intercept	2,957.36	2,924.46	2,957.36	22,039.29	22,179.03	22,199.18
$\hat{\rho}^2(\hat{P}^2)$	.39	.33*	.24	.57	.65*	.60*
n	8	11	11	8	11	11

*Note: Individuals 5, 8, and 9 deleted from all analyses.

*$P < .05$

EXHIBIT 16.3.   Correlation and regression output from data in Exhibit 16.1 given alternative ways to handle missing data.

The regression coefficient for $X1$ is the same in Models 1 and 2. This illustrates that replacing missing $X1$ values with the mean does not increase or decrease the error that may be present in the regression coefficient due to missing data.

Alternatively, the estimated population variance in Y explained by $X1$ decreases in Model 2. In this example, the decrease in the variance explained is more than offset by the increase in power. The coefficient for $X1$ (and $\hat{\rho}^2$) is statistically significant ($p < .05$) in Model 2 but not in Model 1.

Some researchers recommend replacing missing independent variables with the mean. They argue that it is a "conservative" technique, because it tends to attenuate the relationship observed, yet power is increased. Others argue that the increase in power is spurious, because the researcher does not actually have scores for the missing values. There is no definitively correct answer. The only thing certain is the need to report to the research consumer how missing data were handled and why.

Statistical outcomes are not as predictable when there are two or more independent variables involved. Models 4 (listwise deletion) and 5 (mean replacement) in Exhibit 16.3 illustrate the point. Y scores are regressed on $X1$ and $X2$ scores from Exhibit 16.1. The regression coefficients on $X1$ are no longer the same in the two equations. This result is typical. It occurs because the multicollinearity between $X1$ and $X2$ differs between the entire sample (missing $X1$ values replaced with means—Model 5) and the subsample (without mean replacement—Model 4).

Alternative Methods

All the methods described are problematic in various ways as noted. In the last two decades, researchers have worked on alternative methods aimed at improving statistical estimates and at generating more accurate statistical significance values.

A simple illustration of these more advanced techniques uses regression to predict missing values of X. In this procedure, an X variable with missing values is temporarily treated as a dependent variable. A prediction equation is created among cases that have values on this X using other X variables as independent variables. Values predicted by this equation are then entered for cases with missing values on the focal X variable.

Unless the X variable is well predicted by the other X variables, this procedure may not provide results much different than simply replacing missing values with the mean. Furthermore, even when the statistical results are improved by replacement with predicted values (rather than the mean), statistical inference values will remain in error.

Two general alternatives are under development that seek to generate more accurate statistical estimates as well as more accurate inferential statistics. One of these generates multiple estimates of each missing value to improve on the estimate of statistical inference. Both methods are complicated and require substantially more statistical knowledge than is provided in this book. The suggested readings provide sources where you can obtain more information on these methods.

Identify "Missingness"

Another technique that is useful in some instances involves creating a dummy coded variable for "missingness." Cases with scores on an independent variable are coded 0; cases with missing values are coded 1.

Models 3 and 6 in Exhibit 16.3 show statistical outcomes of this procedure for simple and multiple correlation and regression, respectively. Results of Model 3 suggest the procedure is attractive for simple correlation and regression problems. Adding the "missing" variable to the equation in Model 2 does not change the regression coefficient of $X1$. This results because the correlation coefficient of $X1$ and "missing" is necessarily 0.00.

The coefficient for "missing" shows the predicted difference in Y scores between those cases with scores on $X1$ and those without. In the example, nonresponding employees on age ($X1$) are predicted to have a salary $121 less than those who provided their age (this difference is not statistically significant; $p < .05$). The addition of the "missing" dummy variable thus provides additional information about cases without influencing the regression coefficient of $X1$.

The issue is more complicated when there is another independent variable(s) in the equation. This is shown by Models 5 and 6 in Exhibit 16.3. The partial regression coefficients for $X1$ and $X2$ differ between Model 5 and 6. This occurs because there is multicollinearity between $X2$ and "missing."

Replacing missing values with the mean and use of a dummy variable coded for "missingness" thus adds complexity when there are two or more independent variables. This is shown by a comparison of Models 4, 5, and 6 in Exhibit 16.3. Because there is no unambiguously correct way to address the situation, it is important to explain whatever model was used to the reader. The problem is more complex if there are missing data in more than one independent variable. It is technically feasible to create a "missingness" variable for every independent variable, sample size permitting. But, this can make interpretation difficult. "Missingness" variables should be created sparingly. Probably only one such variable should be created for the independent variable most central to the objective of a study.

REPORTING INCOMPLETE DATA

Current Reporting Practices

Organizational researchers do not have a stellar record when addressing and reporting on incomplete data. It is common to see the number of nonrespondents reported and the resulting percentage of respondents. Less common are reports comparing respondents with nonrespondents on data available or data that could be obtained with additional effort.

Reporting practices on missing data typically are less satisfactory. Reports often say nothing about missing data. This leads to a conclusion that listwise deletion was probably used because missing data were almost certainly present. Listwise deletion and mean substitution are most frequently reported when it is acknowledged that there are missing data. However, it is not common to see reports of how much missing data have been addressed by these procedures.

Recommended Practices

Most important, as noted earlier, nonresponse and missing data should be reduced as much as possible. Emphasis here is on activities and reporting practices given the presence of nonresponse and missing data.

Good research reports all known characteristics of a study that may influence the results obtained and the probable domains to which the results may generalize. Because nonresponse and missing data influence both, it is essential that researchers acknowledge and report on these two research challenges. Four suggestions are made to address and provide information about nonresponse and missing data.

First, describe the procedures used to elicit high participation and minimize missing data. These include incentives used to obtain participation and any follow-up efforts used to obtain participation from individuals who did not initially respond. Also describe any measurement procedures designed to minimize missing data. Information on these activities signals how serious efforts were to obtain high response rates and to minimize missing data.

Second, report the amount of nonresponse and missing data because they will remain regardless of the best efforts exercised in their minimization. Because missing data vary by variable, the amount of missing data should be reported by variable. This can be done efficiently in a table that summarizes other descriptive statistics on each variable.

Third, report any comparisons made between respondents and nonrespondents and between cases with and without missing data. As noted, such comparisons add little to confidence that cases in each category are identical. Nevertheless, they signal careful research and serve as an explicit limitation to generalization when they are not identical.

Finally, explain how missing data were addressed. Were means used to replace missing values, was it pairwise deletion, or what? If several procedures were used, as often is the case, make clear which procedure was used for which variable(s). As noted, each of these procedures has consequences and should be an explicit part of the research report. The consequences of alternative methods for handling missing data depend on the objectives of the research and the intended generalizations so this portion of the research report is probably best placed in the discussion section under the general heading of research limitations.

SUMMARY

An incomplete research data set may result because participants do not respond to a researcher's request for participation (***nonresponse***). Or participants may respond but only partially (***missing data***).

Incomplete data results in loss of statistical power. It can also result in statistical output that erroneously describes relations in the entire sample and can provide biased estimates of population parameters.

The most effective method for addressing incomplete data is to prevent them. The research design must be planned and executed to minimize the amount of incomplete data. When present, incomplete data should be investigated for possible implications on the generalizability of results. It may be possible to compare respondents and nonrespondents on variables available to the researcher. This is a desirable research practice even though it is likely to suggest generalization problems.

For practical purposes, cases with missing data on dependent variables are best treated as nonrespondents. Only comparisons with respondents are possible to determine whether generalization problems are likely.

A broader array of procedures is available for missing independent variables. These include dropping variables, dropping cases, either ***listwise*** or ***pairwise***, and/or replacing missing variables in one of several ways. Generally, there are not unambiguously correct or incorrect ways to address missing data among independent variables. Each of the procedures may be warranted in certain circumstances. Because there is no single missing data standard, it is important to report their frequency and to describe the procedures used to handle them.

FOR REVIEW

Terms to Know

Nonrespondents: Cases that provided no data for a research study.

Missing data: Data that are absent in a case for some but not all variables.

Listwise deletion: When an entire case with missing data is removed from a research study.

Pairwise deletion: When a case is deleted only if there are missing data on variables from the specific analyses conducted. The case is retained for any other analyses in which data are present.

Mean substitution: Missing data on a variable are replaced with the mean of the responding cases on that variable.

Questions for Review

1. What problems do nonresponse and missing data present to researchers?
2. Suppose you are able to compare research respondents with nonrespondents on several variables that are not part of your research study. In what way(s) is such a comparison useful?
3. Deleting cases and deleting variables are two ways to address missing data on independent variables. Under what circumstances would you choose one over the other?
4. Listwise and pairwise are two methods for deleting cases. Under what circumstances would you choose one over the other?
5. What are the consequences for simple correlation and regression if the mean for an independent variable is used to replace missing data?
6. A regression of Y is performed on $X1$ and $X2$; $X1$ has missing data. What can you say about the partial regression coefficient on $X1$ if cases with missing data are deleted rather than if missing data are replaced by the mean? Are there any circumstances in which the partial regression coefficients will be the same by using the two procedures?
7. Under what circumstances would the creation of a dummy variable(s) to differentiate between cases with data and cases with missing data be most attractive? Why?

SUGGESTED READINGS

Roth (1994) is a good place to start for a general review of missing data and alternative methods for addressing them. Roth concludes that listwise deletion is often the least satisfactory way to address missing data. Roth (2003) introduces a series of articles in *Organizational Research Methods* on more sophisticated alternative methods for estimating missing data. Cohen, Cohen, West, and Aiken (2003) also describe such methods. The latter two sets of readings will be a challenge for readers who do not have statistical knowledge that transcends the statistics described in this volume.

17

On Reliability

Chapter Outline

- *Reliability Defined*
- *Estimating Reliability*
  - *Internal Consistency*
  - *Interpreting Coefficient Alpha*
  - *Stabililty*
  - *Interrater Reliability*
  - *Reporting Reliability Estimates*
- *Consequences of Unreliability*
  - *Simple Correlation and Regression*
  - *Demonstrations*
    - *Correlation Coefficients*
    - *Correcting for Unreliability in Correlation Coefficients*
    - *Regression Coefficients and Intercepts*
    - *Unreliability in X*
    - *Unreliability in Y*
    - *Correcting for Unreliability in Regression Coefficients*
  - *Unreliability in Multiple Correlation and Regression*
- *Summary*
- *For Review*
  - *Terms to Know*
  - *Formulae to Use*
  - *Questions for Review*
  - *Exercise*
- *Suggested Readings*

This chapter extends the discussion of measurement reliability introduced in part II. Two points introduced in that part are summarized here. First, scores from measures of constructs invariably contain random (unsystematic) error. *Reliability*, the opposite of random error, refers to the systematic or consistent portion of scores. Reliable measurement is thus necessary for construct valid measurement.

Second, there are three contexts in which reliability is often of interest to researchers. These three differ with regard to the type of reliability addressed. *Internal consistency* applies to multiple items in a measure, *stability* applies to multiple time periods, and *interrater reliability* applies to multiple observers or raters. In each case, reliability means that scores obtained across repetitions of measurement (item to item, time to time, observer to observer) are consistent.

This chapter provides a more formal description of reliability. Nevertheless, it does not address many subtleties of reliability theory or techniques to estimate it; these theories and techniques are many and often elegant. Rather, this chapter introduces one commonly articulated way of thinking about reliability and methods to estimate it. The chapter also describes consequences of unreliability for correlation and regression output.

RELIABILITY DEFINED

Several formal theories of reliability are available; these differ in assumptions made about the nature of variability in scores. A simple formulation is presented here. Think of scores obtained on a measure as consisting of a systematic component and a random error component. These components cannot be observed directly, but an observed score can be *thought* of as:

$$x_{oi} = x_{ti} + x_{ei}$$

where x_{oi} = an observed score on the ith case
   x_{ti} = systematic score component of the ith case
   x_{ei} = random error score component of the ith case

The error score x_{ei} is assumed to have two properties. First, it is assumed that the random error is as likely to inflate as deflate scores. Thus, it is expected that $\Sigma x_e = 0$. As a consequence:

$$\mu_{Xo} \approx \mu_{Xt}$$

where μ_{Xo} and μ_{Xt} are the means of the observed and systematic scores, respectively

Second, it is also assumed that the error score is unrelated to the systematic score component of the observed score:

$$\rho_{XtXe} = 0$$

where ρ_{XtXe} = the correlation coefficient between the systematic and random error components

When components are uncorrelated, the variance (σ^2) of the sum of these components is equal to the sum of the variances of each component. Thus,

$$\sigma_{Xo}^2 = \sigma_{Xt}^2 + \sigma_{Xe}^2$$

where σ_{Xo}^2 = variance of observed scores
   σ_{Xt}^2 = variance of systematic scores
   σ_{Xe}^2 = variance in random errors

In words, the variance in observed scores is equal to the sum of the variances of the systematic and random error components of the observed scores. Unreliability thus increases variance in observed scores relative to systematic scores:

$$\sigma_{Xo}^2 > \sigma_{Xt}^2$$

Given this perspective, reliability is formally defined as:

$$\rho_{XX} = \sigma_{Xt}^2 / \sigma_{Xo}^2 \qquad (17.1)$$

where ρ_{XX} = reliability of scores on measure X

Formula 17.1 defines reliability as the proportion of observed score variance that is systematic. Although characterized as a correlation coefficient, an accident of history, ρ_{XX} is really a coefficient of determination; it reports the proportion of observed score variance that is explained by true score variation.

$$\rho_{XX} = \rho_{XoXt}^2 = \text{systematic variance/total variance}$$

Reliability can range from 0.00 (all the observed score variance is random) to 1.00 (all the observed score variance is systematic).

3 types of reliability ESTIMATING RELIABILITY

Methods to estimate reliability differ depending on what type of reliability (internal consistency, stability, interrater reliability) is of interest. While these methods differ in detail, all seek to estimate reliability as defined—namely, the ratio of true (systematic) variance to total variance.

Internal Consistency

Reliability estimates of internal consistency address the degree to which the sum (or average) of scores from a set of items correspond to the scores that would be obtained from a parallel set including an equal number of items measuring the same phenomenon. A widely used method is **coefficient alpha**. One formula estimates coefficient alpha by:

$$\hat{\rho}_{XX} = (k \times \rho_{(Ave)ij}) / (1 + (k - 1) \times \rho_{(Ave)ij}) \qquad (17.2)$$

where $\hat{\rho}_{XX}$ = coefficient alpha estimated from observed scores
       k = number of items
$\rho_{(Ave)ij}$ = average correlation among scores on items

Technically, Formula 17.2 is appropriate only when the variability in all the items is equal. It is used here instead of a less restrictive formula because it shows that reliability, as estimated, is a positive function of the average intercorrelation among items and the number of items. Formula 17.2 shows that alpha increases as the number of items increases, holding the average intercorrelation constant. It also shows that alpha increases as the average intercorrelation increases, holding the number of items constant.

Exhibit 17.1 illustrates how the number of repetitions influences coefficient alpha estimates for three different average intercorrelations among repetitions ($\rho_{(Ave)ij}$ = .25, .50, and .75). The estimates approach asymptotes as the number of repetitions grow larger. For example, with

---

RESEARCH HIGHLIGHT 17.1

Other Estimation Procedures

Coefficient alpha is one of many methods to estimate reliability. Methods similar (or in some cases identical) to coefficient alpha go by names such as the Kudar–Richardson, Spearman–Brown, and Hoyt formulas. These are used in special situations. Coefficient alpha is probably the most frequently used and reported of these methods.

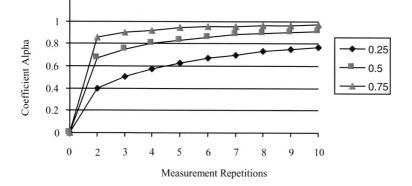

EXHIBIT 17.1.   Factors that influence coefficient alpha: measurement repetitions and average intercorrelations.

an average intercorrelation of .75, there is little improvement in reliability beyond about six repetitions.

Interpreting Coefficient Alpha

There are several ways to interpret coefficient alpha. One useful way is to understand that it provides an estimate of the correlation coefficient that is expected between a summary score from a measure studied and another (hypothetical) measure of the same thing using the same number of items. For example, suppose coefficient alpha is computed on a set of scores obtained from a sample of respondents to the six-item computer satisfaction scale described in chapter 3. In this case, alpha estimates the correlation coefficient between the sum (or mean) of scores from this particular set of items and the sum (or mean) that would be generated on another set of six items measuring the same thing.

This is an important estimate to obtain. Judgments of computer satisfaction should not depend on the particular set of items used to measure it. Researchers want measures that provide comparable scores beyond the immediate items studied. If this is not the case, statements always need to be conditioned on the measure used to obtain the scores. Statements about computer satisfaction would always need to be qualified by "... as measured by this six-item computer satisfaction scale."

Nevertheless, understand that high reliability, as estimated by coefficient alpha, does not ensure construct validity. Reliability does not address systematic errors that may contaminate scores or leave them deficient. Contamination may include systematic variance associated with another construct. Coefficient alpha does not directly address whether the scores are getting at only a single (unidimensional) construct. For example, the six-item computer satisfaction measure may provide reliable scores as estimated by coefficient alpha even though they contain information not related to computer satisfaction as long as they do so consistently.

Stability

The stability of a measure is usually estimated by administering the measure at two points in time. A simple correlation coefficient is then computed to estimate the reliability of the measure over this interval. The square of this coefficient estimates the proportion of true score variance in either measurement.

Stability of measures is sometimes of interest but estimates must be interpreted cautiously. The time interval is critical when measuring phenomena on individuals. If the time interval between administrations is short, the reliability estimate may be inflated by memory. Participants may respond similarly because they recall and repeat responses provided on the measure when first administered.

Alternatively, if the interval is long the estimate may be spuriously low because of change in the underlying construct measured. The probable stability of the construct and the susceptibility of the measure to memory effects are issues to consider when choosing a time interval if estimating stability.

Interrater Reliability

When a construct is measured by having raters provide scores, it is of interest to know whether the scores obtained would generalize to scores provided by another set of raters. Raters are analogous to items on a measure in such contexts.

There are alternative methods to estimate interrater reliability. These vary depending on the design used to obtain the ratings. One design involves different sets of raters for each set of cases to be rated. This is not a particularly good design but sometimes it is the only one available. A better alternative has a single set of raters evaluate all sets of cases to be rated.

The statistical methods use *analysis of variance* (ANOVA). ANOVA is a statistical procedure that is similar to (actually a subset of) correlation and regression. Because ANOVA is not covered in this volume, it is sufficient to say that these methods provide estimates of the ratio of true to total variance just as other methods. These estimates provide information on the reliability of the scores provided by the raters.

Reporting Reliability Estimates

These three types of reliability provide information about different sources of random variance that may influence scores. Consequently, estimates may differ dramatically. For example, administering the six-item measure of computer satisfaction described in chapter 3 to a group of computer owners might provide a high coefficient alpha. However, it could yield a low estimate of stability if the measure were administered to this group again one month later.

Different methods of calculating reliability may also yield different estimates. Alternative methods for calculating interrater reliability, in particular, can lead to substantially different outcomes.

It is thus important to report more than just the reliability estimate obtained. Also report the type of design used and the method used to calculate the reliability estimate. As one example, if stability is calculated with a simple correlation coefficient, it is important to know not only the method but also the time interval.

RESEARCH HIGHLIGHT 17.2

Generalizing Reliability

Standard reliability estimates do not distinguish between different sources of un-systematic error. For example, suppose a researcher estimates the reliability of two intentionally similar measures of a construct (called parallel forms) administered to a group of individuals two weeks apart. A typical measure of reliability does not distinguish between random error generated by differences due to the forms and differences due to time.

Generalizability theory provides a rationale and methods designed to differentiate between sources of unreliability. These sources may be time, items, and individuals providing the scores (observers or research participants) as well as others. The generalizability model thus provides multiple reliability estimates depending on what source(s) of unreliability is of interest to a researcher. Although the objectives of the generalizability model are accessible and desirable, the design and analysis of generalizability studies are typically complex. It is probably for these reasons that the model has not been as widely used as it should be.

Will we apply Standard Reliability or Generalizability Theory within our dissertation on the data sets we are analyzing?

CONSEQUENCES OF UNRELIABILITY

Statistical procedures generally provide misleading information when variables are measured unreliably. Unreliability also leads to errors when statistical inferences are drawn. This section identifies consequences of unreliability for correlation and regression output. Problems of unreliability for statistical inference are discussed in chapter 20.

Simple Correlation and Regression

Consequences of unreliability for simple correlation and regression are well known. Specifically:

1. Unreliability in either X or Y attenuates (reduces) the expected correlation coefficient relative to the correlation coefficient obtained if X and Y are measured with perfect reliability.
2. Unreliability in X attenuates the expected regression coefficient, and increases the intercept, relative to the regression coefficient obtained if X is measured with perfect reliability.
3. Unreliability in Y has no expected effect on the unstandardized regression coefficient and hence no expected effect on the intercept.

Demonstrations

These outcomes are understood by reviewing formulas for simple correlation or regression and by recalling that unreliability has no expected effect on the mean of a variable but that it increases the variance.

$$\mu_{X_o} \approx \mu_{X_t}, \quad \text{and}$$

$$\sigma_{X_o}^2 > \sigma_{X_t}^2$$

where o and t refer to observed scores and systematic scores, respectively

Correlation Coefficients

One formula for the correlation coefficient from chapter 10 using covariance is:

unreliability has no effect on numerator

$$\rho_{YX} = CoVar_{YX}/(\sigma_Y \times \sigma_X) \quad \uparrow \text{unreliability} \uparrow \text{denominator} \quad (10.2b)$$

where ρ_{YX} = correlation coefficient between scores on Y and X
σ_Y and σ_X = standard deviations of Y and X, respectively
$CoVar_{YX}$ = covariance of Y and X

Covariance, in turn, is defined as:

$$CoVar_{YX} = \sum[(Y_i - \mu_Y) \times (X_i - \mu_X)]/N \quad (10.3)$$

where $CoVar_{YX}$ = the average cross-product of the deviations about their respective means of Y and X

Unreliability increases the denominator of Formula 10.2b but leaves the numerator unchanged. Begin with the denominator. Unreliability in either Y or X will increase their variances and hence standard deviations relative to perfectly reliable measurement.

$$\sigma_{X_o} > \sigma_{X_t} \quad \text{and} \quad \sigma_{Y_o} > \sigma_{Y_t}$$

where σ_{X_o} and σ_{Y_o} = observed standard deviations of X and Y, respectively
σ_{X_t} and σ_{Y_t} = true score standard deviations of X and Y, respectively

Alternatively, unreliability does not affect covariance, the numerator in Formula 10.2a. Unreliability serves to inflate some scores and deflate others; these are expected to be offsetting:

$$CoVar_{Y_oX_o} \approx CoVar_{Y_tX_t}$$

where $CoVar_{Y_oX_o}$ = covariance of observed (not perfectly reliable) scores
$CoVar_{Y_tX_t}$ = covariance of true scores

Thus, unreliability in Y and/or X is expected to leave the numerator of Formula 10.2b the same but to increase the denominator. As a consequence, ***unreliability attenuates*** a correlation coefficient relative to what it would be if there were no unreliability. This attenuation occurs whether the unreliability is in X and/or Y. The amount of attenuation is shown by:

$$\rho_{Y_oX_o} = \rho_{Y_tX_t}\sqrt{\rho_{YY}}\sqrt{\rho_{XX}} \quad (17.3)$$

where $\rho_{Y_oX_o}$ = correlation coefficient on observed scores
$\rho_{Y_tX_t}$ = true score correlation coefficient

Do we need to know these formulas for this class, or is the book just introducing concepts?

CONSEQUENCES OF UNRELIABILITY   247

Correcting for Unreliability in Correlation Coefficients

Formula 17.3 can be rearranged to provide an estimated **correction for attenuation** due to unreliability.

$$\rho_{YtXt} = \frac{\rho_{YoXo}}{\sqrt{\rho_{YY}}\sqrt{\rho_{XX}}} \tag{17.4}$$

If the reliability of the Y and X measures are known, Formula 17.4 can be used to estimate the correlation coefficient if Y and X were measured with perfect reliability. However, this estimate can be in substantial error if ρ_{Ye} or ρ_{Xe} is not equal to zero, assumptions of the reliability model noted at the outset of this chapter.

Regression Coefficients and Intercepts

The effect of unreliability in simple regression depends on whether it is in the X or Y variable. From chapter 10:

$$\beta_{YX} = (\rho_{YX} \times \sigma_Y)/\sigma_X \tag{10.4}$$

where β_{YX} = regression coefficient of Y on X

$$\alpha = \mu_Y - \mu_X \times \beta_{YX} \tag{10.5}$$

where α = regression intercept, the predicted value of Y when $X = 0$

Unreliability in X

Given unreliability in X, $\sigma_{Xo} > \sigma_{Xt}$ and $\rho_{YXo} < \rho_{YXt}$ (from Formula 17.3). The former increases the denominator in Formula 10.4 (relative to reliable measurement of X) and the latter decreases the numerator. Both serve to decrease the regression coefficient in Formula 10.4.

$$\underbrace{\beta_{YXo}}_{\text{unreliability}} < \underbrace{\beta_{YXt}}_{\text{reliable}}$$

where β_{YXo} = the regression coefficient when X is measured unreliably
β_{YXt} = the regression coefficient when X is measured with perfect reliability

The decrease in the regression coefficient of Formula 10.4 will serve in Formula 10.5 to increase the intercept.

Unreliability in Y

When there is unreliability in Y, $\sigma_{Yo} > \sigma_{Yt}$ and $\rho_{YoX} < \rho_{YtX}$ (from Formula 17.3). Both of these are components of the numerator in Formula 10.4 and they move in opposite directions. Indeed, it can be shown that the effects in the numerator of Formula 10.4 are offsetting.

$$\beta_{YoX} \approx \beta_{YtX}$$

where β_{YoX} = the regression coefficient when Y is measured unreliably
β_{YtX} = the regression coefficient when Y is measured with perfect reliability

Because unreliability in Y has no expected effect on the regression coefficient, it also has no expected effect on the intercept. Unreliability in Y does have implications for statistical inference. Specifically, other things equal, unreliability makes it less likely that an observed regression coefficient will lead to a conclusion to reject the null hypothesis.

Correcting for Unreliability in Regression Coefficients

Where there is unreliability in X, attenuation can be corrected with the formula:

$$\beta_{Y_tX_t} = \beta_{Y_oX_o}/\rho_{XX} \qquad (17.5)$$

where $\beta_{Y_tX_t}$ = estimated true regression coefficient, and
$\quad \beta_{Y_oX_o}$ = observed regression coefficient

As in the case of correction for unreliability in correlation coefficients, the accuracy of this correction is contingent on the assumptions that ρ_{Ye} and $\rho_{Xe} = 0.0$.

Unreliability in Multiple Correlation and Regression

Consequences of unreliability with simple correlation and regression are straightforward as described. They are also straightforward in multiple correlation and regression in those rare instances when there is no multicollinearity among the independent variables. In such cases, the consequences of unreliability mirror their effects in simple correlation and regression.

However, this is not the situation in multiple correlation and regression when there is multicollinearity among the independent variables. Given multicollinearity, unreliability in the X variables may attenuate standardized or unstandardized partial coefficients; but it also may leave them unchanged, inflate them, or even change their sign. Identifying consequences of unreliability in multiple regression is difficult, especially as the number of independent variables becomes large. The challenge is best confronted by the development and use of measures with high reliability.

In our program, who sets the standards of reliability?

RESEARCH HIGHLIGHT 17.3

Reliability Guidelines

Okay, you're convinced; reliability is important. It is important for construct validity and it is important for statistical output. How reliable must measures be?

That's a good question, but it doesn't have a simple answer. First, there are many different kinds of reliability. A reliability value that is acceptable in one situation may not be acceptable in another. For example, the reliability of a measure administered twice, 2 weeks apart, generally will have greater reliability than if it is administered twice, 1 year apart. Second, what is acceptable or unacceptable reliability also depends on how the measure is used. To illustrate, higher reliability is needed to make accurate predictions about individual cases than is needed to draw conclusions about whether two or more groups differ on some measure.

It is often possible to improve reliability in the course of constructing measures. Because of its importance for construct validity, high reliability should be a top measurement priority.

Intro??

SUMMARY

Reliability refers to consistency of measurement. It is formally defined as the proportion of observed score variance that is systematic.

Methods to estimate reliability typically differ by the type of reliability of interest. ***Coefficient alpha*** is commonly used to estimate internal consistency (the reliability of a set of items). Coefficient alpha is interpreted as the correlation coefficient expected between two similar measures of the same phenomena containing the same number of items. It generally increases as the correlation between items increases and as the number of items increases.

Stability (reliability over time) is usually estimated with a correlation coefficient obtained from administrations of a single measure at two points in time. Finally, interrater reliability is typically estimated by ***analysis of variance***, a statistical procedure closely related to correlation and regression. In all cases, measures of reliability estimate the ratio of true to observed score variance.

Unreliability in measurement whatever its source has generally negative consequences for statistical output obtained on those measures. An observed simple correlation coefficient is attenuated by unreliability in the independent and/or the dependent variable. If the reliability of the measures is known, a ***correction for attenuation*** estimates the correlation coefficient to be expected if both measures had perfect reliability. Unreliability in X also attenuates simple regression coefficients. Simple regression coefficients also can be corrected for unreliability in X. Consequences of unreliability in multiple correlation and regression are more complex when the X variables are collinear.

FOR REVIEW

Terms to Know

Reliability: The consistency of measurement. Formally, it is the ratio of systematic score variance to total variance.

Coefficient alpha: An estimate of reliability; it provides an estimate of the correlation coefficient that is expected between a summary score from a measure studied and another hypothetical measure of the same thing using the same number of repetitions.

Attenuation due to unreliability: Formula that estimates the degree to which unreliability in either or both variables reduces a correlation coefficient relative to perfectly reliable measurement of the variables.

Correction for attenuation: Formulae that estimate the correlation coefficient or regression coefficient between two variables if they are measured with perfect reliability; it requires knowledge of reliability.

Formulae to Use

Reliability

$$\rho_{XX} = \sigma_{Xt}^2/\sigma_{Xo}^2 \tag{17.1}$$

where ρ_{XX} = reliability of scores on measure X

Coefficient alpha

$$\hat{\rho}_{XX} = (k \times \rho_{(Ave)ij})/[1 + (k-1) \times \rho_{(Ave)ij}] \tag{17.2}$$

where $\rho_{(Ave)ij}$ = average correlation among scores of items

Attenuation due to unreliability

$$\rho_{Y_oX_o} = \rho_{Y_tX_t}\sqrt{\rho_{YY}}\sqrt{\rho_{XX}}$$ (17.3)

where $\rho_{Y_oX_o}$ = correlation coefficient on observed scores
  $\rho_{Y_tX_t}$ = true score correlation coefficient

Correction for attenuation (correlation coefficient)

$$\rho_{Y_tX_t} = \frac{\rho_{Y_oX_o}}{\sqrt{\rho_{YY}}\sqrt{\rho_{XX}}}$$ (17.4)

Correction for attenuation (regression coefficient)

$$\beta_{Y_tX_t} = \beta_{Y_oX_o}/\rho_{XX}$$ (17.5)

where $\beta_{Y_tX_t}$ = estimated true regression coefficient, and
  $\beta_{Y_oX_o}$ = observed regression coefficient

Questions for Review

1. How does unreliability in an independent variable influence the simple correlation co-efficient, regression coefficient, and regression intercept? How do these conclusions change if the unreliability was in the dependent rather than the independent variable?

2. Simple correlation coefficients among four items designed to measure opinions about the nutritional value of herbal tea are shown.

	Simple Correlation Coefficients			
	X_1	X_2	X_3	X_4
$X1$	1.00	.55	.35	.45
$X2$		1.00	.65	.50
$X3$			1.00	.45

a. Calculate coefficient alpha for the four items.
b. What three items would form the most reliable scale if only three items were used?
c. What is coefficient alpha for these three items?
d. Given your alpha value from Question c, what correlation would you expect between the sum of these three items and the sum of another three items measuring the same thing?

3. You observe that $\rho_{YX} = .35$ and $\rho_{YZ} = .45$. Reliabilities are $\rho_{YY} = .90$, $\rho_{XX} = .80$, and $\rho_{ZZ} = .70$. What has the higher true score relationship, ρ_{YX} or ρ_{YZ}?

4. If you have covered the material in chapter 10: How is the random error term (e_i) different in the regression model than in the reliability model? How is it the same?

Exercise

The following data set shows reliable Y and X scores and Y and X scores with unreliability.[1] (The eight values in parentheses are included only to show how the variables are influenced by unreliability. Do not include them in your analysis.)

Reliable Y	Unreliable Y	Reliable X	Unreliable X
2	2	1	1
2	3 (*up 1*)	2	1 (*down 1*)
2	1 (*down 1*)	3	4 (*up 1*)
2	2	4	4
4	4	3	3
4	3 (*down 1*)	4	5 (*up 1*)
4	5 (*up 1*)	5	4 (*down 1*)
4	4	6	6

Use the data set to calculate the following statistics.

1. Descriptive statistics that provide means and standard deviations for each variable. What is noteworthy about these statistics in terms of your knowledge of reliability?
2. Simple correlation coefficients between all the variables. What is noteworthy about these statistics in terms of your knowledge of reliability?
3. Regress reliable Y on reliable X. Then, regress unreliable Y on reliable X. Finally, regress reliable Y on unreliable X. What is noteworthy about these statistics in terms of your knowledge of reliability?

SUGGESTED READINGS

Reliability has received a great deal of attention by researchers, probably because it can be addressed with mathematics more rigorously than many other construct validity topics. Two good general discussions of reliability that go beyond the level of presentation here but are nevertheless accessible are provided by Ghiselli, Campbell, & Zedeck (1981) and by Nunnally (1978). I also like Campbell's (1976) chapter on reliability.

There are also many writings on specific topics discussed in the chapter. Cortina (1993) presents a nice discussion of the use and limitations of coefficient alpha. Cohen et al. (2003) have an understandable discussion of problems presented by unreliability for multiple correlation and regression. Problems created by unreliability are discussed by Schmidt & Hunter (1996). Finally, Shavelson, Webb, & Rowley (1989) provide an introduction to Cronbach, Rajaratnam, & Gleser's (1963) complex generalizability theory.

---

[1] The random appearing errors in this data set are really not random at all. With such a small sample of observations, unreliability can have *unexpected* results. This data set is constructed to have *expected* unreliability consequences for correlation and regression.

18

On Multicollinearity

Chapter Outline

- *Consequences of Multicollinearity*
- *A Demonstration*
  - *Population Parameters*
  - *Sample Statistics*
- *Multicollinearity Misconceived*
- *Addressing Multicollinearity*
- *Summary*
- *For Review*
  - *Terms to Know*
  - *Formula to Use*
  - *Questions for Review*

Multicollinearity is a big word to describe a simple concept; it means that independent variables are correlated (e.g., $r_{X1X2} <> 0$). This chapter elaborates on chapter 11, which introduced multicollinearity in a multiple correlation/regression context. It also extends chapters 12 and 13, which described statistical inference. It begins with a brief summary of consequences of multicollinearity. These consequences are then illustrated through a simulation. Next, a common multicollinearity misconception is identified. Finally, suggestions for addressing multicollinearity are offered.

CONSEQUENCES OF MULTICOLLINEARITY

Chapter 11 explained that the multiple coefficient of determination (P^2_{YX1X2}) is not equal to the sum of the simple coefficients of determination ($\rho^2_{YX1} + \rho^2_{YX2}$) when there is multicollinearity

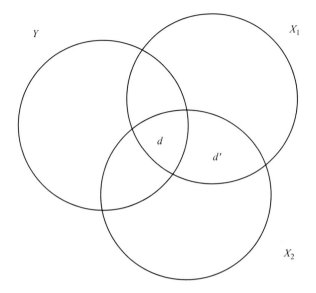

EXHIBIT 18.1.   Multicollinearity with two independent variables.

in a two-independent-variable case. Typical consequences of multicollinearity are shown in Exhibit 18.1 where multicollinearity between $X1$ and $X2$ is shown by the area $d + d'$. Some variance that each explains in Y is redundant (the area d). Consequently, the total variance explained in Y is less than the simple sum of the variance that each X_i explains. This two-independent-variable case generalizes to three or more independent variables.

It is also the case that the standard error of any partial coefficient for X_i (regression or correlation) increases as multicollinearity in X_i increases. A standard error is a standard deviation of a sampling distribution (chapter 12). The larger the standard error, the greater the variability in sample estimates of a parameter. As a consequence, the partial coefficients (e.g., β_{YX_i}) from one sample may not be similar to coefficients calculated on another sample drawn from the same population. Because of this, standardized regression coefficients calculated when independent variables are collinear are sometimes called ***bouncing betas***.

A DEMONSTRATION

Data for two populations were created to illustrate several multicollinearity outcomes. Both populations have 6,000 cases. Both have a standardized ($\mu = 0$; $\sigma = 1$) dependent variable (Y) and three standardized independent variables ($X1$, $X2$, and $X3$). Each X_i was specified to correlate with its respective Y, $\rho_{YX_i} = .30$. However, Population 1 was specified to have no multicollinearity (simple correlation coefficients among the Xs equal zero). Population 2 was specified to have multicollinearity of $p_{X_iX_j} = .50$ for all three pairs of relationships. Descriptive statistics summarized in Exhibits 18.2 and 18.3 show that the populations created conform closely to specification.

Population Parameters

Exhibits 18.4 and 18.5 show results of a regression of Y on all X_i in Populations 1 and 2, respectively. Standardized partial regression coefficients (betas) and the multiple coefficient of

Coefficients Variables	μ	σ	Correlation Coefficients			
			Y	X1	X2	X3
Y	0.00	1.00	1.00			
X1	0.00	1.00	.28	1.00		
X2	0.00	1.00	.32	.00	1.00	
X3	0.00	1.00	.30	-.01	-.00	1.00

N = 6,000.

EXHIBIT 18.2.   Population 1: Descriptive statistics.

Coefficients Variables	μ	σ	Correlation Coefficients			
			Y	X1	X2	X3
Y	0.00	1.00	1.00			
X1	0.00	1.00	.30	1.00		
X2	0.00	1.00	.30	.51	1.00	
X3	0.00	1.00	.31	.51	.50	1.00

N = 6,000.

EXHIBIT 18.3.   Population 2: Descriptive statistics.

determination (P^2) are shown in each. No inferential statistical values (e.g., t or F statistics) are shown because these coefficients are population parameters.

Beta coefficients in Exhibit 18.4 correspond closely to the simple correlation coefficients in Exhibit 18.2. This result occurs because all variables are standardized and there is nearly zero correlation among the independent variables. Also observe that $P^2_{YX1X2X3}(=.28)$ is about equal to the sum of the simple coefficients of determination ($\Sigma[p^2_{YXi}] = .28^2 + .32^2 + .30^2 = .27$). This result also obtains because the independent variables have nearly zero multicollinearity.

Contrast the population results in Exhibit 18.4 with Exhibit 18.5. The standardized regression coefficients in Exhibit 18.5 are all smaller than their counterparts in Exhibit 18.4. And, they are all smaller than the zero-order correlation coefficients of X_i with Y. These outcomes result from multicollinearity among the independent variables. Some of the variance explained in Y by each X variable is redundant with variance explained by others. Thus, Y variance explained in Population 2 ($P^2_{YX1X2X3} = .14$) is smaller than in Population 1 and smaller than the sum of the simple coefficients of determination ($\Sigma[p^2_{YXi}] = .30^2 + .30^2 + .31^2 = .28$).

Sample Statistics

Twenty-five random samples of 25 cases each were drawn from each population to illustrate the implications of multicollinearity for statistical inference. Exhibits 18.6 (Population 1) and 18.7 (Population 2) summarize statistics calculated on these samples. The exhibits show standardized regression coefficients, standard errors, and the corrected coefficient of determination, $\hat{P}^2_{YX1X2X3}$.

Variable	Beta
$X1$	.28
$X2$	.32
$X3$	.30
P^2	.28

$N = 6,000.$

EXHIBIT 18.4. Population 1: Regression output.

Variable	Beta
$X1$	.14
$X2$	.15
$X3$	.17
P^2	.14

$N = 6,000.$

EXHIBIT 18.5. Population 2: Regression output.

The corrected coefficient of determination $\hat{P}^2$, called **adjusted R^2**, is a better estimate of the population coefficient of determination than unadjusted R^2. $\hat{P}^2$ is found by:

$$\hat{P}^2 = R^2 - [k \times (1 - R^2)]/(n - k - 1) \qquad (18.1)$$

where $\hat{P}^2$ = adjusted coefficient of determination
$\quad R^2$ = sample coefficient of determination
$\quad n$ = sample size
$\quad k$ = number of independent variables

Average $\hat{P}^2$ and beta values obtained in the 25 samples from the two populations are shown near the bottom of Exhibits 18.6 and 18.7. These averages illustrate the unbiasedness of population estimates obtained from random samples. Average $\hat{P}^2$ from samples of both populations are close to the population parameters. Further, with one exception (b_{YX1}, Population 2), average betas are also close to their respective population parameters.

The mean standard errors associated with the betas are informative about multicollinearity. On average, these errors are all larger in Population 2 with multicollinearity. This shows that statistical power is reduced by multicollinearity.

Exhibits 18.6 and 18.7 reveal results of multicollinearity in three additional ways. All are consistent with the standard error results, and all are associated with loss of power due to multicollinearity.

1. Beta estimates for all three independent variables have larger standard deviations in samples drawn from the population with multicollinearity (Population 2).

Sample	$\hat{P}^2$	X1	SE X1	X2	SE X2	X3	SE X3
1	.44**	.43*	.13	.37*	.21	.48*	.12
2	.31*	.29	.15	.38	.17	.34	.11
3	.04	.19	.22	.40	.19	.01	.26
4	.54**	.64**	.17	.30*	.17	.58**	.17
5	.27*	.08	.25	.29	.21	.43*	.23
6	.33*	.25	.22	.39*	.16	.40*	.19
7	.24*	.57**	.14	-.04	.15	.05	.18
8	.27*	.38	.17	.51*	.16	.16	.16
9	.26*	.26	.13	.34	.11	.40*	.12
10	.57**	.36*	.13	.56**	.10	.52*	.14
11	.58**	.60**	.18	.35*	.13	.44*	.17
12	.24*	.57	.16	.21	.16	.06	.21
13	.10	.18	.15	.11	.16	.44*	.17
14	.47**	-.04	.23	.69**	.17	.13	.17
15	.11	.34	.26	.26	.24	.32	.21
16	.00	.09	.22	.11	.19	.03	.20
17	.23*	.45	.21	.44*	.20	.50*	.22
18	.48**	.43*	.16	.38*	.17	.52**	.16
19	.37**	.36	.22	.14	.25	.44*	.18
20	.22*	.32	.16	.40*	.18	.27	.20
21	.04	-.10	.19	.05	.16	.39	.17
22	.44**	.48*	.14	.56**	.15	-.12	.17
23	.33*	.26	.16	.57**	.19	.27	.20
24	.30*	.37	.22	.27	.18	.29	.18
25	.00	.06	.23	.22	.16	.23	.19
Mean	.29	.31	.18	.33	.17	.30	.18
Std Dev	.17	.20	.04	.18	.03	.19	.03

$*P < .05$
$**P < .01$

EXHIBIT 18.6.   Population 1: Sample regression output from 25 samples ($n = 25$).

2. An examination of the signs of the beta coefficients is also revealing. Although the population betas are all positive, 23 of the sample beta coefficients are negative in Population 2. Only 4 of the sample betas are negative in Population 1.

3. Power is low in statistical tests from both populations (the sample sizes are only 25 in each case), but it is lower in the population with multicollinearity. Thirty of the 75 partial coefficients are statistically significant ($p < .05$) in samples from Population 1 (Exhibit 18.6); only 6 are statistically significant in samples from Population 2 (Exhibit 18.7). Keep in mind, all X_i are related in the populations (see Exhibits 18.4 and 18.5). Thus, only Type II error is possible (failing to conclude H_1 when H_1 is true).

MULTICOLLINEARITY MISCONCEIVED

If discussed, multicollinearity is almost always described as problematic by statistics and research methods books. Indeed it is; as shown, multicollinearity attenuates multiple correlation and regression coefficients and makes any sample estimates less reliable predictors of population parameters (i.e., reduces power).

However, absence of multicollinearity is not an assumption of multiple correlation and regression as is sometimes suggested. Standard errors remain correct even with multicollinearity

Sample	$\hat{P}^2$	X1	SE X1	X2	SE X2	X3	SE X3
1	.08	-.13	.23	.18	.17	.39	.23
2	.03	-.44	.28	.36	.27	.06	.29
3	.00	-.32	.27	.40	.27	-.09	.26
4	.14	.06	.30	.38	.26	.13	.33
5	.26*	.03	.14	-.17	.16	.63*	.18
6	.30*	.13	.23	.48	.30	.08	.25
7	.00	.23	.28	.11	.38	-.15	.29
8	.03	-.42	.30	.18	.30	.41	.33
9	.06	-.12	.25	.56	.29	-.19	.29
10	.32*	.73**	.25	-.08	.23	-.16	.20
11	.14	.14	.20	-.15	.18	.47*	.15
12	.08	.27	.22	.34	.24	-.48	.17
13	.26	.27	.17	.45	.21	-.04	.21
14	.06	.14	.32	.07	.39	.30	.28
15	.14	-.51	.22	.06	.18	.61*	.20
16	.14	.39	.20	.23	.20	-.11	.21
17	.02	.14	.24	.07	.28	.26	.23
18	.23*	.26	.23	-.35	.21	.58*	.18
19	.16	.20	.29	.27	.31	.19	.25
20	.50	.10	.14	-.02	.27	.70**	.15
21	.53	.76	.20	.07	.15	-.05	.19
22	.08	-.13	.23	.18	.17	.39	.23
23	.03	-.44	.28	.36	.27	.06	.29
24	.00	-.32	.27	.40	.27	-.09	.26
25	.14	.06	.30	.38	.26	.13	.33
Mean	.15	.04	.24	.19	.25	.16	.23
Std Dev	.14	.33	.05	.23	.06	.31	.06

*$P < .05$
**$P < .01$

EXHIBIT 18.7.   Population 2: Sample regression output from 25 samples ($n = 25$).

(although larger than they otherwise would be). Hypothesis tests and confidence intervals thus remain correct.

Think of it another way: With zero multicollinearity, we could obtain R^2 simply by summing the simple $r^2_{YX_i}$ (see Formula 11.1). Furthermore, any simple regression coefficient would be the same as its corresponding partial coefficient. If multicollinearity were not present, multiple correlation and regression would provide no information beyond what we can learn from simple correlation and regression.

But multicollinearity is no virtue. Although multicollinearity does not invalidate multiple correlation and regression, it nevertheless has the undesirable consequences identified. Researchers prefer less to more.

ADDRESSING MULTICOLLINEARITY

The best way to address multicollinearity is to view it in conceptual terms before data are collected and analyses are performed. Design, measurement, and data analysis responses to multicollinearity should be driven by the conceptual model of interest. For example, suppose an interest in some work attitude and a conceptual model suggests that employee age and work experience affect this attitude but for different reasons. That being the case, both variables should be included in the model, even though they are typically related (collinear).

Alternatively, a conceptual model may not distinguish between the roles of age and experience. They may only represent approximations (proxies) for longevity in some sense. If so, one might include only one of the two variables in a statistical model, or the two could be combined in a single index representing longevity.

SUMMARY

Multicollinearity refers to the correlation among independent variables. It presents two problems for multivariate data analysis procedures. First, it reduces the dependent variable variance explained relative to what would be the case if the independent variables have the same simple relationships with the dependent variable but less multicollinearity. Second, multicollinearity results in sample statistics that are less stable estimates of population parameters. A simulation demonstrated both effects.

Your approach to multicollinearity should be guided by the conceptual model explaining relationships among the variables. Independent variables may be collinear. However, if they are important to the conceptual model they should be retained in the analysis.

It is wise to aim for a large sample when there is multicollinearity. The increase in standard errors of the partial coefficients associated with the collinear independent variables reduces power.

FOR REVIEW

Terms to Know

Bouncing betas: Instability in sample standardized partial regression coefficients resulting from multicollinearity.

Adjusted R^2: Multiple coefficient of determination adjusted for sample size and number of independent variables. It is a better estimate of the parameter than is the unadjusted sample multiple coefficient of determination.

Formula to Use

Adjusted coefficient of determination

$$\hat{P}^2 = R^2 - [k \times (1 - R^2)]/(n - k - 1) \tag{18.1}$$

where $\hat{P}^2$ = adjusted coefficient of determination
R^2 = sample coefficient of determination
n = sample size
k = number of independent variables

Questions for Review

1. Multicollinearity leads to an increase in the standard error of partial correlation and regression coefficients. What are the implications of this increase for statistical inference?

2. Two studies are performed by drawing random samples from two populations. Selected characteristics of the studies are summarized below.

Study 1   Study 2

$R^2 = .35$ $R^2 = .45$

$n = 1,500$ $n = 150$

$k = 4$ $k = 6$

where n = sample size; k = number of independent variables

At a population level, how much of the variance in the dependent variable do you estimate is accounted for in each study?

19

On Causal Models and Statistical Modeling

Chapter Outline

- *Causal Models*
  - *Illustrative Data Set*
  - *Evaluating Causal Models*
- *Four Illustrative Models*
  - *Direct Effects Models*
  - *Mediated Models*
  - *Moderated Models*
    - *Subgrouping*
    - *Moderated Regression*
    - *Centering*
    - *A Final Requirement*
  - *Hierarchical Models*
- *A Closing Caution*
- *Summary*
- *For Review*
  - *Terms to Know*
  - *Questions for Review*
- *Suggested Readings*

This chapter introduces **statistical modeling**: the study of the structure of scores on variables using statistics and statistical inference. Multiple correlation and regression serve as the statistics throughout, consistent with the statistical methods covered in the book. The chapter also explains how statistical inference is used in the modeling process.

The chapter is also consistent with the orientation of the book—namely, that empirical research most often is aimed at causal understanding (chapter 2). Thus, it focuses on using statistical models to evaluate **causal models**. A causal model specifies linkages between independent and dependent *constructs* in a causal chain; it is thus a conceptual model. Statistical models are used to help evaluate the tenability of causal models.

CAUSAL MODELS

Causal models take a variety of forms. Four simple but frequently investigated models are described. These four are all **recursive models**; causal influence is assumed to go in only one direction, from the independent to the dependent variable.

Two terms commonly characterize variables in causal models. **Endogenous variables** are explained by the causal model. Thus, dependent variables are always endogenous. Independent variables are also endogenous if they depend on some other independent variable(s) in the model. Alternatively, independent variables are **exogenous** when their cause(s) is not specified by the causal model.

Illustrative Data Set

Procedures used to evaluate causal models are illustrated with a hypothetical data set. These data represent information on a random sample of 100 low- to middle-level managers from a simulated population of 4,861 managers in a large organization.

Statistics on the variables are summarized in Exhibit 19.1. Yearly salary serves as the dependent variable in all models. Depending on the model evaluated, independent variables include the following:

- Years of experience at the organization
- Job level; scaled from 1 (first level supervisor) to 4 (highest level middle manager). (The relationship between salary and job level in this data set is linear; hence, it is treated as a scaled variable. If the relationship is not linear, three dummy variables could be created to account for the four job levels.)
- Performance rating; provided by each manager's supervisor ranging from 1 (poor performance) to 7 (superior performance)
- Gender; dummy coded, male = 1, female = 0
- Set of occupations; finance/accounting, dummy coded, finance/accounting = 1, all other occupations = 0; similar dummy variables are created for the other occupations; human resources, manufacturing, and sales/marketing
- Two variables formed by multiplying independent variables together: (1) gender times years of experience, and (2) job level times years of experience. The motivation for these variables is explained in the discussion of moderator variables.

Several different conceptual models are hypothesized to illustrate the statistical methods. Focus on the statistical methods; do not take the veracity of the illustrative conceptual models too seriously.

Evaluating Causal Models

Empirical researchers obtain scores on measures of the causal variables and identify relationships between them. Statistical inference (part V) is used to help in the evaluation process. Support for a causal link is claimed if a relationship under investigation is statistically significant at some specified level (e.g., $p < .05$). Confidence intervals are an alternative inferential procedure; they are used infrequently.

		M	SD	Simple Correlation Coefficients										
				Y	X1	X2	X3	X4	X5	X6	X7	X8	X9	X10
Y	Yearly salary	63,800.00	9,000.70	1.00										
X1	Years experience	9.20	3.02	.44*	1.00									
X2	Job level	2.36	1.07	.58*	.66*	1.00								
X3	Performance	4.62	1.81	.13	.12	.17	1.00							
X4	Gender	.70	.46	.20*	.15	.06	.03	1.00						
X5	Finance/accounting	.24	.43	.17	-.08	-.04	-.02	-.14	1.00					
X6	Human resources	.24	.43	-.03	.04	-.15	-.09	.16	-.32*	1.00				
X7	Manufacturing	.28	.45	-.33*	.07	.02	.08	-.13	-.35*	-.35*	1.00			
X8	Sales/marketing	.24	.43	.21*	-.04	.16	.03	.11	-.32*	-.32*	-.35*	1.00		
X9	Gender × years of experience	6.65	5.04	.40*	.54*	.35*	.10	.87*	-.10	.13	-.11	.09	1.00	
X10	Job level × years of experience	23.83	15.77	.58*	.85*	.93*	.16	.12*	-.04	-.0 6	.02	.08	.49*	1.00

Note. $^*p < .05$ (two-tailed).

Job level ranges from 1 (first level supervisor) to 4 (top middle manager).

Performance ranges from 1 (marginal performance) to 7 (highest performance).

Gender dummy coded (male = 1; female = 0).

Accounting dummy coded (finance/accounting = 1; other = 0); likewise for the other occupational areas.

Gender × years of experience is an interaction (moderator) term formed by multiplying gender times years of experience.

Job level × years of experience is an interaction (moderator) term formed by multiplying job level times years of experience.

EXHIBIT 19.1.   Summary statistics on hypothetical managerial data set.

Typically, researchers also look to some measure of the importance of a relationship between variables. Importance is assessed by the size of a regression coefficient, by the variance an independent variable explains in a dependent variable, or in other ways. Criteria for judging importance are not as standardized as in the case of statistical inference. Consequently, researchers' judgments about importance are made more subjectively.

For example, a model might hypothesize that years of experience influences salary. Support for this expectation from a research study is claimed if the observed relationship (e.g., simple regression coefficient from salary regressed on years of experience) is statistically significant (e.g., $p < .05$). The size of the coefficient will also likely be discussed as further evidence of its importance.

FOUR ILLUSTRATIVE MODELS

Four causal models are described. Causal models represented by these four are frequently hypothesized in organizational research. The models are illustrative only. In most situations, causal models hypothesized contain more variables than are used here to illustrate. In addition, the models here are often combined in various ways to form more complex models for testing.

Direct Effects Models

A ***direct effect*** refers to a causal relationship between an independent and a dependent variable that is not mediated by some other variable(s). It is observed after other independent variables are controlled. Thus, when there are two or more independent variables in a model, the direct effect of any one independent variable is represented by its *partial* coefficient.

To illustrate, researcher A specifies a model shown in Exhibit 19.2. It is a direct effects model involving two independent variables. Researcher A hypothesizes that managerial salary levels depend on years of work experience and level in the job hierarchy of an organization. The independent variables are exogenous because A offers no explanation of their causes.

RESEARCH HIGHLIGHT 19.1

Empirical Models

The models described in this chapter all depend on a researcher's prior specification of a causal model. Statistical tests help researchers evaluate whether the model specified is plausible given the data obtained on a group of cases. The causal model dominates; statistical tests only help the researcher decide if the data do or do not provide support for the model.

Alternatively, in ***empirical models*** independent variables are chosen by using statistical criteria. Researchers using empirical modeling identify only the dependent variable and a *tentative set* of independent variables that may account for variance in it. Results from statistical analyses are used to decide which specific independent variables are retained in the final model. Several such modeling procedures are available; they are often called ***stepwise*** procedures.

Procedures that rely exclusively on statistical criteria to identify independent variables are not recommended for most research situations. They are definitely inappropriate for testing causal models. Statistical significance, even when appropriately used, and variance explained are not substitutes for conceptual model building.

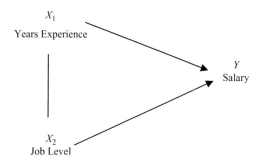

EXHIBIT 19.2. Direct causal effects model.

Model	(1)	(2)	(3)
Variable	b_{YXi}	b_{YXi}	$b_{YXi \cdot Xj}$
$X1$ Years of experience	1,320.99*		324.19
$X2$ Job level		4,850.96*	4,242.48*
Intercept (a)	51,646.92*	52,351.74*	50,805.17*
r^2 (R^2)	.20	.33	.34
$\hat{\rho}^2$ ($\hat{P}^2$)	.19*	.32*	.32*

*$p < .05$ (two-tailed).

Job level ranges from 1 (first level supervisor) to 4 (top middle manager).

EXHIBIT 19.3.   Three statistical models of salary as a function of years of experience and job level.

Arrows in Exhibit 19.2 represent causal linkages in the model. Years of work experience and job level are both expected to have positive causal influences on salary level. The line between years of experience and job level acknowledges there may be a relationship between these two variables. However, A's causal interest does not go beyond explaining salary as a joint function of the two independent variables.

Statistical information on direct effects can be obtained from partial regression (standardized or unstandardized) or squared partial or semipartial correlation coefficients. Exhibit 19.3 shows three models reporting unstandardized regression coefficients. Model 3 shows statistical output addressing A's model. For comparison, Models 1 and 2 show results from simple regressions of salary on years of work experience and job level, respectively.

The first partial regression coefficient in Model 3 estimates the direct effect of years of experience, holding job level constant, as $324.19. This coefficient is smaller than the coefficient in the simple regression of salary on years of experience (Model 1) because years of experience and job level are collinear ($r_{X1X2} = .66$; see Exhibit 19.1). Furthermore, although the simple regression coefficient for years of experience is statistically significant ($p < .05$) in Model 1, its partial regression coefficient is not statistically significant in Model 3.

Exhibit 19.3 also shows that, the direct effect of job level is $4,242.48 holding years of experience constant. This coefficient is statistically significant ($p < .05$). Researcher A concludes that support is obtained for job level but not for years of experience by using a statistical inference criterion.

Finally, Exhibit 19.3 shows that Model 3 explains 34% of the salary variance in the sample (R^2). It estimates that 32% of salary variance is jointly explained by years of experience and job level in the population of managers ($\hat{P}^2$). (See Formula 18.1 for an explanation of $\hat{P}^2$.)

Mediated Models

Researcher B posits an alternative model shown in Exhibit 19.4. It includes the same three variables as A's model but has a different hypothesized causal explanation. Job level is exogenous in A's model. However, B hypothesizes that years of experience influences both salary

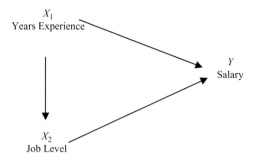

EXHIBIT 19.4.   Mediated effects model.

and job level. B reasons that increases in years of experience have both a direct and an ***indirect effect*** on salary. An indirect effect operates through a mediator (chapter 5) variable. In this case, years of experience affects job level (the mediator), which in turn influences salary. B reasons that more senior employees are more likely to obtain promotions to higher job levels, other things equal.

In B's model, salary and job level are endogenous; both are consequences of another independent variable in the model. Only years of experience is exogenous.

The combined direct effects of years of experience and job level on salary are estimated just as for researcher A (Model 3 in Exhibit 19.3). Each partial regression coefficient shows the direct effect of its variable on salary.

However, in B's conceptual model (Exhibit 19.4), years of experience also has an indirect effect. Direct and indirect (through job level) effects of years of experience on salary can be estimated as follows:

1. Take the partial regression for years of experience from Model 3 as its direct effect, $324.19, as before.
2. Estimate the influence of years of experience on job level. To do this, regress job level on years of experience. The equation is,

$$\text{job}^{\wedge}\text{level} = .20 + .23 \times \text{ (years of experience)}$$

3. Estimate the indirect effect of years of experience on salary by multiplying its direct effect on job level times the direct effect of job level on salary (.23 × $4,242.48 = $975.77). A unit change in years of experience is expected to increase job level by .23. In turn, a .23 increase in job level is expected to increase salary by $975.77.

The ***total effect*** of years of experience on salary is the sum of the direct and indirect effects ($975.77 + $324.19 = $1,299.96). Except for rounding error, this total effect equals the simple regression coefficient in Model 1 (Exhibit 19.3) when salary is regressed just on years of experience. The sum of the direct and indirect effects equals the coefficient from the simple regression of salary on years of experience.

A more general procedure for identifying direct and indirect effects capitalizes on this relationship between total, direct, and indirect effects. The simple regression coefficient of an exogenous independent variable represents its total effect. Its partial regression coefficient represents its direct effect when all other appropriately specified endogenous independent variables are in the equation. The difference between the total and direct effects represents the indirect effects of this exogenous variable through the endogenous variables in the model.

RESEARCH HIGHLIGHT 19.2

The Conceptual Model Dominates

Researchers A and B have different conceptual models and accordingly test them with different statistical models. Furthermore, both researchers obtain some support for their prior (but differing) expectations. But the variables and data are identical! The point? Statistical models make no independent contribution to the specification of conceptual models. They are of use only in evaluating causal models once developed.

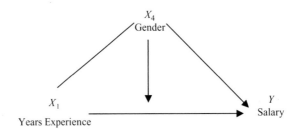

EXHIBIT 19.5.   Moderated model: Gender as a moderated variable.

Moderated Models

Like A and B, researcher C expects that years of experience increases salary level. However, C's model includes gender (a nominal dichotomy) rather than job level as a causal variable. C hypothesizes that men obtain higher salaries than women, other things equal.

Furthermore, C expects that gender *moderates* (chapter 5) the relationship between years of experience and salary. Specifically, C hypothesizes that the relationship between years of experience and salary is larger for men than for women; men benefit more from an additional year of experience in the salary setting process.

The model is diagrammed in Exhibit 19.5. Arrows pointing from gender and years of experience to salary signal direct effects as before. The arrow from gender to the *line* connecting years of experience and salary indicates that gender is expected to moderate (influence) this relationship. The line linking gender and years of experience indicates that C believes the two variables may be related but has no reason to believe a causal relationship exists.

Direct effects of years of experience and gender can be addressed statistically as already seen with years of experience and job level. Model 3 in Exhibit 19.6 shows these results on all sample members. In this model, the direct effect of years of experience on salary is $1,257.20, gender held constant. This effect is statistically significant ($p < .05$). The direct effect of gender is $2,742.80. Given the dummy coding of gender (male = 1), the results indicate a $2,742.80 salary advantage for men, controlling for years of experience; this is not statistically significant.

Subgrouping

Because gender is a nominal dichotomy, its status as a moderator can be assessed by dividing the sample into two subgroups (male and female). Salary is then regressed on years of experience in each. Exhibit 19.6 shows results from a simple regression of salary on years of experience among men (Model 1) and women (Model 2). The relationship between years of experience is stronger among men than women, as hypothesized. A statistical test, whether the relationship

Model	(1)	(2)	(3)	(4)
Participants	Males	Females	All	
Variable	b_{YmXm}	b_{YfXf}	$b_{YXi \cdot Xj}$	$b_{YXi \cdot Xj}$
$X1$ Years of experience	1,626.79*	377.84	1,257.20*	377.84
$X4$ Gender			2,742.80	-8,242.78
$X9$ Gender × years of experience				1,248.94*
Intercept (a)	49,545.54*	57,788.32*	50,313.79*	57,788.32*
r^2 (R^2)	.29	.02	.22	.25
$\hat{\rho}^2 (\hat{\rho}^2)$	.28*	.00	.20*	.23*

*$p < .05$ (two-tailed).

Gender dummy coded (male = 1; female = 0).

EXHIBIT 19.6. Four statistical models of salary as a function of years of experience and gender.

RESEARCH HIGHLIGHT 19.3

An Inappropriate Test of Moderation

Researchers sometimes perform an inappropriate test of moderation when sub-grouping. Specifically, they conclude there is a moderated relationship if the co-efficient is statistically significant in one group but not in the other, as is the case with researcher C's data (the coefficient is statistically significant in the male sub-sample but not in the female subsample). However, a moderator expectation is that the relationships *differ* from each other and not whether a relationship is greater than zero in only one population. The appropriate test therefore must compare the results obtained in one group with the results obtained in the other group.

---

between years of experience and salary observed among men is greater than the relationship observed among women is statistically significant, as hypothesized by researcher C ($p < .05$). (This test is described in the appendix to chapter 13.)

Moderated Regression

Moderated regression is a second, more general method, to address potential moderator vari-ables. A moderated regression accounts for the contingent relationship brought about by a moderator variable. It does so with the help of a new variable that is the product of the two variables (gender × years of experience). Given the scaling, this variable has values of 0.0 for all female participants in the sample; it has values equal to years of experience for all males. This new variable indicates whether men and women obtain different salary returns for experience by using a linear regression model.

Results of a regression of salary on all three variables are shown in Model 4 of Exhibit 19.6. Given the way the moderator variable was formed, the partial regression coefficient means males obtain \$1,248.94 more than females for each additional year of experience. The same result is obtained (except for rounding error) if you subtract the coefficient on years of experience in the female (Model 2) subgroup from the same coefficient in the male (Model 1) subgroup (\$1,626.79 − \$377.84 = \$1,248.95). The tests of statistical significance (the difference in coefficients in the simple regression models and the magnitude of the coefficient on the moderator variable in the multiple regression model) are mathematically equivalent. Both are statistically significant ($p < .05$), supporting researcher C's moderator hypothesis.

In summary, moderated regression provides a direct test of the moderator hypothesis. It also can be used to reproduce simple regression results obtained from subgrouping on nominal variables (see Research Highlight 19.3).

RESEARCH HIGHLIGHT 19.4

Moderated Regression Provides All Information Available from Subgrouping

The equation in Model 4 can also be used to reproduce the other results from subgrouping on gender and calculating simple regression models. Model 4 predicts salaries for males:

$$\hat{Y}_m = 57,788.32 + 377.84(X1) - 8,242.78(X4) + 1,248.94(X9)$$

However, because, for males, $X9 = X1$ and $X4 = 1$,

$$\hat{Y}_m = 57,788.32 + 377.84(X1) - 8,242.78(1) + 1,248.94(X1)$$

or,

$$\hat{Y}_m = 49,545.54 + 1,626.78(X1)$$

This result is identical (except for rounding error) to the simple regression equation of salary on years of experience in the male subsample (Model 1, Exhibit 19.6). For females:

$$\hat{Y}_f = 57,788.32 + 377.84(X1) - 8,242.78(X4) + 1,248.94(X9)$$

In this case $X4 = X9 = 0$ for females,

$$\hat{Y}_f = 57,788.32 + 377.84(X1) - 8,242.78(0) + 1,248.94(0)$$

or,

$$\hat{Y}_f = 57,788.32 + 377.84(X1)$$

As in the male subsample, results reproduce simple regression results in the female subsample (Model 2).

On the problematic side, the product term in moderated regression is often collinear with one or both of the components that form the product. Exhibit 19.1 shows that the moderator variable is collinear with gender, $r_{X4X9} = .87$. While the moderator is statistically significant in the example ($p < .05$), multicollinearity reduces statistical power as noted in chapter 18. Centering, discussed next, addresses multicollinearity and another challenge often present in moderated regression.

Centering

When there is an interaction (moderated relationship), the effect of an independent variable on the dependent variable is not constant across all values of the other independent variable(s) as it is when the relationship between the variables is linear. The contribution of $X1$ to the prediction of Y depends on the value of $X2$ (and vice versa). This follows directly from the definition of moderation and can be seen in

$$\hat{Y}_{X1 \cdot X2(X1X2)} = \alpha + \beta_{YX1 \cdot X2(X1X2)} \times X1 + \beta_{YX2 \cdot X1(X1X2)} \times X2 + \beta_{Y(X1X2) \cdot X1X2} \times X1X2$$

The impact of $X1$ on Y depends on both $\beta_{YX1 \cdot X2(X1X2)}$ and the partial regression coefficient for the moderated term $\beta_{Y(X1X2) \cdot X1X2}$.

However, if $X2 = 0.0$, $X1 \times X2 = 0.0$ and $\beta_{Y(X1X2) \cdot X1X2}$ drops out; the predicted influence of $X1$ on Y is determined solely by $\beta_{YX1 \cdot X2(X1X2)}$. The partial regression coefficient reported for $X1$ thus unambiguously indicates its contribution to the explanation of Y, but only when $X2 = 0.0$. Similarly, $\beta_{YX2 \cdot X1(X1X2)}$ unambiguously indicates the predicted contribution of $X2$ only when $X1 = 0.0$.

The partial regression coefficients in Model 4 (Exhibit 19.6) of the previous example are meaningful because of some unusual characteristics of the variables. The two independent variables are (1) a dummy coded independent variable (gender) and (2) a continuous variable with an interpretable zero value (years of experience). With the interaction term included (Model 4), the partial coefficient on years of experience indicates the predicted salary change when gender is equal to zero. Given the scaling, it refers to the change in salary resulting from an additional year of experience for men. Similarly, the gender coefficient indicates the predicted difference between men's and women's salary at the time of hire (zero years of experience). In both cases, the direct contribution of the independent variable when the interaction term drops out (by virtue of the other independent variable taking a meaningful value of zero) provides useful information.

Suppose, however, that both independent variables forming the interaction term do not have meaningful zero values. For example, researcher D specifies a model where years of experience and job level have direct effects on salary. In addition, D hypothesizes that years of experience moderate the relationship between job level and salary. D reasons that job level has a larger effect on salary among managers with more years of experience. This model is diagrammed in Exhibit 19.7.

EXHIBIT 19.7.   Years of experience as a moderator variable.

	Model 1	Model 2	Model 3	Model 4
Variable	Uncentered		Centered	
$X1$ Years of experience	324.19	-176.68	324.19	375.75
$X2$ Job level	4,242.48*	1,964.15	4,242.48*	4,117.68*
$X10$ Years of experience $\times$ job level	--	234.08	--	234.08
Intercept (a)	50,805.17*	55,211.10*	63,800.00*	63,303.37*
R^2	.34	.34	.34	.34
$\hat{P}^2$	.32*	.32*	.32*	.32*

*$p < .05$ (two-tailed).

EXHIBIT 19.8.   Four statistical models of salary as a function of years of experience and job level.

This model differs from the previous one only because it involves job level rather than gender. Two scaling differences between these variables are noteworthy. First, gender is a nominal dichotomy; job level is an ordered variable, it may have nearly interval qualities. Second, gender has a meaningful zero value (females). Job level has no zero value; it is scaled from 1 (first-level supervisor) to 4 (highest-level middle manager).

Despite this, a moderated regression can be conducted exactly as in the case with gender and years of experience. A moderator variable is created by multiplying years of experience by job level. Exhibit 19.8 shows results from the regression of salary on years of experience and job level (Model 1) and salary on years of experience, job level, and the moderator (Model 2).

It is difficult to interpret Model 2 because of the way job level is scaled. As before, the partial regression coefficient for years of experience (−$176.68) provides the predicted change in salary for an additional unit of years of experience only when job level is zero. However, unlike gender, job level cannot be zero given its scaling. Thus, the partial years of experience coefficient in Model 2 does not provide information about a plausible state of affairs.

Better information from the regression analysis can be obtained if the independent variables are first **centered** by subtracting the average of each variable from every value of the variable ($X_i - X_{Bar}$). These centered variables are multiplied to form the interaction variable. When the dependent variable is regressed on the two centered independent variables and interaction, the partial regression coefficients on the independent variables indicate the predicted change in the dependent variable for a unit change in one independent variable at the *mean* of the other independent variable (because the mean is now zero). The partial regression coefficients for the independent variables are now meaningful however they may be scaled.

To illustrate, years of experience and job level are centered. A variable representing the interaction is created by multiplying the centered variables; the interaction itself is *not* centered. Salary is then regressed on these variables. The results are shown as Models 3 and 4 in Exhibit 19.8 for comparison with the analyses using the uncentered variables.

Several differences and similarities between results from the uncentered (Models 1 and 2) and centered (Models 3 and 4) regression results are noteworthy. First, partial regression coefficients for years of experience and job level differ in models containing the interaction term (Model 2 versus 4). For example, the coefficient for years of experience in Model 4 ($375.75) differs from Model 2 ($−176.68) because it indicates the predicted change in salary given a unit change in years of experience for a manager with an average job level. This is true because centering shifted the mean of the job level to zero. The partial coefficient for job level also differs between the two models. In Model 4, its value ($4,117.68) reflects the predicted change in salary given a unit change in job level for a manager with an average level of years of experience.

Alternatively, the partial regression coefficients on the interaction terms are identical in the two models. This is always the case following centering. In addition, the amount of salary variance explained by the independent variables jointly is the same whether they are centered or not (compare Models 1 with 3, and 2 with 4). This observation also generalizes.

In this example, the variance explained in Model 1 (Model 3) is the same as the variance explained in Model 2 (Model 4) because the interaction term does not add to variance explained. This does not occur when the moderator hypothesis obtains support.

A Final Requirement

Multiple regression/correlation tests of moderated relationships must include the linear components of the product variable as well as the product variable in any statistical model. In the last example, the regression equation must include years of experience, $X1$ and job level, $X2$, along with their product, $X10$. If $X1$ and $X2$ are not included, the product variable will reflect any linear influence of the variable(s) not included as well as the nonlinear influence. It will thus be a biased estimate of the nonlinear influence.

Hierarchical Models

In **hierarchical modeling** researchers examine changes in dependent variable variance explained as independent variables are added or deleted from two or more statistical models. This differs from a focus on the statistical significance of individual independent variables characteristic of the previous models.

When used to evaluate a causal model, the first equation regresses the dependent variable on the exogenous independent variable(s). To illustrate using B's model (Exhibit 19.3), this is a regression of salary on years of experience (Model 1). Endogenous independent variables are then entered sequentially, beginning with those directly influenced by the exogenous variable(s). Again, using B's model, salary is regressed on both years of experience and job level (Model 3).

Explanations of hierarchical models focus on dependent variable variance explained and changes in variance explained from model to model. Years of experience alone explains 20% of the variance in salary (Model 1). Adding job level in Model 3 increases salary variance explained from 20% to 34%. This increment is a squared semipartial correlation coefficient (Formula 11.6b), $sr^2_{YX2 \cdot X1} = R^2_{YX2 \cdot X1} - r^2_{YX1} = .34 - .20 = .14$; it is statistically significant ($p < .05$) providing support for the hierarchical model. [An incremental F test is used, see the appendix to chapter 13 (Formula 13A.15).]

Hierarchical analysis is especially attractive when a researcher can specify sets of variables in causal order but not necessarily variables within sets. As an example, researcher E believes three sets of independent variables influence salary as shown in Exhibit 19.9. Years of experience and gender are believed to be exogenous direct determinants of salary. In addition, these two independent variables are expected to indirectly influence salary through their effects on the occupation managers enter. Occupations, in turn, are expected to have direct and indirect effects on salary through job level and manager performance ratings.

Three equations can be created to evaluate this model, as shown in Exhibit 19.10. Model 1 includes just the exogenous variables. Their total effects are estimated as $1,257.20 and $2,742.80 for years of experience and gender, respectively. They explain 22% of the salary variance in the sample, and they are estimated to explain 20% of the salary variance in the population.

Model 2 adds occupation dummy variables (manufacturing is omitted) and Model 3 adds job level and performance rating. The change in R^2 is .16 between Models 1 and 2, and .11 between Models 2 and 3. These changes are statistically significant ($p < .05$). The addition

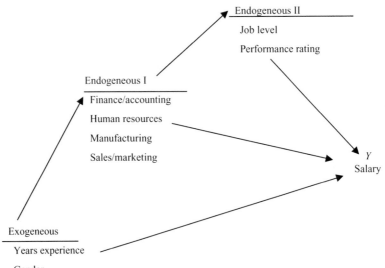

EXHIBIT 19.9. Hierarchical model.

Model	(1)	(2)	(3)
Variable	$b_{YXi \cdot Xj}$	$b_{YXi \cdot Xj}$	$b_{YXi \cdot Xj}$
$X1$ Years of experience	1,257.20*	1,388.23*	430.81
$X4$ Gender	2,742.80	2,296.26	2,666.79
$X5$ Finance/accounting		8,633.72*	8,375.51*
$X6$ Human resources		3,884.11	4,999.62*
$X8$ Sales/marketing		8,350.39*	6,728.62*
$X2$ Job level			3,871.48*
$X3$ Performance rating			292.33
Intercept (a)	50,313.79*	44,412.49*	42,657.62*
R^2	.22	.38	.49
$\hat{P}^2$	.20*	.34*	.45*
R^2 change		.16*	.11*

*$p < .05$ (two-tailed).

Job level ranges from 1 (first level supervisor) to 4 (top middle manager)

Performance ranges from 1 (marginal performance) to 7 (highest performance).

Gender dummy coded (male = 1; female = 0).

Finance/accounting dummy coded (finance/accounting = 1; other = 0); likewise for the other.

EXHIBIT 19.10. Hierarchical models with sets of independent variables.

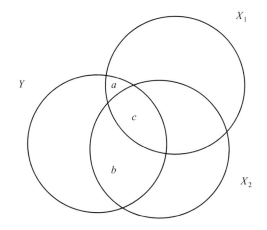

EXHIBIT 19.11. Variance explained in "A's" model.

of each set of independent variables adds to the salary variance explained at a statistically significant level.

Results obtained by the hierarchical method are sensitive to the order in which independent variables are entered whenever there is multicollinearity. This is illustrated with researcher A's models in Exhibit 19.3. Years of experience is credited with explaining 20% of salary variance if it is entered first (Model 1). Job level, entered second, is credited with adding 14% to explained salary variance (Model 3). Alternatively, if job level is entered first (Model 2), it is credited with explaining 33% of salary variance. Years of experience is now credited with explaining only an additional 1% of salary variance.

The reason for these order-sensitive results is seen by examining the representation of these three variables using variance explained circles in Exhibit 19.11. The area c represents the collinear variance in years of experience and job level that overlaps with salary. When years of experience is entered first, it gets credit for areas a and c; when years of experience is entered second, it gets credit only for area a.

A CLOSING CAUTION

Statistical modeling is widely used to assess causal models in research. Such modeling and the conclusions drawn from it must be done cautiously.

Causation is a complex construct as described in chapter 2. Chapter 5 additionally identified potential pitfalls to making legitimate causal claims; some research designs are more vulnerable to these pitfalls than are others. Measurement issues discussed in chapters 3 and 17 also bear on the legitimacy of causal claims.

Appropriate use of statistics and statistical inference must be carried out recognizing the roles of these other research elements for making causal claims. The next chapter elaborates. It addresses challenges to be addressed when statistical procedures are used to evaluate causal models.

SUMMARY

Statistical models using multiple correlation and regression are often used to help researchers evaluate **causal models**. Variables explained by a causal model are **endogenous**.

Exogenous variables help explain endogenous variables but are not themselves explained by the model.

Conceptual models can take several forms when there are three or more exogenous or endogenous variables involved. Two or more independent variables are believed to influence a dependent variable without mediation in *direct effects* models. Such models are often assessed by multiple regression; the partial regression coefficients provide evidence on the direct effects.

A mediated model involves an endogenous independent variable(s). Exogenous variables influence the dependent variable two ways. They influence it directly as already described, and they influence it *indirectly* through their influence on endogenous independent variables. Such models can be evaluated empirically by allowing each endogenous variable to serve as a dependent variable in a series of regression equations.

Models involving moderator variables can be assessed two ways. One method involves subgrouping on the moderator; relationships between other variables in the model are investigated within each subgroup. The other method, *moderated regression* involves creating a new variable that accounts for the interaction between the moderator variable and the independent variable it moderates. This interaction variable is then included with the other variables in the model. *Centering* the independent variables before creating the interaction variable typically makes interpretation of the partial coefficients on the independent variables more meaningful.

Hierarchical models are assessed by examining changes in the explanation of dependent variable variance across two or more statistical models. These models are specified by the causal chain hypothesized. Exogenous variables are entered in the first model followed by a model(s) with the endogenous independent variable(s). Changes in the variance explained in the dependent variable, as independent variables are added to models, typically serve as a criterion using this procedure.

FOR REVIEW

Terms to Know

Statistical modeling: The study of the structure of scores on variables using statistics and statistical inference.

Causal model: A researcher's conceptual specification of how independent variables influence a dependent variable.

Recursive model: Causal model where causal influence is assumed to go in only one direction.

Endogenous variable: Variable explained by a causal model.

Exogenous variable: Independent variable in a causal model that is not explained by the model.

Direct effect: In a causal model, relationship between an independent and a dependent variable that is not mediated by some other variable(s). When there are two or more independent variables in the causal model, a direct effect of any one independent variable in the subsequent statistical model is represented by its partial coefficient.

Indirect effect: In a causal model, the influence of an independent variable that operates through a mediator variable.

Total effect: The sum of the direct and indirect effects for any independent variable in mediated models.

Moderated regression: Regression procedure in which an independent variable is created to capture the nonlinear effects of a moderator variable.

Centering: Used in moderated regression by subtracting the mean of an independent variable from each observation to obtain a new distribution of the same shape and variance but with a mean of zero.

Hierarchical modeling: Researchers examine the change in dependent variable variance explained as independent variables are added or deleted from two or more statistical models.

Empirical models: When researchers retain independent variables in a model based on statistical criteria (e.g., statistical inference); independent variables are not chosen based on conceptual considerations.

Step-wise procedures: Popular methods to assess empirical models statistically.

Questions for Review

1. In what way is an endogenous independent variable a dependent variable?
2. Compare and contrast moderated causal models with mediated causal models.
3. Compare partial regression coefficients on independent variables and interaction variables in centered versus uncentered models involving moderated regression.
4. You read an article in the *New Yorker* that states: "Smoking increases lung cancer among smokers and among persons in close proximity to smokers." Diagram a causal model that accounts for this statement using the variables smoker (versus not smoker), person in proximity (versus not in proximity), and lung cancer.
   a. What type of causal model is this?
   b. What variable(s) is endogenous in this model? What is exogenous?
   c. If data on these three variables are available, how would you assess this model by using correlation/regression?
5. You overhear the following at a party with friends: "Whether you make the basketball team in high school depends on whether the coach likes you. In college it depends on whether you have athletic ability." Diagram this statement with a causal model that has variables for athletic ability, participation on a basketball team (versus no participation), and school level.
   a. What type of causal model is this?
   b. What variable(s) is endogenous in this model? What is exogenous?
   c. If data on these three variables are available, how would you assess this model by using correlation/regression? How else could you assess this model?
6. A researcher investigates a causal model by using a hierarchical approach. In Model 1 Y is regressed on $X1$. If related, all variables are positively related. In Model 2 Y is regressed on $X1$ and $X2$. What can you say about $X2$ and about R^2 in Model 2 compared with R^2 in Model 1 if:
   a. the simple regression coefficient for $X1$ in Model 1 is the same as the partial regression coefficient for $X1$ in Model 2?
   b. the simple regression coefficient for $X1$ in Model 1 is smaller than the partial regression coefficient for $X1$ in Model 2?
   c. the simple regression coefficient for $X1$ in Model 1 is larger than the partial regression coefficient for $X1$ in Model 2?

SUGGESTED READINGS

Cohen et al. (2003) and Frees (1996), two books recommended in part 4, have extensive discussions of statistical modeling by using multiple correlation and regression. Good articles on regression modeling are also provided by Alwin and Hauser (1975) and by Baron and Kenny (1986).

Aiken and West (1991) have a book on interactions that emphasizes centering. They cover a number of more complicated models than are discussed in this chapter. A simulation study on power determinants in moderated regression and references to other studies is provided by Aquinis and Stone-Romero (1997).

20

On Statistical Modeling Challenges

Chapter Outline

- *Specification*
  - *The Conceptual Model*
  - *The Statistical Model*
- *Importance of Independent Variables*
  - *Variance Explained and Coefficient Size*
    - *Correlation and Variance Explained*
    - *Regression Coefficients*
  - *Measurement Issues*
    - *Reliability*
    - *Construct Validity*
  - *Representativeness of the Cases Studied*
- *Design and Statistical Inference*
- *Summary and Conclusions*
- *For Review*
  - *Terms to Know*
  - *Questions for Review*
  - *Issues to Discuss*
- *Suggested Readings*

Portions of this and the next chapter draw on an unpublished paper, "Evidence of meaning and generalizability in single studies: Roles for statistical inference," University of Wisconsin-Madison, 2000 (with J. Paul Peter).

The previous chapter described how statistics and statistical inference are used to assess causal models. This chapter extends that discussion; it addresses challenges when using statistical modeling. These challenges go beyond the mechanics of modeling described in the last chapter. They pertain to judgments required when one draws conclusions from statistical modeling studies. Emphasis is placed on (1) judgments about model specification, (2) assessing the importance of independent variables, and (3) interpreting statistical inference.

SPECIFICATION

The Conceptual Model

To be fair, initial specification of the conceptual model to be investigated is at least as challenging as any empirical tasks that follow. The researcher as theoretician has to answer questions such as the following:

- What dependent variable deserves explanation?
- What independent variables explain variance in this dependent variable?
- Which of these independent variables should be considered endogenous?
- Which exogenous?
- Are some of the hypothesized relationships between independent and dependent variables moderated by other variables?
- Are some independent variables more important than others for explaining variance in the dependent variable?
- Are some of the relationships nonlinear?
- In what population(s) does the theoretical model hold?

These are examples of challenging issues researchers confront as theoreticians.

However, this volume is aimed at explicating empirical methods. Challenges addressed here are those that remain after a conceptual model has been specified. Plenty remain.

The Statistical Model

Proper specification of a conceptual and statistical model is essential if statistics and tests of statistical inference are to provide useful information about causal relationships. ***Proper statistical specification*** requires that the statistical model account for all conceptually relevant collinear independent variables that are also related to the dependent variable. If the model does not, coefficients obtained statistically will be biased as will tests of statistical inference.

The centrality of this requirement is illustrated in tests of researcher A's model in the previous chapter. A's model hypothesized that salary depends on both years of experience and job level. However, if the statistical model includes only years of experience (Model 1 in Exhibit 19.3), conclusions include that its effect is statistically significant ($p < .05$) and large. A unit change in years of experience leads to a predicted change of \$1,321 in yearly salary. However, when both years of experience and job level are included, as hypothesized in A's theory (Model 4 in Exhibit 19.3), the years of experience coefficient is no longer statistically significant and its coefficient is substantially smaller (\$324).

Statistics invariably will be in error, as will statistical inferences, if the model is not properly specified in this respect.

IMPORTANCE OF INDEPENDENT VARIABLES

A major criterion used to evaluate independent variables in statistical modeling has already been identified—namely, statistical inference. In a typical research study—and as a first cut—statistically significant independent variables (typically at $p < .05$ or $p < .01$) are judged to be important. Variables that do not reach the specified level are judged to be not important.

Variance Explained and Coefficient Size

But knowledgeable researchers know that statistical significance alone is not a sufficient criterion. They know the importance of specification as discussed above. They also know that statistical significance does not depend solely on the size of a statistic or its variability. It also depends on the number of cases studied. For example, a simple correlation coefficient of .05 is statistically significant ($p < .05$, one-tailed) in a study using 1,100 cases. Yet, the two variables share only 0.25% common variance. On the other hand, a correlation of .50 is not statistically significant at the same level in a study of ten cases even though the two variables share 25% common variance.

Knowledgeable researchers thus seek additional evidence on the importance of independent variables. Two common approaches are suggested by the examples in the previous chapter.

Correlation and Variance Explained

One approach focuses on the contribution an independent variable (or set of such variables) makes to the explanation of variance in the dependent variable. Regardless of the specific model tested, researchers typically look at the size of multiple coefficient of determination (R^2) to address the importance of the full conceptual model. Importance assessed this way is referred to as the *precision* of the model. R^2 indicates how much dependent variance is accounted for by a researcher's theory when all variables are entered in the statistical model. For example, in researcher A's chapter 19 model, years of experience and job level jointly explained 34% of the salary variance in the cases studied (Model 3, Exhibit 19.3).

Researchers using hierarchical models additionally examine changes in variance explained as independent variables are added to, or deleted from, models in a series of equations. For example, in chapter 19 researcher E added type of job to a model, after accounting for purely exogenous variables, and increased explained salary variance by 16%.

The amount of variance an independent variable adds to the explanation of dependent variable variance can be a useful supplement to statistical significance. However, chapter 19 also showed that this contribution depends on the order in which independent variables are entered into an equation if the independent variables are correlated. Thus, researchers must be confident that the order of entry is causally persuasive.

Regression Coefficients

A second approach seeks evidence for importance from regression. Here emphasis is placed on the *size* of the partial regression (unstandardized) or beta (standardized) coefficients. Size speaks to the direct effect an independent variable has on a dependent variable when other independent variables are controlled. The rank order of the size of standardized versus unstandardized coefficients on a set of independent variables is typically not the same. Furthermore, some sources of error (e.g., unreliability in the dependent variable) bias standardized but not unstandardized regression coefficients. Thus, the decision to focus on one or the other is consequential.

Unstandardized coefficients are preferred when variables are scaled in conceptually meaningful units. Salary, years of experience, and the other variables used in the examples of the previous chapter are illustrative. Partial regression coefficients are useful to understand the effects of these independent variables on salary. For example, it is intuitively understandable to know that a 1-year change in years of experience has a $324 impact on yearly salary, controlling for job level.

Unstandardized coefficients are less helpful when comparing the *relative* importance of independent variables if they are scaled in different units (e.g., in dollars, or as a dichotomy, male or female). Furthermore, independent variables scaled meaningfully can still be expressed with different units. For example, in the same data set the coefficient on experience is larger if scaled in decades rather than years; it is smaller if scaled in months. As a consequence, comparing the size of unstandardized regression coefficients to assess relative importance is not good practice.

If the dependent variable is reliable, partial beta coefficients are better for making comparisons of the relative importance of independent variables. Partial betas are generated after all variables have been standardized to mean = 0.0 and standard deviation = 1.0 (chapter 11). A unit change in one independent variable has the same one standard deviation meaning as a unit change in another independent variable. Comparing importance across independent variables is thus facilitated.

Partial beta coefficients are also preferred when the variables are not scaled in conceptually meaningful units. This often applies when complex constructs are measured. For example, the Cornell Job Description pay satisfaction scale has scores ranging from 9 to 27 (chapter 4). A partial regression coefficient on the scale, whatever its value, is not very meaningful in the abstract. And, it has even less meaning in a comparative context with other independent variables such as years of experience. However, following standardization a meaningful comparison can be made between the consequences of a one standard deviation change in pay satisfaction compared with a one standard deviation change in any other independent variable.

Despite the advantages of standardized regression coefficients, they do have a disadvantage. Standard partial coefficients are more sample dependent than unstandardized coefficients because standard deviations can vary from sample to sample.

Measurement Issues

Reliability

Measurement is also an issue when assessing the importance of an independent variable or when comparing the importance of different variables. The first of these involves reliability. Chapter 17 showed that unreliability in measures of independent variables leads to biased coefficients. Typically, such bias reduces (attenuates) relationships observed; however, if there are two or more independent variables some coefficients may actually be inflated. In either event, unreliability among independent variables results in biased coefficients and erroneous significance levels. Unreliability thus generates error in all the indicators of importance identified.

The situation differs if the dependent variable is unreliable. Chapter 17 demonstrated that unreliability in the dependent variable does not bias unstandardized regression coefficients. However, unreliability in the dependent variable does lead to erroneous statistical significance levels.

Construct Validity

Causal models are aimed at the conceptual level, the level constructs and intellectual understanding. Consequently, assessing importance on scores from measures must additionally assume that the scores represent the underlying constructs of interest. Absent construct validity,

Structural Equation Modeling

Structural equation modeling (SEM) provides another way to investigate causal models with statistical procedures. SEM goes by different terms; often it is called LISREL. LISREL is actually a widely used statistical software package to perform this sort of modeling.

The main extension of SEM over regression/correlation procedures discussed here is that it makes possible the integration of measurement models with statistical models representing causal models. LISREL or similar programs use *factor analysis* and multiple regression or regression-like analyses.

Factor analysis (there are many types) is a statistical procedure used in measurement research. It captures a dimension or multiple dimensions (chapter 3) from the items on a measure (or measures among multiple measures). These dimensions are called *factors*. Factors are sets of scores generated to optimally (using several statistical criteria) capture the shared variance in a set of items or measures.

In SEM the statistical analyses use factor scores (confusingly called *latent variables*) rather than scores from the original items or measures. These analyses often conduct the measurement and statistical tests of the causal model simultaneously. However, it is also done sequentially beginning with a factor analysis. Once factors are identified, the statistical test of the causal model proceeds analogously to the procedures described using regression in the previous chapter.

SEM models to assess direct and mediated models have been available for some time. Recently, SEM models have also been developed to test moderated models.

SEM has several advantages over multiple regression for conducting statistical assessments of causal models. First, the measurement steps in SEM allow researchers to identify and account for unreliability in the measures used. It can estimate a statistical model unbiased by unreliability. SEM also can be used to account for certain systematic biases. It can provide help in construct validation by addressing nomological networks (chapter 3).

Finally, SEM can be used to estimate how well the entire model fits the researcher's causal model. In models of any complexity, multiple regression is constrained to estimating fit on an equation-by-equation basis.

Nevertheless, more is often claimed for SEM than is warranted. Researchers sometimes claim that SEM accounts for construct invalidity. This is erroneous. Constructs are mental representations of variables, and factors are numerical functions of the scores obtained among the fallible items or measures. Although some measurement errors can be modeled and hence controlled, it is not true that SEM can account for construct invalidity.

the statistical results observed may provide misleading information about importance at the level of understanding one seeks. This is true even if all variables are measured with perfect reliability.

Chapter 3 noted that addressing construct validity is more difficult than addressing reliability. There is no single statistical test that identifies construct validity as there is to identify reliability. Researchers must rely on more, but necessarily indirect, evidence for construct validity.

Representativeness of the Cases Studied

Representativeness of the cases studied is another issue when assessing the importance of independent variables in a causal model. An important issue is *restriction of range* introduced in chapter 5.

Correlation (simple or multiple) and beta coefficients (simple or partial) are biased downward if the range of either the dependent or the independent variable is restricted relative to the range of cases one wants to generalize to. For example, consider the relationship between years of education and salary level. Assuming a linear relationship, a correlation or beta coefficient invariably will be larger when persons representing all education levels are studied than when only persons with a high school education or more are studied. In the latter situation, the magnitude of the relationship will be attenuated because the range of education is restricted. The size of a coefficient and hence its statistical significance will be misrepresented relative to the size and statistical significance of a coefficient representing all levels of education.

Outcomes for unstandardized regression coefficients are more complex in the presence of restriction of range. If the restriction occurs in the dependent variable unstandardized simple and partial regression coefficients are biased downward. However, if the restriction occurs in the independent variable(s) the simple or partial regression coefficients should remain approximately the same.

RESEARCH HIGHLIGHT 20.2

Restriction of Range in Measurement

Restriction of range is also an issue in studies in which a researcher manipulates the values of one or more independent variables. Larger effects are observed when greater range is built into the manipulation(s).

For example, an experimental study was conducted in which the researchers were interested in how starting salary, geographical location, and type of job influenced decisions to apply for employment (Rynes, Schwab, & Heneman, 1983). In different versions of the study, participants were exposed to substantially different salary ranges. Not surprisingly, salary explained more variance in application decisions when its range was larger.

In such studies the objective should not be to make the range as large as possible. Rather, the objective should be to make the range correspond to the range to be expected in the population of cases one wants to generalize to.

DESIGN AND STATISTICAL INFERENCE

Data on 100 cases were used to illustrate statistical tests of causal models in the previous chapter. In this instance statistical inference is legitimately used to address statistical generalization because these cases were drawn randomly from a larger population of cases. In the examples, statistical hypothesis tests address the question: is the relationship observed in the sample of sufficient size to suppose that some nonzero relationship obtains in the population from which the cases were drawn?

Although generalization is important and of interest, statistical generalization to a specific population is not the goal of most causal modeling studies. Rather, the objective of statistical inference in causal modeling is closer to its purpose in experiments.

In experiments, cases are randomly assigned to levels of an independent variable(s) (chapter 5). The probabilistic foundations that justify inference in experiments pertain to *internal* statistical validity, not *external* statistical validity (chapter 13). Internal statistical validity addresses whether one can be confident a relationship is large enough to conclude it is not due to the chance allocation of cases to levels of the independent variable(s).

Because the allocation of cases is done randomly, it is possible that cases will not be similar across different levels of the independent variable(s). For example, suppose an experiment contrasts a training group with a control group. Student cases are randomly assigned to one group or the other. By chance the most able students may be assigned disproportionately to the training group; less able students are then assigned disproportionately to the control group. The trained group subsequently performs better on the dependent variable. However, they do so because of the initial unequal assignment on ability and not because of differences between the training and control conditions. Statistical inference helps assess whether such a chance is a probable explanation for the differences on the dependent variable observed.

Statistical inference as used in experiments falls short of establishing causation (chapter 2). It speaks only to the tenability of a relationship and not whether one variable causes another. Nevertheless, it is the closest a purely statistical test gets to addressing causation.

Experiments are powerful because they can be properly specified without being *fully specified*. Full specification means all independent variables that influence the dependent variable in a causal model are included in the statistical model investigated. Experiments can achieve proper specification without full specification when randomization results (as expected) in no multicollinearity between the independent variables manipulated experimentally and other independent variables not controlled. This is true even though the other independent variables would otherwise influence the dependent variable. (Quasi-experiments can also be designed so that collinear independent variables are controlled through design rather than statistically.)

Interestingly, most organizational researchers who investigate causal models use field study designs as defined in chapter 5. Such designs use judgment or convenience samples, not probability samples. Furthermore, field studies (or quasi-experiments) do not randomly assign cases to levels of independent variables. Thus, they fail to meet the probability requirements for either statistical generalization validity or internal statistical validity.

What does this imply for the use of statistical inference in a typical field or quasi-experimental study? First, it is difficult to argue that statistical inference contributes to generalizability when cases are chosen by convenience. Examples include statistical inference tests when cases include all responding (1) students in a class, (2) work teams in an organization, or (3) members of Fortune 500 firms.

Researchers typically want to generalize from field studies such as these. For example, a researcher who studies all work teams in one organization may wish to generalize results to work teams in other organizations. It may be appropriate to do so. However, the basis for such generalization must be made on grounds other than statistical inference because probability sampling wasn't used to choose those studied. When an intact group of cases is studied, the design is more appropriately thought of as an investigation of a population; there is no sampling error to estimate. Claims for generalization in these situations rely on *judgments* about the similarity of cases studied to those one wants to generalize to.

The use of statistical inference in field studies and quasi-experiments may more appropriately address internal statistical validity. Key here is whether it is reasonable to assume the statistical model tested is sufficiently well specified to assume the remaining error is random. If so, it may be plausible to use statistical inference to help address whether the coefficients observed are large enough to assume they didn't arise by chance.

One thing is certain: statistical inference is never a sufficient criterion for judging the quality of a research study or the veracity of its results. Even in surveys and experiments where its two purposes are straightforward, one must additionally evaluate the quality of measurement (manipulations), sampling, and the general craftsmanship by which the study is conducted. Field studies and quasi-experiments bear the additional burden of not satisfying the probabilistic foundations on which statistical inference is constructed.

SUMMARY AND CONCLUSIONS

Researchers specify conceptual models representing hypothesized causal relationships among constructs. Empirical researchers investigate such models with statistical models.

Variables in statistical models are evaluated several ways. Statistical inference is almost always used as one criterion for evaluating the importance of the overall model (e.g., the statistical significance of R^2) and individual independent variables (e.g., the statistical significance of a regression coefficient). In addition, researchers look to the **precision** of a model, the amount of variance explained by the overall model (e.g., R^2), and by individual independent variables or sets of variables within the overall model. Researchers also evaluate the size of the coefficients on individual independent variables (e.g., partial beta or partial regression coefficients).

These alternative criteria do not necessarily lead researchers to the same conclusion about the contribution of the overall statistical model or individual variables in it. Conclusions drawn from statistical inference information in particular may vary from the other ways of estimating contribution because it depends on the number of cases studied along with the size of the coefficients assessed. Thus, it is good practice to assess statistical models using all the criteria available.

Evaluation is further challenged by a number of factors that can result in statistical models providing erroneous information about causal models. Factors discussed in this chapter are summarized in Exhibit 20.1.

Exhibit 20.1 shows four criteria used to evaluate statistical models. The two leftmost columns show the variance explained by the full model and its standard error. These columns also apply to standardized (beta) regression coefficients. When the standard error is incorrect, statistical significance levels will be in error as will the width of confidence intervals. The two rightmost columns show the simple or partial *unstandardized* regression outcomes and the standard error for these coefficients.

Many factors can lead to erroneous estimates of the underlying conceptual model from statistical models, beginning with specification. **Proper statistical specification** requires that the statistical model tested includes all collinear independent variables that are also related to the dependent variable. Estimates of the total variance explained and regression coefficients

Source	r^2/R^2		Regression Coefficient	
	Value	Std. Error	Value	Std. Error
Specification				
Omitted collinear X	Bias	Bias	Bias	Bias
Omitted uncorrelated X	?[1]	?[1]	Correct	Correct
Measurement				
Unreliability in X	Bias	Bias	Bias	Bias
Unreliability in Y	Bias	Bias	Correct	Bias
Construct invalidity in X	Bias	Bias	Bias	Bias
Construct invalidity in Y	Bias	Bias	Bias	Bias
Sampling				
Restriction of range in X	Bias	Bias	Correct	Bias
Restriction of range in Y	Bias	Bias	Bias	Bias

Note: Erroneous standard error means that statistical significance levels are in error as are confidence intervals.

[1] If the omitted independent variable is related to the dependent variable, bias results. If it is not related to the dependent variable, there is no bias.

EXHIBIT 20.1.   Sources of bias in correlation/regression estimates of causal models using statistical models.

will be in error as will their standard errors if models are not properly specified. Even if an omitted independent variable is not correlated with independent variables in the model, the estimate of the overall relationship will be biased if the omitted variable is related to the dependent variable.

Unreliability poses another challenge for statistical models. Unreliability in an independent variable leads to erroneous estimates of all criteria in both simple and multiple regression contexts. Unreliability in the dependent variable is also problematic. It leads to biased estimates of the relationship expressed in variance explained terms and erroneous standard errors in all cases. It does provide an unbiased estimate of regression coefficients. However, standard errors will be in error.

Because unreliability can be modeled, its effect on correlation and regression output is well developed. Alternatively, construct invalidity is more difficult to model and substantially more complex. Thus, although the specific implications of construct invalidity are not as well known as those for unreliability, it is clear that such invalidity generates errors in all correlation and regression output.

Finally, restriction of range creates problems for correlation and regression output. Restriction in either the dependent or the independent variables biases correlation and standardized regression coefficients downward. Restriction in the dependent variable also biases unstandardized regression coefficients, although restriction in the independent variable does not.

These challenges make it clear that statistical models can, and often do, provide estimates of causal models that contain substantial error. This should not discourage statistical modeling. But it should make you sensitive to the importance of all facets of the design and conduct of research studies. And, even when studies are carefully designed and executed, it should make you cautious about the veracity of findings from any single study.

Problems with outcomes from single studies are major reasons why meta-analysis (chapter 14) is attractive. All meta-analysis techniques assume that averages generated across studies are better estimates than can be obtained from single studies. In addition, some meta-analysis techniques try to correct for errors introduced by factors such as unreliability and restriction of range.

FOR REVIEW

Terms to Know

Proper statistical specification: In causal modeling when all collinear independent variables that influence the dependent variable are included in the model tested.
Model precision: Variance explained by the statistical model.
Misspecification: When a statistical model does not include all collinear independent variables in the underlying causal model.
Fully specified model: All independent variables that influence the dependent variable in the causal model are included in the statistical model investigated.
Structural equation models: Combines measurement models with statistical models to assess causal models.
Factor analysis: Statistical procedure for reducing information from a set of items in a measure to a smaller number of factors that represent common dimensions in the larger set.
Latent variable: Term in structural equation modeling for a factor.

Questions for Review

1. Under what conditions might you consider an independent variable to be important in a causal model when it was not statistically significant in an empirical test of the model?
2. Explain how construct invalidity leads to biased estimates in statistical inference tests of causal models.
3. Compare the consequences of unreliability in Y and X with consequences of restriction of range in Y and X for simple correlation and regression coefficients.
4. When can a statistical model be properly specified yet not fully specified?

Issues to Discuss

Discuss the use of standardized (beta) versus unstandardized partial regression coefficients for making comparisons on the relative importance of independent variables in a statistical model.

A causal model consists of direct positive effects of $X1$ and $X2$ on Y. However, a researcher tests the model by regressing Y only on $X1$.

Suppose $X1$ and $X2$ are positively related. Discuss the implications of the researcher's misspecification for the regression coefficient on $X1$ and for the variance explained by the model overall. What are the implications for the statistical significance level of the coefficient on $X1$ and for the statistical significance level of the variance explained overall?

Suppose now that $X1$ and $X2$ are not related. Discuss the implications of the researcher's misspecification for the regression coefficient on $X1$ and for the variance explained by the model overall. What are the implications for the statistical significance level of the coefficient on $X1$ and for the statistical significance level of the variance explained overall?

SUGGESTED READINGS

Statistical inference is a topic that has generated a substantial amount of controversy in the social sciences. Contentious issues involve, when statistical significance testing is appropriate, preferences for statistical hypothesis testing versus confidence intervals, and contributions of significance testing to the advancement of knowledge. Although some of this controversy arises because of misunderstandings about basic issues covered in this book, some revolve around more subtle issues. Those interested in obtaining more detailed knowledge on these topics may read books by Oakes (1986) and by Morrison and Henkel (1970). Cohen (1994), Hagen (1997), and Schmidt (1996) have written papers that address these issues from very different perspectives.

21

On Good Research

Chapter Outline

- *What Makes Research Good?*
- *An Illustration Using the Research Model*
  - *Causal Conceptual Relationships*
  - *Generalizability of Causal Conceptual Relationships*
- *Elements of a Persuasive Research Study*
  - *Theoretical Justification*
    - *Contributions of Theory*
    - *If There Is No Theory*
  - *Prior Research Evidence*
  - *Research Design*
  - *Research Execution*
    - *Sensitivity Analysis*
    - *The Research Report*
- *Summary*
  - *Causal Relationships*
  - *Generalization*
- *For Review*
  - *Terms to Know*
  - *Questions for Review*
  - *Issues to Discuss*
- *Suggested Readings*

You're eager to conduct a research study. Or, you're reading a study conducted by someone else. You do so because you are interested in a particular topic. Your first motivation in conducting, or reading about, research is personal or professional interest.

This chapter picks up after you have chosen an interesting topic. Given that topic, how do you go about conducting a good research study? If the study is by someone else, how do you decide whether it is good?

WHAT MAKES RESEARCH GOOD?

This book argues that most research is aimed at understanding causal relationships at the conceptual level of our intellectual (between the ears) understanding. Such research is good if the causal conclusions reached are persuasive.

Thus, a good research study must first be convincing about the validity of relationships between the central variables of interest. Because truth cannot be known with certainty, validity means only very similar to the truth (verisimilitude, chapter 2).

Validity does not require that a relationship(s) be large. The magnitude of an expected relationship, large or modest, depends on the phenomena studied. For example, a relationship between education and subsequent financial attainment may not be large because other variables also influence financial attainment.

Indeed, validity does not even require that a relationship between the variables is obtained. After all, research is conducted to *investigate* relationships. In some situations a valid conclusion is that no consequential relationship(s) exists. Validity thus refers to the confidence one can have in whatever relationship is claimed.

It is true that you typically have some hypothesized relationship(s) in mind when you begin a study. Finding support for your expectations is more satisfying than not. But unexpected or unsupportive findings alone do not mean that the study is without value.

A second criterion for judging the quality of a research study, generalizability, is relevant if the validity of a causal conclusion is persuasive. Generalizability of a causal conceptual relationship represents one overarching form of external generalization discussed in chapter 2. It includes the probable generalizability of the statistical conclusions to the population from which cases were drawn, if drawn probabilistically. It also includes generalization to other populations, other times, other conditions, and using other measures.

Generalizability is almost always of interest. After all, research studies report results from data obtained in the past. Except in purely historical investigations there is always an interest in whether the results hold in the future. Whether the causal conceptual relationship is valid for other types of cases and situations is usually also of interest.

Just as the magnitude of a causal relationship does not determine its validity, the breadth of generalization claimed does not determine its persuasiveness. A study is persuasive when the degree of generalizability (narrow or wide) is believably presented. It is true that the results are more broadly applicable if the generalizability of the causal conceptual relationship is wide.

In summary, a good research study makes a persuasive case for the (1) probable validity of the causal conceptual relationship(s) claimed, and (2) degree of generalizability claimed for the relationship(s). Consequently, when evaluating contributions of a study, attend carefully to these two criteria.

The remainder of this chapter is devoted to helping you think about persuasive research. Attention to the issues raised can help you conduct good research and can help you decide whether the research you read is good. To begin, the research model introduced in chapter 2 is reviewed and applied to an example. This example explains when validity of a causal conceptual relationship and its generalizability are tenable. Second, four research components are identified. These components can improve the quality of any research investigation when skillfully used.

AN ILLUSTRATION USING THE RESEARCH MODEL

A research study typically investigates several causal relationships. These relationships often address moderated and/or mediated relationships as well as direct effects. Multiple control variables are also common. However, most of the issues critical to conducting or evaluating research can be identified with a simple model that contains a dependent variable and two independent variables.

The hypothesized positive relationship between education and financial attainment from human capital theory is used to illustrate a causal relationship.[1] After the initial model is reviewed, innate ability is added to illustrate a second independent variable that serves as a control. Education is hypothesized to have a positive impact on financial attainment, controlling for innate ability.

Causal Conceptual Relationships

Exhibit 21.1 shows the model from chapter 2 modified to represent the hypothesis of interest in human capital theory. The relationship designated by line a illustrates the first criterion to evaluate research. That line, with its arrow linking the education and financial attainment constructs indicates the direction of the relationship and that it is causal. The line is broken to signal that the relationship results from an inference, not an empirical observation. An inference about a causal conceptual relationship between education and financial attainment is appropriate when conceptual and empirical evidence support it.

Suppose a researcher administers a questionnaire to a group of employees. The questionnaire asks for highest year of schooling completed (to measure education) and for last year's gross salary (to measure financial attainment). The resulting scores are analyzed to determine the strength and direction of the relationship. Line d in Exhibit 21.1 linking scores on the two measures represents this relationship. It is solid to indicate that it can be observed directly through empirical procedures. It has no arrow because a relationship between scores on measures demonstrates only covariation, not causation.

Two additional types of evidence are required to establish a causal conceptual relationship between the constructs (line a). First, evidence is needed that the measures represent their respective constructs. There must be evidence of construct validity as represented by relationships for education (b_1) and for financial attainment (b_2). These relationships are shown as broken lines because they involve inferences about the relationships between scores on measures and unobservable constructs. They have arrows because constructs are believed to determine measures.

Construct validity inferences are best if based on evidence from both conceptual (e.g., nomological network) and operational (e.g., reliability) levels. Although construct validity evidence is always incomplete, it is the only link between the empirical operations and the constructs. If there is evidence to infer validity for both constructs, an observed relationship between scores on the measures of years of schooling and salary suggests a relationship between the education and financial attainment constructs.

---

[1] References on human capital theory include Becker (1964; 1993) and Card (1998). Market signaling theory is discussed by Spence (1973); it is an alternative theoretical explanation for the relationship between education and financial attainment.

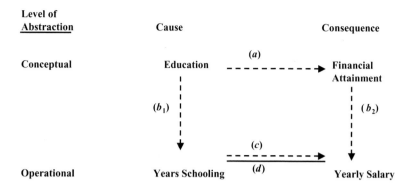

EXHIBIT 21.1.   Research model applied to human capital theory.

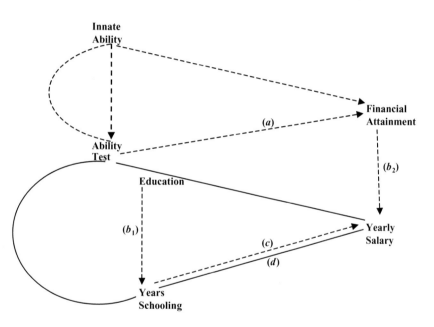

EXHIBIT 21.2.   Empirical research model with confounding variable.

Second, there must be evidence that the covariation observed is causal, that variation in education *leads to* variation in financial attainment. As with construct validity, evidence of causation is most persuasive when provided at both conceptual and operational levels. In the example, conceptual arguments that education leads to financial attainment have been made with both human capital and market signaling explanations. For either explanation, the plausibility of causation is driven largely by the conceptual arguments sustaining it.

Internal validity addresses causal relationships at the operational level (chapter 2). Support for internal validity is present when there is evidence (1) of covariation (line *d*), (2) that years of schooling precedes salary in time, and (3) that alternative explanations for observed relationships between scores are implausible. Most plausible alternative explanations involve other variables that may covary with education and financial attainment.

The latter possibility is shown in Exhibit 21.2 where innate ability and an ability test to represent the construct and operationalization, respectively, are added to the model. When uncontrolled, ability will bias the observed relationship between years of education and salary

---

RESEARCH HIGHLIGHT 21.1

The Model Applied to Experiments and Quasi-experiments

The research scenario used to illustrate Exhibits 21.1 and 21.2 represents a survey or field study; measures on both independent and dependent variables are obtained from the cases studied. However, the model is equally useful for research that employs an experimental or quasi-experimental design. For example, a researcher proposes that variation in a cognition (e.g., perceived equity) leads to variation in the intensity of some behavior (e.g., job performance). Perceived equity and job performance are the independent and dependent constructs, respectively, and their relationship is hypothesized to be causal (line *a*). A researcher could arrange for groups of participants to experience different treatments representing various levels of equity and evaluate scores on a measure of performance to assess differences among the groups (line *d*).

Inferences drawn about a causal conceptual relationship from an experiment or quasi-experiment are assessed against the same criteria. Is there a relationship among scores at the operational level? Is there conceptual and empirical evidence of construct validity? In experiments, there must be evidence that the manipulation represents the independent variable construct. Finally, is there conceptual and empirical evidence that the relationship is causal (i.e., evidence of concomitant variation, temporal ordering, and elimination of alternative explanations)?

---

if it influences salary and is related to education as shown in Exhibit 21.2. (The value of this control also depends on the construct validity of the measure of innate ability.)

The line *c* in Exhibits 21.1 and 21.2 represents internal validity. It is distinct from line *d* because it requires more than a demonstration of covariation or its strength per se. It is distinct from line *a* because it is at the operational level and not the conceptual level. It has an arrow to indicate that it is causal, although it is broken to acknowledge that internal validity is based on researcher inferences.

Generalizability of Causal Conceptual Relationships

Formal treatments of generalizability focus on the operational level of scores. For example, generalizability theory addresses domains (e.g., attributes, measurement methods, time periods) over which relationships between scores obtain (Research Highlight 17.2). External validity as defined in chapter 2 addresses the generalizability of relationships between scores over times, settings, and cases or participants. In terms of the model, the focus of these treatments is on the generalizability of line *d* as shown in Exhibits 21.1 and 21.2.

However, the second major criterion is aimed at generalizing a causal conceptual relationship (line *a*), not merely relationships obtained on operational scores. Suppose a researcher performs a study on an employee group and finds a positive relationship between years of schooling and last year's gross salary as hypothesized. Empirically, this relationship is limited to the employees studied, the measures used, the model investigated (e.g., whether ability was controlled), and the time period of the study. Yet, researchers are seldom interested in specific research conditions and obtained scores. They are interested in whether the evidence supports a causal relationship between education and financial attainment and its generalizability. In the example, the researcher wishes to conclude that educational attainment is a cause of financial attainment in general.

This claim may be warranted. However, its validity depends on judgments that go beyond the empirical results obtained in this one study. It must be based on persuasive theoretical argumentation and other evidence as discussed below.

ELEMENTS OF A PERSUASIVE RESEARCH STUDY

Both conceptual and operational levels contribute to interpretations of, and inferences about, a causal conceptual relationship and its generalizability. Four sources can help a study persuasively address these criteria. The first two, theory and prior research, represent sources to use before you carry out a study. The third, design, represents your overall plan for the study. Finally, execution consists of carrying out the plan and summarizing the results in a research report. Judging whether research conclusions are persuasive depends on how successfully research studies develop these four sources.

Theoretical Justification

Contributions of Theory

Theory may help address a causal conceptual relationship or generalizability of a causal conceptual relationship in four ways. First, it helps explain *why* the constructs should be causally related as hypothesized (line *a* in Exhibit 21.1 or 21.2). It explains the logic for why more education leads to higher financial attainment in the example. Such explanations often depend on mediating processes. The human capital explanation depends largely on the increase in knowledge and problem-solving skills that education provides to make individuals more valuable in the workplace.

Second, theory provides evidence for generalizability in an analogous manner. For example, it follows from the preceding mediating explanation that a relationship between education and financial attainment should be observed in any labor market that values knowledge and problem-solving skills.

Third, theory may help specify a broader causal network. This network, in turn, is important to identify control variables in empirical investigations and for subsequent evaluation of results from such studies. For example, human capital theory acknowledges that innate ability also influences financial attainment. Further, it predicts that ability and education will be positively related. Consequently, an empirical test of the relationship between education and financial attainment will be biased if ability is not accounted for.

Fourth, theory helps define constructs; hence, theory suggests ways measures of constructs may be developed. Education is expected to increase knowledge and problem-solving skills in human capital theory. This, in turn, suggests that education should be operationalized in terms of what is learned in the educational process. Years of education are widely accepted as an indicator of learning.

Different theoretical explanations may call for different ways of defining and measuring constructs. For example, market signaling theory hypothesizes an alternative mechanism linking education to financial attainment. It hypothesizes that education serves as a signal to employers of employee ability and trainability. In this formulation, educational degrees attained, rather than years of education, may be an appropriate way to measure education.

If There Is No Theory

You may be interested in a topic for which no theory is available. This need not discourage your research activities. But it does make research more challenging.

Absent theory, researchers must engage in theory-like activities before conducting the empirical portions of a research study. These are needed to develop hypotheses, specify constructs, and identify variables to control.

Empirical procedures and outcomes inevitably play a more influential role when research is not motivated by theory. Such studies are often *exploratory*. Exploratory research studies are aimed at discovering interesting relationships that may obtain in a set of data.

Exploratory research is warranted when an interesting issue has not been subject to prior theory or empirical research. However, findings from exploratory research must be interpreted with extra caution. Indeed, findings from exploratory research are better thought of as hypothesis generating than hypothesis testing. They best serve as a basis for additional research. The validity of exploratory findings is more persuasive if replicated in subsequent research.

Prior Research Evidence

A thorough review of the literature is always appropriate before conducting a research study. A study you contemplate falls on a continuum of novelty. The research may be truly seminal. More likely, it will be the most recent in a stream of research already conducted. For example, there is a large volume of research on human capital theory. Failure to review this research before doing a study could easily result in duplicative effort with little contribution to knowledge.

When available, prior research serves many of the same roles as theory. Indeed, when theory is missing or primitive, prior research is often the best source for conceptualizations justifying both causal relationships and generalization.

Greater credibility is given to a hypothesized relationship between constructs if it has been inferred in previous studies. In addition, previous research often provides evidence of construct validity for measures employed, which adds to the evidence for the conceptual relationship.

When there is consistency across studies, prior research provides the best evidence for making inferences about generalizability. Claims of generalizability are particularly persuasive when empirical results are consistent in direction and magnitude but methods, measures, cases, and contexts differ. This illustrates research triangulation (Research Highlight 14.1).

Of course, there are times when a study does not obtain findings anticipated either by theory or by prior research. This may be valuable. The cases or other contextual features of the study may suggest theoretical boundary conditions not previously recognized.

Alternatively, unanticipated results may simply mean that the study was deficient in some important respect. For example, the design may not adequately account for variables requiring control. Thus, unexpected findings should be treated as findings from exploratory research. They should be viewed as input for hypotheses that deserve additional research investigation.

Research Design

The research design provides an opportunity to plan the overall study. In formulating it you should attend carefully to the state of theory and previous research. These two provide the best help as you decide on a design that most effectively adds to knowledge.

For example, suppose existing research is not compelling about causal direction. Further, suppose previous research consists largely of field studies. In such situations an experiment or quasi-experiment may provide the best opportunity to generate new knowledge.

Alternatively, if causal direction is not theoretically at issue there is less reason to be concerned about using a design that is strong on assessing causal direction. Design planning may be more effectively directed to other issues.

For example, a substantial amount of human capital research has been conducted on explaining wage levels of individuals who work for organizations (i.e., employees). Less is known about the determinants of salary among the self-employed. A study designed to assess income determinants in the latter group will thus more likely add to knowledge than will an additional investigation of employees.

Thus, questions from, or gaps in, existing theory and research can serve as effective stimuli for research design. However, keep the key questions for good research in mind: are the causal claims persuasive? Are the claims for generalization persuasive? Typically, research designs should not be so novel that they cannot benefit from prior research or theory.

Research Execution

You have an interesting topic. Theory related to this topic has been thoroughly and thoughtfully reviewed as has prior research. A design is developed that addresses the topic of interest and takes advantage of both theory and prior research. The table is set to conduct a good research study. One ingredient remains—execution.

Measures must be assembled. Cases must be motivated to participate. Procedures must be followed to obtain scores on measures. Analyses must be performed. A report summarizing the study must be prepared.

Executing a research study is analogous to custom home building. Each design and site is different. Conditions vary from one site to another and from one time period to another. Materials (e.g, cases and measures) perform differently in different settings. A good researcher, much as a master builder, is sensitive to these subtle differences that make each research study unique.

Thus, even though a strong design, faithfully followed, is necessary, it is typically not sufficient to ensure good research execution. Unanticipated events invariably occur during the execution stage. As one example, nonresponse and missing data likely will pose problems even after procedures designed to motivate high participation are used. Both nonresponse and missing data serve as threats to generalization. When they are not randomly distributed through a data set, as is typical, they also may serve to bias relationships observed.

Nonresponse and missing data illustrate typical methodological problems in the sense that they have no unambiguously correct solution. Although there are several ways to address nonresponse and missing data, none is entirely satisfactory (chapter 16).

Sensitivity Analysis

In situations such as this, it is good practice to engage in **sensitivity analysis**. Sensitivity analysis consists of conducting analyses different ways to see if results vary as a function of alternative specifications. Greater confidence is justified in believing that missing data are not a problem if results are similar using different ways to account for them.

Sensitivity analysis is often appropriate when there are alternative ways that methodological issues might be addressed. It is also attractive in situations in which conceptual issues are ambiguous. For example, the most appropriate set of control variables often is not clear even in well-developed conceptual models. Sensitivity analyses using control variables in different combinations can address conceptual ambiguity of this sort.

Findings are characterized as **robust** if they do not differ as a function of different ways of addressing a research issue. Robust findings represent a form of generalization. They generalize across the different ways a research issue is addressed.

The Research Report

It is difficult to overstate the importance of the written report summarizing a study. It represents the "tip of the iceberg," the only visible portion of a study. Decisions about whether the research is good or not good necessarily depend on it.

Because of the importance of the report in this respect, negative inferences about the quality of the entire project may hinge on small report imperfections. Common examples include unwarranted claims of generalizability, inconsistencies between values reported in the body of the report and tables, errors in tables (e.g., an exhaustive set of proportions that do not add to 1.0), and inconsistencies in references found in the body of the text with those in the bibliography.

The written report is also important because the very act of writing it is a central part of the research process. It does not stand alone or outside that process. Theory and prior research carefully reviewed, a plan skillfully designed, procedures masterfully conducted, conclusions about causal relationships and their generalizability thoughtfully drawn are all known and persuasive only if the research report communicates them.

Attention needs to be given to the final report from the very beginning of a research study. Indeed, if theory and prior research are used as recommended, extensive notes should be taken on these issues before the empirical procedures are undertaken. Notes should also be recorded while the study is under way. Subtle decisions are often made while a study is in progress that can easily be forgotten if not recorded as they are made.

Suggestions for report organization and style made in chapter 15 can help you prepare a report. The report must be understandable and include all the information needed to evaluate a study. The review of theory and prior research and the description of methods used are as important in judging research quality as are the findings and conclusions.

SUMMARY

The chapter suggests ways to evaluate empirical research; it assumes the topic investigated is of interest. Given an interesting topic, two criteria are appropriate to evaluate research investigations. These are (1) whether a causal conceptual relationship is judged valid, and (2) the validity of its generalization. The first criterion is most important, because the second becomes relevant only if the first is judged to be valid.

Causal Relationships

The research model suggests three key questions that must all be answered affirmatively to conclude that an empirical study makes a persuasive claim about a causal conceptual relationship.

1. Is there an unambiguous relationship between the variables?
2. Is the relationship causal?
3. Does the relationship apply at the conceptual level?

The theory motivating a research study helps provide answers to all three questions. Even the first question benefits because the identification of variables requiring control depends primarily on theoretical specification. Theory is also the main source of causal arguments in all but true experiments. Finally, theory in the form of nomological networks is important for construct validity. Construct validity, in turn, is required to move from empirical operations to the conceptual level.

Absent theory, ***exploratory research*** may be justified when an interesting research issue occurs. Findings from exploratory research must be viewed as tentative because they are not motivated by prior conceptual or empirical evidence.

Prior research can also help address issues involving causal conceptual relationships. Findings in a study are more persuasive when they are consistent with prior research findings. Prior research is also helpful in identifying variables that require control.

Research design is important to answer questions about causal conceptual relationships because it involves decisions about all operational aspects of a study. Decisions about variables to measure, combined with analysis, help address the first question about unambiguous relationships among variables. Administration of measures to cases can address the first and second question involving causal direction. Finally, decisions about measures to use and analyses to perform on those measures have implications for construct validity and hence whether observed relationships apply at the conceptual level.

Research execution is the final step in the research process. The quality of this execution determines how well the study benefits from theory development, the review of prior research, and the design.

Where there are alternative ways to address methodological or conceptual issues execution benefits from ***sensitivity analysis***, carrying out analyses several ways. Findings are more persuasive when they are ***robust*** (similar) across the alternative specifications investigated.

The research report is an especially important part of the execution phase. First, during the act of writing a research report a researcher combines all previous components of the study. To a considerable extent a researcher learns what was found and how persuasive the findings are during the writing process. Second, the research report once completed provides the only publicly available information on how the study was conducted and what it found.

Generalization

Generalization becomes an issue if a study is persuasive about the validity of the causal conceptual relationship. Again, all four elements of research studies identified (i.e., theory, prior research, design, and execution) can contribute; however, now theory and prior research play even more prominent roles. Theory helps specify the probable domains over which the causal conceptual relationship may generalize. It can help do so by specifying the mediating processes that explain why a causal system operates. It also does so if it explicitly specifies limiting boundary conditions of the theory.

Technically, prior empirical research addresses generalization only at the operational level. However, even at this level, evidence from such studies can broaden the domains (e.g., cases, time periods) over which operational results may be expected to hold. Moreover, when prior research uses different measures and research methods, as is typically the case, there can be greater confidence that results apply at the conceptual level.

FOR REVIEW

Terms to Know

Exploratory research studies: Research studies conducted without benefit of theory to help guide the development of hypothesized relationships among variables of interest.
Sensitivity analysis: Conducting analyses different ways to see if results depend on particular methods (e.g., ways of measuring a variable) or specification models.
Robust findings: When findings obtained are consistent across different ways of carrying out analyses in sensitivity analyses.

Questions for Review

1. Why is generalization a second-order criterion for judging research?
2. How can theory help make empirical research studies persuasive?
3. What are limitations to exploratory research?

Issues to Discuss

1. Discuss the following statement: experimental designs are inherently superior to alternative designs for research aimed at addressing causal conceptual models.
2. Discuss the importance of the research report to persuasive research.

SUGGESTED READINGS

I find two discussions of the material covered in this chapter to be excellent. Both address the criteria discussed here for evaluating research. Chapter 2 of Cook & Campbell (1979) is particularly good on the first issue having to do with the persuasiveness of causal claims made within a study. Sackett & Larson (1990) are particularly good on the issue of generalization.

Glossary

Adjusted R^2 Multiple coefficient of determination adjusted for sample size and number of independent variables. It is a better estimate of the parameter than is the unadjusted sample multiple coefficient of determination.

Analyses Used to describe scores on single measures and to identify relationships that may exist between scores across different measures; typically involve the use of statistics.

Assignment error Results because the random allocation of cases to levels of an independent variable typically does not exactly equalize scores on the dependent variable across groups.

Attenuation due to unreliability Formula that estimates the degree to which unreliability in either or both variables reduces a correlation coefficient relative to perfectly reliable measurement of the variables.

Bar chart A graph that reports the values of a discrete variable on one axis and the frequency (number and/or percentage) of cases on the other.

Beta coefficient A standardized (mean = 0.0, standard deviation = 1.0 of all variables in the model) regression coefficient. In simple regression, the beta coefficient is identical to the simple correlation coefficient.

Between-cases design Design that uses two or more cases or groups of cases; each case or group experiences different levels of an independent variable. Effect of an independent variable is assessed by comparing dependent variable scores across the cases or groups of cases.

Biased relationship An observed relationship between an independent and dependent variable that under- or overstates the causal relationship. Occurs if a nuisance variable is causally related to the dependent variable and is related to the independent variable(s).

Binomial probability distribution Discrete probability distribution that results from a set of trials where the values of each trial are independent, the probability remains constant from trial to trial, and each trial can lead to one of two values.

Bouncing betas Instability in sample standardized partial regression coefficients resulting from multicollinearity.

Boundary condition Synonym for moderator variable. A relationship between an independent and a dependent variable depends on the value (boundary) of another independent variable.

Box-score method In meta-analysis, the use of statistical significance values as the dependent variable. Its use is not recommended.

Cases Entities (e.g., individuals, groups, organizations, transactions) investigated in research.

Causal conceptual relationship A relationship in which variation in the independent construct is responsible for variation in the dependent construct.

Causal model Refers to variables that operate in a causal system and to their true relationships.

Causal relationship When variation in one factor is responsible for variation in another.

Centering Used in moderated regression by subtracting the mean of an independent variable from each observation to obtain a new distribution of the same shape and variance but with a mean of zero.

Central limit theorem States that as sample sizes randomly obtained become larger, the sampling distribution becomes less variable and more normally distributed. Applies to several, but not all, sampling distributions.

Central tendency The middle of a distribution of scores.

Central tendency error Present when an observer clusters responses in the middle of a scale when more variable responses should be recorded.

Closed-ended response format Questionnaire scaling in which the researcher provides participants with fixed response categories.

Coefficient alpha An estimate of reliability; it provides an estimate of the correlation coefficient that is expected between a summary score from a measure studied and another hypothetical measure of the same thing using the same number of repetitions.

Coefficient of determination The square of the correlation coefficient. A statistic that reports the proportion of linear variance in one variable that is explained or associated with variance in another variable.

Comparison groups Groups of research cases thought to be comparable on levels of potential nuisance variables.

Conceptual variable; also a ***construct*** A mental definition of a characteristic of some object that can vary.

Confidence intervals A range of statistical values that likely include the population parameter.

Confidence level Refers to the likelihood that a confidence interval includes the population parameter.

Construct validation Methods used to estimate a measure's construct validity.

Construct validity Present when there is a high correspondence between cases' scores on a measure and the mental definition of the construct the measure is designed to represent.

Contamination In measurement, the portion of scores that measures something other than the defined construct.

Content validation Procedures employed to obtain content validity.

Content validity When a measure is judged to be construct valid, usually by individuals who are thought to be subject matter experts.

Continuous probability distribution Probability distribution where probabilities are assigned to regions of the continuous random variable.

Continuous variable Variable that is infinitely divisible between any two values.

Convenience sampling (also judgment sampling) The selection of cases (usually an intact group) to study by using nonprobability methods.

Convergent validity Is present when there is a high correspondence between scores from two different measures of the same construct.

Correction for attenuation   Formulas that estimate the correlation coefficient or regression coefficient between two variables if they are measured with perfect reliability; it requires knowledge of reliability.

Correlation coefficient (product moment)   A statistic that describes the degree of linear relationship between two variables in a standardized form ranging from ± 1.00.

Covariance   A statistic that provides information about how values of two variables go together. It is the average cross-product of the deviations of the values of each variable about its respective mean.

Covariate   A synonym for an independent variable that is not manipulated by a researcher in experiments and quasi-experiments.

Criterion-related validity   Is present when the measure of interest is related to another measure judged to be more construct valid.

Cross-sectional design   Design in which the independent and dependent variables are measured only once. The relationship between the variables is taken as evidence of the influence of X on Y.

Data   Scores characterizing cases obtained on measures. *Datum* refers to one score.

Data matrix   A rectangular array of scores with cases in the rows and variables in the columns.

Deficiency   In measurement, the portion of the defined construct that is not captured by scores on a measure of the construct.

Degrees of freedom (d.f.)   Refer to the amount of information available to estimate population parameters from sample statistics. They are used to identify the appropriate sampling distribution for statistical hypothesis tests and confidence intervals.

Demand characteristics   Characteristics of a research study that motivate participants' expectations about what is investigated; a threat to internal validity.

Dependent variable   Research outcome; the consequence in a causal relationship.

Direct effect   In a causal model, relationship between an independent and a dependent variable that is not mediated by some other variable(s).

Discrete probability distribution   Probability distribution has a probability associated with each value of the discrete random variable.

Discrete variable   Variable with a countable number of values.

Discriminant validity   Is present when measures of constructs that are supposed to be independent are found to have a low correspondence.

Distribution shape   Degree to which a distribution is symmetrical/asymmetrical and the degree to which it is peaked or flat. These characteristics are defined by skew and kurtosis.

Dummy variable   A nominal variable with two values coded 0 and 1.

Empirical models   When researchers retain independent variables in a model based on statistical criteria (e.g., statistical inference); independent variables are not chosen based on conceptual considerations.

Empirical relationship   The correspondence between scores obtained from cases on measures.

Empirical research   Systematic study of relationships between scores obtained from cases on measures.

Endogenous variable   Variable explained by a causal model.

Exhaustive values When one of the values on a variable must result.

Exogenous variable Independent variable in a causal model that is not explained by the model.

Expectancy effects A nuisance variable that influences the dependent variable because a researcher treats some cases differently than others based on assumptions made about expected research results; a threat to internal validity.

Experiments A research design in which cases are randomly assigned to levels of an independent variable(s).

Exploratory research studies Research studies conducted without benefit of theory to help guide the development of hypothesized relationships among variables of interest.

External validation Methods used to estimate external validity.

External validity Present when findings obtained in a research study, other than statistical generalization, are correctly generalized.

F distributions A set of asymmetrical sampling distributions with positive skew. *F* distributions are designed to test the equality of variances from two populations.

Face validity When a measure appears to be construct valid by individuals who use it, including participants.

Factor analysis Statistical procedure for reducing information from a set of items in a measure to a smaller number of factors that represent common dimensions in the larger set.

Factorial design Studies with two or more independent variables. *Factor* is a synonym for *independent variable,* which is under the control of a researcher.

Field study A research design in which values of the independent variable(s) are characteristics of the cases studied and in which cases are not randomly selected from some larger population.

Forced choice scales Scales in which response categories are equated on favorability or other characteristics to control for response styles.

Frequency table Provides a summary of cases' scores from a data matrix by reporting the number (and/or percent) of cases at each level of a discrete variable or within each interval of a continuous variable.

Full mediation The relationship between an independent and a dependent variable operates only through a mediator variable. The independent variable has no direct effect on the dependent variable.

Fully specified model All independent variables that influence the dependent variable in the causal model are included in the statistical model investigated.

Halo error Present when an observer evaluates an object in an undifferentiated manner.

Hierarchical modeling Researchers examine the change in dependent variable variance explained as independent variables are added or deleted from two or more statistical models.

Histogram A graph that reports values of a continuous variable placed in intervals on one axis with the frequency (number and/or percentage of cases) on the other.

History An exogenous event that occurs between measurements of the dependent variable; a threat to internal validity in longitudinal designs.

Hypothesis An expected relationship between an independent and a dependent variable.

Independence Two variables are independent when information about the value on one variable provides no information about the probability of values on the other variable.

Independent variable Variable that helps explain or predict a dependent variable; it is a cause in a causal relationship.

Indirect effect In a causal model, the influence of an independent variable that operates through a mediator variable.

Instantaneous models Time series model in which changes in the independent and dependent variables are assumed to occur without an intervening time interval.

Instrumentation A threat to internal validity in longitudinal designs when the measure of the dependent variable changes over time.

Interaction variable Synonym for *moderator variable*. A relationship between an independent and a dependent variable depends on the value of another independent variable.

Internal consistency A form of reliability that addresses the consistency of scores from a set of items in a measure.

Internal statistical validity Present when an empirical relationship is not due to chance.

Internal validation Methods used to determine whether internal validity is likely.

Internal validity Present when variation in scores on a measure of an independent variable is responsible for variation in scores on a measure of a dependent variable.

Interrater reliability A form of reliability that addresses the consistency of scores from a set of observers.

Interval variable Variable with ordinal properties, and the distance between values is meaningful.

Interviews Measuring instruments in which another individual (the interviewer) asks the questions verbally and is responsible for recording responses.

Intragoup history An exogenous event(s) that affects a group of cases that experience one level of an independent variable differently than it influences groups experiencing other levels of the independent variable; a threat to internal validity.

Kurtosis Describes the flatness or peakedness of a distribution relative to a normal distribution. Kurtosis > 0.0 when a distribution is more peaked than a normal distribution. Kurtosis < 0.0 when a distribution is less peaked than a normal distribution.

Lagged models Time series model in which changes in the independent variable are assumed to take some time to influence the dependent variable.

Latent variable Term in structural equation modeling for a factor.

Least-Squares Criterion A rule that establishes the regression line so that the sum of the squared deviations between the actual dependent variable values and the values predicted are minimized.

Leniency error Present when an observer systematically inflates ratings of a group of objects.

Level of measurement Refers to the amount of information provided by scores.

Listwise deletion When an entire case with missing data is removed from a research study.

Longitudinal design Design in which the dependent (and perhaps, independent) variable is measured more than once.

Matching Cases are selected for research so that those who experience different levels of an independent variable(s) are equated on levels of nuisance variables.

Maturation Changes in cases between measurements of the dependent variable; a threat to internal validity in longitudinal designs.

Mean A statistic describing central tendency; the sum of the values of each score divided by the number of scores.

Mean substitution Missing data on a variable are replaced with the mean of the responding cases on that variable.

Measurement Activities associated with measuring cases.

Measures Instruments used to obtain scores from participants.

Median A statistic describing central tendency; the middle score in a distribution (or if there are an even number of scores, the sum of the two middle-most scores divided by 2).

Mediator variable Also *intervening variable,* comes between an independent and a dependent variable in a causal chain.

Meta-analysis Procedures to review and evaluate prior research studies that depend on quantitative research methods.

Missing data Data that are absent on a case.

Misspecification When a statistical model does not include all collinear independent variables in the underlying causal model.

Mode A statistic describing central tendency; the most frequent score in a distribution of discrete values.

Model precision Variance explained by the statistical model.

Moderated regression Regression procedure in which an independent variable is created to capture the nonlinear effects of a moderator variable.

Moderator variable A variable whose values are associated with different relationships between an independent and a dependent variable. May or may not be an independent variable.

Mortality Occurs when some cases leave between measurements of the dependent variable; a threat to internal validity in longitudinal designs.

Multicollinearity Nonzero correlation among independent variables in a multiple correlation or regression context.

Multidimensional constructs Construct that contains more specific but related one-dimensional constructs.

Multiple coefficient of determination Describes the proportion of linear variance in one ordered dependent variable that is accounted for jointly by two or more independent variables. It ranges from 0.0 to 1.0.

Multiple correlation coefficient Describes the degree of linear relationship between one ordered dependent variable and two or more independent variables. It describes the relationship in standardized form and ranges from 0.0 to 1.0.

Multiple regression Describes relationships between a dependent and two or more independent variables in units of the dependent variable.

Multiple regression intercept The predicted value of Y when all independent variables $=$ 0.0.

Mutually exclusive values When the presence of one value precludes the presence of another value, and vice versa.

Narrative research review A review of prior research studies that depends largely on a reviewer's knowledge of the topic and research methods. The review typically includes a summary and evaluation of the previous research.

Noisy relationship Occurs when a nuisance variable is related to the dependent variable, but not to the independent variable(s).

Nominal (categorical) variable Variable in which similar values signal the same thing, different values signal different things.

Nomological network Relationships between a construct under measurement consideration and other constructs. It is the measurement analog to a conceptual model of interest to causal research.

Nonrespondents Cases that provided no data for a research study.

Normal distribution A distribution of a continuous variable that is unimodal, symmetrical around its middle, and has 68.3% of scores falling within ±1 standard deviation of the mean, 95.5% of scores falling within ±2 standard deviations, and 99.7% of scores falling within ±3 standard deviations.

Normal probability distribution Continuous probability distribution in which probabilities assigned to regions conform to a normal distribution.

Nuisance variable A variable in the causal model that is not controlled in a research study.

Null hypothesis (H_0) The hypothesis of no relationship (or no difference) in the population.

Omitted category The value of a nominal variable assigned zeros to all dummy variables established to account for the nominal variable in multiple correlation and regression.

Omitted variable An independent variable that operates in the causal system studied but is not included in the model studied. Serves as a threat to internal validity in the same way selection is a threat.

One-dimensional constructs Construct that represents a single domain or dimension.

One-tailed hypothesis A research hypothesis that is directional; the researcher believes a relationship is positive or negative.

Open-ended response format Questionnaire scaling that has participants respond in their own words.

Operational variable Variable with a measure to obtain scores from cases.

Ordinal variable Variable with nominal properties, and values signal order from highest to lowest (or lowest to highest).

Pairwise deletion When a case is deleted only if there are missing data on variables from the specific analyses conducted. The case is retained for any other analyses where data are present.

Panel studies Independent and dependent variables are measured two or more times on a group of cases; design to measure changes in the dependent variable as a function of changes in an independent variable(s).

Parameter Statistic that describes a statistical inference drawn by a researcher.

Partial mediation The relationship between an independent and dependent variable operates partially through a mediator variable. The independent variable has a direct effect on the dependent variable and an indirect effect through the mediator.

Partial regression coefficient The predicted change in Y for a unit change in one independent variable when all other independent variables in the equation are held constant.

Percentile Reports a score in percentage terms relative to the lowest score in the distribution.

Phi coefficient A correlation coefficient, sometimes calculated when both variables are dichotomous.

Point-biserial correlation coefficient A correlation coefficient, sometimes calculated when one variable is ordered and the other has two values.

Probability (P_r) Specifies the likelihood that a particular value of a variable will be obtained. It can range from 0.0 to 1.0.

Probability distribution A distribution that summarizes probabilities associated with values of a random variable.

Probability sample Obtained when the likelihood that each case in the population is chosen for the sample is known.

Probability sampling The selection of a subset of cases obtained from a larger population of cases using rules of probability.

Product moment correlation coefficient A statistic that describes the degree of linear relationship between two variables in a standardized form ranging between ± 1.00.

Proper statistical specification In causal modeling when all collinear independent variables that influence the dependent variable are included in the model tested.

Qualitative research Empirical research procedure that investigates a small number of cases, typically with substantial interaction between the cases and the researcher.

Quasi-experiments A research design in which cases do not control the levels of the independent variable(s) they experience; cases are not randomly assigned to levels of the independent variable(s).

Questionnaires Measuring instruments that ask individuals to respond to a set of questions in verbal or written form.

Random assignment Allocation of cases to levels of an independent variable(s) without order; a procedure designed to match cases on levels of nuisance variables.

Random errors In measurement, also called *unreliability*, errors in scores on a measure that are unsystematic. Random errors are uncorrelated with *true (systematic)* scores.

Random variable A variable whose values are not known exactly but are described by probability.

Randomization test Used to develop a null probability distribution by generating all possible ways cases may be assigned to levels of the independent variable.

Ratio variable Variable with interval properties, and there is a true zero point.

Recursive model Model in which causal influence is assumed to go in only one direction.

Regression As a statistic, describes relationships between an independent and a dependent variable in the scale values of the variables.

Regression As a threat to internal validity in longitudinal designs when (a) groups are chosen for levels of the independent variable based on dependent variable performance on a first measurement and (b) there is unreliability in the dependent variable measure.

Regression coefficient A statistic that reports the predicted change in the value of the dependent variable for a unit change (change of 1.0) in the independent variable.

Regression intercept A statistic that reports the predicted value of the dependent variable when the independent variable is equal to 0.0.

Reliability The consistency of measurement. Formally, it is the ratio of systematic score variance to total variance.

Replication A research study that addresses the same research issue(s) as an earlier study.

Research confederate A member of the research team who interacts with participants but is not known by participants to be a member of the research team.

Research design Overall plan of a study. Establishes procedures to obtain cases for study and to determine how scores are obtained on measures of cases.

Research hypothesis (H_1) Represents a researcher's expectation about what is true of the population parameter.

Response acquiescence (also **yea-saying**) A self-report response style in which the respondent tends to agree with a questionnaire item regardless of its content.

Restriction of range A reduction in the variance of a variable through selection of cases.

Rho coefficient A correlation coefficient, sometimes calculated when the variables represent only rank order.

Robust findings When findings obtained are consistent across different ways of carrying out analyses in sensitivity analyses.

Sampling distribution A probability distribution of a sample statistic obtained on all possible probability samples of a given sample size.

Sampling distribution of the mean A sampling distribution created by calculating means for all possible probability samples of a given size.

Sampling error The difference between a sample statistic and population parameter brought about because the sample size is smaller than the population. The size of this error can be estimated when probability sampling is used.

Scores (also, **data**) Numerical information about cases obtained on measures.

Secondary data Information used for research purposes but that has been collected for other purposes.

Selection A threat to internal validity when there are preexisting differences between groups experiencing different levels of an independent variable. These differences may account for differences observed on the dependent variable.

Self-report questionnaires Questionnaires that ask respondents to provide information about themselves.

Sensitivity analysis Conducting analyses different ways to see if results depend on particular methods (e.g., ways of measuring a variable) or specification models.

Severity error Present when an observer systematically deflates ratings of a group of objects.

Simple random sample A probability sample in which every unique sample of a given size from a population has an equal chance of being selected.

Simultaneity When causal influence goes from the independent to the dependent variable and vice versa.

Skew Describes the symmetry or asymmetry of a distribution relative to a normal distribution. When a distribution is symmetrical skew $= 0.0$. When the distribution is asymmetrical and the tail is toward the right skew > 0.0; when the tail is to the left skew < 0.0.

Social desirability A self-report response style designed to present the respondent in a publicly favorable light.

Spurious relationship An observed relationship between an independent and a dependent variable but with no causal relationship. Occurs when a nuisance variable accounts for all the observed relationship between a dependent and an independent variable(s).

Squared partial correlation coefficient Represents the proportion of Y variance explained by an independent variable that is not otherwise explained.

Squared semipartial (or part) correlation coefficient Represents the proportion of the total variance in Y that is uniquely (nonredundantly) explained by an independent variable.

Stability reliability A form of reliability that addresses the consistency of scores across time periods.

Standard deviation The average variability of scores around the mean.

Standard error Standard deviation of a sampling distribution.

Standard normal distribution A normal distribution with a mean $= 0.0$ and a standard deviation $= 1.0$.

Standard error of the correlation coefficient Standard deviation of a sampling distribution of the correlation coefficient.

Standard error of the mean Standard deviation of a sampling distribution of the mean.

Standard score A score that results by subtracting its distribution mean and dividing the result by the distribution standard deviation.

Standard score distribution A distribution of scores on a variable that have been transformed to mean $= 0.0$ and standard deviation $= 1.0$.

Statistical generalization validity Present when an empirical relationship observed on a sample of cases provides a correct estimate of the relationship in the population of cases from which the sample was drawn.

Statistical hypothesis test Estimates whether a relationship (or difference) observed on a sample of cases suggests there is a relationship (difference) in the population from which the sample was drawn.

Statistical inference Use of statistics and probability theory to draw conclusions about population parameters or the likelihood that observed relationships (differences) are due to chance.

Statistical modeling The study of the structure of scores on variables using statistics and statistical inference.

Statistical power The likelihood that a statistical hypothesis test will lead to rejection of the null hypothesis when the research hypothesis is true in the population.

Statistical significance level Level of risk a researcher takes when rejecting the null hypothesis.

Statistical validation The use of probability theory to investigate internal statistical validity or statistical generalization validity.

Statistics Refers to a field of study, procedures to analyze data, or a term to describe outcomes of statistical procedures. It also refers to a summary characteristic of scores.

Step-wise procedures Popular methods to assess empirical models statistically.

Structural equation models Combines measurement models with statistical models to assess causal models.

Student's t distributions A set of symmetrical sampling distributions that are shaped as a standard normal distribution but more variable. Student's *t* distributions become more like a standard normal distribution as the sample size gets larger.

Suppressor variable A nuisance variable that biases an observed relationship between an independent variable downward; usually occurs when a nuisance variable has a positive relationship with the independent variable and a small negative relationship with the dependent variable.

Survey study A research design in which values of the independent variable(s) are characteristics of the cases studied and in which cases are randomly selected from some larger population.

Systematic errors In measurement, when scores from a measure consistently vary from construct validity because of contamination and/or deficiency.

Testing A threat to internal validity in longitudinal designs when the initial measurement of a dependent variable influences participants' responses to the dependent variable on a subsequent measurement of it.

Theory Provides a tentative explanation for why a causal relationship(s) obtains.

Threats to internal validity Characteristics of research studies that make a causal claim that an independent variable leads to a dependent variable vulnerable to alternative explanations.

Time series Design to investigate longitudinal changes in a dependent variable; independent and dependent variables are measured more than once over time.

Total effect The sum of the direct and indirect effects for any independent variable in mediated models.

Treatment contamination Occurs when a level of an independent variable assigned to one group of participants is communicated to another; a threat to internal validity.

Triangulation In research, a form of replication that seeks to discover whether research findings generalize across different research methods.

True scores Also called ***systematic,*** the consistent (repeatable) portion of scores obtained from participants on a measure.

Two-tailed hypothesis A research hypothesis that is not directional; the researcher believes there is a relationship but does not speculate on whether it is positive or negative.

Type I error, also ***α error*** In hypothesis testing, the error of concluding a relationship exists in the population when it does not.

Type II error, also ***β error*** In hypothesis testing, the error of failing to conclude a relationship exists in the population when it does.

Validity In research, when a conclusion or inference is true.

Variability The spread in a distribution of scores.

Variables Characteristics of objects that can take on two or more values.

Variance The standard deviation squared.

Verisimilitude Having the appearance of truth. In research validity is best thought of as verisimilitude.

Within-cases design Design that uses one case or one group of cases. Effect of an independent variable is assessed by measuring the dependent variable before and after a change in the level of the independent variable.

References

Abelson, R. P. (1995). *Statistics as principled argument*. Hillsdale, NJ: Erlbaum.

Aiken, L. S., & West, S. G. (1991). *Multiple regression: Testing and interpreting interactions*. Newbury Park, CA: Sage.

Alwin, D. F., & Hauser, R. M. (1975). The decomposition of effects in path analysis. *American Sociological Review, 40*, 37–47.

American Psychological Association (1994). *Publication manual of the American Psychological Association* (4th ed.). Washington, D.C.

Aquinis, H., & Stone-Romero, E. F. (1997). Methodological artifacts in moderated multiple regression and their effects on statistical power. *Journal of Applied Psychology, 82*, 192–205.

Baron, R. M., & Kenny, D. A. (1986). The moderator-mediator variable distinction in social psychological research: Conceptual, strategic, and statistical considerations. *Journal of Personality and Social Psychology, 51*, 1173–1182.

Barrett, G. V. (1992). Clarifying construct validity: Definitions, processes and models. *Human Performance, 5*, 13–58.

Becker, G. S. (1964). *Human capital: A theoretical and empirical analysis with special reference to education*. New York: Columbia University Press.

Becker, G. S. (1993). *Human capital: A theoretical and empirical analysis with special reference to education* (3rd ed.). Chicago: University of Chicago Press.

Blalock, H. M. Jr. (1968). The measurement problem: A gap between the languages of theory and research. In H. M. Blalock, Jr., & A. B. Blalock (Eds.), *Methodology in social research* (pp. 5–27). New York: McGraw-Hill.

Bobko, P. (1995). *Correlation and regression: Principles and applications for industrial/organizational psychology and management*. New York: McGraw-Hill.

Bretz, R. D., Jr. (1989). College grade point average as a predictor of adult success: A meta-analytic review and some additional evidence. *Public Personnel Management, 18*, 11–21.

Campbell, D. T., & Fiske, D. W. (1959). Convergent and discriminant validation by the multitrait-multimethod matrix. *Psychological Bulletin, 56*, 81–105.

Campbell, D. T., & Stanley, J. C. (1963). *Experimental and quasi-experimental designs for research*. Chicago: Rand-McNally.

Campbell, J. P. (1976). Psychometric Theory. In M. D. Dunnette (Ed.), *Handbook of industrial and organizational psychology* (pp. 185–222). Chicago: Rand McNally.

Card, D. (1998). The causal effect of education on earnings. In O. Ashenfelter & D. Card (Eds.), *Handbook of labor economics*. Vol. 3a. Amsterdam, NY: Elsevier, pp. 1801–1863.

Cochran, W. G. (1982). *Planning and analysis of observational studies*. New York: Wiley.

Cohen, J. (1988). *Statistical power analysis for the behavioral sciences* (2nd. ed.). Hillsdale, NJ: Erlbaum.

Cohen, J. 1994. Things I have learned (so far). *American Psychologist, 45*, 1304–1312.

Cohen, J., Cohen, P., West, S. G., & Aiken, L. S. (2003). *Applied multiple regression/correlation analysis for the behavioral sciences* (3rd ed.). Mahwah, NJ: Erlbaum.

Cook, T., & Campbell, D. T. (1979). *Quasi-experimentation: Design and analysis issues for field settings*. Boston: Houghton Mifflin.

Cook, T. D., & Shadish, W. R. (1994). Social experiments: Some developments over the past fifteen years. *Annual Review of Psychology, 45*, 545–580.

Cortina, J. M. (1993). What is coefficient alpha? An examination of theory and application. *Journal of Applied Psychology, 78*, 98–104.

Cronbach, L. J., & Meehl, P. E. (1955). Construct validity in psychological tests. *Psychological Bulletin, 52*, 281–302.

Cronbach, L. J., Rajaratnam, N., & Gleser, G. C. (1963). Theory of generalizability: A liberalization of reliability theory. *The British Journal of Statistical Psychology, 16*, 137–163.

Cryer, J. D., & Miller, R. B. (1993). *Statistics for business: Data analysis and modeling* (2nd ed.). Belmont, CA: Brooks Cole.

Daft, R. L. (1985). Why I recommended that your manuscript be rejected and what you can do about it. In L. L. Cummings & P. Frost (Eds.). Publishing in the organizational sciences. Homewood, IL: Irwin.

Frees, E. W. (1996). *Data analysis using regression models: The business perspective.* Upper Saddle River, NJ: Prentice-Hall.

Ghiselli, E. E., Campbell, J. P., & Zedeck, S. (1981). *Measurement theory for the behavioral sciences.* San Francisco: Freeman.

Glass, G. V., McGaw, B., & Smith, M. L. (1981). *Meta-analysis in social research.* Newbury Park, CA: Sage.

Hackett, R. D., & Guion, R. M. (1985). A reevaluation of the absenteeism-job satisfaction relationship. *Organizational Behavior and Human Decision Processes, 35,* 340–381.

Hagen, R. L. (1997). In praise of the null hypothesis statistical test. *American Psychologist, 52,* 15–24.

Hays, W. L. (1988). *Statistics* (4th. ed.). New York: Holt, Rinehart & Winston.

Hedges, L. V., & Olkin, I. (1985). *Statistical methods of meta-analysis.* Orlando, FL: Academic Press.

Hunt, M. (1997). *How science takes stock: The story of meta-analysis.* New York: Russel Sage.

Hunter, J. E., & Schmidt, F. L. (1990). *Methods of meta-analysis.* Newbury Park, CA: Sage.

Keppel, G. (1982). *Design & analysis a researcher's handbook* (2nd ed.). Englewood Cliffs, NJ: Prentice-Hall.

Kish, L. (1987). *Statistical design for research.* New York: Wiley.

Lowin, A., & Craig, J. R. (1968). The influence of level of performance on managerial style: An experimental object-lesson in the ambiguity of correlational data. *Organizational Behavior and Human Performance, 3,* 440–458.

McEvoy, G. M., & Cascio, W. F. (1987). Do good or poor performers leave: A meta-analysis of the relationship between performance and turnover. *Academy of Management Journal, 30,* 744–762.

Miller, C. C., & Cardinal, L. B. (1994). Strategic planning and firm performance: A synthesis of more than two decades of research. *Academy of Management Journal, 37,* 649–665.

Morrison, D. E., & Henkel, R. E. (Eds). (1970). *The significance test controversy.* Chicago: Aldine.

Nunnally, J. C. (1967). *Psychometric theory.* New York: McGraw-Hill Book Company.

Nunnally, J. C. (1978). *Psychometric theory* (2nd ed.). New York: McGraw-Hill Book Company.

Nunnally, J. C., & Bernstein, I. H. (1994). *Psychometric theory* (3rd ed.). New York: McGraw-Hill.

Oakes, M. (1986). *Statistical inference: A commentary for the social and behavioural sciences.* Chichester, UK: Wiley.

Olian, J. D., Schwab, D. P., & Haberfeld, Y. (1988). The impact of applicant gender compared to qualifications on hiring recommendations: A meta analysis of experimental studies. *Organizational Behavior and Human Decision Processes, 41,* 180–195.

Payne, S. L. (1951). *The art of asking questions.* Princeton, NJ: Princeton University Press.

Pedhazur, E. J. (1982). *Multiple regression in behavioral research: Explanation and prediction* (2nd ed.). New York: Holt, Rinehart & Winston.

Petty, M. M., McGee, G. W., & Cavender, J. W. (1984). A meta-analysis of the relationships between individual job satisfaction and individual performance. *Academy of Management Journal, 9,* 712–721.

Price, J. L., & Mueller, C. W. (1986). *Handbook of organizational measurement.* Marshfield, MA: Pitman.

Rosenthal, R. (1991). *Meta-analytic procedures for social research* (revised ed.). Beverly Hills, CA: Sage.

Rosenthal, R. (1995). Writing meta-analytic reviews. *Psychological Bulletin, 118,* 183–192.

Rosnow, R. L., & Rosenthal, R. (1989). Statistical procedures and the justification of knowledge in psychological science. *American Psychologist, 44,* 1276–1284.

Roth, P. L. (1994). Missing data: A conceptual review for applied psychologists. *Personnel Psychology, 47,* 537–560.

Roth, P. L. (2003). Introduction to the feature on problematic data. *Organizational Research Methods, 6,* 279–281.

Roth, P. L., BeVier, C. A., Switzer, F. S., III, & Schippmann, J. S. (1996). Meta-analyzing the relationship between grades and job performance. *Journal of Applied Psychology, 80,* 548–556.

Sackett, P. R., & Larson, J. R., Jr. (1990). Research strategies and tactics in industrial and organizational psychology. In M. D. Dunnette & L. M. Hough (Eds.), *Handbook of industrial and organizational psychology* (2nd ed.). Vol. 1. Palo Alto, CA: Consulting Psychologists Press.

Schmidt, F. L. (1996). Statistical significance testing and cumulative knowledge in psychology: Implications for training of researchers. *Psychological Methods, 1,* 115–129.

Schmidt, F. L., & Hunter, J. E. (1996). Measurement error in psychological research: Lessons from 26 research scenarios. *Psychological Methods, 1,* 199–223.

Schmidt, F. L., Law, K., Hunter, J. E., Rothstein, H. R., Pearlman, K. & McDaniel, M. (1993). Refinements in validity generalization methods: Implications for the situational specificity hypothesis. *Journal of Applied Psychology, 78,* 3–13.

Schwab, D. P. (1980). Construct validity in organizational behavior. In B. M. Staw & L. L. Cummings (Eds.), *Research in organizational behavior* (pp. 3–43). Vol. 2. Greenwich, CT: JAI Press.

Schwab, D. P., Gottlieb-Olian, J. D., & Heneman, H. G., III. (1979). Between subject expectancy theory research: A statistical review of studies predicting effort and performance. *Psychological Bulletin, 86,* 139–147.

Schwarz, N., & Sudman, S. (Eds.). (1994). *Autobiographical memory and the validity of retrospective reports.* New York: Springer.

Scott, K. D., & Taylor, G. S. (1985). An examination of conflicting findings on the relationship between job satisfaction and absenteeism: A meta-analysis. *Academy of Management Journal, 28,* 599–612.

Shavelson, R. J., Webb, N. M., & Rowley, G. L. (1989). Generalizability theory. *American Psychologist, 44,* 922–932.

Smith, P. C., Kendall, L. M., & Hulin, C. L. (1969). *The measurement of satisfaction in work and retirement.* Chicago: Rand McNally.

Spence, M. A. (1973). Job market signaling, *Quarterly Journal of Economics, 87,* 355–374.

Steel, R. P., & Griffeth, R. W. (1989). The elusive relationship between perceived employment opportunity and turnover behavior: A methodological or conceptual artifact? *Journal of Applied Psychology, 74,* 846–854.

Sudman, S., & Bradburn, N. M. (1982). *Asking questions.* San Francisco: Jossey-Bass.

Van Eerde, W., & Thierry, H. (1996). Vroom's expectancy models and work-related criteria: A meta-analysis. *Journal of Applied Psychology, 81,* 575–586.

Weiss, D. J., Dawis, R. V., England, G. W., & Lofquist, L. H. (1967). *Manual for the Minnesota Satisfaction Questionnaire.* Minneapolis: Industrial Relations Center, University of Minnesota.

White, A. G. (1986). *Survey and questionnaire design: A bibliography.* Monticello, IL: Vance Bibliographies.

Author Index

Note: Numbers in *italics* indicate pages with complete bibliographic information.

A

Abelson, R. P., 200, *311*
Aiken, L. S., 154, 200, 239, 251, 275, 276, *311*
Alwin, D. F., 276, *311*
American Psychological Association, 220, 222, 223, *311*
Aquinis, H., 276, *311*

B

Baron, R. M., 276, *311*
Barrett, G. V., 49, *311*
Becker, G. S., 290, *311*
Bernstein, I. H., 49, *312*
BeVier, C. A., 216, *312*
Blalock, H. M., Jr., 49, *311*
Bobko, P., 154, *311*
Bradburn, N. M., 50, *313*
Bretz, R. D., Jr., 216, *311*

C

Campbell, D. T., 93, 276, 298, *311*
Campbell, J. P., 49, 251, *311*, *312*
Card, D., 290, *311*
Cardinal, L. B., 216, *312*
Cascio, W. F., 216, *312*
Cavender, J. W., 216, *312*
Cochran, W. G., 93, *311*
Cohen, J., 154, 200, 239, 251, 275, 287, *311*

Cohen, P., 154, 200, 239, 251, 275, *311*
Cook, T., 93, 298, *311*
Cook, T. D., 93, *311*
Cortina, J. M., 251, *311*
Craig, J. R., 55, *312*
Cronbach, L. J., 49, 251, *311*
Cryer, J. D., 154, *311*

D

Daft, R. L., 224, *312*
Dawis, R. V., 42, *313*

E

England, G. W., 42, *313*

F

Fiske, D.W., 276, *311*
Frees, E. W., 154, 275, *312*

G

Ghiselli, E. E., 49, 251, *312*
Glass, G. V., 212, 216, *312*
Gleser, G. C., 251, *311*
Gottlieb-Olian, J. D., 216, *312*

Griffeth, R.W., *313*
Guion, R. M., 214, 216, *312*

H

Haberfeld, Y., 216, *312*
Hackett, R. D., 214, 216, *312*
Hagen, R. L., 287, *312*
Hauser, R. M., 276, *311*
Hays, W. L., 154, *312*
Hedges, L. V., 216, *312*
Heneman, H. G., III., 216, *312*
Henkel, R. E., 287, *312*
Hulin, C. L., 42, *313*
Hunt, M., 216, *312*
Hunter, J. E., 212, 216, 251, *312*

K

Kendall, L. M., 42, *313*
Kenny, D. A., 276, *311*
Keppel, G., 93, *312*
Kish, L., 93, *312*

L

Larson, J. R., Jr., 298, *312*
Law, K., 216, *312*
Lofquist, L. H., 42, *313*
Lowin, A., 55, *312*

M

McDaniel, M., 216, *312*
McEvoy, G. M., 216, *312*
McGaw, B., 212, 216, *312*
McGee, G. W., 216, *312*
Meehl, P. E., 49, *311*
Miller, C. C., 216, *312*
Miller, R. B., 154, *311*
Morrison, D. E., 287, *312*
Mueller, C. W., 50, *312*

N

Nunnally, J. C., 49, 251, *312*

O

Oakes, M., 287, *312*
Olian, J. D., 216, *312*
Olkin, I., 216, *312*

P

Payne, S. L., 50, *312*
Pearlman, K., 216, *312*
Pedhazur, E. J., 154, *312*
Petty, M. M., 216, *312*
Price, J. L., 50, *312*

R

Rajaratnam, N., 251, *311*
Rosenthal, R., 216, *312*
Rosnow, R. L., 175, *312*
Rosenthal, R., 175, *312*
Roth, P. L., 216, 239, *312*
Rowley, G. L., 251, 252, *313*

S

Sackett, P. R., 298, *312*
Schippmann, J. S., 216, *312*
Schmidt, F. L., 212, 216, 251, 287, *312*
Schwab, D. P., xv, 49, 216, *312*
Schwarz, N., 50, *313*
Scott, K. D., 214, 216, *313*
Shadish, W. R., 93, *311*
Shavelson, R. J., 251, 252, *313*
Smith, M. L., 212, 216, *312*
Smith, P. C., 42, *313*
Spence, M. A., 290, *313*
Stanley, J. C., 93, *311*
Steel, R. P., *313*
Stone-Romero, E. F., 276, *311*
Sudman, S., 50, *313*
Switzer, F. S., III, 216, *312*

T

Taylor, G. S., 214, 216, *313*
Thierry, H., 216, *313*

V

Van Eerde,W., 216, *313*

W

Webb, N. M., 251, 252, *313*
Weiss, D. J., *313*

West, S. G., 154, 200, 239, 251, 275, 276, *311*
White, A. G., 50, *313*

Z

Zedeck, S., 49, 251, *312*

Subject Index

A

Abbreviations, 226
Abstraction, 12, 28
Adjusted coefficient of determination, 258
Adjusted R^2, 255, 257, 258
Affability, 58
Analysis
  empirical research, 6, 9, 10
  report writing, 222, 225
Analysis applications
  multiple correlation and regression
    formulae, 148–150
    graphical representation, 135
    more than two independent variables,
      142–143
    multiple correlation, 135–139
    multiple regression, 139–142
    nominal independent variables, 143–146
    partial coefficients, 152–154
    single independent variables, 150–152
  scores on single variable
    data matrix, 107–108
    formulae, 115–116
    relationships between statistics, 113–114
    statistical representations, 110–113
    tables and graphs, 108–109
  simple correlation and regression
    formulae, 121–124, 127–128, 132–133
    graphical representation, 119–120
    nominal independent variables, 128–130
    regression model, 126–127
    variance explained, 124–126
Analysis of variance (ANOVA), 244, 249
And, avoiding use, 44
ANOVA, *see* Analysis of variance
Areas under the curve, 111–112, 163, 165
Arrow symbol, 13
Assertiveness, 63
Assessment, 41
Assignment error, 188, 189, 191, 192, 212
Attenuation, reliability, 245, 246, 247, 249
Attenuation due to unreliability, 250
Average, 110

Average Y values, 129, *see also* Y
Averaging out, 29

B

Bar chart, 108, 109, 113, 114, 115
Behaviorally anchored observation, 46, 47
Beta coefficients
  demonstration of multicollinearity, 253, 254, 255, 256
  formula for two independent variables, 149
  multiple regression, 141, 142, 147, 148
  partial in statistical modeling challenges, 280
Between-cases designs
  design applications
    experiments/quasi-experiments, 70, 71, 82
    surveys/field studies, 85–86
  internal validity threats, 73–74
Bias
  causal challenges and design foundations, 56–57, 63
  coefficients and statistical modeling, 278, 285
  design foundations, 66
  multiple regression, 142
  problems of incomplete data, 232
  surveys/field studies, 88, 89–90
Biased coefficients, 280
Biased relationships, 56, 57, 59, 67
Biasing variable, 80
Binomial probability distribution, 162, 169
Bouncing betas, 253, 258
Boundary conditions, 66, 67
Box-score method, 210, 215

C

Cases
  construct definitions, 26
  deleting and missing data, 234–235
  empirical research, 5–6, 10
  representativeness in statistical modeling, 282
  research report writing, 220–221, 225
  surveys and field studies, 85
  using design for causal challenges, 63–64

Categorical variables, *see* Nominal variables
Causal challenges
  design foundations in empirical research,
    54–60
  using design to address, 61–64
Causal conceptual relationship
  causal challenges and design foundations,
    55
  empirical research model, 14, 20
  good research studies, 290–292, 297
Causal direction, 65, 66, 89, 92, 294–295
Causal modeling, 283
Causal models and statistical modeling
  evaluation, 261–262, 273
  four illustrative models, 262–271
  hierarchical models, 271–273
  illustrative data set, 261
Causal relationships
  empirical level and empirical research model,
    14–16
  influence, 4, 9, 10
  persuasive research study, 296–297
  suppressor variables, 57
Causation, variables, 13
Centered variables, 270
Centering, 269–271, 274, 275
Central limit theorem, 168, 170
Central tendency, 110, 113–114, 115, 176
Central tendency error, 46, 47, 49
Change, external generalization, 205
Clean data, 104–105
Closed-ended response format, 44, 48, 49
Codification, 209, 210
Coding task, 211
Coefficient alpha, 242, 243–244, 249–250
Coefficient of determination
  multicollinearity, 252
  multiple correlation/regression, 142
  nominal independent variables, 129
  simple correlation, 124, 125, 126, 131,
    132
Comparisons, 233
  groups, 62, 67
Complexity, surveys versus field studies, 85
Conceptual model, 278
Conceptual relationships, 14,129
Conceptual validity, 16
Conceptual variables, 12, 19
Confidence interval for Beta$_{YXi \cdot Xj}$ (B$_{YXi \cdot Xj}$),
    199–200
Confidence interval for B$_{YX}$, 198
Confidence interval ρ_{YX}, 195–197
Confidence intervals
  causal models, 261
  example, 185–187
  hypothesis testing and statistical power, 187–188,
    191, 192
  logic and procedures, 185

Confidence level, 185, 192
Construct
  definition, 26, 27
  empirical research model, 12, 19, *see also* Conceptual
    variables
  persuasive research study, 293
  questionnaire construction, 43
Construct domain, 26
Construct invalidity, 281, *see also* Construct validity
Construct validation
  empirical research model, 20
  measurement applications, 30–35
Construct validity
  causal conceptual relationships, 290, 296
  challenges, 29, 30
  empirical research model, 16, 19, 20
  independent variables and statistical modeling, 280,
    282, 285
  measurement applications, 27–30
  reliability, 32, 243
  research report, 221
  threat to internal validity, 90
Construction, questionnaires, 42–45
Constructive replications, 206
Contamination, 29, 36, 243
Content domain, 43
Content validation, 31, 36
Content validity, 31, 36
Continuous probability distributions, 162–163,
    169
Continuous random variables, 163
Continuous scales, 108, 109
Continuous variables, 101, 103, 269
Convenience, causal challenges, 61, 67
Conventions, data analysis/statistics, 101
Convergent validity, 32–33, 36, 37
Correcting for unreliability, 247
Correction for attenuation, 247, 249, 250
Correlation coefficient
  coefficient alpha interpretation and reliability,
    243
  data analysis and statistics, 98
  formula, 132
    correction for attenuation, 250
  hypothesis testing
    calculation and example, 178
    statistical power, 180
  internal statistical inference and meta-analysis,
    213
  simple correlation, 121
  standard scores and simple correlation, 123
  unreliability, 245, 246, 247, 249
Cost/time, questionnaire construction, 40
Courses of action, 4
Covariance, 132, 246
  method, 122, 131
Covariates, 79, 81, 83
Credibility, 294

Criteria, empirical research, 54
    model, 14–16
Criterion distribution, 175
Criterion-related validity, 34, 36, 37
Critical values
    formula for standard normal and F distributions, 194,
        195
    hypothesis testing, 178, 180, 181, 191
    identifying for null sampling distribution, 176,
        177
Critique, report writing, 225
Cross-sectional between-cases design, 85–86
Cross-sectional design, 70, 71
    with covariate, 79–80, 81, 82
Cross-sectional factorial design, 77–79
Cumulative knowledge, 207

                    D

d.f., see Degrees of freedom
Data, see also Scores
    empirical research, 6, 10, see also Scores
    secondary and alternatives to questionnaire
        construction, 40, 48, 49
    within-cases time-series studies, 87
Data analysis, foundations
    clean data, 104–105
    conventions, 101–103
    properties of scores, 99–101
    statistics, 98–99
Data error sources, 104
Data file errors, 104–105
Data matrix, 102–103, 107–108, 232
Data set, causal modeling, 261, 262
Deficiency, 29, 36
Degrees of freedom (d.f.), 176, 177, 192, 194,
        195
Delete cases, see Cases, deleting
Delete variables, see Variables, deleting
Demand characteristics, 73, 81, 82
Demand effects, 89
Demographic information, 44
Demonstrations, unreliability, 245–248
Dependent variables, see also Independent
        variables
    addressing missing data, 233–234
    causal challenges and design foundations, 54, 57, 58,
        59, 60
    design applications and
        experiments/quasi-experiments, 70, 71
    direct effects model, 263
    meta-analysis, 209
        inappropriate, 210
    regression model, 126
    relationship and empirical research model,
        12–13, 19
    simple correlation and regression, 119

Design
    basic and field studies/surveys, 85–88
    empirical research, 6, 9, 10
    extensions, 80
    persuasive research study, 294–295, 297
    statistical inference, 283–284
    types and empirical research, 64–65
    use to address causal challenges, 61–64
Design applications
    experiments and quasi-experiments
        additional designs, 75–80
        basic designs, 70–71
        threats of internal validity, 72–75
    field studies and surveys
        basic designs, 85–88
        praise for, 90–91
        threats to internal validity, 88–90
Design constraints, 91
Deviation scores, 122, 123, see also Scores
Dichotomous variables, 121
Direct effect, 265
Direct effects models, 263–264, 274
Directional research hypothesis, 174
Discrete probability distributions, 160–162, 169
Discrete variables, 101, 103
Discriminant analysis, 128
Discriminant validity, 33–34, 36, 37
Discussion, report writing, 223, 225
Distributions, scores on single variable, 107, 110–113,
        114
Drafts, report writing, 225
Dummy codes, 212
Dummy coding, 266, 269
Dummy variables
    addressing missing data, 237
    hierarchical models, 271
    nominal independent variables, 143, 144, 147
    simple correlation and regression, 128, 129, 130, 131,
        132

                    E

Empirical models, 263, 275
Empirical relationships, 14, 20, 54
Empirical research
    activities, 6–7
    design foundations
        addressing causal challenges, 61–64
        causal challenges, 54–60
        design types, 64–65
    expected relationships, 5, 9, 10
    model
        characterization, 13–17, 19
        generalizing, 17–19
        research variables, 12–13
    shortcomings and meta-analysis, 213
Endogenous variables, 265, 273, 274

Equal-appearing categories, avoiding, 44
Error score, 241
Errors
    hypothesis testing, 179
    multiple regression, 140
    questionnaire construction and use, 47
    score readiness, 107
    simple regression, 127
    structural equation modeling, 281
Execution, persuasive research, 295, 297
Exhaustive values, 160, 169
Exogenous variables, 265, 271, 274, 274
Expectancy effects, 73, 82
Experimental design, research report, 221
Experiments, 64–65, 66, 67, 292
Exploratory studies, 294, 297
External generalizations, *see also* Generalizability
    addressing through replication studies,
        207
    challenges, 204–205, 207
    empirical research model, 18, 19
External statistical inference, 158
    meta-analysis, 212, *see also* Statistical inference
External validation, 19, 20
External validity
    empirical research model, 19, 20
    generalization challenges, 204–205
    generalization from single studies, 205–206
    meta-analysis, 208–214
    replication, 206–208

F

F distributions
    formula, 194, 195
    probability samples and statistical inference, 168,
        169, 170
Face valid, 31–32
Face validation, 31
Face validity, 37
Factor analysis, 281, 284, 286
Factorial designs, 77, 78, 81, 82
Field studies, 65, 66, 67, 85
Findings, research reports, 223
Forced-choice scales, 47, 49
Frequency tables, 108, 114, 115
Full mediation, 66, 67
Full specification, 283, 286

G

Generalizability
    causal conceptual relationships, 292–293
    good research studies, 289, 293, 297
Generalization, problem, 235

Generalizing theory, 245, *see also* Reliability
Graphical representation, 119–120, 135
Graphs, 108–109
Guidelines, 43–44

H

Halo error, 46, 49
Headings, tables, 226
Hierarchical models, 271–273, 274, 275
Histograms, 108, 109, 113, 114, 115
History, 74, 81, 82, 88
Honesty, 43–44
Human capital theory, 290, 291, 293
Hypothesis
    empirical research, 14, 17, 20
    testing, 187–188, 189, 191

I

Incomplete data
    addressing missing data, 233–237
    avoiding, 232–233
    evaluating nonresponse, 233
    reporting, 237–238
Incremental R^2, 200
Independent random variables, 160, *see also* Probability
Independent variables, *see also* Dependent variable
    addressing missing data, 234–237
    causal challenges and design foundations, 54, 57, 58,
        59, 60, 62–63, 66
    cross-sectional factorial designs, 77, 78
    design applications
        experiments/quasi-experiments, 70, 71
        surveys/field studies, 85
    dichotomy, 128
    direct effects model, 263
    empirical models, 263
    formula for multiple correlation/multiple regression,
        148
    hierarchical models, 272
    importance and statistical modeling challenges,
        279–282, 284
    meaning and use by researchers, 160, 169
    meta-analysis, 209, 211
    more than two, 142–143
    multicollinearity, 252, 253
    multiple correlation, 135–139
    multiple regression, 139, 140
    regression model, 126
    relationship and empirical research model,
        12–13, 19
    scores from field and survey studies, 84
    simple correlation and regression, 118, 119
    single in multiple correlation, 150–152

Indirect effect, 265, 274
Inferences, 16, 27
Instantaneous models, 87, 92
Instrumentation, 75, 81, 82
Interaction variables, 67
Intercept, 140, 145, 148
Internal causal criteria, 54
Internal consistency, reliability, 241, 242–243
    measurement applications, 32, 36, 37
Internal statistical inference, 158
    meta-analysis, 212–213, *see also* Statistical inference
Internal statistical validity, 15, 188–190, 283
Internal validation, 15, 19, 20
Internal validity
    causal challenges and design foundations, 54, 62, 66
    causal conceptual relationships, 291, 292
    empirical research model, 14–15, 20
    research report writing, 221
    surveys/field studies, 92
        lack of concern, 91
    threats
        cross-sectional design with covariate, 80
        experiments/quasi-experiments, 72–75, 81, 82
        surveys/field studies, 88–90
Interpretations, meta-analysis, 211–212
Interrater reliability, 241, 244
    measurement applications, 32, 36, 37
Interval variables, 100, 103, 119
Intervening variables, 58–59, 66
Interviewees, 42, 48
Interviews, 39, 41–42, 48
Intragroup history, 73, 81, 82, *see also* History
Introduction, report writing, 220, 225
Intuition, 142
Item sequence, 44
Item wording, 43–44, 90
Items, questionnaire construction, 43–45

J

Judgment sampling, 61, 67

K

Kurtosis, 113, 114, 115

L

Lagged models, 87, 92
Latent variables, 281, 286
Least-squares criterion, 127, 131, 132, 135
Legal analogy, 178
Leniency error, 46, 47, 48, 49
Letter conventions, statistics, 102

Levels of measurement, 99–101, 103
Likert Scale, 46
Likelihood, 185
LISREL, *see* Structural equation modeling
Listwise deletion, 234, 238–239
Logit regression models, 128
Longitudinal between-cases design, 75–76
Longitudinal between-cases panel studies, 87–88
Longitudinal designs, 70, 71, 81, 82, 74–75

M

Manipulation, measurement, 31
Matching, 63, 66, 67
Math symbol conventions, 101
Maturation, 74, 81, 82, 88
Mean
        central tendency and scores on single variable, 110,
            114, 115
        data analysis and statistics, 98
        formula, 115
        sampling distribution and statistical inference,
            164–168
Mean replacement, 235
Mean substitution, 235–236, 239
Measurement
    construct definition, 26–27
        illustration, 27
        construct validation, 30–35
        construct validity challenges, 27–30
    decisions and using design to address causal,
        62–63
    empirical research, 6
    independent variables and statistical modeling
        challenges, 280, 282
    research questionnaires
        construction, 42–45
        decisions, 39–42
        pilot testing, 47
        response styles, 45–47
Measures
    empirical research, 5, 6, 9, 10
    research report writing, 221, 225
Measuring instruments, 104
Median, 110, 114, 115
Mediated effects models, 264–265, 274
Mediator, 58–59
Mediator variables, 66
Memory, 244
Meta-analysis
    empirical research model, 19, 20
    external validity, 208–214, 215
Methodological characteristics, 209, 211, 213,
        see also Meta-analysis
Methods, report writing, 220–222, 225
Minnesota Satisfaction Questionnaire (MSQ),
        42, 44

Missing data
    addressing, 233–237, 238, 239
    data matrix, 232
    errors and clean data, 104
Missing values, 105
Missingness, 234, 237
Missingness variables, 237
Misspecification, 56, 57, 66, 67, 286
Mode, 110, 115
Moderated models, 266–271
Moderated regression, 267–269, 274
Moderated variable, 266, 267, 269, 270, 274
Moderating effect, 80
Moderation, 267
Moderator, 266
Moderator variable
    design to address causal challenges, 59–60, 61,
        66, 67
    cross-sectional factorial designs, 78, 79
    generalization from single studies, 206
    internal statistical inference and meta-analysis,
        212–213
    limits of external generalization, 214
Mortality, 74, 81, 82, 89
Motivation, participants, 233
MSQ, see Minnesota Satisfaction Questionnaire
Multicollinearity
    addressing, 257–258
    consequences, 252–253
    demonstration, 253–256
    hierarchical models, 272
    misconceived, 256–257
    moderated model, 269
    multiple correlation, 138, 139, 147, 148
        single independent variables, 150
    unreliability, 248
Multidimensional constructs, 28, 37
Multiple coefficient of determination
    formula, 198–199
        for two independent variables, 148
    independent variables and statistical modeling
        challenges, 279
    multicollinearity, 253–254, 255
    multiple correlation, 136–139, 147
Multiple correlation, multiple coefficient of
        determination, 136–138
    examples, 138–139, 148
Multiple correlation coefficient, 135–136, 146,
        147
Multiple correlation/regression, 248, 257
Multiple regression
    characterization, 139, 147, 148
    examples, 141–142
    intercept, 140, 147
    partial beta coefficients, 140–141
    partial regression coefficients, 140
    structural equation modeling, 281

Multiple regression intercept, 140, 141, 143
Multiple regression prediction model, 139, 148
Mutually exclusive values, 160, 168, 169

N

Narrative reviews, 207, 213, 215
Nearly interval measurement, 100
Noise variable, 79–80
Noisy relationship, 57–58, 66, 67
Nominal dependent variables, 128
Nominal dichotomy, 270
Nominal independent variables, 128–130, 143–146
Nominal variables, 99, 103, 268
Nomological networks, 26–27, 34–35, 36
Nondirectional research hypothesis, 175
Nonrespondents, 232, 239
Nonresponse, 233, 238
Normal distribution, 111–112, 114, 115
Normal probability distribution, 163, 169
Nuisance variable, 56, 60–64, 66, 67
Null hypothesis
    confidence intervals versus hypothesis
        testing/statistical power, 188
    erroneously accepting, 180
    hypothesis testing example, 177
    internal statistical validity, 189, 190
    statistical hypothesis testing, 174, 175, 191, 192
Null sampling distribution
    determining whether sample statistic is false, 176
    estimating, 175, 176
    hypothesis testing example, 177, 178
    identifying critical regions, 176
    statistical power, 181
Numbering, tables, 226

O

Observations, 40–41, 46–47
Observed score variance, 242
Omitted category, 144–145, 147, 148
Omitted variables, 74, 81, 82
One-dimensional constructs, 28, 37
One-tail hypothesis
    hypothesis testing example, 177–179
    identifying critical regions of null sampling
        distribution, 176, 177
    statistical hypothesis testing, 174, 191, 192
One-tailed test, 180, 188, 195, 197
Open-ended response format, 44, 48, 49
Operational relationships, 14–16
Operational variables, 12, 19
Ordered dependent variables, 135–136, see also
        Dependent variables
Ordered independent variable, 145, 146
Ordered scales, 107, 108, 109

Ordinal variables, 100, 103
Organizations, secondary data collections, 40
Organizing, research report writing, 224
Other questionnaires, 40
Outcomes
    hypothesis testing, 179
    populations and multicollinearity, 253–256
    research report writing, 224
    statistical and missing data, 236

P

P, *see* Multiple correlation coefficient
Pairwise deletion, 235, 238–239
Panel studies, 87, 92
Parameters, statistics, 164, 170, 179
Partial beta coefficients, 140–141, 142, 143, 199–200,
    see also Beta coefficients
Partial coefficients, 152–154, 253
Partial mediation, 58, 66, 67
Partial regression coefficient
    direct effects model, 263
    independent variables
        formula for two, 148
        statistical modeling, 280
    moderated model, 268, 269, 270–271
    multiple correlation/regression, 140, 142, 147,
        148
    nominal independent variables, 145
Partial replications, 206
Participant information, 221
Participants, 72–73, 104
Participation, missing data, 232
Percentiles, 114, 115
Persuasive research study, 289, 293–296
Phi coefficient, 121, 131
Pilot testing, 47
PM, *see* Product moment correlation coefficient
Point-biserial correlation, 121, 131
Population
    confidence intervals, 185, 186, 187
    multicollinearity, 253–256
    relationship, 181, 182, 183
    sampling distributions, 165–166
    statistical hypothesis testing, 175
Precision, 284
Precision of model, 279, 286
Predisposition differences, 90
Prime symbol, 13
Probability
    conceptual constructions, 163
    statistical inference, 159–160, 168, 169
        requirements and design, 283
Probability distributions, 160–163, 169
Probability sample, 164, 170, 175, 185, 186
Probability sampling, 61, 67
Probability theory, 157
Probability tree, 161

Probit regression models, 128
Problems, nonresponse, 232
Procedures, report writing, 221, 225
Product moment (PM) correlation coefficient, 121, 127,
    131
Proper specification, 283
Proper statistical specification, 278, 284, 286

Q

Qualitative research, 7, 10
Quantitative information, tables, 226
Quantity adjectives, avoiding, 44
Quasi-experiments, 64, 65, 66, 67, 292
    design, 221
Questionnaires
    alternatives to construction, 39–40
    construction, 42–45, 48
    decisions, 39–42
    measurement applications, 39
    response styles, 45–47

R

R square, 137
r square, 124
Random assignment, 64, 65, 66, 67
Random errors, 27, 28–29, 36, 241
Random samples, 165, 168, 254–256
Random variables, 159–160, 169
Randomization tests, 188–189, 190, 191, 192
Ratio variables, 100, 103
Reading ability, written questionnaires, 41
Recommended practices, missing data, 238
Recursive model, 274
Regression, internal validity threats, 75, 81, 82
Regression coefficient
    attenuation and unreliability, 245, 247, 248
    confidence interval example, 185
        calculation, 186, 187
    confidence interval formula, 193
    formula, 132
        correction for attenuation, 250
    independent variables and statistical modeling,
        279–280, 284–285
    multicollinearity, 254
    simple correlation/regression, 127, 129,
        131, 132
    unstandardized and direct effects model, 263
Regression intercept
    consequences of unreliability, 247
    formula, 132
    simple regression, 126–127, 128, 131, 132
Regression model, 126–127
Regression prediction model, 126–127,
        132, 141

Relationships, 12, *see also* Individual entries
Reliability
    consequences of unreliability, 245–248
    construct validation and measurement applications,
        32, 36, 37
    definition, 241–242, 249
    estimation, 242–245
    formula, 249
    formulae, 249–250
    independent variables and statistical modeling
        challenges, 280
    nominal independent variables, 129
    research report, 221, 222
Repetitions, 242
Replication, 206–206, 215
Reporting, 237–238, 244
Research
    construct validity and misconceptions, 35
    elements of persuasive study, 293–296
    illustration using a model, 290–293
    what makes it good, 289–290
Research confederate, 55, 63, 67
Research environment, 72, 88
Research hypothesis, 174, 175, 191, 192
Research problem, stating, 220
Research report writing
    additional suggestions, 224–225
    format, 220–223
        alternative, 223–224
    table construction, 226–228
Researcher, expectations, *see* Expectations
Researcher effects, 88
Respondent, 43
Response acquiescence, 45, 48, 49
Response formats, 41
Response styles, 45–47
Restriction of measurement range, 282, 285
Restriction of range, 61–62, 66, 67
Results
    research report writing, 222, 225
    table summary, 226, 227
Rewriting, 225
Rho coefficient, 121, 131
Robust findings, 295, 297

S

Sample correlation coefficient, 192
Sample size
    estimating if null hypothesis is true,
        175–176
    hypothesis testing, 178
    inclusion in research report, 221
    statistical power, 181, 182, 183–184
    standard error and statistical inference, 168
Sample size internal statistical validity, 189
Sample statistic, 185

Sampling, 61–62
Sampling distribution
    confidence interval example, 185
    estimating if null hypothesis is true, 175–176
    estimation and confidence intervals, 185
    formulas, 194
    hypothesis testing example, 178
    statistical inference, 164–168, 169, 170
    statistical power, 181
Sampling error, 165, 166, 170, 176, 212,
        see also Errors
Satisfaction, measurement, 27, 28
Scaling, 44, 221, 280
Scatterplot, 124, 129, 135, 137
Scientific method, 8
Scores, *see also* Data
    construct validation and measurement applications,
        32, 33
    critical nature and measurement, 29–30
    empirical research, 5, 6, 9, 10
    obtaining and research report writing, 221
    properties and data analysis/statistics, 99–101,
        103
    single variables, 107–114
Secondary data, *see* Data, secondary
Secondary data sets, 105
Selection, internal validity threats
    between-cases designs, 73, 74, 81, 82
    cross-sectional design with covariate, 80
Self-report questionnaires, 39, 40–41, 47, 48
Self-reports, 45–46
SEM, *see* Structural equation modeling
Semantic differential scale, 46
Sensitivity analysis, 295, 297
Severity error, 46, 48, 49
Shape, 111–113, 176, 177, 178
Significance level
    hypothesis testing
        errors, 179
        example, 177–179
        statistical power, 180–181, 182
        statistical, 174–175
    independent variables and statistical modeling,
        280
Simple correlation coefficient
    formulas, 194–197
        statistical inference, 194–195
    meta-analysis, 211
Simple coefficient of determination, 254
Simple correlation
    consequences of unreliability, 245
    demonstration of multicollinearity, 257
    formulae, 121–124
    variance explained, 124–125
Simple random sample, 164, 170
Simple regression, 126–128, 245, 257
Simple regression coefficient, 142, 197–198
Simplicity, 43

Simultaneity, 55, 67
Single studies, generalization, 205–206
Size, coefficients, 279
Skew, 112, 113–114, 115
Slope coefficient, 127
Social desirability, 45, 47, 48, 49
Specificity, questionnaire wording, 43
Spurious relationships, 57, 66, 67, 90
Squared partial correlation coefficient, 148, 149, 151
Squared semipartial correlation coefficient, 142, 149, 151
Stability, 241, 244, 249
    measurement applications, 32, 36, 37
Standard normal distribution, 112, 115, 194
Standard deviation
    formula, 116
    multicollinearity, 255
    probability samples and statistical inference, 167
    representations of scores on single variable, 110, 111, 112, 114, 115
Standard error
    hypothesis testing example, 178
    multicollinearity, 253, 254, 255, 256–257
    probability samples and statistical inference, 167–168, 169
    statistical modeling challenges, 284
Standard error of the correlation coefficient, 167, 170, 178, 192
Standard error of the mean, 167, 170, 176
Standard error of the regression coefficient, 186, 187, 193, 198
Standard score deviation, 123, 132
Standard scores, 123–124, 132
Standardized regression coefficients, 280, 284
Statistical control, 63
Statistical generalization validity, 158–159
    empirical research model, 17, 19, 20
Statistical generalization, 17–19, 189
Statistical hypothesis testing
    example, 177–179, 192
    logic and procedures, 174–177
    outcomes, 179
    statistical power, 179–184, 191
Statistical inference
    applications
        confidence intervals, 184–188
        formulas, 194–200
        internal statistical validity, 188–190
        statistical hypothesis testing, 173–184
    design, 283–284
    formulas, 170, 194–200
    foundations
        probability, 159–160
        probability distributions, 160–163
        sampling distributions, 164–168

tests
    confidence interval for ρ_{YX}, 195
    incremental R^2, 200
    multiple coefficient of determination, 198–199
    partial beta coefficients, 199
    simple correlation coefficient, 194–197
    simple regression coefficient, 197–198
Statistical information, 98–99
Statistical model, 278
Statistical modeling, challenges, *see also* Causal modeling and statistical modeling
    design and statistical inference, 283–284
    independent variables importance, 279–282
    specification, 278
Statistical power
    hypothesis testing, 179–184, 191, 192
        confidence intervals comparison, 187–188
    loss and multicollinearity, 255, 256
    moderated model, 269
    when analysis is essential, 183
Statistical significance
    causal models, 261, 262
    direct effects model, 263
    independent variables and statistical modeling, 279, 282
    moderated model, 268
    research report writing, 222
    statistical hypothesis testing, 175, 192
Statistical validation, 15, 17, 19, 20
Statistics
    calling attention to and table construction, 227
    sample and multicollinearity, 254–256
    use, 98, 103
Stepwise procedures, 263, 275
Strength of relationship, 121
Structural equation modeling (SEM), 281
Students' t distributions, 168, 169, 170
Subgrouping, 266–267, 268
Suppressor variables, 57, 67, 140
Surveys, 65, 66, 67, 85, 205
Systematic errors, 27–28, 29, 36, 243
Systematic score, 241

T

t distribution
    confidence interval example, 187
    formula, 194
    hypothesis testing example, 177, 178
    identifying critical regions of null sampling distribution, 176, 177
    probability samples and statistical inference, 168
Tables, 108–109, 222, 226–228
Testing, validity threats, 74, 81, 82
Tests, theory, 15
Text–table integration, 226
Theoretical justification, persuasive research, 293–294

Theory, 15, 20, 294
Three-value nominal variable, 144
Thurstone scale, 46
Time–series studies, 86–87, 92
Title, table, 226
Total effect, 265, 274
Training, 78, 79
Treatment contamination, 73, 81, 82,
    see also Contamination
Trends, systematic, 88–89
Triangulation, 208, 215, 294
True score variance, 29, 36
Two-tailed hypothesis, 175, 176, 177, 191, 192
Two-tailed test
    formula for simple correlation coefficient, 195, 197
    hypothesis testing, 180, 181, 182, 188
Type I error, 179, 181, 183–184, 191, 192
Type II error, 179, 180, 181, 183–184, 191, 192

U

Uncontrolled variable, 56–61, 63
Understanding, information, 232–233
Unreliability
    consequences, 245–248
    reliability defined, 242, 249
    structural equation modeling, 281, 285
Unstandardized coefficients, 279–280, 282, 284

V

Validity, 14, 20, 159, 289, *see also* Individual entries
Variability
    estimating reliability, 242
    estimating sampling distribution if null hypothesis is
        true, 176
    probability samples, 166–167
    replication studies, 207
    scores on single variable, 110, 114, 115
    simple correlation, 125
Variables, *see also* Individual entries
    deleting and addressing missing data, 234
    empirical research model, 12, 19
    inclusion in research report, 221
    knowledge and generalization from single studies,
        205
    questionnaire construction, 43
    relationships and causal models, 262
    uncontrolled, *see* Uncontrolled variables
    varying and data analysis/statistics, 98

Variance
    consequences of unreliability, 245–246
    direct effects model, 263
    empirical models, 263
    formula, 115
    hierarchical models, 271
    independent variables and statistical modeling,
        279–280, 284
    multicollinearity, 253, 254
    multiple correlation/regression, 138–139, 142
    reliability, 241
    scores on single variable, 110, 114, 115
    simple correlation, 124–125
    single independent variables in multiple correlation,
        162
Versimilitude, 14, 19, 20

W

Within-cases studies, 70, 71, 81, 211
Within-cases time series, 86–87
Words, avoiding, 44
Written report, 296

X

X
    causal challenges and design foundations, 55, 62
    centering and moderated model, 269
    confidence interval example, 187
    consequences of unreliability, 246, 247, 248, 249
    dependent/independent variables and empirical
        research model, 13
    design applications
        experiments/quasi-experiments, 70, 71, 75–76
        surveys/field studies, 85, 86, 87
    internal validity threats, 72–74
    multicollinearity, 253, 254
    multiple correlation/regression, 135–145
    nominal independent variables, 129
    simple correlation, 119–125
    simple regression, 126–128

Y

Y
    causal challenges and design foundations,
        55, 62
    centering and moderated model, 269
    confidence interval example, 187
    consequences of unreliability, 246, 247–248
    dependent/independent variables and empirical
        research model, 13
    design applications

experiments/quasi-experiments, 70, 71, 75–76
surveys/field studies, 85, 86, 87
internal validity threats, 72–75
multicollinearity, 253, 254
multiple correlation/regression, 135–145
nominal independent variables, 129
simple correlation, 119–125

Yea-saying, 45, 48
You, avoiding, 44

Z

Zero point, 100
z_r transformations, 195–196